DISCOVER PERL 5

DISCOVER PERL 5

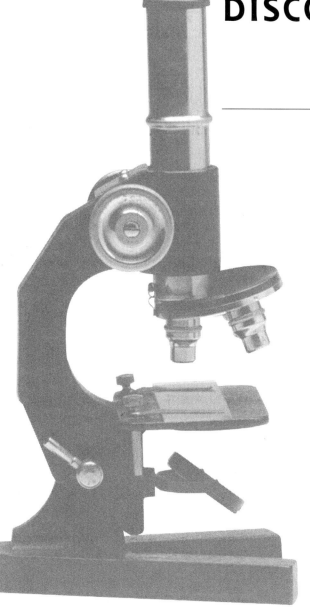

NABA BARKAKATI

IDG BOOKS WORLDWIDE, INC.

AN INTERNATIONAL
DATA GROUP COMPANY

FOSTER CITY, CA CHICAGO, IL
INDIANAPOLIS, IN SOUTHLAKE, TX

Discover Perl 5

Published by

IDG Books Worldwide, Inc.

An International Data Group Company

919 E. Hillsdale Blvd.

Suite 400

Foster City, CA 94404

www.idgbooks.com (IDG Books Worldwide Web site)

www.dummies.com (Dummies Press Web site)

Library of Congress Catalog Card No.: 97-73218

ISBN: 0-7645-3076-3

Printed in the United States of America

10 9 8 7 6 5 4 3 2 1

1B/SV/QX/2X/FC

Distributed in the United States by IDG Books Worldwide, Inc.

Distributed by Macmillan Canada for Canada; by Transworld Publishers Limited in the United Kingdom; by IDG Norge Books for Norway; by IDG Sweden Books for Sweden; by Woodslane Pty. Ltd. for Australia; by Woodslane Enterprises Ltd. for New Zealand; by Longman Singapore Publishers Ltd. for Singapore, Malaysia, Thailand, and Indonesia; by Simron Pty. Ltd. for South Africa; by Toppan Company Ltd. for Japan; by Distribuidora Cuspide for Argentina; by Livraria Cultura for Brazil; by Ediciencia S.A. for Ecuador; by Addison-Wesley Publishing Company for Korea; by Ediciones ZETA S.C.R. Ltda. for Peru; by WS Computer Publishing Corporation, Inc., for the Philippines; by Unalis Corporation for Taiwan; by Contemporanea de Ediciones for Venezuela; by Computer Book & Magazine Store for Puerto Rico; by Express Computer Distributors for the Caribbean and West Indies. Authorized Sales Agent: Anthony Rudkin Associates for the Middle East and North Africa.

For general information on IDG Books Worldwide's books in the U.S., please call our Consumer Customer Service department at 800-762-2974. For reseller information, including discounts and premium sales, please call our Reseller Customer Service department at 800-434-3422.

For information on where to purchase IDG Books Worldwide's books outside the U.S., please contact our International Sales department at 415-655-3200 or fax 415-655-3295.

For information on foreign language translations, please contact our Foreign & Subsidiary Rights department at 415-655-3021 or fax 415-655-3281.

For sales inquiries and special prices for bulk quantities, please contact our Sales department at 415-655-3200 or write to the address above.

For information on using IDG Books Worldwide's books in the classroom or for ordering examination copies, please contact our Educational Sales department at 800-434-2086 or fax 817-251-8174.

For press review copies, author interviews, or other publicity information, please contact our Public Relations department at 415-655-3000 or fax 415-655-3299.

For authorization to photocopy items for corporate, personal, or educational use, please contact Copyright Clearance Center, 222 Rosewood Drive, Danvers, MA 01923, or fax 508-750-4470.

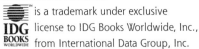 is a trademark under exclusive license to IDG Books Worldwide, Inc., from International Data Group, Inc.

ABOUT IDG BOOKS WORLDWIDE

Welcome to the world of IDG Books Worldwide.

IDG Books Worldwide, Inc., is a subsidiary of International Data Group, the world's largest publisher of computer-related information and the leading global provider of information services on information technology. IDG was founded more than 25 years ago and now employs more than 8,500 people worldwide. IDG publishes more than 275 computer publications in over 75 countries (see listing below). More than 60 million people read one or more IDG publications each month.

Launched in 1990, IDG Books Worldwide is today the #1 publisher of best-selling computer books in the United States. We are proud to have received eight awards from the Computer Press Association in recognition of editorial excellence and three from *Computer Currents*' First Annual Readers' Choice Awards. Our best-selling *...For Dummies*® series has more than 30 million copies in print with translations in 30 languages. IDG Books Worldwide, through a joint venture with IDG's Hi-Tech Beijing, became the first U.S. publisher to publish a computer book in the People's Republic of China. In record time, IDG Books Worldwide has become the first choice for millions of readers around the world who want to learn how to better manage their businesses.

Our mission is simple: Every one of our books is designed to bring extra value and skill-building instructions to the reader. Our books are written by experts who understand and care about our readers. The knowledge base of our editorial staff comes from years of experience in publishing, education, and journalism — experience we use to produce books for the '90s. In short, we care about books, so we attract the best people. We devote special attention to details such as audience, interior design, use of icons, and illustrations. And because we use an efficient process of authoring, editing, and desktop publishing our books electronically, we can spend more time ensuring superior content and spend less time on the technicalities of making books.

You can count on our commitment to deliver high-quality books at competitive prices on topics you want to read about. At IDG Books Worldwide, we continue in the IDG tradition of delivering quality for more than 25 years. You'll find no better book on a subject than one from IDG Books Worldwide.

John Kilcullen
CEO
IDG Books Worldwide, Inc.

Steven Berkowitz
President and Publisher
IDG Books Worldwide, Inc.

WINNER

*Eighth Annual
Computer Press
Awards 1992*

IX WINNER

*Ninth Annual
Computer Press
Awards 1993*

X WINNER

*Tenth Annual
Computer Press
Awards 1994*

XI WINNER

*Eleventh Annual
Computer Press
Awards 1995*

IDG Books Worldwide, Inc., is a subsidiary of International Data Group, the world's largest publisher of computer-related information and the leading global provider of information services on information technology. International Data Group publishes over 275 computer publications in over 75 countries. Sixty million people read one or more International Data Group publications each month. International Data Group's publications include: **ARGENTINA:** Buyer's Guide, Computerworld Argentina, PC World Argentina; **AUSTRALIA:** Australian Macworld, Australian PC World, Australian Reseller News, Computerworld, IT Casebook, Network World, Publish, Webmaster; **AUSTRIA:** Computerwelt Osterreich, Networks Austria, PC Tip Austria; **BANGLADESH:** PC World Bangladesh; **BELARUS:** PC World Belarus; **BELGIUM:** Data News; **BRAZIL:** Annuário de Informática, Computerworld, Connections, Macworld, PC Player, PC World, Publish, Reseller News, Supergamepower; **BULGARIA:** Computerworld Bulgaria, Network World Bulgaria, PC & MacWorld Bulgaria; **CANADA:** CIO Canada, Client/Server World, ComputerWorld Canada, InfoWorld Canada, NetworkWorld Canada, WebWorld; **CHILE:** Computerworld Chile, PC World Chile; **COLOMBIA:** Computerworld Colombia, PC World Colombia; **COSTA RICA:** PC World Centro America; **THE CZECH AND SLOVAK REPUBLICS:** Computerworld Czechoslovakia, Macworld Czech Republic, PC World Czechoslovakia; **DENMARK:** Communications World Danmark, Computerworld Danmark, Macworld Danmark, PC World Danmark, Techworld Denmark; **DOMINICAN REPUBLIC:** PC World Republica Dominicana; **ECUADOR:** PC World Ecuador; **EGYPT:** Computerworld Middle East, PC World Middle East; **EL SALVADOR:** PC World Centro America; **FINLAND:** MikroPC, Tietoverkko, Tietoviikko; **FRANCE:** Distributique, Hebdo, Info PC, Le Monde Informatique, Macworld, Reseaux & Telecoms, WebMaster France; **GERMANY:** Computer Partner, Computerwoche, Computerwoche Extra, Computerwoche FOCUS, Global Online, Macwelt, PC Welt; **GREECE:** Amiga Computing, GamePro Greece, Multimedia World; **GUATEMALA:** PC World Centro America; **HONDURAS:** PC World Centro America; **HONG KONG:** Computerworld Hong Kong, PC World Hong Kong, Publish in Asia; **HUNGARY:** ABCD CD-ROM, Computerworld Szamitastechnika, Internetto online Magazine, PC World Hungary, PC-X Magazin Hungary; **ICELAND:** Tolvuheimur PC World Island; **INDIA:** Information Communications World, Information Systems Computerworld, PC World India, Publish in Asia; **INDONESIA:** InfoKomputer PC World, Komputek Computerworld, Publish in Asia; **IRELAND:** ComputerScope, PC Live!; **ISRAEL:** Macworld Israel, People & Computers/Computerworld; **ITALY:** Computerworld Italia, Macworld Italia, Networking Italia, PC World Italia; **JAPAN:** DTP World, Macworld Japan, Nikkei Personal Computing, OS/2 World Japan, SunWorld Japan, Windows NT World, Windows World Japan; **KENYA:** PC World East African; **KOREA:** Hi-Tech Information, Macworld Korea, PC World Korea; **MACEDONIA:** PC World Macedonia; **MALAYSIA:** Computerworld Malaysia, PC World Malaysia, Publish in Asia; **MALTA:** PC World Malta; **MEXICO:** Computerworld Mexico, PC World Mexico, Publish in Asia; **MYANMAR:** PC World Myanmar; **NETHERLANDS:** Computer! Totaal, LAN Internetworking Magazine, LAN World Buyers Guide, Macworld Netherlands, Net, WebWereld; **NEW ZEALAND:** Absolute Beginners Guide and Plain & Simple Series, Computer Buyer, Computer Industry Directory, Computerworld New Zealand, MTB, Network World, PC World New Zealand; **NICARAGUA:** PC World Centro America; **NORWAY:** Computerworld Norge, CW Rapport, Datamagasinet, Financial Rapport, Kursguide Norge, Macworld Norge, Multimediaworld Norge, PC World Ekspress Norge, PC World Nettverk, PC World Norge, PC World ProduktGuide Norge; **PAKISTAN:** Computerworld Pakistan; **PANAMA:** PC World Panama; **PEOPLE'S REPUBLIC OF CHINA:** China Computer Users, China Computerworld, China InfoWorld, China Telecom World Weekly, Computer & Communication, Electronic Design China, Electronics Today, Electronics Weekly, Game Software, PC World China, Popular Computer Week, Software Weekly, Software World, Telecom World; **PERU:** Computerworld Peru, PC World Profesional Peru, PC World SoHo Peru; **PHILIPPINES:** Click!, Computerworld Philippines, PC World Philippines, Publish in Asia; **POLAND:** Computerworld Poland, Computerworld Special Report Poland, Cyber, Macworld Poland, Networld Poland, PC World Komputer; **PORTUGAL:** Cerebro/PC World, Computerworld/Correio Informático, Dealer World Portugal, Mac*In/PC*In Portugal, Multimedia World; **PUERTO RICO:** PC World Puerto Rico; **ROMANIA:** Computerworld Romania, PC World Romania, Telecom Romania; **RUSSIA:** Computerworld Russia, Mir PK, Publish, Seti; **SINGAPORE:** Computerworld Singapore, PC World Singapore, Publish in Asia; **SLOVENIA:** Monitor; **SOUTH AFRICA:** Computing SA, Network World SA, Software World SA; **SPAIN:** Communicaciones World España, Computerworld España, Dealer World España, Macworld España, PC World España; **SRI LANKA:** Infolink PC World; **SWEDEN:** CAP&Design, Computer Sweden, Corporate Computing Sweden, Internetworld Sweden, it branschen, Macworld Sweden, MaxiData Sweden, MikroDatorn, Nätverk & Kommunikation, PC World Sweden, PCAktiv, Windows World Sweden; **SWITZERLAND:** Computerworld Schweiz, Macworld Schweiz, PCtip; **TAIWAN:** Computerworld Taiwan, Macworld Taiwan, NEW ViSiON/Publish, PC World Taiwan, Windows World Taiwan; **THAILAND:** Publish in Asia, Thai Computerworld; **TURKEY:** Computerworld Turkiye, Macworld Turkiye, Network World Turkiye, PC World Turkiye; **UKRAINE:** Computerworld Kiev, Multimedia World Ukraine, PC World Ukraine; **UNITED KINGDOM:** Acorn User UK, Amiga Action UK, Amiga Computing UK, Apple Talk UK, Computing, Macworld, Parents and Computers UK, PC Advisor, PC Home, PSX Pro, The WEB; **UNITED STATES:** Cable in the Classroom, CIO Magazine, Computerworld, DOS World, Federal Computer Week, GamePro Magazine, InfoWorld, I-Way, Macworld, Network World, PC Games, PC World, Publish, Video Event, THE WEB Magazine, and WebMaster; online webzines: JavaWorld, NetscapeWorld, and SunWorld Online; **URUGUAY:** InfoWorld Uruguay; **VENEZUELA:** Computerworld Venezuela, and PC World Venezuela, and **VIETNAM:** PC World Vietnam. 3/24/97

Welcome to the Discover Series

D o you want to discover the best and most efficient ways to use your computer and learn about technology? Books in the Discover series teach you the essentials of technology with a friendly, confident approach. You'll find a Discover book on almost any subject — from the Internet to intranets, from Web design and programming to the business programs that make your life easier.

We've provided valuable, real-world examples that help you relate to topics faster. Discover books begin by introducing you to the main features of programs, so you start by doing something *immediately*. The focus is to teach you how to perform tasks that are useful and meaningful in your day-to-day work. You might create a document or graphic, explore your computer, surf the Web, or write a program. Whatever the task, you learn the most commonly used features, and focus on the best tips and techniques for doing your work. You'll get results quickly, and discover the best ways to use software and technology in your everyday life.

You may find the following elements and features in this book:

Discovery Central: This tearout card is a handy quick reference to important tasks or ideas covered in the book.

Quick Tour: The Quick Tour gets you started working with the book right away.

Real-Life Vignettes: Throughout the book you'll see one-page scenarios illustrating a real-life application of a topic covered.

Goals: Each chapter opens with a list of goals you can achieve by reading the chapter.

Side Trips: These asides include additional information about alternative or advanced ways to approach the topic covered.

Bonuses: Timesaving tips and more advanced techniques are covered in each chapter.

Discovery Center: This guide illustrates key procedures covered throughout the book.

Visual Index: You'll find real-world documents in the Visual Index, with page numbers pointing you to where you should turn to achieve the effects shown.

Throughout the book, you'll also notice some special icons and formatting:

A Feature Focus icon highlights new features in the software's latest release, and points out significant differences between it and the previous version.

Web Paths refer you to Web sites that provide additional information about the topic.

Tips offer timesaving shortcuts, expert advice, quick techniques, or brief reminders.

The X-Ref icon refers you to other chapters or sections for more information.

Pull Quotes emphasize important ideas that are covered in the chapter.

Notes provide additional information or highlight special points of interest about a topic.

The Caution icon alerts you to potential problems you should watch out for.

The Discover series delivers interesting, insightful, and inspiring information about technology to help you learn faster and retain more. So the next time you want to find answers to your technology questions, reach for a Discover book. We hope the entertaining, easy-to-read style puts you at ease and makes learning fun.

Credits

ACQUISITIONS EDITOR
Gregory S. Croy

DEVELOPMENT EDITOR
Greg Robertson

TECHNICAL EDITOR
Sally Neuman

COPY EDITORS
Pamela Clark
Carolyn Welch

PRODUCTION COORDINATOR
Katy German

GRAPHICS AND PRODUCTION SPECIALIST
Edmund B. Penslien

PROOFREADER
Mary Clarc Oby

INDEXER
Donald Glassman

BOOK DESIGN
Seventeenth Street Studios
Phyllis Beaty
Kurt Krames

About the Author

Naba Barkakati is an expert programmer and successful computer book author with experience in a wide variety of systems, from MS-DOS and Windows to UNIX and the X Window System. He bought his first personal computer — an IBM PC-AT — in 1984 after graduating with a Ph.D. in electrical engineering from the University of Maryland at College Park, Maryland. While pursuing a full-time career in engineering, Naba dreamed of writing software for the emerging PC software market. As luck would have it, instead of building a software empire like Microsoft, he ended up writing *The Waite Group's Microsoft C Bible* — one of the first 1,000-page tutorial-reference books that set a new trend in the computer book publishing industry.

Over the past nine years, Naba has written 21 computer books on a number of topics, ranging from Windows programming with Visual C++ to tutorials for the Webmaster. He is the author of several bestselling titles, such as *The Waite Group's Turbo C++ Bible*, *Object-Oriented Programming in C++*, *X Window System Programming*, *Visual C++ Developer's Guide*, and *Borland C++ 4 Developer's Guide*. His books have been translated into several languages, including French, Russian, Italian, Dutch, Polish, Greek, Japanese, Chinese, and Korean. Naba's last two books are *Linux SECRETS* and *UNIX Webmaster Bible*, both published by IDG Books Worldwide in 1996.

Naba lives in North Potomac, Maryland, with his wife, Leha, and their children Ivy, Emily, and Ashley.

THIS BOOK IS DEDICATED TO MY WIFE, LEHA,
AND MY DAUGHTERS IVY, EMILY, AND ASHLEY.

PREFACE

Perl (which officially stands for *Practical Extraction Report Language*) was originally created to extract information from text files and then use that information to prepare reports. Perl is a scripting language, which means the programmer does not have to compile and link a Perl script (a text file containing Perl commands). Instead, an interpreter executes the Perl script. This makes it easy to write and test Perl scripts because programmers do not have to go through the typical edit-compile-link cycles to write Perl programs.

Besides ease of programming, another reason for Perl's popularity is that Perl is distributed freely and is available for a variety of computer systems, including UNIX, Windows 95, Windows NT, and Macintosh. Until recently, Perl has been popular among system administrators (primarily on UNIX systems) as a scripting language. System administrators typically use Perl to automate routine system administration tasks, such as looking for old files that could be archived and deleted to free up disk space.

When the World Wide Web became popular and the need for Common Gateway Interface (CGI) programs arose, Perl became the natural choice for those already familiar with the language. The recent growth in the number of Web sites has transformed Perl from a previously obscure scripting language into a mainstream tool for CGI programming. Many new and experienced Webmasters are now beginning to learn Perl. The number of Perl beginners is growing fast because many Internet Service Providers allow anyone with a home page to use CGI programs. That means even relatively inexperienced users want to learn Perl and add CGI programs to their home pages.

Like any programming language, it takes considerable time and effort to learn everything about Perl. Anyone with some computer experience, however, can become familiar with Perl and write simple Perl scripts very quickly. The trick is to start with just a small amount of relevant information and build up your knowledge slowly.

Because Perl is popular, there is no shortage of books on Perl. All these books, however, tend to overwhelm the beginner by providing a tremendous amount of detail right from the start. Even the books that claim to teach Perl in two weeks can be daunting to the beginner because the volume of information is too much to assimilate in two weeks. What a Perl beginner needs is a gentle introduction from someone who has gone through the experience of learning Perl.

What This Book Can Offer You

*D*iscover Perl 5 addresses the unique needs of a Perl beginner by providing a quick but thorough introduction to the basics of Perl. The book's goal is to provide just the right amount of information to get the reader up and running quickly. The book comes with a companion CD-ROM that includes the most recent Perl 5 sources and executable programs (*binaries*), along with instructions on how to install Perl 5 on Windows 95, Windows NT, and UNIX systems.

Discover Perl 5 describes clearly and concisely how to write and execute Perl programs, from very simple to reasonably advanced ones. Instead of going through a litany of syntactical details (which can confuse a beginner), *Discover Perl 5* uses real-world examples to illustrate Perl syntax and programming techniques. These examples will help you create useful Perl scripts. You will also find these Perl programs on the companion CD-ROM.

How This Book Is Organized

*D*iscover Perl 5 has 15 chapters organized into three parts, as well as two appendixes.

Part One, "Getting Started with Perl," includes five chapters that cover the basics of Perl. This part begins with a complete overview of Perl, as well as a step-by-step introduction to writing and running a Perl script. Basic concepts of computer programming are also outlined. Perl variables, control structures, and basic input and output are covered in this part.

Part Two, "Learning to Use Perl," has six chapters that introduce the reader to more advanced features of Perl. This part begins with a gentle introduction to regular expressions — one of the most powerful and useful features of Perl. Other chapters in Part Two teach the reader how to write Perl subroutines, use the built-in functions to perform useful tasks, and work with files and directories. Chapter 11 is devoted to the unique features of Perl 5, which is the latest version of Perl.

Part Three, "Using Perl in Web Programming" has four chapters that show you how to use Perl scripts to implement CGI programs at Web sites. This part shows you how to run other programs from a Perl script and how to format reports in Perl. You will learn the inner workings of CGI, receive step-by-step instructions on writing Perl CGI programs, and see how an HTML document can make use of a Perl CGI program to provide dynamic content — Web pages whose content depends on what a user requests through HTML forms.

Appendix A, "Perl Resources on the Internet," lists Perl resources on the Internet.

Appendix B, "How to Use the CD-ROM," discusses how to install Perl 5 from the CD-ROM on Windows 95, Windows NT, and Unix systems.

You are expected to proceed sequentially through the book. If you have some exposure to Perl programming, you may proceed to Part II and learn more about key features of Perl. If you already know Perl programming, you may jump to Part III and get started with CGI programming with Perl.

It's time to start your Perl adventure. Take out the companion CD-ROM and install Perl. Then turn to a relevant chapter, and let the fun begin. Before you know it, you'll become a Perl expert!

I hope you enjoy reading this book as much as I enjoyed writing it!

Acknowledgments

I am grateful to Greg Croy for providing me the opportunity to write this introductory guide to Perl. As the project editor, Pat O'Brien got me going with the manuscript submission process. Greg Robertson took care of the development editing and ensured the consistency of the book's content. I appreciate the guidance and support all three of you have given me during this project.

I would like to thank Sally Neuman for reviewing the manuscript for technical accuracy and for providing many useful suggestions to improve the book's content.

Thanks to everyone at IDG Books Worldwide who worked behind the scenes to transform my raw manuscript into this well-edited and beautifully packaged book. In particular, thanks to Pamela Clark for the thorough copyediting.

Finally, and as always, I am most thankful to my wife, Leha, and my daughters Ivy, Emily, and Ashley — it is their love and support that keep me going.

CONTENTS AT A GLANCE

PART THREE—USING PERL IN WEB PROGRAMMING

CONTENTS

15 WRITING CGI PROGRAMS IN PERL, 339

QUICK TOUR

W elcome to Perl 5 — the language of choice for writing applications for the World Wide Web.

Perl is a scripting language, which means you do not have to compile and link a Perl script (a text file containing Perl commands). Instead, an interpreter executes the Perl script. This makes it easy to write and test Perl scripts, because you do not have to go through the typical *edit-compile-link* cycles to write Perl programs.

Besides ease of programming, another reason for Perl's popularity is that Perl is distributed freely and is available for a wide variety of computer systems, including UNIX, Windows 95, Windows NT, and Macintosh.

Discover Perl 5 introduces you to Perl programming by providing a quick but thorough introduction to Perl. The book's goal is to provide just the right amount of information to get you up and running quickly. The first part of the book gets you started with Perl; the second part shows you some advanced features such as regular expressions; and the third part teaches you the inner workings of CGI programs and provides step-by-step instructions on how to create a CGI program in Perl.

As with any computer programming language, the best way to learn Perl is to start using it. The Perl 5 Quick Tour takes you through the process of creating a simple Perl program.

Getting Ready to Go

When you write and run Perl programs, you will be working in an MS-DOS prompt window (in Windows 95 or Windows NT). In UNIX, you'll use a terminal window. For example, to verify if Perl is installed on your system, type the following command in an MS-DOS prompt window:

```
perl -v
```

Figure 1 shows a typical output from this command. The output should tell you the version of Perl. If you see something similar to what Figure 1 shows, Perl is installed on your system.

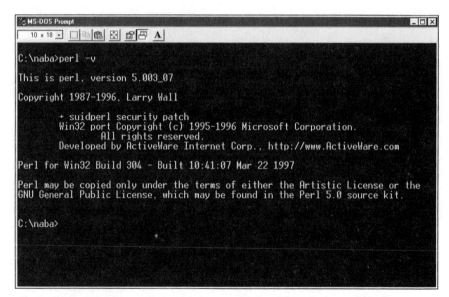

Figure QT-1   Checking whether Perl is installed on a Windows 95 system

Let's assume that you have already installed Perl 5 on your computer and are ready to begin programming in Perl.

If you have not yet installed Perl 5, you'll find Perl 5 for Windows 95, Windows NT, and UNIX on the companion CD-ROM. To install Perl from the CD-ROM, consult Appendix B, "How to Use the CD-ROM."

Creating a Perl Program

A Perl program starts out as a text file containing Perl commands or statements. It's easy to write a simple Perl program. Let's begin by writing a Perl program that displays Hello, World! on your monitor.

The first step is to prepare the text file containing the Perl program. Then you can use the Perl interpreter to run the program.

Follow these steps to prepare your first Perl program:

1. Start a text editor. On a Windows 95 or Windows NT system, you can use the MS-DOS EDIT editor (just type **EDIT** in the MS-DOS prompt window) or the Notepad program. On a UNIX system, you may use a text editor such as vi or emacs.

2. Type the following lines in the text editor:

```
# hello.pl
#
# A Perl program that prints Hello, World!

print "Hello, World!\n";
```

3. Save that text in a file named hello.pl (the exact command to save a file depends on your text editor).

Figure 2 shows this Perl program in the EDIT program running in an MS-DOS prompt window in Windows 95.

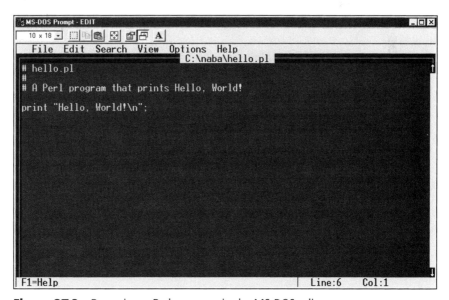

Figure QT-2   Preparing a Perl program in the MS-DOS editor

Running a Perl program

In Windows 95 or Windows NT, you typically double-click on icons to start programs. That's not the way to run a Perl program, however. Instead, you type a specific command in the MS-DOS prompt window to run a Perl program.

To run the `hello.pl` program, you have to type the following command:

```
perl hello.pl
```

This command runs the Perl interpreter, which, in turn, runs the Perl program `hello.pl`. After you type this command, you should see the following message on-screen:

```
Hello, World!
```

At this point, if you look back at the content of the `hello.pl` program, you can see the `print` command that causes the `Hello, World!` output.

Figure 3 shows an MS-DOS prompt window with the result of running the `hello.pl` program.

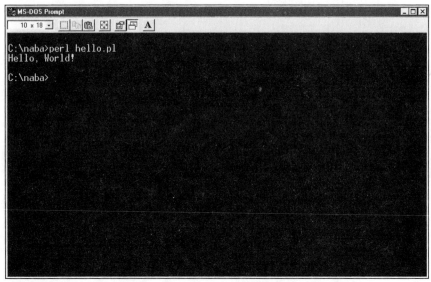

Figure QT-3 Running a Perl program in the MS-DOS prompt window

GETTING STARTED WITH PERL

THIS PART CONTAINS THE FOLLOWING CHAPTERS

So, what kind of background does it take to create a programming language like Perl? Appropriately enough, Perl's creator, Larry Wall, has a background in natural and artificial languages, as well as graduate-level training in linguistics. Maybe that's why so many programmers feel right at home with Perl — it just feels so natural!

O'Reilly & Associates was justifiably proud on November 21, 1996, when the company announced the hiring of Larry Wall as a software developer in O'Reilly's Software Products Group. After all, among UNIX aficionados, Wall has a reputation as a tool builder par excellence.

Over the past ten years or so, Larry Wall has written quite a few popular free programs for UNIX. His creations include the rn news reader and the patch utility. He is best known, however, as the father of Perl. As the story goes, it all started when Larry was asked to develop a configuration management (CM) system for a bicoastal software development team. Wall improvised a CM system using the news software, but he also needed a reporting tool. The CM information was stored in news articles, which, in turn, were in a number of text files. The software team, however, really needed a data extraction and reporting tool — one that could process text files well. That's when Wall created Perl as a reporting language. The year was 1986, and Larry Wall had worked about a year to create the language.

During the intervening years, Wall continued to nurture Perl as he applied it to various tasks. Perl turned out to be a useful tool for UNIX system administration — UNIX traditionally uses a great many text files to store various pieces of system information, and Perl excels in text processing. By 1991, Perl was popular enough that O'Reilly had decided to release the Programming Perl book, which Larry Wall cowrote with Randall Schwartz. That book covered Perl version 4 (Perl 4). By the time Larry Wall joined O'Reilly, he had released Perl 5, a completely overhauled version of Perl. And that is what this book covers.

CHAPTER ONE

PERL IN FIFTEEN MINUTES

IN THIS CHAPTER YOU LEARN THESE KEY SKILLS

You must have heard a lot about Perl lately. Maybe you have seen job announcements asking for Perl programming experience. Or, you may have seen phrases such as "CGI programming in Perl" and wondered why everyone's talking about Perl — and what exactly is "CGI programming"? In fact, that last phrase — *CGI programming* — is the reason why Perl has suddenly become popular. CGI stands for Common Gateway Interface, which is a standard way to write programs for World Wide Web (or, simply, Web) servers. Perl happens to be a programming language that many Webmasters — the folks who keep the Web servers up and running — use to write CGI programs. Webmasters like to use Perl for a good reason. Unlike traditional programming languages such as C or C++, Perl does not need a compiler to create executable programs. A Perl program is a plain text file that can be executed as is (using the Perl interpreter). This makes Perl programming quick and easy. If you are puzzled by this explanation, don't despair. You don't have to brave the world of Perl programming on your own. You have this book, *Discover Perl 5*, as your personal guide.

Just as a guide takes you to the major attractions, the 15 chapters of this book show you how to use the key features of Perl 5 (the latest version of Perl). Instead of taking you through a boring list of syntactical details, this book shows you how to solve real-world problems using Perl. First, you learn how to work with text and numbers in Perl. Then you learn to use Perl for more complex tasks, such as searching for text in a file or creating a formatted report. Finally, you see how Perl is useful in Web programming — this is where you'll learn about CGI programming.

As with any computer programming language, the best way to learn Perl is to start using it. This chapter takes you on a whirlwind tour of Perl, introducing you to many of the key topics that the rest of *Discover Perl 5* describes in detail.

Understanding Perl

B y now, you must have guessed that Perl is a programming language. Officially, Perl stands for *Practical Extraction and Report Language*, but Larry Wall, the creator of Perl, says people often refer to Perl as *Pathologically Eclectic Rubbish Lister*. As these names might suggest, Perl was originally designed to extract information from text files and generate reports.

Perl began life in 1986 as a system administration tool created by Larry Wall. Over time, Perl grew by accretion of many new features and functions. The latest version of Perl — Perl 5 — supports object-oriented programming and enables anyone to extend Perl 5 by adding new modules in a specified format.

True to its origin as a system administration tool, Perl has been popular with UNIX system administrators for many years. More recently, when the World Wide Web (Web, for short) became popular and the need for Common Gateway Interface (CGI) programs arose, Perl became the natural choice for writing CGI programs. The recent surge in Perl's popularity is primarily due to the use of Perl in writing CGI programs for the Web. Of course, as people pay more attention to Perl, they discover that Perl is useful for much more than CGI programming. That, in turn, has made Perl even more popular among users.

In addition to the increased use of Perl for CGI programming on the Web, another key reason for Perl's popularity is that it's freely available and it may be freely distributed. To top it off, Perl is also available for a wide variety of systems, from Windows 95 and Windows NT to UNIX and Macintosh.

All these factors have made Perl a "must learn" language for programmers. As you will learn from the rest of this chapter, you can pick up Perl easily, especially if you already know how to program in another language.

Looking for Perl

B efore you can start using Perl, you must have the Perl software installed on your computer. The first step, then, is to find out whether Perl is already installed on your system. If you are lucky, you'll find Perl ready to go and you'll be all set to learn Perl programming. Otherwise, you have to install Perl (or arrange to have it installed) on your system.

Follow these steps to find out whether Perl is installed on your system:

1. If you are on a UNIX workstation, make sure that you are at a UNIX shell prompt. (On a graphics workstation, this means you have a terminal window open and in that window you can type UNIX commands such as `ls` or `w`). If you are running Windows 95 or Windows NT 4.0, open an MS-DOS window (click `Start` → `Programs` → `MS-DOS Prompt`).

2. Type the following command:

   `perl -v`

3. On a typical UNIX system with Perl properly installed, you should see output similar to that shown in Figure 1-1 (this output is from a Linux system).

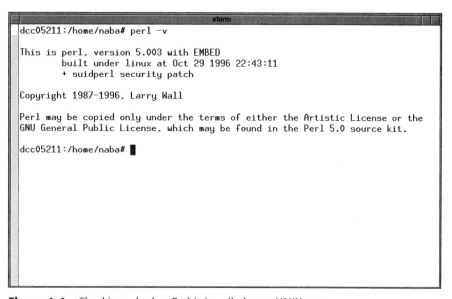

```
dcc05211:/home/naba# perl -v

This is perl, version 5.003 with EMBED
        built under linux at Oct 29 1996 22:43:11
        + suidperl security patch

Copyright 1987-1996, Larry Wall

Perl may be copied only under the terms of either the Artistic License or the
GNU General Public License, which may be found in the Perl 5.0 source kit.

dcc05211:/home/naba#
```

Figure 1-1 Checking whether Perl is installed on a UNIX system

On a Windows 95 or Windows NT system with Perl already installed, the output should appear as shown in Figure 1-2.

As you can see, if Perl is installed on your system, these steps should show you the version number of Perl. In fact, the `perl -v` command runs the `perl` program and instructs it to display the version number. The `perl` program is the Perl interpreter (the computer program that interprets and runs Perl programs, which are text files containing Perl commands).

```
┌─────────────────────────────────────────────────────────────────────┐
│ ⁵⁄ₛ MS-DOS Prompt                                          _ ⟋ ⊠     │
├─────────────────────────────────────────────────────────────────────┤
│ [ 10 x 18 ▾ ] ⬚ 🗈 🗇 ⊠ 🗗 🗖 A                                        │
├─────────────────────────────────────────────────────────────────────┤
│ C:\naba>perl -v                                                       │
│                                                                       │
│ This is perl, version 5.003_07                                        │
│                                                                       │
│ Copyright 1987-1996, Larry Wall                                       │
│                                                                       │
│         + suidperl security patch                                     │
│         Win32 port Copyright (c) 1995-1996 Microsoft Corporation.     │
│              All rights reserved.                                     │
│         Developed by ActiveWare Internet Corp., http://www.ActiveWare.com │
│                                                                       │
│ Perl for Win32 Build 304 - Built 10:41:07 Mar 22 1997                 │
│                                                                       │
│ Perl may be copied only under the terms of either the Artistic License or the │
│ GNU General Public License, which may be found in the Perl 5.0 source kit. │
│                                                                       │
│                                                                       │
│ C:\naba>_                                                             │
│                                                                       │
└─────────────────────────────────────────────────────────────────────┘
```

Figure 1-2 Checking for Perl from an MS-DOS prompt window

TIP The `perl -v` command might show a version number that begins with a 4 or a 5. These numbers correspond to Perl 4 and Perl 5, respectively. Although this book's goal is to teach you about Perl 5 (the latest version of Perl), most of the examples work in Perl 4 as well.

If the `perl -v` command generates an error message (for example, in Windows 95, you might see the message `Bad command or file name`), then chances are that Perl is not installed on your system. Another reason for the error message might be that even though Perl may be on your system somewhere, a crucial installation step was not completed and the system cannot locate the Perl interpreter. Your best bet is to install Perl again from this book's companion CD-ROM.

X-REF To install Perl software, follow the instructions outlined in the "Installing Perl from the CD-ROM" section.

Learning Programming

Assuming that you found Perl on your system, you are now ready to begin learning Perl programming. If you have written programs in any other programming language, you can pick up Perl programming very quickly. If you have never written a computer program, however, you first need to understand the basics of programming. You also need some familiarity with computers and the major parts that make up a computer. This section gives you an overview of computer programming — just enough to get you going.

X-REF If you are already familiar with the concept of computer programming, skip the next few sections and jump to the "Writing Your First Perl Program" section.

A simplified view of a computer

Before you get a feel for computer programming, you need to understand where computer programs fit into the rest of your computer. Figure 1-3 shows a simplified view of a computer, highlighting the major parts that are important to you as a programmer.

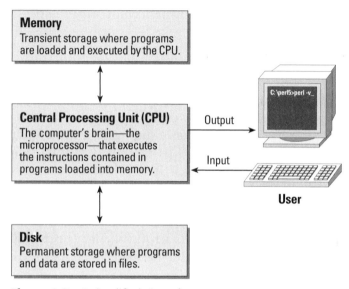

Figure 1-3 A simplified view of a computer

At the heart of a computer is the *central processing unit* (*CPU*), which performs the instructions contained in a computer program. In a Pentium PC, the Pentium microprocessor is the CPU. In a Sun SPARC workstation, the CPU is a SPARC microprocessor. In an HP 9000 workstation, the CPU is a PA-RISC microprocessor.

Random-access memory (RAM), or just *memory*, serves as the storage area for computer programs while the CPU executes them. The contents of the memory are not permanent; they go away when the computer is shut down or when a program is no longer running.

The *hard disk*, or disk, serves as the permanent storage space for computer programs and data. The disk is organized into files, which are, in turn, organized in a hierarchical fashion into directories and subdirectories (somewhat like organizing paper folders in the drawers in a file cabinet). Each file is essentially a block of storage space capable of holding a variety of information.

For example, a file may be a human-readable text file or it may be a collection of computer instructions that make sense only to the CPU, such as an executable file. When you create computer programs, you work with a great many files. As you see later in this book, each Perl program is a text file that contains Perl commands (of course, that's what you are going to learn in the rest of this book).

For a programmer, the other two important items are the *input and output* — the way a program gets input from the user and displays output to the user. The user provides input through the keyboard, and output appears on the monitor. A program, however, may accept input from a file and send output to a file.

Role of the operating system

The *operating system* is a special collection of computer programs whose primary purpose is to load and run other programs. All operating systems include one or more command processors that enable users to type commands and perform tasks, such as running a program or printing a file. Many operating systems also include a graphical user interface (GUI) that enables the user to perform most tasks by clicking on graphical icons. Windows 95, Windows NT, and various versions of UNIX are examples of operating systems.

It is the operating system that gives a computer its personality. For example, you can run Windows 95 or Windows NT on a PC. On that same PC, you could also install and run Linux, which is a UNIX clone that runs on 486 and Pentium PCs. That means, depending on the operating system installed on it, a PC could be a Windows 95, Windows NT, or a UNIX system.

Computer programs are built on top of the operating systems. That means a computer program makes use of the operating system's capabilities. For example, computer programs read and write files by using built-in capabilities of the operating system.

Although the details vary, most operating systems support a number of similar concepts. As a programmer, you need to be familiar with the following handful of concepts:

* A *process* is a computer program that is currently running in the computer. Most operating systems can run multiple processes simultaneously.

* A *command processor* is a special program that enables the user to type commands and perform various tasks, such as run any program, look at a list of files, or print a file. The term *shell* is also used for a command processor. In Windows 95 or Windows NT, you can type commands in an MS-DOS prompt window. When writing Perl programs, you work with the command processor a great deal, because Perl programs are typically run by using the command processor.

* The term *command-line* refers to the commands that a user types to the command processor. Usually, command-lines contain a command and

one or more options — the command is the first word in the line and the rest are the options.

✴ *Environment variables* are essentially text strings (sequences of characters) with a name. For example, the PATH environment variable refers to a string that contains the names of directories. Operating systems use environment variables to provide useful information to processes. To see a list of environment variables in a Windows NT or Windows 95 system, type **SET** in an MS-DOS prompt window. On UNIX systems, you can type the printenv command to see the environment variables.

Basics of computer programming

A computer *program* is a sequence of instructions for performing a specific task. Consequently, computer programming involves creating that list of instructions to complete a specific task. The exact instructions depend on the programming language that you use. For most programming languages, you must go through the following steps to create a computer program:

1. Use a text editor to type in the sequence of commands from the programming language. This is the sequence of commands that accomplishes your task. This human-readable version of the program is called the *source file* or *source code.* You can create the source file by using any application (such as a word processor) that can save a document in plain text (ASCII) form.

2. Use a compiler to convert that text file — the source code — from human-readable form into machine-readable object code (*object code* refers to the sequence of machine instructions). Typically, this step also combines several object code files into a single machine-readable computer program, something that the computer can actually run.

3. Use a special program called a debugger to track down any errors and to find which lines in the source file might have caused the errors.

These three steps are referred to as the *edit-compile-debug* cycle of programming, because most programmers must repeat this sequence several times before a program works correctly.

Perl programming is a bit different from the traditional edit-compile-debug cycle. Perl programs do not need the compile step; instead, a special program known as the *Perl interpreter* can compile and run the Perl source file (that's the text file with Perl commands). That means you can run a Perl program as soon as you finish typing the Perl commands in a text file. This is one of the reasons why many programmers find Perl attractive — you get going faster than the traditional compiled languages, such as C and C++.

PERL PROGRAM OR PERL SCRIPT?

The term *script* simply is a synonym for *program*. Unlike programs written in programming languages such as C and C++, Perl programs do not have to be compiled; the Perl interpreter interprets and executes the Perl programs. The term *script* often is used for such interpreted programs. (Strictly speaking, the Perl interpreter does not simply interpret a Perl program; it converts the Perl program into an intermediate form before executing the program.)

In addition to learning the basic programming steps, you also need to be familiar with the following terms and concepts:

* *Variables* store different types of data. You can think of each variable as being a placeholder for data — kind of like a mailbox, with a name and room to store data. The content of the variable is its *value.*

* *Expressions* combine variables by using *operators.* One expression might add several variables; another might extract a part of a string.

* *Statements* perform some action, such as assigning a value to a variable or printing a string.

* *Flow-control statements* enable statements to be executed in various orders, depending on the value of some expression. Typically, flow-control statements include for, do-while, while, and if-then-else statements.

* *Functions* (also called *subroutines* or *routines*) enable you to group several statements and give them a name. This feature, therefore, enables you to execute the same set of statements by invoking the function that represents those statements. Typically, a programming language provides many predefined functions to perform tasks such as opening a file reading from it.

Installing Perl from the CD-ROM

Before you can start using Perl, you must have the Perl software installed on your computer. The first step is to check to find out whether Perl is already installed on your system. If you are lucky, you'll find Perl ready to go and you'll be all set to learn Perl programming. Otherwise, you have to install Perl (or arrange to have it installed) on your system. The installation steps for Windows NT or Windows 95 systems are different from those for UNIX systems.

Installing Perl in Windows NT or Windows 95

The companion CD-ROM includes a ready-to-run version of Perl 5 (that's version 5 — the latest version — of Perl).

Follow these steps to install Perl 5 on your Windows 95 or Windows NT system:

1. Insert the CD-ROM into your system's CD-ROM drive.

2. Open an MS-DOS window. Assuming that you want to install Perl on the current drive, create a directory for Perl 5 with the following commands:

   ```
   cd \
   md perl5
   ```

3. Change to the newly created directory and copy the Perl 5 software from the CD-ROM with the following commands (this step assumes that D is your system's CD-ROM drive):

   ```
   cd \perl5
   xcopy /s d:\perl5
   ```

   Note that if your CD-ROM drive is not D, you must replace d: with the drive letter for your CD-ROM drive.

4. Complete the final installation steps by typing the following command:

   ```
   bin\perlw32-install
   ```

   This step executes an installation batch file that displays an informative message and asks whether you want to proceed. Press Y to continue. There are a few more questions as well; in each case, press Y to continue with the installation.

The installation process updates the search path — the names of directories that Windows 95 or Windows NT searches to locate any program. You have to reboot your PC for the new search path to take effect.

Installing Perl in UNIX

If you work on a UNIX system, you probably have a system administrator who takes care of installing software on the system. The companion CD-ROM includes an archive (latest.tar) with the source code for Perl 5. Your system administrator has to copy the source code archive to the system, unpack the archive, and compile the files to create the executable file. (Unfortunately, there are too many varieties of UNIX systems to provide ready-to-run Perl software for each UNIX variant.)

Ask your system administrator to follow these steps to install Perl 5 on the UNIX system:

1. Mount the CD-ROM. A typical UNIX command to mount the CD-ROM on the directory named /cdrom might be as follows:

```
mount -r /dev/devname /cdrom
```

where you must replace devname with the actual device name of the CD-ROM drive.

2. Unpack the source code in a directory of your choice. For example, you might decide to place the source code in the /usr/local/src directory. To do this, type the following commands:

```
cd /usr/local/src
tar xvf /cdrom/latest.tar
```

This step assumes that the CD-ROM is mounted on /cdrom. After this step finishes, you'll find the Perl source code in a directory whose name begins with perl (the rest of the directory name depends on the exact version number of Perl).

3. Change to the Perl source directory by using the following command:

```
cd perl*
```

4. Configure the Perl software for your system with the following command:

```
sh configure
```

5. To compile and link the Perl software, your system must have a C compiler. Type the following command to build Perl:

```
make
```

6. Complete the installation steps with the following command, which copies the executable files (often referred to as *binaries*) to an appropriate directory:

```
make install
```

After the system administrator completes these steps, you should be able to try out Perl with the perl -v command.

Writing Your First Perl Program

Like any computer program, a Perl program starts out as a file containing commands or statements — in this case, they are Perl commands or statements. It's easy to write a simple Perl program. Let's begin by writing a Perl program that displays `Hello, World!` on your monitor.

The first step is to prepare the text file containing the Perl program. Then you can use the Perl interpreter to run the program.

Preparing the Perl program

Follow these steps to prepare your first Perl program:

1. Start a text editor. On a UNIX system, you may use an editor such as `vi` or `emacs`. On a Windows 95 or Windows NT system, you can use the MS-DOS EDIT editor (just type **EDIT** in the MS-DOS prompt window) or the Notepad program.

2. Type the following lines in the text editor:

```
#!/usr/local/bin/perl
#
# A Perl program that prints Hello, World!
#
# The \n is a newline character (causes the
# printing to advance to the next line)

print "Hello, World!\n";
```

3. Save that text in a file named `hello.pl` (the exact command to save a file depends on your text editor).

Now you have a Perl program in the file `hello.pl`. You learn how to run this program in the next section, but first take a moment to note the following features of a Perl program:

* The `#` character indicates a comment. The remainder of a line following the `#` character is ignored when the Perl program is executed. You should make it a habit to use comments liberally in your Perl programs.

* Blank lines and extra spaces are ignored, so you can add blank lines or spaces to make your program more readable.

* Every Perl statement ends with a semicolon (;).

* On UNIX systems, the first comment line has a special form that enables you to start the Perl interpreter and run the Perl program easily. As you see in the next section, this feature makes a Perl program directly

executable in UNIX (in other words, you can run the Perl program by typing the program's name at the UNIX prompt).

In the `hello.pl` program, nearly every line is a comment (as indicated by the # character at the beginning of the comment lines). The program displays `Hello, World!` with a single Perl statement:

```
print "Hello, World!\n";
```

You could probably guess that this statement prints a text string and the text appears inside double quotes. The only odd-looking character is the \n just before the closing quote mark. That's a special notation for a line feed character (also known as *newline* among UNIX programmers). The \n character causes the output to advance to the next line (the concept is a holdover from the days of line printers, when a computer program explicitly had to move the print head to the next line by issuing a line feed command).

That's probably more than enough explanation for such a simple program. Now you should try to run the program.

Running a Perl program

To run a Perl program, you must start the Perl interpreter and provide your Perl program as input to the interpreter. This approach to running a Perl program works on both Windows 95 (or Windows NT) and UNIX systems. On a UNIX system, however, you also can run a Perl program in a somewhat simpler manner. The next two sections show you the details of using the Windows 95 (or Windows NT) and UNIX systems, respectively.

RUNNING A PERL PROGRAM IN WINDOWS 95

You may have some experience running programs in Windows 95 or Windows NT. Because Windows 95 and Windows NT have nice graphical interfaces, you typically double-click on icons to start programs. That's not the way to run a Perl program in Windows 95, however. Instead, you type a specific command in the MS-DOS prompt window to run a Perl program.

To run the `hello.pl` program, for example, you have to type the following command:

```
perl hello.pl
```

The message you see on-screen is as follows:

```
Hello, World!
```

You should interpret these two lines as follows:

✳ The first line runs `perl.exe`, the Perl interpreter, and provides `hello.pl` as the input to the Perl interpreter.

✳ The second line shows the result of running `hello.pl` — it prints the `Hello, World!` message.

At this point, if you look back at the contents of the `hello.pl` program, you can see the `print` function that causes the `Hello, World!` output. That print function is one of Perl's many built-in functions (or commands) that you can use in any Perl program.

Figure 1-4 shows an MS-DOS prompt window with the result of running the `hello.pl` program.

Figure 1-4 Running a Perl program in the MS-DOS prompt window

If you get an error message when you try to run a Perl program, the Perl software may not be properly installed on your system. You should consult the "Installing Perl in Windows NT or Windows 95" section and install Perl from this book's companion CD-ROM.

RUNNING A PERL PROGRAM IN UNIX

On a UNIX system, you must run a Perl program from a UNIX shell prompt. If you are working on a UNIX system with a graphical user interface, you need to be in a terminal window to run the Perl script. As is the case with a Windows 95 or Windows NT system, you can run the Perl program with the following command:

```
perl hello.pl
```

The program, in turn, prints the following message:

```
Hello, World!
```

The UNIX shell (command processor) also provides for another way to run a Perl program. You can run the Perl program simply by typing its name at the UNIX shell prompt.

Follow these steps to make a Perl program executable in UNIX:

1. Add the following line at the very beginning of the Perl program:

```
#!/usr/local/bin/perl
```

That's a comment line in the Perl programming language, but the UNIX shell treats the `#!` combination in a special way. The shell runs the program whose name follows the `#!` characters. In this case, the program name is `/usr/local/bin/perl`, which is the usual location of the Perl interpreter. On some UNIX systems, the Perl interpreter is installed in the `/usr/bin` directory. On such systems, you have to specify `#!/usr/bin/perl` on the first line of the Perl program.

2. Use the UNIX `chmod` command to mark the Perl program as an executable file. For example, to make the `hello.pl` file executable, type the following command:

```
chmod +x hello.pl
```

Now you should be able to run the Perl program by typing its name. For example, after you perform the preceding steps for the `hello.pl` program, you can run it by typing the following:

```
hello.pl
```

The program then prints the `Hello,World!` message.

Figure 1-5 shows a typical UNIX terminal window with the result of running the `hello.pl` program in two different ways: by typing `perl hello.pl` and by typing `hello.pl` alone.

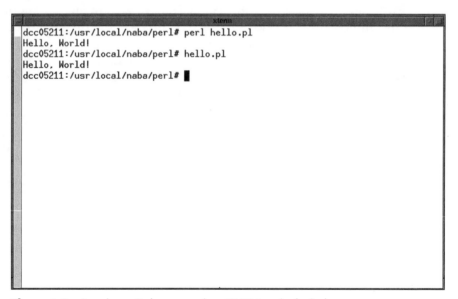

Figure 1-5 Running a Perl program in a UNIX terminal window

On UNIX systems, it is customary to set up Perl programs to be executable by adding the special comment line at the beginning of the file and then making the file executable with the `chmod +x` command.

Exploring Perl

The simple `Hello, World!` example shows very little of what Perl can do. That basic example is meant to show you the mechanics of how to create a Perl program and then run it. Perl, of course, can do a lot more than print simple messages. Although you learn the key features of Perl by reading this book, you may find it helpful to get an overview of Perl's features. In particular, you should see some simple examples of these features to get a feel for Perl. For now, just examine the sample code and read the brief explanations. Don't fret if everything is not clear. The subsequent chapters cover these topics in greater detail.

Understanding Perl versions

Before you go through the overview of Perl, you should know that there are two common versions of Perl: Perl 4 and Perl 5. The actual version number (which you can see with the `perl -v` command) has more digits. As of this writing, for example, the latest version of Perl 5 is 5.003. The extra digits refer to new releases with bug fixes that have occurred since version 5 of Perl became available.

Although Perl 5 is slowly becoming the most commonly used version of Perl, many sites still use Perl 4. Perl 5 introduces important new features, such as support for object-oriented programming, but it also supports all the basic programming features that Perl 4 supports. The bottom line is that you can learn Perl with either Perl 4 or Perl 5.

X-REF In Chapter 11, you learn about the new features of Perl 5. You need Perl 5 to try out the sample programs in that chapter.

Learning basic Perl syntax

Perl is relatively easy to learn and use because there are not that many syntax rules. Nevertheless, as outlined in this section, you have to follow some simple rules in a Perl program.

Perl is free-form; there are no constraints on the placement of any keyword. That means there are no rules for the exact number of spaces or lines. You don't even have to place parentheses around the arguments in a function call (you learn about function calls in the section "Using subroutines or functions," later in this chapter). All you need to do is end each Perl statement with a semicolon (;).

Comments begin with a hash mark (#). The Perl interpreter disregards the rest of the line beginning with the #.

Sometimes, a group of Perl statements must be treated as a block. You have to enclose such groups of Perl statements in braces ({ ... }). For example, you may want to check some condition and execute a group of statements only when the condition is true. Using the `if` statement, such a group of statements appears as follows:

```
if (condition)
{
    ... group of Perl statements ...
}
```

Of course, this is not real Perl code; it's meant to show you the syntax only.

Perl programs often are stored in files with names that end in `.pl`, but there is no restriction on the filenames that you can use. When you run a Perl program, you have to specify the full filename, including any extension.

Storing data

The primary purpose of writing a Perl program is to do something with data. For example, you might have to write a program that counts the number of times a customer has ordered from your company (imagine that each transaction is recorded in a file and your job is to search through that file and count the number of times a specific customer has had any transactions with your company). When you try to solve such a problem using a Perl program, you have to read and store data in your program. You have to read data from the file, you have to keep a count that you can increment whenever you find a transaction for the selected customer, and so on.

In Perl programs, you store data in *variables.* Each variable has a name, and you can store any type of data in a variable. You can easily recognize a variable in a Perl program, because each variable name begins with a special character: a dollar sign ($), an at symbol (@), or a percent sign (%). The special character denotes the variable's type. The three variable types are as follows:

* *Scalar variables* are used to store single data items, such as numbers or text strings. The name of a scalar variable begins with a dollar sign ($). Here are some Perl statements that use scalar variables:

```
$num_pages = 256;
$price = $24.99;
$title = "Discover Perl 5";
```

* *Array variables* are collections (or lists) of scalar variables. An array variable has an at symbol (@) as a prefix. Thus, the following are arrays:

```
@pages = (62, 26, 22, 24);
@commands = ("start", "stop", "draw", "exit");
```

* Because an array is a list of scalar variables, the value of each array is a number of comma-separated data items enclosed in parentheses.

* *Associative arrays* are collections of key-value pairs in which each key is a string and the value is any scalar variable. If you see a percent-sign (%)

prefix, then you are looking at an associative array. You can use associative arrays to associate a name with a value. For example, you might store the amount of disk space used by each user in an associative array such as the following:

```
%disk_usage = ("root", 147178, "naba", 28547,
               "emily", 55, "ivy", 60, "ashley", 45);
```

As you can see, each element is separated by commas, and they must be kept in the correct, associative order.

Because each variable type has its own special character prefix, you can use the same name for different variable types. Thus, %disk_usage, @disk_usage, and $disk_usage can appear within the same Perl program.

 X-REF **In Chapter 2, you learn more about variables and how to use them in Perl programs.**

Processing data

To process data, you store the data in variables and then work with those variables. For example, to compute the price of a number of books, you use the following formula:

```
total_price = number_of_books x unit_price
```

The right-hand side of that formula is an *expression.* You need to use the multiplication operator in that expression. As in this formula, you use *operators* in Perl programs to combine Perl variables. Typical mathematical operators are addition (+), subtraction (-), multiplication (*), and division (/). In a Perl program, therefore, you might compute the price of a number of books with the following statement:

```
$total_price = $number_of_books * $unit_price;
```

Here, the right-hand side of the equal sign is a Perl expression. Here are a few more typical Perl expressions:

```
$count == 10          comparison operator
$count + $i           arithmetic expression
$users[$i]            array index
```

These expressions are examples of the *comparison operator* (the first line), the *arithmetic operator,* and the *array-index operator.* That last operator is the way you access an element of an array.

In addition to the common mathematical and comparison operators, Perl has some unique operators. A good example is the dot operator (.), which concatenates two strings, as illustrated by the following Perl program:

```
#!/usr/local/bin/perl

$part1 = "Hello, ";
$part2 = "World!";
$message = $part1.$part2;   # $message = "Hello, World!"
print "$message\n";
```

When you run this Perl program, it prints:

```
Hello, World!
```

As this output illustrates, the dot operator creates a new string by concatenating two strings.

 In Chapter 3, you learn more about other operators and how to use them in data processing.

Controlling program flow

The Perl interpreter executes the statements in a Perl program in a serial fashion, one after another. Sometimes, however, you need to perform some computation only when a specific condition exists. Suppose that you want to write a Perl program to print a message if the value of a variable exceeds a threshold. In this case, you use an if statement to check the variable and then execute a block of Perl code only if that variable exceeds the threshold. The code would take the following form:

```
if ($variable > $threshold)
{
    print "Warning: $variable exceeds $threshold\n";

... other Perl statements to be executed when variable exceeds
    threshold...
}
```

This is an example of code that controls the flow of the Perl program — the block of code within the curly braces is executed only if the condition specified by the if statement is true.

Perl provides a number of ways to control the program's flow. Here are some of Perl's flow-control statements:

* The if and else statements enable you to check a condition and execute a specific block of code. Suppose that you have to report a different service charge, depending on the account balance. Here's how you might do this with the if and else statements:

```
if ($balance > 1000)
{
    print "Your monthly service charge is \$2.00\n";
}
else
{
    print "Your monthly service charge is \$7.00\n";
}
```

* The `unless` statement is useful when you have to execute a block of code only if a condition is false. Here is a simple example:

```
unless ($user eq "root")
{
    print "You must be \"root\" to run this program.\n";
    exit;
}
```

In this case, unless the string `user` is `"root"`, the program exits.

* The `while` statement enables you to repeat a block of code as long as some condition remains true. This is known as *looping*. For example, if you want to add the numbers from 1 to 10, you might use the following Perl program with a `while` statement:

```
#!/usr/local/bin/perl

# Define the variables to hold the sum
# and keep count
$sum = 0;
$i = 1;

# Add the numbers from 1 through 10
while ($i <=10)
{
    $sum = $sum + $i;
    $i = $i + 1;
}

# Print the result
print "Sum of 1 through 10 is $sum\n";
```

When you run this Perl program, it prints the following text:

```
Sum of 1 through 10 is 55
```

* The `for` statement also enables you to write loops. The syntax is a bit more complicated than `while`. For example, the following `for` loop adds the numbers from 1 to 10:

```
for($i=0, $sum=0; $i <= 10; $sum += $i, $i++) {}
```

In this example, the actual work of adding the numbers is done in the third expression ($sum += $i, $i++), and the statement controlled by the for loop is an empty block ({}). You might want to compare this for loop with the while loop that performs the same task.

 X-REF **Perl has several other flow control statements; you learn about them in detail in Chapter 4.**

Using regular expressions

The "Understanding Perl" section mentions that Perl originated as a programming language for processing text. One of the common text-processing tasks is to look for occurrences of a text string. For example, you may want to find all occurrences of a name in a file (assuming that the file records transactions and you are interested in all transactions for a specific person). To implement such text-search capabilities, Perl adopts a strategy from UNIX. The strategy is based on regular expressions. To understand regular expressions, you need to learn about a UNIX command that uses regular expressions a great deal.

UNIX has a command called grep that enables you to search files for a pattern of strings. You can use the grep command to locate all files that have any occurrences of a specified string. Suppose that you want to find all occurrences of the strings make or Make on any line of all Perl 5 source files. On your Linux system, you have loaded the latest Perl 5 source code in the /usr/local/src/ perl5.003 directory. Therefore, you use the following two commands to accomplish this task under UNIX:

```
cd /usr/local/src/perl5.003
grep "[Mm]ake" *.c
```

This grep command finds all occurrences of make and Make in the files whose names end in .c.

The grep command's "[Mm]ake" argument is known as a *regular expression*, which is a pattern that matches a set of strings. You construct a regular expression with a small set of operators and rules that are similar to the ones for writing arithmetic expressions. A list of characters inside brackets ([...]), for example, matches any single character in the list. Thus, the regular expression "[Mm]ake" is a set of two strings, as follows:

```
make    Make
```

Perl supports regular expressions just as the grep command does. Many other UNIX programs, such as the text editors vi and sed (stream editor), also support regular expressions. The purpose of a regular expression is to search for a pattern of strings in a file.

In a Perl program, you can use the same type of regular expressions that the UNIX grep command uses. For example, to test whether a text string contains the words make or Make, you write the following Perl code:

```
if ( $string =~ /[Mm]ake/ ) { print $string; }
```

This code prints the text string if it contains one of the strings make or Make. The expression inside the parentheses shows how you look for an occurrence of a regular expression in a text string:

```
$string =~ /[Mm]ake/
```

 X-REF   **Regular expressions are one of the most powerful features of Perl. You'll find them useful even if you are only beginning to learn Perl. Unfortunately, regular expressions look rather forbidding because they contain many special characters. The rules for constructing regular expressions, however, are fairly simple. You'll learn to define and use regular expressions in Chapters 6 and 7.**

Using subroutines or functions

A common programming practice is to break programs into smaller parts known as *functions* or *subroutines*. A Perl subroutine is basically a group of statements that perform a specific task. You can refer to that group of Perl statements by a name, and whenever your program has to perform that task, you can call that subroutine. An example should make this technique clear.

Suppose that you want to write a subroutine that accepts a first and a last name and prints a welcome message. The idea is that you'll call the subroutine whenever you need to display a welcome message. Let's call the subroutine hello. Here's how you might write the hello subroutine:

```
sub hello
{
# Obtain the arguments from the @_ array
# and give them the names $first and $last
    local ($first, $last) = @_;

# Print the welcome message with the full name
    print "Hello, $first $last\n";
}
```

To use the hello subroutine, you have to call it by using a special syntax and provide it with the first and last names to be used in the welcome message.

Here is an example:

```
$a = Jane;
$b = Doe;

&hello($a, $b);    # Call the hello subroutine
```

This code displays the following output:

```
Hello, Jane Doe
```

From this example of a subroutine, you should make the following observations:

* A Perl subroutine declaration begins with the `sub` keyword, followed by the name of the subroutine.

* The body of the subroutine is a group of Perl statements enclosed in curly braces ({ . . . }).

* The special array variable @_ — you can tell this is an array because of the "at" sign prefix — contains any arguments passed to the subroutine.

* Inside the subroutine, you can assign the arguments to a local array of scalar variables by using the `local` keyword (see the body of the `hello` subroutine).

* To call a subroutine, place an ampersand (&) before its name. Thus, the subroutine `hello` is called by `&hello`.

X-REF **Subroutines are a good way to package code that you (or others) may use in many different Perl programs. You learn more about subroutines in Chapter 8.**

Using Perl's built-in functions

When you process data (whether numbers or text strings) in a Perl program, you may need to perform a variety of computations. For example, you may need to compute mathematical functions such as sines and cosines, or you may need to run a command from the operating system (for example, the command to list the contents of a directory). Perl makes it easy for you to perform these types of tasks by providing built-in functions. These are functions that are already defined; all you have to do is call the function.

You have already seen one of these built-in functions — `print` — which you use to generate output from a Perl program. Besides `print`, Perl includes more than 160 built-in functions that can perform a host of tasks, such as the following (the sample code shows a typical use of the function to accomplish the task):

* Find the number of characters in a text string:

  ```
  $num_characters = length($string);
  ```

* Convert a string to all lowercase:

  ```
  $lc_string = lc($string);
  ```

* Remove the last character of a string (used to get rid of the newline character that ends many strings):

  ```
  chop($string);
  ```

* Compute the cosine of an angle (in radians):

  ```
  $cos_theta = cos($theta);
  ```

* Reverse the items in an array:

  ```
  @reverse_array = reverse(@array);
  ```

* Open a file:

  ```
  open(DATAFILE, "sales.dat");
  ```

* Execute an operating system command:

  ```
  system("dir");  # Runs the DIR command in Windows 95
  ```

This handful of examples shows you the variety of tasks that you can perform with Perl's built-in functions. The examples also illustrate how to use a built-in function — you call the function by its name and provide a list of arguments in parentheses (although you can skip the parentheses if you want — this is an example of Perl's flexibility).

X-REF In Chapter 9, you become familiar with a larger selection of Perl's built-in functions.

Accessing files

Because most data resides in files, you often must work with files in your Perl programs. Perl identifies files by a name that's known as a *filehandle.* Just so that these names do not conflict with other Perl variables, the convention is to use all uppercase for filehandles. A Perl program can immediately use a number of predefined filehandles:

* STDIN denotes the standard input — by default, the keyboard.
* STDOUT is the standard output and refers to the display screen, by default.
* STDERR is used for printing error messages.

To read from a file, you write the filehandle inside angle brackets (<>). Thus, <STDIN> reads a line from the standard input.

You can open other files by using the open function. The following example shows you how to open the /etc/passwd file on a UNIX system and display the lines in that file:

```
#!/usr/local/bin/perl
# Works only on a UNIX system
#
open (PWDFILE, "/etc/passwd"); # filehandle is PWDFILE
while ($line = <PWDFILE>)
{
    print $line;                # Input line is in $line
}
close PWDFILE;                  # Close the file
```

If you run this Perl program on a UNIX system, it displays all the lines in the /etc/passwd file (that's the file with passwords of all users — in encrypted form, of course).

 By default, the open function opens a file for reading. In Chapter 10, you learn how to open files for other types of operations, such as writing or appending. Also, you learn how to obtain directory listings in a Perl program.

Accessing the operating system

Sometimes you want to run an existing program or execute an operating system command from a Perl program. For example, to get a listing of the files in a directory, you might want to run the ls command under UNIX (on Windows 95, you might use the DIR command to do the same task). Or, you might want your Perl program to automatically display a text file in the Notepad program (on Windows 95 or Windows NT). Perl includes facilities for such tasks.

To run another program or to execute an operating system command, a Perl program needs to access the operating system, because the operating system performs these tasks. Perl programmers can access these operating system capabilities through a number of built-in functions.

The simplest way to execute any operating system command in your Perl program is to use the system function with the command in a string. The command can be one of the standard operating system commands (such as the UNIX ls or Windows 95 DIR) or the name of a program (such as Notepad in Windows 95) that you want to run.

To see the system function in action, type the following code and save it in a file named run.pl:

```
# Run excel
system "notepad run.pl";
```

That `system` function call executes the command: `notepad run.pl`. On a Windows 95 or Windows NT system, that command should start the Notepad program and cause it to load the `run.pl` file.

To try out this example, type the following command in an MS-DOS prompt window:

```
perl run.pl
```

You should see the Notepad program's window appear with the contents of the `run.pl` file in that program's window. To quit the Notepad program, click File → Exit .

X-REF **As this example shows, the capability to run any operating system command is very powerful, because that enables you to run virtually anything from a Perl program. You learn to exploit this capability more in Chapter 12.**

BONUS

Using Perl at a Web Site

At the beginning of this chapter, I mentioned that Perl is popular because it is the language of choice for CGI programming. Although you learn more about CGI programming in Chapters 14 and 15, I don't want to leave you wondering what a CGI program does. This section shows you a simple CGI program that displays a welcome message in an HTML page. (HTML stands for HyperText Markup Language — the notation used to describe the layout of a Web page).

On the World Wide Web, when you use a Web browser to view a document, it sends the request for the document to a specific Web server. The server sends back the requested document, which the browser interprets and displays. When certain special document names are used, the Web server launches a CGI program instead of returning an existing document. The CGI program can create a document on the fly and send back that document.

To communicate with the CGI program, the Web server sets up a number of environment variables with useful information (such as the system from which the request came, the name and version of the Web browser making the request, and so on). The CGI program is supposed to retrieve that information from the environment variables. The sample CGI program includes an example of how to access environment variables. Perl uses a special type of variable called an *associative array* to hold the environment variables. You learn about associative arrays in Chapter 2.

NOTE **To run a CGI program, you need access to a Web server. If you have an account with an Internet Service Provider (ISP) and the ISP offers you a Web page, you may be able to try out the CGI program.**

Now you'll see how to write a CGI program that displays a welcome message in an HTML page. By using a few special environment variables, the Perl program even customizes the hello message with the name of the user's system, as well as provides a link back to your Web page.

To implement this simple CGI program, all you need to do is create a Perl script that prints a Multipurpose Internet Mail Extension (MIME) header followed by the message. Use a text editor to type the following text, and then save it as the hello.pl file:

```perl
#!/usr/local/bin/perl

# A simple Perl script that displays
# "Hello!" in an HTML page

# First, send the MIME header. Remember to
# end header with an extra newline

print "Content-type: text/html\n\n";

# Next, send the HTML document with
# appropriate tags

print "<html>\n";
print "<head>";
print "<title>Hello from ", $ENV{SERVER_NAME}, "</title>\n";
print "</head>\n";
print "<body>\n";
print "<h3>Hello from ", $ENV{SERVER_NAME}, "</h3>\n";

# Send some interesting information from
# the environment variables that the Web
# server sets up before running this
# script
```

```
print "<pre>\n";
print "You're visiting from: ", $ENV{REMOTE_HOST}, "\n";
print "Your browser is:      ", $ENV{HTTP_USER_AGENT}, "\n";
print "</pre>\n";

print "<hr>\n";

print "Return to: <a href=\"http://", $ENV{SERVER_NAME}, "/\">\n";
print $ENV{SERVER_NAME}, "</a>\n";

print "</body>\n";
print "</html>\n";
```

As the listing shows, this Perl script first prints a MIME header to indicate the document type. The script writes an extra newline (\n) character to mark the end of the header. Then the script prints lines of an HTML document. The script uses several environment variables (accessed through the $ENV{...} syntax) to prepare a dynamic HTML document whose content changes depending on who accesses the script.

You can best understand the script's output when you see the script in action. To test the hello.pl script, perform the following steps:

1. Make sure that your system has Perl installed and the perl program is in the /usr/local/bin directory. If not, edit the first line of hello.pl to reflect the name of the directory where perl resides.

2. Place the script in a directory where your Web server expects CGI programs. For example, my ISP has set up the Web server to recognize scripts in the /exec-bin/ directory, so I place the script in that directory.

3. Use a Web browser (you can run the browser on any system on the Internet) to access the script with an appropriate URL. For my Web server, the URL is http://www.lnbsoft.com/exec-bin/hello.pl. (Go ahead and try this; it should work.)

Figure 1-6 shows the HTML document generated by the hello.pl script for a typical access.

If you access http://www.lnbsoft.com/exec-bin/hello.pl from a different system, the script displays the name of your system instead of what Figure 1-6 shows. Also, if you copy the script and run it on your Web server, the script generates an HTML document with a hello message from your server instead of from www.lnbsoft.com, as shown in Figure 1-6.

This simple script gives you an idea of how to write CGI programs in Perl. The hello.pl script, however, does not show how to process a query from the user. In Chapters 14 and 15, you learn more about CGI programming in Perl and how to create interactive forms for your home page.

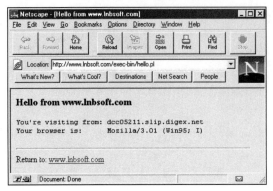

Figure 1-6 An HTML document created by the `hello.pl` script

Summary

Perl is gaining popularity primarily because of the popularity of the World Wide Web. Perl happens to be the language of choice for CGI programming. CGI stands for *Common Gateway Interface*, which is a standard way of writing programs that provide unique services (such as access to a database) on the World Wide Web. Another reason for Perl's popularity is that Perl is freely available, and Perl runs on nearly all systems, including UNIX, Windows 95, Windows NT, and Macintosh. You'll find Perl for UNIX as well as Perl for Windows NT and Windows 95 on this book's companion CD-ROM.

This chapter provided a quick introduction to Perl, with the caution that details follow in the rest of the book. You learned how to find out whether Perl is installed on your system and, if not, how to install Perl from the companion CD-ROM. You learned the basics of Perl programming and, if you do not know programming yet, this chapter even provided a brief introduction to computer programming.

As a bonus, you experienced a Perl CGI program that prints a customized welcome message on a Web page. You needed access to a World Wide Web server to try out this CGI program.

The next chapter introduces you to the concept of variables — the storage bins for data — and shows you how to define and use variables in Perl programs.

STORING DATA IN PERL

IN THIS CHAPTER YOU LEARN THESE KEY SKILLS

C hapter 1 provides an overview of Perl programming. As you might infer from that overview, much of what you do in a Perl program is store and manipulate data. To work with data, you must use *variables* — storage bins that can hold various types of information, such as numbers and lines of text.

This chapter shows you the various ways in which you can store data in a Perl program. It also tells you a bit about printing from a Perl program, because you'll want to print out values of variables in example programs.

Understanding Perl Variables

I n a Perl program, you need variables to hold data while the program performs various computations using the data. Think of a variable as a storage bin — a place in the computer's memory where one or more pieces of data can be stored. A variable has a name and a value. The value is the data, and you use the name to refer to that data in a Perl program.

You have to use variables in nearly all Perl programs. For example, if you are computing the average travel expense of the employees in your company, you need a variable to keep a running total of the expenses, another to count the number of employees whose travel expenses you have counted so far, and a third variable for the average expense. You can refer to each variable by its name and perform the computations using these names.

Many programming languages have strict rules about variable names and the types of data that a variable can store. Although Perl is not strict about the type of data a variable can store, it does have different types of variables depending on whether the variable stores a single value or an aggregate of values. Figure 2-1 shows the three types of variables in Perl.

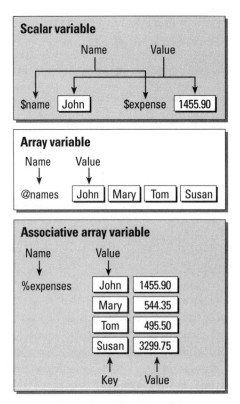

Figure 2-1   Types of Perl variables

As Figure 2-1 illustrates, each variable has a name and a value. Each type of variable name has a unique special character:

* *Scalar variables* have names that begin with a dollar sign ($). A scalar can store single values, such as a number or a text string.

* *Array variables* have names that begin with an "at" sign (@). Each array stores a list of scalar values. You can individually access the scalar values in an array.

* *Associative arrays* have names that begin with a percent sign (%). An associative array holds a list of key-value pairs. Each key-value pair is simply a pair of scalar variables, where the first item serves as a key and

the second item is the corresponding value. For example, in Figure 2-1, the associative array %expenses enables you to access the expenses of a person by that person's name.

Scalars are the most commonly used type of variable. Arrays are useful when you need to store a number of related values. When creating a form letter to all the employees in your organization, for example, you might store the names of the employees in an array.

An associative array is a special type of array that enables you to access a value by a key name. As Figure 2-1 shows, you might store the travel expenses of employees in an associative array with the employee name as the key. Then you can get the expense amount for an employee by using that employee's name as the key.

That was a quick overview of Perl's variable types. In the rest of this chapter, you learn how to use each type of variable.

Defining Scalar Variables

A scalar variable can store a single value, such as the number *24.99*, or the text string *Discover Perl 5 is a great book for learning Perl*. Here's how you might define and use these two variables in a Perl program:

```
#!/usr/local/bin/perl
# Define some scalar variables
$price = 24.99;
$comment =
"Discover Perl 5 is a great book for learning Perl";

# Print the variables
print "The book costs \$$price\n";
print "Comment: $comment\n";
```

When you run this program, it displays the following output:
```
The book costs $24.99
Comment: Discover Perl 5 is a great book for learning Perl
```

NOTE Note the print statement that displays the price of the book. To display the dollar sign, you have to type \$ (with a backslash in front of the dollar sign). The backslash indicates that the next character is to be interpreted specially. In this case, the Perl interpreter treats \$ as a plain dollar sign instead of expecting it to start the name of a scalar variable.

As the example program shows, it's simple to use a scalar variable. You pick a name for the variable, add a $ prefix to the name, and begin using the variable. A variable name usually begins with a letter followed by any number of letters and digits. You can also use underscores in variable names. Thus, the following are typical scalar variables in Perl:

```
$number_of_pages
$disk_usage
$unit_cost
$employee_name
```

NOTE **Although I have been using lowercase variable names in most examples, you can use both upper and lowercase letters in variable names. Note, however, that in Perl, variable names are case-sensitive. Thus $price and $Price are considered two different variables.**

You can store any single value in a scalar variable. Some common values are integers, real numbers (numbers with decimal points), and text strings. Note that a single value does not mean a single character — a whole line of text is considered a single value.

Storing integer values

Integers are whole numbers that you typically use for counting. For example, the number of pages in this book is an integer value. You can store such an integer value in a scalar variable, as follows:

```
$pages = 350;
```

NOTE **You can even embed underscores in integer values; the Perl interpreter automatically gets rid of the underscores when copying the value into the variable. Here is an example:**

```
$population = 220_000_000;
print "Population is: $population\n";
```

When this code runs, it displays the following output (unfortunately, as you can see, the print function does not print with commas separating the digits in long numbers):

```
Population is: 220000000
```

The idea is similar to that of using parentheses and hyphens as punctuation marks in a U.S. telephone number, such as (301) 555-1212. You can use the underscore as a punctuation mark in an integer value.

Storing real numbers

Real numbers are numbers with a fractional part — you can think of real numbers as numbers with a decimal point. They are also called *floating-point numbers.*

Many real-world numbers are floating-point numbers. For example, the price of this book, today's Dow Jones Industrial Average, the price of a cup of coffee — these are all floating-point numbers.

As with integers, you can store a floating-point number in a variable by assigning the value to the variable. Here are some examples:

```
$unit_price = 24.99;
$DJIA = 6958.29;
$bit_error_rate = 1.57e-6;
```

That last value — 1.57e-6 — shows how a floating-point number is written in scientific notation. As you probably know, 1.57e-6 stands for 1.57×10^{6}. In Perl, you can specify floating-point values in scientific notation.

Storing text strings

In most Perl programs, you process data and generate results. You use the `print` function to display the results, and you typically use text strings to explain the results. Of course, you can also store text strings in a variable, such as a variable that holds the title of this book. You can recognize the text strings by the double quotes that enclose the strings. For example, a simple Perl program might use text strings as follows:

```
#!/usr/local/bin
   $title = "Discover Perl 5"; # book's title
   $price = 24.99;             # price of one book
   $sales_tax_rate = 0.05;     # 5% sales tax
   $num_books = 10;            # number of books

# Compute the total cost for the books
   $total_amount = $num_books *
                $price * (1 + $sales_tax_rate);
# Display the result (notice the text string in
# double quotes with embedded variable names)
   print
   "$num_books copies of $title cost $total_amount\n";
```

When you run this Perl program, it prints the following output:

```
10 copies of Discover Perl 5 cost 262.395
```

Compare this output with the text string used in the `print` statement in the Perl program. As you can see, each scalar variable (identified by a name, such as `$title`, that begins with a $) is replaced by its value.

You might want to add double quotes around the book's title and a dollar sign in front of the total amount. Because double quotes mark the beginning and the end of a text string, you need to add a backslash prefix and type `\"` for any quote that you want Perl to print literally. Similarly, a $ signals the beginning of a scalar variable, so you must type `\$` to print a dollar sign. With these additions, the print statement becomes:

```
print "$num_books copies of \"$title\" cost ",
      "\$$total_amount\n";
```

In this example, I have also split the string into two parts because the entire line of the Perl statement is too long to fit on a single line. Here is the output resulting from this `print` function:

```
10 copies of "Discover Perl 5" cost $262.395
```

As you can see, the two comma-separated strings (each enclosed in double quotes) are concatenated by the print function. Also, each `\"` is printed as `"`, and the `\$` that precedes the `$total_amount` variable is printed as a $.

X-REF You might have wanted to print that dollar amount with two decimal places (as $262.39 instead of $262.395), but the `print` function does not enable you to control the formatting to that extent. You learn about other ways of formatting output in Chapter 13.

ENCLOSING STRINGS IN DOUBLE QUOTES

Until now, you have seen example programs that use strings enclosed in a pair of double quotes (`". . ."`). Such double-quoted strings are commonly used because they have some useful behavior:

* Scalar and array variables embedded in double-quoted strings are replaced by their values. Thus, you can write `"Total = $total"` and Perl treats that string as `"Total = 10"` (assuming that the value of the variable `$total` is 10).

* In double-quoted strings, characters with a backslash prefix are replaced by a single special character. For example, `\n` becomes a newline and `\t` is replaced by a tab character.

The term *escape sequence* refers to a single backslash followed by one or more characters. Escape sequences are used inside a double-quoted string. You can use escape sequences to insert special characters (such as tabs or newlines) into the string. Table 2-1 lists some commonly used escape sequences in Perl.

Table 2-1 Escape sequences in double-quoted strings

Escape sequence	Interpretation
\a	Causes the bell to sound.
\b	Moves backward by one space (backspace).
\cn	Inserts the Ctrl+*N* character (where *N* is any character).
\e	Prints an escape character (ASCII code 27 decimal or 33 octal).
\f	Moves to the beginning of the next page (form feed).
\l	Converts next letter to lowercase.
\n	Moves to the next line (newline).
\r	Moves to the beginning of current line (carriage return).
\t	Moves to the next tab position (tab).
\u	Converts next letter to uppercase.
\L	Converts all subsequent characters (up to the next \E) to lowercase.
\U	Converts all subsequent characters (up to the next \E) to uppercase.
\E	Ends case conversion started by \L or \U.
\"	Prints a quote.
\$	Prints a dollar sign.
\\	Prints a single backslash.
\0nn	Inserts the octal digits nn.
\xnn	Inserts the hexadecimal digits *nn*.

Here are some examples of situations in which you have to use escape sequences:

* To end a line and begin a new one, you use the \n escape sequence.
* To insert double quotes in a string, you use the \" sequence.
* To insert a dollar sign in the output, you use the \$ sequence.

ENCLOSING STRINGS IN SINGLE QUOTES

Sometimes, you may not want to display values of variables embedded in a string. Instead, you may want to print a text string exactly as is without any special attention being paid to characters such as $, @, or \. To store and print such strings, you should enclose the string in single quotes (' . . .'). For example, if you write the following Perl statement:

```
print
    '$num_books copies of $title cost $total_amount\n';
```

where the text string is enclosed in a pair of single quotes, the resulting output is:

```
$num_books copies of $title cost $total_amount\n
```

In other words, Perl displays a single-quoted string verbatim without replacing variable names with corresponding values. You might use single quotes to print strings that contain special characters, such as $ and @.

ENCLOSING STRINGS IN BACKQUOTES

A third type of string quoting is useful when you want to display the output of an operating system command. Suppose that you want to store the output of the UNIX ls command (the ls command lists the files in the current directory) in a string variable named $lsout. You can do so by using the following Perl statement:

```
$lsout = `ls`;   # Store output of ls in string $lsout
```

As you can see, the convention is to enclose the command within a pair of backquotes (` . . .`). The following Perl program illustrates how you might use a backquoted string:

```
#!/usr/local/bin/perl

# Store output of ls in a string variable
    $lsout = `ls`;

# Display the text string
    print "Directory listing:\n$lsout\n";
```

Here is typical output when I ran this Perl program in a directory containing several files:

```
Directory listing:
hello.pl
prls.pl
prpasswd.pl
var1.pl
```

NOTE The output is different when you run the program, of course, because it displays whatever the directory contains. If you want to try this program on a Windows NT or Windows 95 system, simply replace the ls command with DIR.

Defining Arrays

For single values, such as the name of an employee or the travel expense of an employee, you can use scalar variables. Sometimes, however, your program has to store multiple values, such as 30 employee names, 50 expense reports, or 20 e-mail addresses. When you need to store multiple values in a Perl program, you can use an array. A single array of names, for example, can hold as many employee names as you want.

An *array* is a collection of scalars. In Perl, you must start the name of an array with an at symbol (@). Figure 2-2 illustrates an array variable — @file_names — that holds four filenames.

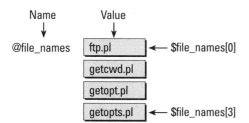

Figure 2-2 An array variable in Perl

The Perl statement that creates the @file_names variable shown in Figure 2-2 is as follows:

```
@file_names = ("ftp.pl", "getcwd.pl", "getopt.pl",
               "getopts.pl");
```

NOTE As this statement illustrates, you initialize (assign the initial value of) the array with a sequence of comma-separated scalar values (in this case, text strings) enclosed in parentheses. That sequence of strings in parentheses is called a *list*.

X-REF Another way to initialize an array is to read the contents of an entire file into the array. In this case, each line becomes an element in the array. You learn to read files in Chapter 10.

NOTE You can also store all the output of a command in an array. For example, consider the following Perl statement:

```
@perl_files = `ls *.pl`;
```

This statement causes the Perl interpreter to run the UNIX command `ls *.pl` and store the output in the `@perl_files` array. That means the `@perl_files` array will contain all filenames that end with `.pl`.

All the items in an array need not be of the same type; you can store any collection of scalar values — strings or numbers — in an array. Usually, however, you use an array to store scalar values of the same type.

Accessing array elements

The reason you store a sequence of scalar values in an array is to access the elements and use them in some computation. For example, you might store the filenames in an array and print out the size of each file. To perform these operations, you have to access individual elements in the array.

Each element in an array is a scalar variable and, as such, you can access an element by its position in the array. The element's position is known as the *index*: The first element is at index 0, the second one is at index 1, and so on. Thus, if you have four elements in an array (as shown in Figure 2-2), the fourth element is at index 3.

NOTE When you want to refer to the first element (index 0) of the array `@file_names`, you have to write `$file_names[0]` — replace the `@` with a `$` and then append the index within square brackets. As a beginner, you might find this notation for referring to an array element a bit confusing; I know *I* found it confusing. You can get over the initial confusion if you remember that each element of an array is a scalar, and scalar variable names begin with a `$`. Figure 2-2 shows how you would refer to the elements of the `@file_names` array using an index.

TIP If you want to access the last item in an array, just use the `-1` index. In other words, `$file_names[-1]` refers to the last element in the `@file_names` array.

Although I have shown only examples of accessing arrays with specific numbers as index, you can use a scalar variable as index. For example, if the `$i` variable is set to 3, then `$file_names[$i]` refers to the fourth element in the `@file_names` array.

Counting elements in an array

Suppose that you want to access each element of the `@file_names` array and perform some operation (such as determine the file size) for each element. As you learn in Chapter 4, you can use a `for` loop to do the job.

To write `for` loops, you need to know the number of elements in the array. Although you might know the number of elements in the array when you have explicitly initialized the array, situations will occur when you do not know the number of elements (for example, when you initialize an array using the output of a command, such as the UNIX ls command). In any case, Perl provides a way to find the number of elements in an array.

If you initialize a scalar variable with the array's name, Perl evaluates the array name as the count of elements in that array. The following Perl program illustrates how this feature works:

```
#!/usr/local/bin/perl

# Initialize an array with a list of strings
@commands = ("start", "stop", "draw" , "exit");

$numcmd = @commands;
print "There are $numcmd commands.",
      "The first command is: $commands[0]\n";
```

When you run this Perl program, it produces the following output:

```
There are 4 commands. The first command is: start
```

As you can see, equating a scalar variable to the array's name sets that scalar to the number of elements in the array. The first element of the @commands array is referenced as $commands[0] because the index starts at zero. Thus, the fourth element in @commands is $commands[3].

You can print an entire array with a print statement like this:

```
print "@commands\n";
```

When the Perl interpreter executes this statement, it displays the following output:

```
start stop draw exit
```

NOTE Note how the Perl interpreter treats the name of the array @commands differently in different contexts. When you set a scalar variable equal to @commands, the Perl interpreter evaluates @commands to be the number of elements in the array. When @commands appears in the print function, however, the Perl interpreter treats @commands as the sequence of scalar elements in the array. Thus, depending on the context, the Perl interpreter handles the array name in the most appropriate way.

Another way to get the count of elements in an array is to use the scalar variable $#arrayname (where arrayname is the name of an array variable) that has the last array index as the value. Because the array index starts at 0, the last index is one less than the number of elements in the array. For the four-element @commands array, for example, $#commands is 3.

Understanding the @ARGV array

When you use operating system commands, you typically type the command followed by one or more arguments. To make a copy of a file in a UNIX system, for example, you use the `cp` command, as follows:

```
cp oldfile newfile
```

That entire line is called a *command-line:* `cp` is the command, and `oldfile` and `newfile` are the command-line *arguments.* In this context, these two command-line arguments should be filenames.

Just as the `cp` command accepts command-line arguments, so you can write Perl programs that accept arguments on the command-line. Suppose that you are writing a Perl program (let's call it `thanks.pl`) that prints out a Thank You note, and you want to personalize the note with the recipient's name. You might decide to pass the recipient's name as a command-line argument to the `thanks.pl` program. In other words, to thank Joe, you want to run the `thanks.pl` program with the following command-line:

```
perl thanks.pl Joe
```

Perl automatically defines the @ARGV array using all the command-line arguments used when the Perl program is launched. For this `thanks.pl` example, @ARGV is an array with a single item — "Joe". Inside the Perl program, then, you can refer to the first argument as `$ARGV[0]`. With this information in hand, you could write the `thanks.pl` script as follows:

```
#!/usr/local/bin/perl

print "Dear $ARGV[0],\n";
print "Thank you for your suggestions.\n";
print "    Webmaster\n";
```

If you run this Perl program by typing `perl thanks.pl Joe`, the program prints the following output:

```
Dear Joe,
Thank you for your suggestions.
    Webmaster
```

If you compare this output with the `print` statements in the `thanks.pl` program, you'll notice that `$ARGV[0]` is equal to `Joe` — the first argument used on the command-line that launches the `thanks.pl` program.

You can use the @ARGV array whenever your Perl program has to access the command-line arguments. As the simple `thanks.pl` program shows, you can use command-line arguments as inputs to a Perl program.

@ARGV contains all the command-line arguments as elements in the array. Suppose that you run a Perl program (named `progname`) with the following command-line:

```
perl progname one two 3
```

Here, @ARGV is equal to (`"one"`, `"two"`, `3`). As you can see, Perl defines the @ARGV array using the list of arguments that appear immediately after the program name.

Working with Arrays

After you store a collection of scalar variables in an array, you can work with the array. Suppose that you have stored a list of employee names in an array; here are some ways in which you might want to manipulate the elements:

* Remove array elements one by one and perform some operation on each element (the operation could be as simple as printing the element).
* Add new elements to an array.
* Sort the elements in the array.
* Reverse the order of the elements in the array (you could use this operation, for example, to convert an ascending array of numbers to one sorted in descending order).
* Append one array to another. For example, you may have the list of employee names from two divisions of your company and you want to create a single consolidated list.

 Perl includes a number of built-in functions that enable you to manipulate arrays. You don't need to learn exhaustively about these functions, but you'll find it helpful to know that they exist. You learn about these built-in functions again in Chapter 9.

Removing array elements

You have already seen how to access array elements using indices — to access the first element of the @names array, you write $names[0]. There are a few other ways of accessing the array elements. For example, you may want to remove the array elements one by one and process each element. Perl provides some built-in functions to remove (and add) array elements.

Suppose that you have an array of names:

```
@names = ("John", "Bill", "Mary", "Susan");
```

and you want to extract the first element from the @names array. You can use the shift function to do this. To remove an element using shift, you might write the following:

```
$employee = shift @names; # First name is removed
```

The shift function removes the first element from @names and decreases the size of the @names array by one. Thus, after this Perl statement executes, $employee will have the value "John" and the @names will have three elements: ("Bill", "Mary", "Susan"). Each time you use shift on an array, the number of elements is reduced by one.

TIP **If you keep using the shift function on an array after the array runs out of elements, shift returns an undefined scalar value. You can check to see whether shift has returned a valid value by using the built-in function named** defined. **The following example shows how you can print all the elements in an array by using shift and** defined:

```perl
#!/usr/local/bin/perl

@names = ("John", "Bill", "Mary", "Susan");

while(1)  # loop continuously
{
    $employee = shift @names;

    if(defined($employee))
    {
        print "$employee\n";
    }
    else
    {
        last;  # end the loop
    }
}
```

X-REF **This example uses a** while **statement as well as** if and else **statements, which are further described in Chapter 4. Essentially, the** while **loop is set up to run continuously. Each time through the loop, an array element is extracted into the** $employee **variable using** shift. **The** if **statement uses the** defined **function (with** $employee **as the argument) to check whether the** $employee **is defined. As soon as the array runs out of**

elements, `shift` **returns an undefined value and the** `else` **statement ends the** `while` **loop with a** `last` **statement.**

If you want to process the array elements from last to first; you can do so by using the `pop` function — `pop` removes the last element of an array and decreases the count of array elements by one. You can use `pop` just as you use `shift`, as follows:

```
@names = ("John", "Bill", "Mary", "Susan");
$employee = pop @names; # Last name is removed
```

After this Perl statement executes, `$employee` will have the value `"Susan"` and the `@names` array will have three elements: (`"John"`, `"Bill"`, `"Mary"`).

Adding array elements

To add elements to the array, you can use the reverse of the `shift` and `pop` functions that you encountered in the preceding section. The reverse of `shift` is the `unshift` function, which adds one or more elements to the beginning of an array and increments the count of elements by one. You can add a single scalar value as the first element of an array by using the `unshift` function like this:

```
@names = ("John", "Bill", "Mary", "Susan");
unshift(@names, "Joe"); # Add to beginning of array
```

After this statement executes, the `@names` array will contain five elements in the following order: (`"Joe"`, `"John"`, `"Bill"`, `"Mary"`, `"Susan"`).

You can add more than one element with the `unshift` function. For example, if you write the following:

```
@names = ("John", "Bill", "Mary", "Susan");
unshift(@names, "Joe", "Tom");
```

then the `@names` array becomes (`"Joe"`, `"Tom"`, `"John"`, `"Bill"`, `"Mary"`, `"Susan"`).

The other function to add to an array is `push` — the reverse of `pop`. Just as `pop` removes the last element from an array, the `push` function adds one or more elements to the end of an array. For example, if you write the following:

```
@names = ("John", "Bill", "Mary", "Susan");
push(@names, "Joe", "Tom");
```

then the `@names` array contains six elements in the following order (`"John"`, `"Bill"`, `"Mary"`, `"Susan"`, `"Joe"`, `"Tom"`).

Sorting the array elements

Sorting is one of the common tasks you have to do when generating reports. If you are printing a report showing the travel expenses of all employees, you may want to sort the names in alphabetic order before printing the report. If you have the names in an array, you can sort them by using the sort function.

The sort function returns a sorted array, but does not alter the original array. In practice, this means that you must save the result of the sort in another array, as shown in the following program:

```
#!/usr/local/bin/perl
@names = ("Joe", "Tom", "John", "Bill", "Mary", "Susan");
@sorted_names = sort(@names);  # save the sorted array
print "@sorted_names\n";
```

The last print statement prints the sorted array of names. When the program runs, it prints the following:

```
Bill Joe John Mary Susan Tom
```

As you can see, this is an alphabetically sorted version of the @names array.

If you have an array of numbers, the sort function rearranges the items in ascending order. Here is an example of sorting an array of numbers:

```
#!/usr/local/bin/perl
@cost = (24.99, 19.95, 49.95, 44.99);
@sorted_cost = sort @cost;
print "@sorted_cost\n";
```

This program prints the following sorted array:

```
19.95 24.99 44.99 49.95
```

Reversing the order of array elements

If you have an array sorted in ascending order, you can turn it into a descending array by using the reverse function. You use the reverse function by providing an array as the argument. The result of calling reverse is another array with the elements in reverse order. You have to store the result in another array variable, as shown in the following example:

```
@ascending_array = (19.95, 24.99, 44.99, 49.95);
@descending_array = reverse(@ascending_array);
print "@descending_array\n";
```

This Perl code prints the following array as the result:

```
49.95 44.99 24.99 19.95
```

Although the reverse function is most useful when converting an ascending order array into descending order, you can use the reverse function to reverse the order of elements in any array. For example, if you reverse an array of strings like this:

```
@an_array = ("this", "and", "that");
@reverse_array = reverse(@an_array);
print "@reverse_array\n";
```

the result is the following:

```
that and this
```

Appending arrays

Suppose that you have two lists of employee names from two divisions of your company and you want to create a single consolidated list. If you have the two lists of names in arrays, you can create the combined list by appending one array to another. Perl provides the splice function for this purpose.

Actually, the splice function can do more than simply append one array to another. With splice, you can replace a portion of an array with another array. Figure 2-3 illustrates how splice works.

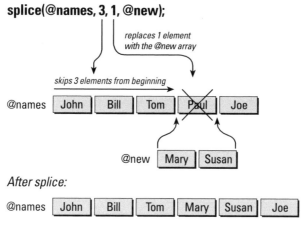

Figure 2-3 Splicing two arrays with the splice function

The following Perl program implements the splicing operation shown in Figure 2-3:

```
#!/usr/local/bin/perl
```

```
# Define two arrays
  @names = ("John", "Bill", "Tom", "Paul", "Joe");
  @new = ("Mary", "Susan");

# Splice the two arrays and print the result
  splice(@names, 3, 1, @new);
  print "@names\n";
```

When you run this program, it prints the following result:

```
John Bill Tom Mary Susan Joe
```

This is the result of splicing the array `@new` into the `@names` array after skipping the first 3 elements and replacing one element (`Paul`). The `splice` function has the following syntax:

```
splice(@old, offset, length, @new);
```

The `splice` function first removes `length` items from the `@old` array, starting with the item at the position specified by `offset`. Then `splice` inserts the `@new` array in place of the elements that were removed.

You can think of appending one array to another as a special case of splicing with the following constraints:

* All the elements of the first array are skipped.
* None of the elements of the first array are replaced.

Remember that for the array `@names`, the number of elements is `$#names+1` (`$#names` is the last array index, which is one less than the number of elements in the array). Thus, the following Perl program illustrates how you might append the `@new` array to the `@names` array:

```
#!/usr/local/bin/perl

# Define two arrays
  @names = ("John", "Bill", "Tom", "Paul", "Joe");
  @new = ("Mary", "Susan");

# Append @new to @names and print the result
  splice(@names, $#names+1, 0, @new);
  print "@names\n";
```

When executed, this program prints the following result:

```
John Bill Tom Paul Joe Mary Susan
```

which is the result of appending the `@new` array to the `@names` array.

Learning about Associative Arrays

Suppose that you are processing the travel expense reports of your company's employees and you want to keep track of the travel expenses by employee name. You might want a Perl program that enables you to enter an employee name and look up the corresponding travel expense amount. To do this, you need to associate each employee's travel expenses with that employee's name. Perl includes a unique type of array — the associative array — that enables you to store associated pairs of scalar variables, such as an employee name and the amount of travel expenses incurred by that employee.

Figure 2-4 illustrates a typical associative array.

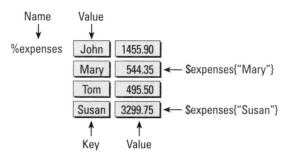

Figure 2-4 An associative array in Perl

The `%expenses` variable is an associative array that stores "name-expense" pairs. Here, the name is the key and the number representing the expense is the associated value.

In a Perl program, you declare and use the associative array `%expenses`, as follows:

```
#!/usr/local/bin/perl
%expenses = ("John",   1455.90,
             "Mary",    544.35,
             "Tom",     495.50,
             "Susan", 3299.75);

$mary_spent = $expenses{"Mary"};
print "Mary spent \$$mary_spent\n";
```

As this example illustrates, you must declare an associative array variable with a percent-sign (%) prefix. You can initialize the associative array with pairs of scalars — in this case, each pair has a name and a number (which, presumably, is the amount of travel expenses incurred by the named person).

When you run this Perl program, it displays the following output:

```
Mary spent $544.35
```

If you look back at the initialization of the %expenses variable, you'll see that 544.35 is the number that goes with Mary's name.

NOTE The example program and Figure 2-4 also illustrate how to refer to a scalar value by a key, which, in this case, is the name. As the example shows, you can refer to the expenses incurred by Mary with the variable $expenses{"Mary"} — by replacing the % with a $ and appending the key within curly braces. Note that you have only to enclose the key (such as "Mary") in quotes if it has embedded blanks. Thus, you could write

```
$expenses{Mary}
```

NOTE If you want to show a visual association between the key-value pairs in an associative array, you can use => in place of the comma. For example, you can define the %expenses associative array as follows:

```
%expenses = ("John"   =>   1455.90,
             "Mary"   =>    544.35,
             "Tom"    =>    495.50,
             "Susan"  =>   3299.75);
```

With this notation, you can easily see the key-value pairs in the associative array.

It's very easy to add the expenses of a new employee to the %expenses associative array. For example, to add the expense amounts of Bill, all you need to do is write:

```
$expenses{"Bill"} = 1327.65;
```

From then on, the %expenses associative array contains an entry for Bill.

Using the %ENV associative array

You can use an associative array to store anything that you need to access using an arbitrary key. The environment variables, commonplace in operating systems such as UNIX, Windows NT, and Windows 95, fit the model of associative array. An environment variable has a name and a value. For example, an environment variable named PATH has a value that's a list of directory names. The command processor searches the directories in PATH to locate programs. On a UNIX system, the PATH environment variable may be defined to be the following string:

```
/usr/local/bin:/bin:/usr/bin:/usr/etc:/usr/X11/bin:.
```

With Windows 95, PATH might be as follows:

```
C:\WINDOWS;C:\WINDOWS\COMMAND;C:\JAVA\BIN;.;C:\PERL5\BIN;
```

By convention, many programs use environment variables to accept input parameters. For example, an e-mail program might automatically forward all messages to the addresses specified in an environment variable named DISTLIST.

Because each environment variable is a name-value pair, you can easily store environment variables in an associative array with the name as the key. In fact, that's what Perl does for you. Perl automatically defines the %ENV associative array with all the currently defined environment variables.

ACCESSING AN ENVIRONMENT VARIABLE BY NAME

You can access the value of any environment variable from %ENV by using the environment-variable name as an index. For example, in a Perl program you can print the value of the PATH environment variable as shown in the following program:

```
#!/usr/local/bin/perl
# Print the PATH environment variable
    print "Current PATH = $ENV{PATH}\n";
```

When the Perl interpreter executes the print statement, it prints the current setting of PATH. On a UNIX system, the typical output might be as follows:

```
Current PATH =
    /usr/local/bin:/bin:/usr/bin:/usr/etc:/usr/X11/bin:.
```

NOTE Note that environment variables are also used in Common Gateway Interface (CGI) programs that are commonplace at World Wide Web sites. For example, when a user fills out a form and sends a query to a Web server, the Web server might invoke a Perl program to handle the query. By convention, that query is provided as the value of the QUERY_STRING environment variable whose value you can print with the following Perl statement:

```
print "QUERY_STRING = $ENV{QUERY_STRING}\n";
```

To retrieve the value of QUERY_STRING into a variable, you would write the following:

```
$query_string = $ENV{QUERY_STRING};
```

X-REF When you learn CGI programming in Chapters 14 and 15, you learn how to use associative arrays to handle the input that users provide through interactive forms on a Web page.

PRINTING ALL ENVIRONMENT VARIABLES

Although you can access the value of any environment variable by its name, Perl also provides some functions that enable you to access all the items in an associative array. For example, you can use the `keys` function and a `foreach` statement to print out all the environment variables. The following Perl program illustrates how to do this:

```perl
#!/usr/local/bin/perl

foreach $name (keys(%ENV))
{
    $value = $ENV{$name};
    print "$name = $value\n";
}
```

The `keys` function accepts an associative array as an argument and returns all the keys in that array. Thus, `keys(%ENV)` is a list of the environment-variable names.

X-REF

The `foreach` statement enables you to go through a list of items, copy the item into a named variable (in this case, that variable is $name), and use that variable in any computations you might want to perform. (Chapter 4 explains more about the `foreach` statement.) After you have a list of keys, you can access the values by using each key as index for the %ENV associative array. Thus, if a key is in the variable $name, you can refer to the corresponding value by writing $ENV{$name}.

When you run the example program, it prints out the name and value of all environment variables. On a Windows 95 system, a typical output might appear something like the following:

```
WINBOOTDIR = C:\WINDOWS
TMP = C:\WINDOWS\TEMP
PROMPT = $p$g
CLASSPATH = .;c:\java\lib\classes.zip
TEMP = C:\WINDOWS\TEMP
COMSPEC = C:\WINDOWS\COMMAND.COM
CMDLINE = perl prenv.pl
PATH = C:\WINDOWS;C:\WINDOWS\COMMAND;C:\JAVA\BIN;.;C:\PERL5\BIN;
WINDIR = C:\WINDOWS
```

Working with Associative Arrays

As you learn more about Perl programming, you'll discover that associative arrays are one of Perl's most useful features. You can use an associative array as a mini-database — to store information indexed by an arbitrary string (be it a numeric identifier or a name). From the previous section on the %ENV associative array, you have already seen some of the ways in which to work with associative arrays. Perl includes several built-in functions that enable you to manipulate associative arrays. Using these built-in functions, you can perform tasks such as the following:

* List all the keys in an associative array. You can then use the keys to obtain the corresponding values. You might also want a list of the values.

* Retrieve all the key-value pairs, one by one. You might want this to perform some operation on all the entries in an associative array. That operation, for example, could be simply to print each key-value pair.

* Delete an element from the associative array.

Accessing keys and values

To access an element in an associative array, you need a key. It's like trying to find your bank balance — you need an account number before you can get the account balance. When you want to go through all the items in an associative array, you need the keys. Perl includes a keys function, which takes the name of an associative array as argument and returns an array with all the keys. Here's a program that prints out the keys in an associative array:

```
#!/usr/local/bin/perl

# Define an associative array
   %expenses = ("John"  =>  1455.90,
               "Mary"  =>   544.35,
               "Tom"   =>   495.50,
               "Susan" =>  3299.75);
#Get the keys and print them out
   @names = keys(%expenses);
   print "@names\n";
```

When you run this program, it prints the following array:

```
Tom Mary Susan John
```

If you examine the %expenses associative array, you'll notice that those are exactly the keys used in that associative array. You'll also notice that the keys are not in the same order as they were defined. That's another characteristic of associative arrays: the order in which elements are returned is arbitrary.

The `keys` function is most often used to access all the elements in an associative array. You have already seen how to use the `keys` function to print all the items in the `%ENV` associative array (see the "Printing all environment variables" section).

TIP **Suppose that you want to access all the elements in the associative array and print the items in sorted order. To do this, you can first get the keys and then use the `sort` function to sort the keys. Then you access the items from the associative array by using the sorted keys. The following program illustrates this idea:**

```perl
#!/usr/local/bin/perl

# Define an associative array
   %expenses = ("John"   =>   1455.90,
                "Mary"   =>    544.35,
                "Tom"    =>    495.50,
                "Susan" =>   3299.75);

#Get the keys and sort them
   @names = keys(%expenses);
   @sorted_names = sort(@names);

# Print the elements one by one
   foreach $name (@sorted_names)
   {
      print "$name spent \$$expenses{$name}\n";
   }
```

This program makes use of the `foreach` statement that you learn about in Chapter 4. For now, just run the program and note that it prints the following expense report sorted by name:

```
John spent $1455.9
Mary spent $544.35
Susan spent $3299.75
Tom spent $495.5
```

Analogous to the `keys` function, Perl provides a `values` function that returns an array with all the values in an associative array. You can use the `values` function the same way you use `keys`. Here is an example:

```
@amounts = values(%expenses);
print "@amounts\n";
```

Given the %expenses associative array defined earlier in this section, these statements print the following output:

```
495.5 544.35 3299.75 1455.9
```

As you can see, these are the values shown in the %expenses associative array (although not in that exact order — the values are returned in arbitrary order).

Retrieving key-value pairs

One way you can access all the items in an associative array is by getting the keys first and then getting the values one by one. Perl provides another way to access the contents of an associative array (a recurring theme in Perl is that you have more than one way to do the same thing). You can use the each function to access key-value pairs one by one.

The following program illustrates a typical way to use the each function:

```perl
#!/usr/local/bin/perl

# Define an associative array
  %expenses = ("John"   =>  1455.90,
               "Mary"   =>   544.35,
               "Tom"    =>   495.50,
               "Susan"  =>  3299.75);

# Print the key-value pairs one by one
  while(($name, $amount) = each(%expenses))
  {
    print "$name spent \$$amount\n";
  }
```

This program makes use of a while loop to retrieve key-value pairs and print them out. The following expression retrieves the key-value pairs:

```perl
($name, $amount) = each(%expenses)
```

Each time this expression is evaluated, $name and $amount holds a key-value pair. When no more items are in the associative array, the each function returns an empty array and the while loop ends.

Here's a typical output from this program:

```
Tom spent $495.5
Mary spent $544.35
Susan spent $3299.75
John spent $1455.9
```

Those are indeed the key-value pairs in the %expenses associative array. Note that the each function returns the key-value pairs in arbitrary order, reflecting how Perl internally stores an associative array.

Deleting an associative array element

If you maintain information in an associative array, you might have to remove items. For example, if the associative array stores travel expenses for employees, you may want to remove the entry for an employee who's no longer with the company. Perl provides the delete function for removing an element from an associative array.

Suppose that you have the travel expense amounts in the %expenses associative array and you want to delete the entry corresponding to the key Tom because he no longer works for your company. Here's a Perl program that illustrates how you can use delete to get rid of an entry in an associative array:

```perl
#!/usr/local/bin/perl

# Define an associative array
  %expenses = ("John"  =>  1455.90,
               "Mary"  =>   544.35,
               "Tom"   =>   495.50,
               "Susan" =>  3299.75);
# Print the current keys
  @names = keys(%expenses);
  print "(Original keys): @names\n";

# Delete the entry corresponding to "Tom"
  delete($expenses{"Tom"});

# Now, print the keys again
  @names = keys(%expenses);
  print "(After deleting entry): @names\n";
```

When you run this program, it prints the following output:

```
(Original keys): Tom Mary Susan John
(After deleting entry): Mary Susan John
```

As you can see, the delete function gets rid of Tom's entry.

BONUS

Understanding the Special Variables in Perl

Perl has a large number of special variables that contain useful information that you may need to use in a Perl program. You have already seen the @ARGV array and the %ENV associative array in earlier sections. Table 2-2 lists a few more special variables that you might find in Perl programs. You will encounter some of these special variables later in the book.

By going through the list in Table 2-2, you get a feel for the kind of special variables that Perl already defines for your use. You can use these variables just like any variable you might define. For example, the following program prints the name of the Perl interpreter and its version number:

```
#!/usr/local/bin/perl
# Print the full pathname of the Perl interpreter
# and its version number
   print "$^X Version $]\n";
```

When I run this program on my Windows 95 PC, it prints the following message:

```
C:\PERL5\BIN\PERL.EXE Version 5.001
```

TABLE 2-2 A few special variables in Perl

Variable name	Description
@ARGV	Array of strings that contains the command-line arguments used to start the Perl program. The first option is $ARGV[0], the second one is $ARGV[1], and so on.
%ENV	Associative array that contains the environment variables. You can access this array by using the environment-variable name as a key. Thus, $ENV{HOME} is the home directory, and $ENV{PATH} is the current search path that the shell uses to locate commands.

(continued)

TABLE 2-2 A few special variables in Perl (*continued*)

Variable name	Description
`$_`	Default argument for many functions. If you see a Perl function being used without any argument, the function is probably expecting its argument in the `$_` variable.
`@_`	List of arguments passed to a subroutine (you learn more about subroutines in Chapter 8).
`$0`	Name of the file containing the Perl program.
`$]`	The version number of Perl you are using (for example, if you are using Perl version 5.003, `$]` will be "5.003").
`$<`	User ID (an identifying number) of the user who is running the script. This is useful on UNIX, where each user has an ID.
`$^X`	Full path name (filename together with the complete directory name) of the Perl interpreter being used to run the Perl program. For example, on Windows 95, `$^X` might be defined to be `C:\PERL5\BIN\PERL.EXE`.

Summary

When you write a Perl program, you typically want to process data, which means the Perl program must store the data as it works with the data. Variables are the storage bins for data. This chapter shows you how to use three basic types of variables — scalar, array, and associative array — in Perl.

Scalar variables store single values, such as a number or a text string. The names of scalar variables begin with a `$`.

Arrays are useful for storing a collection or list of scalar values. In Perl, array names begin with an `@`.

Associative arrays are a collection of pairs of scalars — one scalar is the key and the other one is the corresponding value. Names of associative arrays begin with a `%`.

Through simple examples, this chapter shows you how to define and use scalar, array, and associative array variables in Perl programs. This chapter also introduces you to the special array `@ARGV`, which stores command-line arguments, and the associative array `%ENV`, which stores environment variables.

As a bonus, you learn about some of the other special variables that are often used in Perl programs. Knowledge of the special variables helps you read and understand Perl programs, because these special variables occur often in many Perl programs.

The next chapter introduces you to the operators and expressions that you must use to process data in Perl programs.

2

CHAPTER THREE

PROCESSING DATA IN PERL

IN THIS CHAPTER YOU LEARN THESE KEY SKILLS

WORKING WITH NUMBERS   PAGE 65

USING THE MATHEMATICAL FUNCTIONS   PAGE 75

WORKING WITH TEXT   PAGE 79

USING THE STRING FUNCTIONS   PAGE 83

After you have the data stored in a Perl program, you'll want to perform various operations on the data. For example, you may be adding up some numbers or preparing some text for a report. To perform these operations, you have to learn how to write *expressions — formulas —* that combine variables, using operators such as addition and multiplication. To work with text strings, you have to learn about string operations, such as concatenating and comparing strings.

This chapter teaches you various ways to process numerical and text data in Perl programs. The focus is on operators that enable you to manipulate data in Perl programs.

Working with Numbers

You may have to work with numbers in many Perl programs. One of the most common operations is to keep count by incrementing an integer variable. You also can compute various numerical formulas. Consider, for example, the conversion of a temperature from Fahrenheit to Celsius. The formula is as follows:

$$T_c = (T_f - 32) \times 5/9$$

where T_c is the temperature in Celsius and T_f is the temperature in Fahrenheit.

Suppose that you want to perform this Fahrenheit-to-Celsius computation in a Perl program. You can do so easily by defining scalar variables to hold the temperature in Fahrenheit and Celsius and then writing an expression using Perl's arithmetic operators. Figure 3-1 illustrates the translation of a formula into Perl statements.

A formula

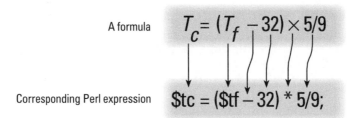

Corresponding Perl expression

Figure 3-1 Writing a formula as a Perl expression

A look at Figure 3-1 should tell you that it's straightforward to convert any mathematical formula into a Perl expression. In this case, the Perl variables $tc and $tf denote temperature in Celsius and Fahrenheit, respectively. To write the rest of the expression, you use Perl's arithmetic operators, such as addition (+), subtraction (-), multiplication (*), and division (/). The Perl statement for the Fahrenheit-to-Celsius conversion formula ends up as the following:

```
$tc = ($tf - 32) * 5 / 9;
```

In this statement, the equal sign (=) represents an operator — the assignment operator that assigns a value to a variable. Here, the value of the expression to the right-hand side of the equal sign is assigned to the variable named $tc (the temperature in Celsius).

You learn about some of the simple operations in the next few sections.

Performing basic arithmetic operations

Nearly all Perl programs have to add, subtract, multiply, or divide values. As you may have noticed in the simple Fahrenheit-to-Celsius conversion example, your Perl programs can perform arithmetic operations on constants (such as 5 / 9) or on variables (such as $tf - 32). Table 3-1 summarizes Perl's basic arithmetic operators and shows an example of a Perl statement that performs the operation and assigns the result to a variable.

TABLE 3-1 Perl's basic arithmetic operators

Operator	Name	Example
+	Addition	`$amount = $price + $sales_tax;`
-	Subtraction	`$over_payment = $payment - $balance;`
*	Multiplication	`$sales_tax = $price * $tax_rate;`
/	Divide	`$average = $total_amount / $number_of_items;`

The following Perl program performs arithmetic operations using constants as well as variables:

```
#!/usr/local/bin/perl
# Define some variables
   $price = 24.99;
   $payment = 30;

# Compute sales tax at 5% rate
   $sales_tax = $price * 0.05;

# Compute total amount and change
   $amount = $price + $sales_tax;
   $change = $payment - $amount;

# Print result
   print "Total = \$$amount\n";
   print "Payment = \$$payment\nChange = \$$change\n";
```

As you can see, this program defines several variables and assigns them numerical values. Then the program performs several arithmetic operations to compute the total amount, including the sales tax and the change owed to the customer.

When you run the program, it prints the following result:

```
Total = $26.2395
Payment = $30
Change = $3.7605
```

You may have noticed that the dollar amounts are printed with four digits after the decimal point instead of the usual two digits after the decimal point. To print a value with a specified number of digits after the decimal point, you can use the `printf` function. Chapter 5 shows you how to use the `printf` function. Another way to print nicely formatted dollar values is to use Perl's report formatting capabilities, described in Chapter 13.

Incrementing a variable by 1

A common operation in many Perl programs is to increment a variable by 1 — usually to keep count. Suppose that you are writing a Perl program that counts the number of times a specific word occurs in a file. You might use a variable named $count to keep track of the number of words. Each time your program finds an occurrence of that word, it adds 1 to the current value of $count. Using the addition operator, you can increment the $count variable's value as follows:

```
$count = $count + 1;
```

Because incrementing a variable is a common operation, Perl provides a shortcut — the *auto-increment* operator, denoted by a double plus sign (++). The following Perl statement, thus, increments the value of $count by 1:

```
$count++;
```

POST-INCREMENT VERSUS PRE-INCREMENT

You can use the auto-increment operator in two ways:

* As a suffix to the variable (such as $count++): The value of the variable is incremented *after* the variable has been used in the current expression. This is called *post-increment*.

* As a prefix to the variable (such as ++$count): The value of the variable is incremented *before* the variable has been used in the current expression. This is called *pre-increment*.

The meaning is clearer when you see an example. Consider the following Perl statements:

```
$count = 100;

# The following is same as the sequence:
#      $count_now = $count;
#      $count++;

$count_now = $count++;
print "count_now = $count_now\ncount = $count\n";
```

The result of these statements is as follows:

```
count_now = 100
count = 101
```

As you can see, the $count_now variable was assigned the old value of $count and then $count was incremented by 1. That's the characteristic of the post-increment operation where you append the ++ to the variable name.

Now consider the pre-increment operator, where you use ++ as a prefix to the variable's name. The following Perl statements demonstrate pre-increment:

```
$count = 100;

# The following is same as the sequence:
#       $count++;
#       $count_now = $count;

$count_now = ++$count;
print "count_now = $count_now\ncount = $count\n";
```

When these statements are executed, the result is as follows:

```
count_now = 101
count = 101
```

In this case, $count is incremented before the value is used. Thus, $count changes from 100 to 101 *before* the value is assigned to $count_now. As a result, $count_now is set to the $count after the increment.

Notice that as far as incrementing $count goes, both $count++ and ++$count accomplish the same task. The difference between the two forms is in the way the value of $count is used in the current expression. If the ++ occurs after the variable name (as in $count++), the variable is incremented after it has been used in the expression. On the other hand, if ++ occurs before the variable name (as in ++$count), the variable is incremented before it is used in the expression.

TIP   You should be aware of the distinction between the two forms of the auto-increment operator so that you can read and understand Perl programs that use these operators. If you want to avoid being confused by post- and pre-increment operators, you should not use the auto-increment operator in any complicated expressions. Instead, always use the auto-increment operator in a standalone statement to increment a variable. Then use the appropriate variable (before or after the increment operation) in various expressions.

AUTO-DECREMENT OPERATOR

Analogous to the auto-increment (++) operator, Perl also includes an auto-decrement operator, denoted by a double minus sign (--). The auto-decrement operator is for decrementing the value of a variable by 1. The auto-decrement operator is useful when you want to count down (for example, 10, 9, 8, ... and so on). To decrement the value of the variable named $count by 1, you can write one of the following:

```
$count--;
--$count;
```

As is the case with the two variants of the auto-increment operator, these two statements are examples of post- and pre-decrement operators. The value of

$count is reduced by 1 in both cases. The difference is in the order in which the decrement operation is performed:

* With $count, the value of $count is decremented after the old value of $count has been used in the current expression.
* If you write $count, the value of $count is decremented before evaluating the current expression.

Learning other Perl operators

So far, you have seen the basic arithmetic operators and the increment and decrement operators. Perl also includes many more operators that work with numbers. Table 3-2 lists some of the operators you might commonly encounter in Perl programs.

TABLE 3-2 Some common Perl operators for working with numbers

Operator	Example	Description
%	$x % $y	Modulo or remainder operator; computes the remainder of $x divided by $y (for example, 16%5 = 1).
**	$x ** $y	Exponentiation operator; raises $x to the power of $y (for example, 2**4 = 16).
~	~$x	Bitwise NOT operator; changes all 1 bits to 0s and all 0 bits to 1s in the binary representation of a number (for example, ~1 = 4294967294, which is one less than 4294967295, the largest 32-bit integer).
&	$x & $y	Bitwise AND operator; performs the AND operation between corresponding bits of $x and $y in their binary representations (for example, 2 & 3 = 2, because in binary notation 2 is 10 and 3 is 11, the AND operation results in a 1 bit only when both bits are 1).
|	$x | $y	Bitwise OR operator; performs the OR operation between corresponding bits of $x and $y in their binary representations (for example, 2 & 3 = 3, because in binary notation 2 is 10 and 3 is 11, the OR operation results in a 1 bit whenever any one of the bits is a 1).

^	$x ^ $y	Bitwise exclusive OR operator; performs the exclusive OR operation (result has 1 where corresponding bits differ) between corresponding bits of $x and $y in their binary representations (for example, 2 & 3 = 1, because in binary notation 2 is 10 and 3 is 11, the exclusive OR operation results in a 1 bit only when the bits differ).
<<	$x << $y	Left shift operator; shifts the bits of $x (in its binary representation) to the left by $y number of times (for example, 1 << 3 = 8, because three left shifts of the 1 bit produces 1000 in binary, which is 8 in decimal).
>	$x > $y	Right shift operator; shifts the bits of $x (in its binary representation) to the right by $y number of times (for example, 8 > 3 = 1, because 8 is 1000 in binary and three right shifts produces a 1).

You may not use the bitwise operators much, but you might need to use the exponentiation and modulo operators in your Perl programs.

USING THE EXPONENTIATION OPERATOR

Sometimes you'll encounter formulas that require the exponentiation operator. Suppose that you want to compute how your money grows with compound interest. If P is the principal amount, R is the yearly interest rate (in percentage per year), and the interest is compounded yearly, then the amount at the end of N years is given by the following formula:

$$\text{Ending balance} = P \times (1 + R/100)^N$$

To evaluate this formula in Perl, you have to use the exponentiation operator when raising the expression (1 + R/100) to the power N. The following Perl program illustrates how much you can expect to get after 10 years, from a $1,000 deposit earning interest at the rate of 4% compounded annually:

```
#!/usr/local/bin/perl
# Initialize variables
    $principal = 1000;   # $1,000 deposit
    $rate = 4;           # 4% interest rate
    $years = 10;         # 10 years duration

# Compute the final amount
    $amount = $principal * (1 + $rate/100) ** $years;

# Print the result
```

```
    print "\$$principal at $rate% compounded annually
yields \$$amount after $years years\n";
```

When you run this program, it prints the following result:

```
$1000 at 4% compounded annually
yields $1480.24428491834 after 10 years
```

USING THE MODULO OPERATOR

The modulo operator is useful whenever you want to check the remainder of a division operation. A situation that may not be obvious is when you want to check if a number is a multiple of some other number. Suppose that you want to print a line of text with a special mark every 10th character. You can use a for statement that prints one character at a time and increments a count after each character. Whenever that count is a multiple of 10 (a number is a multiple of 10 when the remainder after dividing by 10 is zero), you can print the special mark. You can understand this better by looking at the following Perl program, which implements this logic:

```
#!/usr/local/bin/perl

for($i = 0; $i <= 50; $i++)
{
    if($i % 10)
    {
        print "-";
    }
    else
    {
        print "|";
    }
}
```

Although the program uses for and if statements (which you learn about in Chapter 4), you will understand what the program does after you see it in action. When you run this program, it prints the following:

Here's what the program does:

* It counts from 0 through 50 (that's what the $i variable in the for statement does).
* It uses the modulo operator to determine if the count is a multiple of 10 (that's what the expression $i % 10 does).

* If the count is not a multiple of 10 (that means $i % 10 is not zero), it prints a dash (-).
* Otherwise, it prints a vertical bar (|).

TIP   **As you can see, the modulo operator is useful when you check if a number is an exact multiple of another number. For exact multiples, the modulo operator yields a zero remainder; otherwise, the remainder is non-zero.**

Learning operator shortcuts

Sometimes you have to keep performing an arithmetic operation on the same variable. Suppose that you are writing a Perl program to compute the total amount of travel expenses incurred over the past year. You might have a variable named $expenses where you accumulate the total. As the program reads an expense amount (assume the monthly expense reports are stored in a file) into a scalar variable named $amount, it adds the amount to the $expenses variable, as follows:

```
# Assume that $amount holds an expense amount
# to be added to the total

$expenses = $expenses + $amount;
```

Perl provides a shortcut operator to accomplish this computation. You can use the += operator (that's a plus sign followed by an equal sign) and write this expression as follows:

```
$expenses += $amount;
```

TIP   **This expression adds the value of $amount to the $expenses variable.**

Whenever you want to perform an operation with a variable and then save the result in the same variable, you can make use of the shortcut operators — also known as *assignment operators*. The general syntax of the shortcut version is to write the operator immediately followed by an equal sign. Table 3-3 summarizes the assignment operators corresponding to the common arithmetic and bitwise operators.

TABLE 3-3   Assignment operators for working with numbers

Operator	Example	Description
+=	$x += $y	Add assign operator; adds $y to $x and stores the result in $x.
-=	$x -= $y	Subtract assign operator; subtracts $y from $x and stores the result in $x.
*=	$x *= $y	Multiply assign operator; multiplies $y and $x and stores the result in $x.
/=	$x /= $y	Divide assign operator; divides $x by $y and stores the result in $x.
%=	$x %= $y	Remainder assign operator; computes the remainder of $x divided by $y and stores result in $x.
**=	$x **= $y	Exponentiation assign operator; raises $x to the power of $y and stores result in $x.
&=	$x &= $y	Bitwise AND assign operator; performs the AND operation between corresponding bits of $x and $y in their binary representations and stores result in $x.
|=	$x |= $y	Bitwise OR assign operator; performs the OR operation between corresponding bits of $x and $y in their binary representations and stores result in $x.
^=	$x ^= $y	Bitwise exclusive OR assign operator; performs the exclusive OR operation between corresponding bits of $x and $y in their binary representations and stores result in $x.
<<=	$x <<= $y	Left shift assign operator; shifts the bits of $x (in its binary representation) to the left by $y number of times and stores result in $x.
>=	$x >= $y	Right shift assign operator; shifts the bits of $x (in its binary representation) to the right by $y number of times and stores result in $x.

Understanding the order of operations

When an expression contains many different operators, Perl performs the operations in a specific order, depending on the operators. For example, if you were to write

```
$x = 5 + 3 * 4;
```

the result would be 17, because Perl evaluates the multiplication before the addition (which is what you would do as well). This order of operations (such as multiplication before addition) is known as *precedence*.

 TIP For the basic arithmetic operators, you can use your own knowledge of precedence. Although I could show you a table of precedence for the other operators, I won't. There is no point in trying to remember the precedence of all the operators. Instead, use parentheses to explicitly indicate the order in which you want an expression evaluated. For example, if you want to add two numbers first and then multiply by a third, you should write

```
$x = (5 + 3) * 4;
```

In this case, Perl evaluates the addition inside the parentheses first and then performs the multiplication, resulting in a value of 32.

In more complex operations, you may use as many sets of parentheses as necessary to unambiguously specify the order of the operations. For example, here is a more complex expression with several parentheses:

```
$x = ((5 + 3) * (2 + 4)) / 2;
```

This expression evaluates to 24.

TIP By grouping expressions within parentheses, you can explicitly control the order in which Perl performs the operations. An added bonus is that you never have to learn Perl's operator precedence rules.

Using the Mathematical Functions

Although most of your Perl programs may not need anything beyond the basic arithmetic operators, Perl does include many built-in math functions for the occasional trigonometric operation or square root. As you see in the next few sections, Perl's math functions are as easy to use as other Perl functions. Chapter 9 contains a more complete listing of Perl's built-in functions.

Computing trigonometric expressions

Remember those trigonometry problems from high school? Figure 3-2 shows a somewhat practical one.

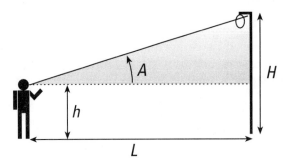

$$H = h + L \times \tan(A), \text{ where } \tan(A) = \frac{\sin(A)}{\cos(A)}$$

Figure 3-2   A simple trigonometry problem

The problem is to measure the height of some object — in this case, a lamp post. You stand at a distance *L* (which you can measure easily with a measuring tape) from the post, stand up straight, and measure the angle *A* — the elevation of the lamp from your perspective. If your height is *h*, then the height of the lamp post (H) is given by the following expression:

```
H = h + L × tan(A)
```

where tan(A) denotes the tangent of the angle A (remember that A has to be in radians). Perl does not include a function to compute tan(A), but you can compute the sine and cosine of A and then use the following formula to compute the tangent of A:

```
tan(A) = sin(A) / cos(A)
```

Now, assume a specific case. Suppose that you are 6 feet tall and, at a distance of 100 feet, you measure the elevation angle for a lamp post to be 12 degrees. That means you have the following data:

```
A = 12 degrees = 0.21 radians
          h = 6 ft
          L = 100 ft
```

You can then compute the height of the lamp post with the following Perl program:

```perl
# Define and initialize variables
   $A = 12;
   $h = 6;
   $L = 100;
# Convert A into radians
   $A *= 3.14159/180;
# Compute height of lamp post
```

```
$H = $h + $L * sin($A) / cos($A);
print "Height = $H feet.\n";
```

When you run this program, it prints the following result:

```
Height = 27.2556376771379 feet.
```

That's an example showing the use of the sin and cos functions. You can also use the atan2 function to compute the arc tangent. For example, you can use atan2 to determine the grade of a terrain given the rise ($h) over a specified distance ($L). The angle would be given by the following Perl expression:

```
$A = atan2($h, $L);
```

Taking the square root

You might remember the Pythagorean theorem from high school. If *x* and *y* are the sides of a right triangle (that is, these two sides meet at a right angle), then the Pythagorean theorem states that the length of the hypotenuse (the third side of the right triangle) is given by the square root of *(x2 + y2)*. You can compute this expression in Perl by using the sqrt function as follows:

```
$x = 3;
$y = 4;
$hypotenuse = sqrt($x**2 + $y**2);
print "Hypotenuse = $hypotenuse\n";
```

When you run this program, it prints the following result:

```
Hypotenuse = 5
```

You can use sqrt whenever you need the square root of a number.

Generating random numbers

Suppose that your community service organization has 20 members — numbered 1 through 20. Each member is going to volunteer a weekend at a nursing home and you want a fair way to determine who gets to volunteer when. One good way to do this is to generate a random sequence of numbers between 1 and 20. This means that the sequence must contain only the numbers 1 through 20 in random order, with no number appearing more than once.

In a Perl program, you can generate such a random sequence by using the srand and rand functions. You also need the int function, which converts a floating-point number into an integer, because the rand function returns random floating-point values. The basic use of srand and rand are as follows:

1. Call `srand` once to initialize the seed of the random number generator. The seed is the starting value for generating a sequence of random numbers.

2. Call `rand` as many times as you need to generate the random numbers. The `rand` function takes an argument and returns a random floating-point value between 0 and the argument.

To use `srand` *and* `rand` *to generate a random sequence of 20 numbers between 1 and 20, you can use the following logic:*

1. Define an empty array to hold the random number sequence:

   ```
   @seq = ();
   ```

2. Call `srand` with the output of the `time` function. The `time` function returns the current time in terms of the number of seconds elapsed since January 1, 1970. The Perl statement to perform this initialization takes the following form:

   ```
   srand(time());
   ```

3. In a loop, keep generating random numbers between 1 and 20. Convert each number to an integer by using the `int` function and check if the number is already in the `@seq` array. If not, add the number to the `@seq` array; else, generate a new random number.

4. Exit the loop when 20 random numbers have been generated.

The following Perl program implements this logic:

```
#!/usr/local/bin/perl

# Define an empty array  to hold the sequence of
# random numbers
  @seq = ();

# Initialize the seed using the output of time
  srand(time());

# Generate 20 unique random numbers between
# 1 and 20
  $count = 0;
  while($count < 20)
  {
# Generate a random number and convert to integer
    $number = int(rand(20) + 1);
```

```
# Check if the number is already in the array
   for($i = 0; $i < $count; $i++)
   {
     if($number == $seq[$i])
     {
       last;   # Number already exists in @seq
     }
   }
   if($i >= $count)   # Not in @seq yet
   {
# Save number in @seq and increment count
     $seq[$count] = $number;
     $count++;
   }
 }


# Print the random sequence
  print "Random sequence (1-20):\n@seq\n";
```

When you run this program, it prints output similar to the following (remember, the numbers are random, so yours probably won't look exactly like this one):

```
Random sequence (1-20):
10 3 19 1 13 12 15 14 16 2 18 17 7 9 5 4 20 11 6 8
```

As you can see, this is a random sequence of 20 numbers between 1 and 20.

NOTE If you were to run this program again, it'll print an entirely different sequence of 20 random numbers, because the srand function initializes the seed with a new value (provided by the time function). Thus, the program generates a unique sequence of random numbers every time you run it. Of course, if you run the program enough times, sooner or later it will duplicate an earlier list of numbers. After all, there are only so many possible combinations of those 20 numbers.

Working with Text

In addition to number crunching, Perl programs also have to deal with text. At a minimum, your Perl program has to display results in text form and, in doing so, may have to manipulate text strings. For example, you may have to combine two text strings to form a third string. In other Perl programs, you may read text data from a file and separate each line of text into various parts.

NOTE Perl is well-known for its capability to process text. Perl's text-processing facilities come from its heritage as a system administration tool for UNIX, where many system configuration files happen to be text files. For example, the UNIX password file (usually the /etc/passwd file) contains a line of text for each user, such as the following:

```
naba:UwbOLxsNWSosd:501:100:Naba Barkakati:/home/naba:/bin/bash
```

As you can see, the line of text contains a number of fields (such as user name, encoded password, home directory, and so on). A colon (:) acts as a separator between fields. Perl excels in manipulating text files formatted like this.

Perl provides some operators as well as a number of built-in functions for processing text. Perl has two basic string operators:

* The concatenation operator joins one or more strings.
* The repetition operator repeats a string a specified number of times.

Concatenating strings

A common text-processing step is to *concatenate,* or *join,* strings. Suppose that you have the first and last names of a customer stored in two separate scalar variables ($firstname and $lastname) and you want to join the two parts into a full name. You can use the string concatenation operator to accomplish this task, as illustrated by the following Perl code:

```
$firstname = "Naba";
$lastname = "Barkakati";

# Concatenate the two strings
$fullname = $firstname." ".$lastname;

print "$fullname\n";
```

The $fullname variable is set to the result of concatenating three strings: $firstname, a blank space (written as a blank space enclosed in double quotes), and $lastname. As you can see from this example, the string concatenation operator is represented by a period (.). To concatenate one or more strings, you simply write the strings with the period in between.

When you run this code, it prints the following result:

```
Naba Barkakati
```

TIP You can use the assignment form of the concatenation operator (.=) to concatenate two strings and store the result back in the first string. For

example, if you want to append "ing" to a string, you should write the following:

```
$str = "cook";
$str .= "ing";  # Now $str is "cooking"
```

You might use string concatenation in a Perl program that needs a complete directory path for a file. For example, you might have the directory name (say, C:\PERL5\BIN) in the string $dirpath. When you find out the filename (such as, PERL.EXE), you append to $dirpath a backslash followed by the filename to complete the full path name (C:\PERL5\BIN\PERL.EXE).

Repeating strings

A curious but useful operator is the *repetition operator*, denoted by x. You can use the x operator to repeat a string a specified number of times. Suppose that you want to initialize a string to 65 asterisks (*) and then use that line of asterisks as a separator in a text file (or the output printed by your Perl program).

The following example shows how you can initialize the string with a repeated number of asterisks by using the x operator:

```
# Define $marker as a string of 65 asterisks
  $marker = "*" x 65;
```

Of course, you can achieve the same result by repeating a string of 5 asterisks 13 times, as follows:

```
$marker = "*****" x 13;
```

You can actually use the string repetition operator in many useful programs. Suppose that you want to generate a simple text plot of some data. You can create a plot by replicating asterisks where the number of asterisks is proportional to the value being plotted. The following Perl program illustrates how you might create a simple plot showing the relative tuition costs for a number of universities:

```
#!/usr/local/bin/perl
# Initialize an associative array of tuition
%tuition = (   "U. Maryland" =>  9700,
               "M.I.T.      " => 22000,
               "UC Berkeley" => 13000,
               "Harvard     " => 21901,
               "Yale        " => 22200,
               "U. Illinois" =>  9100,
               "Georgetown " => 20388 );

  foreach $school (keys(%tuition))
  {
```

```perl
# Initialize the marker
    $marker = "*";

# Retrieve the tuition amount for this school
    $amount = $tuition{$school};

# Compute how many thousands (divide by 1000)
    $amount /= 1000;

# Set up that many asterisks
    $marker x= $amount;
    print "$school: $marker\n";
}


$marker = "-" x 40;
print "$marker\nNote: * = \$1,000\n";
```

When you run this program, it produces the following output:

```
Harvard     : *********************
Georgetown : ********************
Yale        : **********************
UC Berkeley: *************
U. Maryland: *********
M.I.T.      : **********************
U. Illinois: *********
```

_____

```
Note: * = $1,000
```

As you can see, this program's output is quite usable, at least as a way to compare the tuition costs of these schools.

If you study the program, you'll notice that the string of asterisks is prepared in the variable named $marker *in the following manner:*

1. $marker is set to a single asterisk.

2. The amount of tuition is divided by 1000 to convert it to the number of thousands.

3. $marker is repeated by the amount of tuition (in thousands) by using the x= operator (this is the assignment form of the x operator) with the following statement:

   ```perl
   $marker x= $amount;
   ```

Using the String Functions

Although Perl provides only two string operators, you'll find quite a few Perl functions that enable you to manipulate text in various ways. For example, Perl has string functions to extract a part of a string, convert a string to all uppercase, or find the number of characters in a string.

X-REF Chapter 9 contains an overview of Perl's built-in functions. This section shows you how to use some of the common string functions.

Removing the last character of a string

Many Perl programs process the contents of a text file one line at a time. When a Perl program reads a line of text into a scalar variable, that text string includes all the characters on the line plus a newline character at the very end, as shown in step 1 of Figure 3-3.

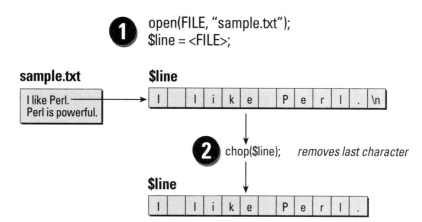

Figure 3-3 Getting rid of the newline character with the chop function

Typically, you will want to remove that newline character, because that character gets in the way of other processing. For example, if you compare that line of text with some other string, the newline character causes the comparison to fail (because Perl does a character-by-character comparison, and the extra newline character in one string causes the comparison to fail).

You can use the chop function to get rid of the newline character at the end of a string read from a file. If the text string is in the $line variable, you can eliminate the last character with the following Perl statement:

```
chop($line);
```

Step 2 in Figure 3-3 illustrates the effect of the chop function.

TIP If you want to remove the last character only if it's a newline, you should use the chomp function instead of chop. Unlike chop, chomp removes the last character only if it matches the current value of $/, which is set to newline by default.

Extracting a substring

Another type of text manipulation is to extract a part of a string. Assume that you have a text file containing suggestions from people. Each suggestion begins with a line that tells you who sent the suggestion, followed by a number of lines of text with the suggestion itself. For example, a suggestion from me begins with the following line:

```
From: Naba Barkakati
```

You want to write a Perl program that reads the suggestion file and prints a "thank you" note to each person who submitted a suggestion. To do this, your Perl program has to read the first line of each suggestion into a text string and then extract the part of the string that follows From: . You can use the substr function to extract the substring. The following Perl program illustrates how you might use substr:

```
#!/usr/local/bin/perl
# Define a string
    $line = "From: Naba Barkakati";

# Extract the part that follows "From: " (in other
# words, extract the text following the first 6 characters)
    $from = substr($line, 6);
    print "$from\n";
```

The substr call in this example skips the first 6 characters of $line and returns the remainder of that text string. When you run this program, it prints the following:

```
Naba Barkakati
```

NOTE A more general form of substring extraction is to pick out a number or characters from the middle of a string. Figure 3-4 illustrates the general form of the substr function call.

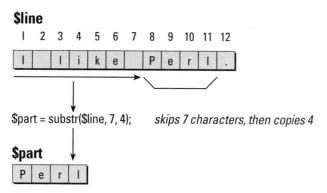

$line

	1	2	3	4	5	6	7	8	9	10	11	12
I		l	i	k	e		P	e	r	l	.	

$part = substr($line, 7, 4);   *skips 7 characters, then copies 4*

$part

P	e	r	l

Figure 3-4   Extracting a substring with the `substr` function

As Figure 3-4 illustrates, if you have the following string:

```
$line = "I like Perl.";
```

you can extract Perl out of this by using `substr` as follows:

```
$part = substr($line, 7, 4);
```

That call to `substr` says skip the first 7 characters in `$line` and return the next 4 characters. After this function call, `$part` contains the string `"Perl"`.

TIP   What if you want to extract "Perl" from "I like Perl.", but you do not want to count the number of characters to skip? You don't have to count, because Perl includes the `index` function, which enables you to find the position where a substring begins. You typically use `index` to find the start of the substring you want and `substr` to extract that substring, as follows:

```
$line = "I like Perl.";
$pos = index($line, "Perl");    # $pos = 7
$part = substr($line, $pos, 4); # $part = "Perl"
```

Finding the length of a string

In many situations, you want the length of a string — the *length* is the number of characters in the string. Consider the problem of extracting a substring from a line of text. Suppose that the variable named $find contains the substring you want to extract from a string named $line. You can use the `index` function to find the start of the substring and then use `substr` to extract the substring. You need to indicate, however, how many characters to specify. This is a situation where you have to use the `length` function.

Here's how you can use the `length` function when locating and extracting a substring:

```
$pos = index($line, $find);  # find start of substring
$nchar = length($find);      # length of substring

# Extract substring by calling substr
$part = substr($line, $pos, $nchar);
```

Consider another problem where you can use the length function. Suppose that you want to print the text in a variable named $title and then print another line with a number of dashes that essentially underlines the text. The following example shows how you can use the length function to solve this problem:

```
# Initialize a string
   $title = "Discover Perl 5";
# Find the length of $title
   $length = length($title);
#Print the title
   print "$title\n";
# Prepare a line of dashes and print it
   $uline = "-" x $length;
   print "$uline\n";
```

When you run this program, it prints the following output:

```
Discover Perl 5
_____
```

As you can see, the line of dashes matches up perfectly with the line of text.

Splitting a string into several parts

In UNIX, text files store much important system information. For example, in most UNIX systems, the /etc/passwd file stores user information (user name, password, home directory, and so forth). Each line in the /etc/passwd file has the following form:

```
naba:UwbOLxsNWSosd:501:100:Naba Barkakati:/home/naba:/bin/bash
```

where each field is separated from the next by a colon (:).

Often UNIX programmers use this approach to store data in a text file — multiple fields are separated by a separator (a character that does not appear in the contents of the fields). The separator is often a colon or a vertical bar (|).

When you write a Perl program that processes data stored in a text file patterned after files such as /etc/passwd, you need to separate the fields. Perl provides the split function for this task. As the name suggests, split can separate a line of text into several parts.

To see `split` in action, try out the following Perl program on a UNIX system:

```perl
#!/usr/local/bin/perl

# Run this program on a UNIX system

# Open the /etc/passwd file
  unless(open(PASSWD, "/etc/passwd"))
  {
    die("Cannot open /etc/passwd\n");
  }
# Read lines from the password file
  while(($line = <PASSWD>))
  {
# Split the line with colons as separators and
# store the result in the @fields array
    @fields = split(":", $line);
# Print the fifth field (full name) and
# the first field (user name). Remember
# first field is at index 0.
    print "$fields[4]  ->  $fields[0]\n";
  }
# Close the file
  close(PASSWD);
```

When you run this program, it prints the full name and the user name (the name that the user types to log in) of each user listed in the `/etc/passwd` file. The following lines show typical output from this program:

```
Naba Barkakati  ->  naba
Ivy Barkakati  ->  ivy
Emily Barkakati  ->  emily
```

X-REF You can actually split a line of text using more complex criteria than a single separator character. In place of the separator character, you can specify a more complex pattern, known as a *regular expression*. Chapters 6 and 7 discuss regular expressions.

BONUS

Operators and Strings

In this chapter, you have seen examples of how many Perl operators work. There are a set of operators for working with numbers, and another, smaller set specifically meant for string operations. Perl, however, does not strictly designate the types of variables. Depending on the context, a variable may be treated as a string or as a numeric value.

You can easily apply a string operator to what appears to be numbers, and vice versa. Typically, Perl produces the most logical result. For example, consider the string concatenation operator, denoted by a period (.). By placing the period between two strings, you create a new string that's the concatenation of the strings. What if you were to use the string concatenation operator with numbers? Here's an example:

```
$x = 12;
$y = 34;
$xy = $x . $y;
$z = $xy + 6;

print "\$xy = $xy  \$z = $z\n";
```

When you execute this code, it generates the following output:

```
$xy = 1234  $z = 1240
```

The result of applying the string concatenation operator to two numbers is a third number created by concatenating the digits of the first and second numbers. You can then continue to use the new number for other numeric operations, such as addition.

When you apply some operators to strings, Perl produces some surprising results. It's good to know the behavior of the operators on strings, because you may be able to make use of such behavior in your Perl programs. The following sections show you the effect of some operators when they are applied to strings.

Some unary operators and strings

The *unary* - operator changes the sign of a number — turns a positive number negative and a negative number positive, as illustrated by the following program:

```
$x = 25;
$y = -30;
```

```
$xm = -$x;
$ym = -$y;
print "\$xm = $xm  \$ym = $ym\n";
```

Here's the output from this program:

```
$xm = -25   $ym = 30
```

The behavior of the unary - operator is different when you apply it to a string. You can see this behavior from the following example:

```
$string1 = "nosign";
$string2 = "+option";
$string3 = "-exclude";

$string1m = - $string1;
$string2m = - $string2;
$string3m = - $string3;

print "\$string1m = $string1m\n";
print "\$string2m = $string2m\n";
print "\$string3m = $string3m\n";
```

When you run this program, it generates the following output:

```
$string1m = -nosign
$string2m = -option
$string3m = +exclude
```

As you can see from this output, the unary - operator works on strings as follows:

* If a string begins with any alphanumeric character besides - or +, the unary - operator adds a minus sign in front of the string.
* If a string begins with a minus (-) or a plus (+) sign, the unary - operator changes that sign to an opposite sign (minus becomes plus and plus turns into minus).

Another unary operator that behaves differently on strings is the bitwise *NOT*, or *negation*, (~) operator. When applied to a number, this operator changes all 1 bits to 0 and vice versa. You may be surprised to learn that when you apply the unary ~ operator to a string, it complements the bits in the binary representation (the ASCII code) of each character in the string.

Bitwise operators and strings

As shown in Table 3-2, Perl has bitwise AND, OR, and exclusive-OR (XOR) operators, denoted by the symbols: &, |, and ^. These operators work differently on numbers than they do on strings.

When you use a bitwise operator on numeric values, Perl converts both numeric values to binary numbers and then applies the bitwise operation to the corresponding bits of the two binary numbers. Consider the following simple example:

```
$x = 10;
$y = 12;
$z = $x & $y;
print "\$z = $z\n";
```

This code prints the following result:

```
$z = 8
```

Here is how the bitwise AND operation works in this case (remember that the bitwise AND of two bits is 1 only if both bits are 1):

```
$x = 1010 (binary representation of decimal 10)
$y = 1100 (binary representation of decimal 12)
$z = 1000 (bitwise AND of $x and $y)
```

If you were to perform a bitwise operation between two strings, Perl performs the bitwise operation between the corresponding bits of each character and generates a result string. Here's an example:

```
$result = "ABC" & "BCD";
print "$result\n";
```

This code prints the following as the result of the bitwise AND of the strings "abc" and "bcd":

```
@B@
```

Figure 3-5 illustrates how such bitwise AND operations between strings work.

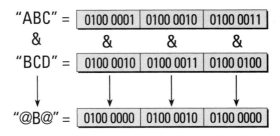

ASCII representation of each character

"ABC" = | 0100 0001 | 0100 0010 | 0100 0011 |
      &   &   &   &
"BCD" = | 0100 0010 | 0100 0011 | 0100 0100 |

"@B@" = | 0100 0000 | 0100 0010 | 0100 0000 |

Figure 3-5   The bitwise AND operation between two strings

In this case, the bitwise AND operation is performed between the ASCII representation of corresponding characters of the two strings.

Summary

Nearly all Perl programs have to process data — numbers and text strings. To work with numbers, you have to use Perl's arithmetic operators and mathematical functions. The arithmetic operators include the basic addition, subtraction, multiplication, and division. Additionally, Perl has an exponentiation operator and a modulo operator. Perl's inventory of mathematical functions includes trigonometric functions such as sine and cosine, square root, and functions to generate random numbers.

True to its reputation as a language for text processing, Perl includes several operators that ease common text-processing tasks, such as concatenation of strings. A set of functions for string manipulation augments the text operators. Perl includes functions for extracting a substring, finding the length of a string, and splitting a string into several parts.

This chapter introduces you to the Perl operators and functions for processing text and numbers. A number of simple examples show you how to work with numbers and text in a Perl program.

As a bonus, you learn how a number of Perl operators interact with strings. You'll be surprised by the way certain operators behave when you apply them on strings.

The next chapter shows you how to make decisions in your Perl programs. You learn how to execute a block of Perl code only when a condition is true.

CHAPTER FOUR

CONTROLLING PROGRAM FLOW IN PERL

IN THIS CHAPTER YOU LEARN THESE KEY SKILLS

Flow of execution, or *program flow,* refers to the sequence in which Perl statements are executed by the Perl interpreter. The Perl interpreter always executes the statements sequentially, in the order of their appearance in a Perl program. In most Perl programs, however, you will want your program to execute one set of Perl statements if a specific condition is true and, possibly, another set of statements if the condition is false.

Suppose that you are writing a Perl program that processes a text file containing expense reports and prints out only those entries that exceed a specified amount (you're looking for the big spenders, in other words). In such a program, you might use the if statement, one of Perl's *conditional statements* — statements that are executed only when certain conditions are true.

You can use conditional statements to control the flow of execution in a program. This chapter shows you how to use the conditional statements in Perl. You also learn how to repeat a block of Perl statements by looping.

Comparing Numbers and Strings

Conditional statements, such as the `if` statement, check the value of an expression and execute a block of statements if the expression is true.

Most of the time, the expression being tested in a conditional statement is a comparison that involves a relational operator. For example, you might use an `if` statement to print a message if the number of errors exceeds a preset threshold. Here's how you might write such an `if` statement:

```
if($error_count > 25)
{
    print "Too many errors!\n";
}
```

The expression `$error_count > 25` is an example of a comparison of two numbers — the value of the variable `$error_count` and 25. The greater-than sign (>) is one of the relational operators in Perl. As you might have guessed, the greater-than sign (>) denotes the greater than operator.

The expression `$error_count > 25` means "`$error_count` is greater than 25." The expression is true (that means the expression's value is nonzero) if `$error_count` exceeds 25; otherwise, the expression is false (the expression's value is zero).

Perl includes two separate sets of relational operators — one set for comparing numbers and the other for comparing text strings.

Performing numeric comparisons

The greater than operator (>) is one of the relational operators you can use to compare numbers in a Perl program. Other numeric comparisons include checking if two numbers are equal or if one number is less than another. Table 4-1 lists Perl's relational operators for numeric comparison.

TABLE 4-1 Relational operators for comparing numbers

Operator	Example	Description
==	$x == $y	Equal to operator; value is true if $x equals $y, else false.
!=	$x != $y	Not equal to operator; value is true if $x and $y are unequal, else false.
<	$x < $y	Less than operator; value is true if $x is less than $y, else false.
<=	$x <= $y	Less than or equal to operator; value is true if $x is less than or equal to $y, else false.
>	$x > $y	Greater than operator; value is true if $x is greater than $y, else false.
>=	$x >= $y	Greater than or equal to operator; value is true if $x is greater than or equal to $y, else false.
<=>	$x <=> $y	Three-way comparison operator; value is -1 if $x is less than $y, 0 if $x equals $y, and 1 if $x is greater than $y.

You can use the relational operators from Table 4-1 in a straightforward manner. For example, if your Perl program is monitoring the stock price and it has to print a warning message whenever the price dips below 10, you write the condition as:

```
($stock_price < 10)
```

where $stock_price is the variable with the current stock price.

Performing string comparisons

In some programming languages, such as C and C++, the relational operators for comparing numbers are the same ones you can use to compare text strings. Not so in Perl. Perl has a complete set of relational operators that you must use when comparing strings.

For example, in a Perl program, you cannot use the == operator to find out whether two strings match; the == operator works only with numbers. To test the equality of strings, Perl includes the eq operator (if you have programmed in FORTRAN, you might remember the eq operator, which you use for a similar purpose in FORTRAN programs). Here is an example of how you might use eq to see whether two strings are identical:

```
if ($input eq "stop") { exit; }
```

Perl includes other operators that can compare two strings in a variety of ways. Table 4-2 summarizes the string comparison operators.

TABLE 4-2   Relational operators for comparing strings

Operator	Example	Description
eq	$x eq $y	Value is true if the strings $x and $y are equal, else false.
ne	$x ne $y	Value is true if the strings $x and $y are not equal, else false.
gt	$x gt $y	Value is true if $x is greater than $y, else false.
ge	$x ge $y	Value is true if $x is greater than or equal to $y, else false.
lt	$x lt $y	Value is true if $x is less than $y, else false.
le	$x le $y	Value is true if $x is less than or equal to $y, else false.
cmp	$x cmp $y	Value is -1 if $x is less than $y, 0 if the strings are equal, and 1 if $x is greater than $y.

Unlike numeric comparisons, string comparisons may be a bit difficult to understand. You can probably guess that two strings are considered equal when each character in the first string matches the corresponding character in the second string.

You might wonder, however, what it means to say that one string is "greater than" another. All string comparisons are done by comparing the numeric value of the characters. For example, the numeric value of uppercase *A* is 65 and that of uppercase *B* is 66. That means, in string comparison, *A* is less than *B*.

NOTE   The numeric values of the characters come from the American Standard Code for Information Interchange (ASCII) code. In fact, the numeric value of a character is referred to as the *ASCII code* of that character.

All the letters are assigned sequential ASCII codes. So, the string comparison operators treat strings as they would appear in a dictionary. All lowercase letters, however, have greater ASCII codes than the uppercase letters. For example, the ASCII code for lowercase *a* is 97, which makes it greater than *A* (ASCII code 65).

Making Decisions in Perl

A Perl program makes decisions by conditional processing. Based on the value of an expression, the program executes a block of statements — statements enclosed in a pair of curly braces ({ . . . }). As you see in the following sections, all conditional statements have the same general form:

```
keyword (expression)
{
... block of statements ...
}
```

Here, `keyword` is a special word (such as `if` and `unless`) that denotes the type of decision the program makes. The `expression` within parentheses is tested before the block of statements within curly braces is executed.

 TIP **A key point to remember is that you must have the curly braces to delineate the statement block, even if there is only one Perl statement in the block.**

In Perl programs, you may use the `if` and `unless` statements to execute a block of code based on the value of an expression. As you see in the next section, you can also use the `elsif` and `else` statements with an `if` statement.

Using the `if` statement

The most common type of conditional statement is the `if` statement, which you have already seen in some example programs in the earlier chapters of this book. The `if` statement executes a block of statements if a condition is true. The condition is usually an expression that compares numbers or strings. Figure 4-1 illustrates the flow control of an `if` statement.

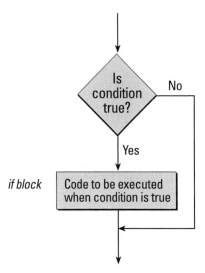

Figure 4-1 Flow control of an if statement in Perl

Suppose that you want to check whether the user name is `root` (the privileged user name in UNIX systems) before running a program. You might use the following `if` statement with a string comparison to implement this logic:

```
# Assume $user has current user name
if($user ne "root")
{
    print "Sorry $user, you must be \"root\" to ",
        "run this program.\n";
    exit;
}
```

In this case, the condition is true when `$user` is not equal to `"root"`. When this is true, the `if` statement executes the block that prints an error message and calls the `exit` function to end the program.

You can add an `else` clause to the `if` statement to handle the case when the condition is false. Figure 4-2 illustrates the flow control of an `if` statement together with an `else` clause.

The form of a combined `if-else` statement is as follows:

```
if(expression)
{
   ...statements to execute if expression is true...
}
else
{
   ...statements to execute if expression is false...
}
```

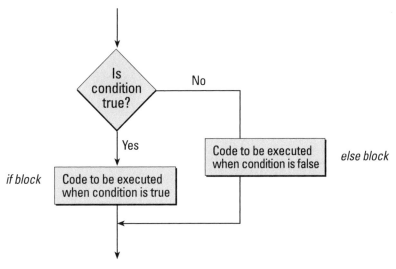

Figure 4-2 Flow control of an if statement with an else clause

Suppose that you want to print a congratulatory message if a student's test score is greater than or equal to 90. If the score is less than 90, however, you want to print a message urging the student to try harder the next time. You can perform this task with an if-else construct, as follows:

```
# Assume $score has the test score
if($score >= 90)
{
   print "Congratulations! You got an A in this test.\n";
}
else
{
   print "Work harder for the next test!\n";
}
```

As you can see, the if-else pair enables you to handle both the true and false cases of a test. Sometimes, however, you need to test for more than two alternatives. Suppose that you are writing a Perl program to handle the upgrade of a software package. You need to consider the following cases:

* If version number is greater than or equal to 10, no upgrade is necessary.
* For versions between 6 and 9, perform a standard upgrade.
* For version numbers 4 and 5, reinstall the software.
* For all other versions, the upgrade is not allowed.

You can use an if statement with several elsif clauses and an else clause to implement this logic, as follows:

```
# Assume that $version contains version number
# Check version number and take appropriate action

if($version >= 10 )
{
   print "No upgrade necessary\n";
}
elsif($version >= 6 && $version <= 9)
{
   print "Standard upgrade\n";
}
elsif($version > 3 && $version < 6)
{
   print "Reinstall software\n";
}
else
{
   print "Sorry, cannot upgrade\n";
}
```

 TIP   **If you want to write an if statement that executes a single Perl statement when an expression is true, you can use the following shorthand form:**

```
statement if(expression);
```

In this case, the Perl interpreter executes the statement only when the expression is true. For example, if you want to increment exit the program if $error_count exceeds 25, you might write:

```
exit if($error_count > 25);
```

As you see in later sections, Perl enables you to use this syntax with unless, while, and until statements as well. This compact form of conditional statements is popular when you want to execute a single statement based on the value of an expression.

Using the unless statement

Sometimes you might want to execute a block of statements if a condition is false. For example, instead of writing *if the user is not root, don't run this program,* you might find it easier to write *unless the user is root, don't run this program.* Perl includes the unless statement precisely for this purpose — so that you can do something when a condition is false.

You could express the statement *unless the user is root, don't run this program* with the following Perl code:

```
unless($user eq "root")
{
    print "You must be \"root\" to run this program.\n";
    exit;
}
```

In this case, unless the string `$user` is `"root"`, the program exits.

TIP A common use of `unless` is to test whether a file has been opened successfully. Although you have not yet seen how to open a file, you should be able to guess the meaning of the following code:

```
unless(open(DATAFILE, "price.dat"))
{
    die "Cannot open price data file\n";
}
```

You can read this conditional statement as follows: *unless the file is successfully opened, stop the program.*

The `unless` statement checks the result of the `open` function, which returns a nonzero value only if the file is successfully opened. The `die` function causes the program to exit after printing the message that you pass as an argument.

NOTE The `unless` statement has the same form as `if`, including the use of `elsif` and `else` clauses. The difference is that `unless` executes its statement block only if the condition is false.

TIP As with the `if` statement, you can use the `unless` statement in the following form:

```
statement unless(expression);
```

which executes the `statement` when the `expression` is false. For example, if you want to exit a Perl program unless the variable `$username` is equal to `"root"`, you could write:

```
exit unless($username eq "root");
```

Here, I am assuming that the `$username` variable contains a string (presumably a user name). If `$username` is not equal to `"root"`, this statement calls the `exit` function, which ends the Perl program.

Repeating a Task by Looping

Sometimes you want to execute a block of statements repeatedly until some condition becomes false. The operation of repeating a block of statements is called *looping*. Figure 4-3 illustrates the flow control of a loop of the type you might implement with the `while` statement.

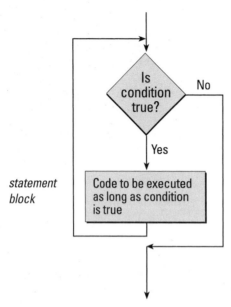

Figure 4-3   Flow control of a loop

To see an example of looping, consider the simple problem of adding the numbers from 1 through 10. You can use the `while` statement to accomplish this task, as follows:

```
#!/usr/local/bin/perl
# Add the numbers 1 through 10 in a loop
while($i <= 10)
{
    $sum += $i;
    $i++;
}
print "Sum of 1 through 10 = $sum\n";
```

If you run this program, it prints the following result:

```
Sum of 1 through 10 = 55
```

In this program, the `while` loop executes the block of code within the curly braces (`{. . .}`) as long as `$i` is less than or equal to 10. Within the block, `$i` is added to a variable named $sum and then incremented. The end result is to add the numbers up to and including 10.

As you can see from this simple example, the while statement has the following general form:

```
while(expression)
{
    ...block of statements to execute as long as expression is true
    ...
}
```

That *expression* could be anything — the value of a variable or the comparison of two strings or numbers. You can use almost anything as the condition to be tested. If you use an array as the condition, for example, the while loop executes until the array has no elements left, as in the following example:

```
# @ARGV has the command-line arguments
while(@ARGV)
{
    $arg = shift @ARGV;          # extract one argument
# Code to process the current argument
    print "$arg\n";
}
```

This while loop prints all the command-line arguments — these are the arguments that you used when you started the program containing this loop. If the program were in a file named argv.pl and you executed it with this command:

```
perl argv.pl one two three
```

then the @ARGV array will be ("one", "two", "three") and the while loop will print the following:

```
one
two
three
```

 X-REF As described in Chapter 2, the shift function removes the first element of an array and returns that element. That means that after all the array elements have been shifted out, the array will have no elements left and the while loop will end.

In addition to the while statement, Perl includes the following statements for looping:

* until
* for
* foreach

Using an `until` loop

The `until` statement is just like `while`, but it repeats a block of statements until a specified condition becomes true. In other words, the `until` statement executes the block as long as that condition is false. You should use the `until` statement whenever you find it most natural to think of repeating a loop until an expression becomes true. Here is an example that illustrates a typical use of an `until` loop:

```
#!/usr/local/bin/perl

# Process commands until "quit" is entered

until($command eq "quit")
{
    $command = <STDIN>; # read command
    chop $command;      # get rid of newline
    print "$command\n";
}
```

When you run this program, it continues accepting commands (and printing them) until you type `quit`. At that point, the expression (`$command eq "quit"`) becomes true and the `until` loop ends.

Using a `for` loop

The `for` statement is another way your Perl program can execute a block of statements any number of times, based on the value of an expression. The syntax of a `for` loop is quite a bit different from that of `while` and `until` loops. For example, here is a `for` loop to add the numbers from 1 to 10:

```
for($i=1; $i <= 10; $i++)
{
    $sum += $i;
}
```

In this example, the actual work of adding the numbers is done in the statement controlled by the `for` loop — the statement that appears within curly braces (`{ }`). The following steps describe what this `for` loop does:

1. `$i` is initialized to 1 before the loop starts.

2. The loop runs as long as `$i` is less than or equal to 10.

3. Each time through the loop, `$i` is added to `$sum`.

4. After each iteration of the loop, `$i` is incremented.

NOTE This is the most common form of a `for` loop. The variable `$i` is used as a counter: it's initialized to a value at the beginning of the loop, incremented each time through the loop, and tested to determine when to end the loop. The `$i` variable is also known as the *loop variable.* Figure 4-4 illustrates various parts of the `for` loop.

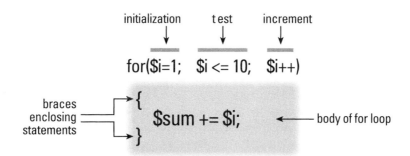

Figure 4-4 A for loop in Perl

As you can see from this example, the syntax of a `for` loop is as follows:

```
for(expr_1; expr_2; expr_3)
{
    statement block
}
```

The *expr_1* expression is evaluated one time, at the beginning of the loop, and the statement block is executed as long as expression *expr_2* is true. The third expression, *expr_3*, is evaluated after each execution of the statement block. You can omit any of these expressions, but you must include the semicolons. Also, the braces around the statement block are required.

TIP You have to use the braces around the statement block even if there are no statements within braces. For example, you can write a `for` loop to add the numbers from 1 to 10 using an empty statement block, as follows:

```
for($i=1, $sum=0; $i <= 10; $sum += $i, $i++) {}
```

As you can see, the initialization statement sets $i to 1 and $sum to 0. Then the last expression adds $i to $sum and increments $i. In this case, the body of the for loop is the empty pair of braces ({ }).

You can use a for loop to perform some operation on each element of an array. Here's a simple example that goes through all the numbers in an array and finds the largest value:

```perl
#!/usr/local/bin/perl

# Define an array of numbers
  @scores = (65, 49, 76, 69, 85, 82, 64, 70, 72);

# Loop through array and find highest score
  for($i=0, $max=0; $i < $#scores; $i++)
  {
    if($scores[$i] > $max)
    {
      $max = $scores[$i];
    }
  }
# Print the highest score
  print "Highest score = $max\n";
```

When you run this program, it prints the following:

```
Highest score = 85
```

If you examine the for loop, you'll notice that the loop processes all the elements of the @scores array as follows:

* $i is the variable that is incremented each time through the loop.
* $i serves as the array index. Inside the for loop's body, each element of the @scores array is accessed with the expression $scores[$i].
* The loop starts at $i=0 and continues as long as $i is less than $#scores. As you'll recall from Chapter 2, $#scores refers to the number of elements in the @scores array. Thus, the for loop goes through all the elements of the @scores array.

Using a foreach loop

Besides while, until, and for, Perl provides the foreach statement to execute a block of code for each element in an array. Of course, you could use a for loop to access each element of an array by its index, but it's much simpler to access each array element with the foreach statement.

To see how `foreach` works, consider the same example as that used in the preceding section. The goal is to find the largest number in an array of numbers. Here's how you might write such a program using a `foreach` loop:

```perl
#!/usr/local/bin/perl
# Define an array of numbers
  @scores = (65, 49, 76, 69, 85, 82, 64, 70, 72);

# Loop through array and find highest score
  foreach $score (@scores)
  {
    if($score > $max)
    {
      $max = $score;
    }
  }
# Print the highest score
  print "Highest score = $max\n";
```

If you compare the `foreach` loop with the `for` loop for processing elements of an array, you'll notice that the `foreach` loop looks simpler because you do not have to use any array index to access the elements of the array. That eliminates all occurrences of expressions such as `$scores[$i]`. Instead, the `foreach` loop has the following clean syntax:

```perl
foreach $Variable (@Array)
{
  statement block
}
```

You can read this `foreach` loop as follows: *for each variable in the array, execute the statement block.*

The `foreach` statement assigns to *$Variable* an element from the @Array and executes the statement block. The `foreach` statement repeats this procedure until no array elements are left.

Here is another simple example of a `foreach` statement, which adds the numbers from 1 to 10:

```perl
foreach $i (1..10) { $sum += $i; }
```

TIP Notice that this example declares the array with the range operator (..). That's an easy way to define an array that's a sequence of numbers.

TIP If you omit the *variable* in a `foreach` statement, Perl implicitly uses the `$_` variable to hold the current array element. Thus, you could use the following `foreach` loop to add the numbers from 1 and 10:

```
foreach (1..10) { $sum += $_; }
```

Breaking Out of a Loop

Sometimes you need to break out of a loop before it has gone through all of its iterations. Suppose that you are searching for a name in an array of names and you want to end the loop as soon as you find a match. Further, suppose that the names are stored in the `@names` array and you want to look for the name stored in the variable `$customer`. Here's how you can break the loop when you find a matching name:

```
foreach $name (@names)
{
# Break the loop if $customer is found
   last if($customer eq $name);
# ... other code ...
}
```

As this example shows, you can break a loop with the `last` command. You can use `last` in all types of loops: `while`, `until`, `for`, and `foreach`. For example, the following `while` loop ends as soon you type a blank line:

```
while($line = <STDIN>)
{
  last if($line eq "\n");
  print $line;
}
```

When this loop is executed, it reads and prints each line that you type. The loop ends as soon as you enter a blank line by pressing Enter on the keyboard.

It's not unusual to have one loop embedded inside another. For example, you may have a `foreach` loop inside a `while` loop. Suppose that you want to end the `while` loop when `$line` matches one of the items in the `@names` array. If you were to write the following code:

```
while($line = <STDIN>)
{
  chop $line; # get rid of the newline

  foreach $name (@names)
```

```
    {
      last if($line eq $name); # ends the foreach loop
    }
  }
```

the `last` command only ends the innermost loop, which, in this case, happens to be the `foreach` loop.

NOTE There is another form of the `last` command that can actually break the outer `while` loop. To use that form, you have to first label the `while` loop — that is, give it a name. Then put the name of the `while` loop after the `last` keyword, as shown in the following example:

```
INPUT: while($line = <STDIN>)
{
  chop $line; # get rid of newline character

  foreach $name (@names)
  {
    last INPUT if($line eq $name); # ends while loop
  }
}
```

TIP In this example, the `while` loop is labeled `INPUT` (note that the label does not have to be all uppercase; you can mix case). To add a label, you have to place the label followed by a colon in front of the statement you are labeling.

Skipping an Iteration of a Loop

When you use loops in a Perl program, you do not necessarily have to perform computations for all iterations of a loop. Typically, you skip some iterations of the loop. For example, you might write a Perl program that generates a message if a user has used more than 2500KB of disk space. Suppose that the user names and the corresponding disk usage are stored in an associative array. In this case, you want to skip an iteration of the loop whenever a user's disk usage is less than 2500KB. The following program shows how to skip an iteration of a loop by using the `next` command:

```
#!/usr/local/bin/perl

# Define an associative array of usernames and
# disk usage
```

```
%disk_usage = ("joe"      => 3500,
               "bill"     => 4800,
               "john"     => 1950,
               "mary"     => 3100,
               "susan"    => 2100);

$limit = 2500;  # Usage must be less than this

# Process the disk usage log and list the users
# who exceed the current limit

print "More than ${limit}KB disk space used by:\n";

foreach $user (keys(%disk_usage))
{
# Skip this iteration if disk use is below limit
    next if($disk_usage{$user} < $limit);

# Otherwise, print the username
    print "  $user\n";
}
```

When you run this program, it prints the following result:

```
More than 2500KB disk space used by:
  mary
  bill
  joe
```

who are the users with more than 2500KB of disk usage.

TIP   **Notice how I write $\{limit\}KB in the print statement that precedes the foreach loop. I use this format because I want to print the value of $limit immediately followed by KB. If I had not used the curly braces, the Perl interpreter would have tried to print the value of the variable $limitKB, which is undefined in this program.**

The following should help you understand how the rest of this program works:

✳ The %disk_usage associative array stores disk space used by each user, with the user name as the key.

✳ The $limit variable is the maximum disk space each user may use.

✳ The foreach loop goes through all the keys in the %disk_usage associative array — the keys function is used to get the array of user names that are the keys for %disk_usage.

* Inside the `foreach` loop's body, the following `next` command is used together with an `if` statement to skip an iteration of the loop if the disk space usage is less than the limit:

```
next if($disk_usage{$user} < $limit);
```

* Finally, for users who exceed the disk usage limit (this is true for any loop iteration that's not skipped with the `next` command), the `foreach` loop prints the user name.

NOTE As with the `last` command that ends a loop prematurely, you can use the `next` command to skip an iteration of a loop with all types of loop statements (`while`, `until`, `for`, and `foreach`). Additionally, in cases where you have one loop inside another, you can use a label with the `next` command to designate which loop you want to skip. When you use `next` without any label, it skips to the next iteration of the innermost loop.

To see how to use `next` with loop labels, consider a somewhat contrived example. Suppose that you want to print a rectangle (6 rows by 15 columns) of asterisks. You can do this with two `foreach` loops, as follows:

```
# Loop over the rows
  foreach $row (1..6)
  {
# Loop over the columns
    foreach $col (1..15)
    {
      print "*";
    }
# Print a newline after each row
    print "\n";
  }
```

The outer `foreach` loop goes through all the rows and the inner `foreach` loop goes through all the columns for each row. When this code runs, it prints the following output:

```
***************
***************
***************
***************
***************
***************
```

Now suppose that you want to skip the second and fifth rows of the asterisks and also skip the second and fourteenth columns. You can label the two loops and then use the `next` command to accomplish this. Here's how:

```perl
# The ROW loop goes through the rows
   ROW: foreach $row (1..6)
   {
# The COLUMN loop goes through the columns
      COLUMN: foreach $col (1..15)
      {
# Skip iterations for 2nd and 5th rows
        if($row == 2 || $row == 5)
        {
           print "\n";
           next ROW;      # skip to next row
        }
# Also skip iterations for 2nd and 14th columns
        if($col == 2 || $col == 14)
        {
           print " ";
           next COLUMN; # skip to next column
        }
        print "*";
      }
# Print a newline after each row
      print "\n";
   }
```

When this code executes, it prints the following pattern of asterisks:

```
* ********** *

* ********** *
* ********** *

* ********** *
```

As you can see, the program skips the second and fifth rows as well as the second and fourteenth columns.

Although the Perl code appears lengthy, the logic for skipping specific rows and columns is implemented by the next commands that appear in the inner foreach loops. For the second and fifth rows, the code prints a newline and uses the following next command to skip the row:

```perl
next ROW;
```

Although this statement appears in the inner foreach loop (labeled COLUMN), this next command causes the Perl interpreter to skip to the next iteration of the outer foreach loop, which is labeled ROW.

BONUS

How Do I Test Multiple Conditions?

This chapter began with an introduction to Perl's numeric and string comparison operators that you use to test for specific conditions in conditional statements and loops. For example, you might check for a simple condition in an `if` statement as follows:

```
if($balance < 1500)
{
    $service_charge = 7.5;
}
```

This might be the implementation of a bank's service charge policy that states: If the balance is below $1,500.00, the service charge is $7.50.

Sometimes, however, you have to test a more complex condition. For example, to compute the service charge for an account, you may also have to test other conditions such as: If the account balance is less than $1,500.00 and the number of transactions (deposits and withdrawals) exceeds 30, the service charge is $7.50.

You could test for multiple conditions by embedding one `if` statement inside another, like this:

```
if($balance < 1500)
{
    if($num_transactions > 30)
    {
        $service_charge = 7.5;
    }
}
```

This is a bit cumbersome to write and not easy to comprehend. A better way to combine multiple tests is by using Perl's logical operators. In this case, you can use the logical AND operator to write the test as follows:

```
if(($balance < 1500) && ($num_transactions > 30))
{
    $service_charge = 7.5;
}
```

In place of the `&&` symbol for the logical AND operator, you can also use the `and` keyword:

```
if(($balance < 1500) and ($num_transactions > 30))
{
  $service_charge = 7.5;
}
```

NOTE **Perl includes the following logical operators:**

```
condition1 && condition2   # logical AND
condition1 || condition2   # logical OR
!condition1                # logical NOT
```

You can write each of these in the following alternate (and more readable) style:

```
condition1 and condition2   # logical AND
condition1 or condition2    # logical OR
not condition1              # logical NOT
```

Summary

The flow of the program refers to the order in which a program's code is executed. Usually, the Perl statements are executed one after another, but sometimes you need to execute a block of code only when a certain condition is true. Perl includes a number of statements — known as *conditional statements* — for controlling the flow of a program.

This chapter shows you how to use Perl's conditional statements to control a program's flow. Because conditional statements need to test conditions, the chapter begins with an introduction to Perl's numeric and string comparison operators.

You learn about the `if` and `else` statements that execute a block of code when a condition is true. You also see how to execute a block of code repeatedly — a programming practice known as *looping* — and how to break a loop or skip an iteration of a loop.

As a bonus, you learn how to test for multiple conditions by using the logical operators such as AND and OR.

The next chapter introduces you to input and output — how to read from standard input and print to the standard output.

CHAPTER FIVE

READING INPUT AND PRINTING OUTPUT

IN THIS CHAPTER YOU LEARN THESE KEY SKILLS

Perl programs are usually designed to read input from the *standard input* and print output to the *standard output*. By default, standard input is the keyboard and standard output is the display screen. Operating systems such as UNIX and Windows, however, enable the user to redirect input and output so that the input may come from a file and the output can be sent to a file. With redirection, you can easily process file-based data with a Perl program that reads input from standard input and prints output to standard output.

Standard input and standard output are also used by the Common Gateway Interface (CGI) programs that are commonplace on the World Wide Web. As you learn in Chapter 14, CGI programs read input from the standard input and print output to standard output. Because you'll be writing CGI programs in Perl, you need to learn how to read input from standard input and print output to standard output.

This chapter shows you how to read lines of text from standard input and use the `print` function to send output to the standard output. You also learn how operating systems such as UNIX, Windows 95, and Windows NT enable you to redirect standard input and standard output.

Understanding STDIN and STDOUT

Perl programs get their input from the standard input and send their output to the standard output. You can think of standard input and standard output as files. In Perl programs, you refer to files by identifiers known as *filehandles.* To obtain a valid filehandle, you have to use the open function with a filename. You learn about opening files in Chapter 10. This chapter's focus is on standard input and standard output, which you can use without opening any files.

To use standard input and standard output, you do not have to explicitly open any files. Instead, Perl automatically defines and opens STDIN and STDOUT as the filehandles for standard input and standard output, respectively. Figure 5-1 illustrates how you can think of STDIN and STDOUT as input and output pipes for a Perl program.

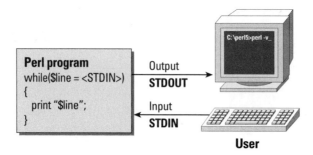

Figure 5-1   Default standard input and output for a Perl program

As Figure 5-1 shows, by default, STDIN is tied to the keyboard and STDOUT is the display screen. That means when your Perl program reads from STDIN, it receives whatever the user types on the keyboard. Similarly, when you use a function, such as print, that sends its output to STDOUT, the output appears on the display screen.

You have already seen how to read from STDIN and use the print function to write to STDOUT. The following Perl program, for example, reads lines from the standard input and prints each line until it reads the string "quit\n" (that's quit followed by a newline character):

```perl
#!/usr/local/bin/perl

while($line = <STDIN>)
{
  print "$line";
  last if($line eq "quit\n");
}
```

If you run this program, it echoes back each line of text you type and exits when you type `quit` (and then press Enter).

Here, the expression `$line = <STDIN>` reads a line from the standard input — the keyboard — into the variable `$line`. The `print` function sends its output to the standard output, which is the display screen. However, you can use operating system commands to connect `STDIN` and `STDOUT` to files rather than to the keyboard or the display, respectively.

Redirecting STDIN and STDOUT

You learn more about reading from `STDIN` and writing to `STDOUT` in the following sections of this chapter, but first you need to understand how a program designed to read from standard input can also process data from a file. You also learn how a program that sends its output to standard output (the display screen) can also send the output to a file.

You have two ways of redirecting `STDIN` and `STDOUT`:

* *Using redirection operators in the command line*: From the command line, you can attach `STDIN` and `STDOUT` to files.

* *Using another program's output as* `STDIN`: From the operating system's command line, you can redirect the output of a program as the standard input for your Perl program. For this to work, the other program must print output to `STDOUT`. Of course, you can also use your Perl program's standard output as the standard input of another program.

Using the UNIX and MS-DOS redirection operators

When you run a Perl program from a UNIX command prompt or an MS-DOS prompt window (in Windows 95 or Windows NT), you can use special operators to attach `STDIN` and `STDOUT` to files instead of the default keyboard and display, respectively.

Suppose that you have written a Perl program, `prog.pl`, that reads input from `STDIN` and prints output to `STDOUT`. If you want to run `prog.pl` with input coming from a file named `infile` and output going to a file named `outfile`, all you have to do is launch `prog.pl` with the following command line:

```
perl prog.pl < infile > outfile
```

The less-than sign (<) is the input redirection operator; the greater-than sign (>) is the output redirection operator. Here's what happens when you use this command line:

* The Perl program reads its input from the file whose name appears after the input redirection operator (<).

✳ The program sends its output to the file whose name appears after the output redirection operator (>).

Figure 5-2 illustrates the concept of input and output redirection through the command line.

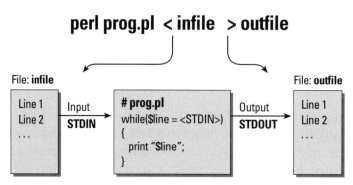

Figure 5-2   Redirecting input and output through the command line

As Figure 5-2 shows, when the command line includes the input and output redirection operators, the operating system hooks up the specified files to STDIN and STDOUT. The Perl program is written as if it always reads input from STDIN and prints output to STDOUT. By using the < and > operators on the command line, you can use the same Perl program to process data from different input files and generate different output files.

NOTE   The syntax for input and output redirection is the same in UNIX as it is in Windows 95 and Windows NT. The concept of input and output redirection was part of the UNIX command-line interface. MS-DOS borrowed the idea of input and output redirection from UNIX. In Windows 95 and Windows NT, you run Perl programs from an MS-DOS prompt window that essentially accepts the MS-DOS commands and, consequently, also accepts the input and output redirection operators.

Connecting STDIN to another program's output

In addition to attaching STDIN to a file, you can use the output of any program as the STDIN of your Perl program. There is only one constraint: The other program must write to its standard output. In other words, you can redirect the STDOUT of any program to the STDIN of your Perl program. To do this, you have to use the vertical bar (|) operator in the command line. Figure 5-3 illustrates the use of the vertical bar operator.

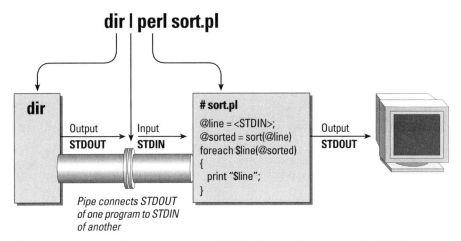

dir | perl sort.pl

Figure 5-3 Connecting one program's STDOUT to another program's STDIN

The vertical bar (|) operator is also called a *pipe*. As Figure 5-3 shows, you can think of this operator as establishing a pipe between the first program's STD-OUT and the second program's STDIN.

To see the pipe in action, consider the following Perl program, named sort.pl, that reads from STDIN into an array, sorts that array, and prints out all the items in the array:

```
#!/usr/local/bin/perl
# sort.pl

# Read all lines into an array
  @line = <STDIN>;

# Sort the array
  @sorted = sort(@line);

# Print all lines from the array
  foreach $line (@sorted)
  {
    print "$line";
  }
```

Feed this program the output of the MS-DOS DIR command. Before doing that, try the DIR command alone. Here's the output when I tried it in a test directory with a few files:

```
Volume in drive C is LNBSOFT
Volume Serial Number is 384C-15D4
Directory of C:\idg\dp\perl\test
```

```
   .                  <DIR>           12-25-96  10:06p  .
   ..                 <DIR>           12-25-96  10:06p  ..
SORT      PL             227  12-25-96  10:23p  SORT.PL
ZFILE     TXT             18  12-25-96  10:07p  ZFILE.TXT
AFILE     TXT             18  12-25-96  10:07p  AFILE.TXT
XFILE     TXT             20  12-25-96  10:07p  XFILE.TXT
              4 file(s)           283 bytes
              2 dir (s)   795,967,488 bytes free
```

Notice that the filenames are not in alphabetical order. Now try the following command in an MS-DOS prompt window:

```
dir | perl sort.pl
```

When I tried this command in my test directory, here's what it printed:

```
              2 dir(s)     795,934,720 bytes free
              4 file(s)            283 bytes
 Directory of C:\idg\dp\perl\test
 Volume Serial Number is 384C-15D4
 Volume in drive C is LNBSOFT
   .                  <DIR>           12-25-96  10:06p  .
   ..                 <DIR>           12-25-96  10:06p  ..
AFILE     TXT             18  12-25-96  10:07p  AFILE.TXT
SORT      PL             227  12-25-96  10:23p  SORT.PL
XFILE     TXT             20  12-25-96  10:07p  XFILE.TXT
ZFILE     TXT             18  12-25-96  10:07p  ZFILE.TXT
```

As you can see, the sort.pl program reads the output of DIR and sorts the lines alphabetically. Lines with blanks at the beginning appear before other lines, which may not be exactly what you want, but the filenames now appear in alphabetical order. (The UNIX ls command, which is similar to the MS-DOS DIR command, generates a sorted list of files, so you cannot see the effect of sort.pl on the output of ls.)

Reading Input from STDIN

In Perl programs, you can read from any open file by enclosing the filehandle in angle brackets (<. . .>). That pair of angle brackets is known as the *input operator,* or *angle operator.*

Reading a single line

To read from a line of text from the filehandle STDIN, you write <STDIN>. When the Perl interpreter evaluates <STDIN>, the result is the next line from standard input. To store the line of text in a variable, all you have to do is assign the value to a variable, like this:

```
$line = <STDIN>;
```

This Perl statement reads the next line from the standard input and stores the text in the $line variable.

The Perl interpreter assumes that the newline character (denoted by \n) marks the end of a line. The angle operator <STDIN> reads all the characters up to and including the newline character. Thus, the text read from STDIN includes the newline as the last character.

REMOVING THE TRAILING NEWLINE

When you first begin using Perl, that trailing newline can be a real pain! Typically, you'll forget about the newline when checking if text read from STDIN (or a file) matches some other string. Luckily, Perl provides an easy way to get rid of the trailing newline. Right after you read a line from STDIN, call the chomp function, as follows:

```
$line = <STDIN>;
chomp $line;
```

The chomp function then removes the trailing newline from $line.

USING THE $_ SPECIAL VARIABLE

Usually, you have to assign <STDIN> to a variable — to store the input text for later use. There is one special case, however, where the line of text provided by <STDIN> is automatically assigned to a special variable named $_. This occurs when you use <STDIN> as the conditional expression of a while loop, as illustrated in the following example:

```
while(<STDIN>)
{
# $_ contains line of text read from standard input.
# Use $_ to refer to the text.
   print $_;
}
```

TIP   When you run this program, it echoes back anything you type until the end of file. For standard input, the end of file is marked by a special character that depends on the operating system. On UNIX systems, run the program, type as much input as you want, and then press Ctrl+D to indicate the end of standard input. In an MS-DOS prompt window, type as many lines of text as you want and then press Ctrl+Z followed by pressing Enter to stop the program.

Here are some key points to note about the automatic assignment of input text to $_:

★ You can use this form of a `while` loop to read text from any file — all you have to do is place the filehandle in angle brackets and use that as the conditional expression of a `while` statement. The line of text read from the file is assigned to $_.

★ The automatic assignment of input text to $_ occurs only with the `while` statement. For example, the expression `if(<STDIN>)` *does not* assign input text to $_.

Reading multiple lines

As you have seen in the examples so far, when you assign the expression `<STDIN>` to a scalar variable with a statement such as this:

```
$line = <STDIN>; # scalar context (one line read)
```

a single line of text is read from `STDIN` and assigned as the value of the scalar variable $line. In this case, Perl interprets the `<STDIN>` expression in a *scalar context,* because the left-hand side of the statement is a scalar variable (remember that you can tell a scalar variable by the $ prefix).

You may also assign `<STDIN>` to an array variable. For example, you could write:

```
@lines = <STDIN>; # list context (many lines read)
```

In this case, Perl evaluates `<STDIN>` in a *list context,* because a list of scalar values is necessary to initialize the @lines array (remember that the @ prefix implies an array variable). The end result is that `<STDIN>` returns a list consisting of all the remaining lines from standard input up to the end of file.

To see how you can read multiple lines into an array, try out the following program:

```
#!/usr/local/bin/perl

# Read multiple lines from STDIN
# Tell user how to end input
    print "In UNIX, press Ctrl+D to end input\n";
    print "In Windows, press Ctrl+Z to end input\n";

    @lines = <STDIN>;   # reads lines until end of file

# Print the @ lines array
    $numlines = @lines;
    print "\nRead $numlines lines:\n";
    foreach $line (@lines) {print "$line";}
```

When you run this program, it displays a message that tells you how to end the input. As you type lines of text, the program reads each line as an element of the @lines array. Depending on your operating system, you have to press a specific key to end the input (Ctrl+D in UNIX or Ctrl+Z in Windows). Then the program prints the lines that you had typed at the keyboard.

You should be careful with the file input statements of the form @array = <FILEHANDLE>; because that single statement loads the entire content of the file into an array. For large files, this statement ends up creating a large array that may take up lots of memory.

Reading with <>

A special way to read from standard input is to skip the filehandle entirely and use the expression <> (just the angle brackets alone). Perl treats this expression as a special type of input. First, try out the following program, which consists of a single Perl statement:

```
# File: print.pl
   print while(<>);
```

Store the program in a file named print.pl. Now run it with the following command:

```
perl print.pl
```

Type lines of text; the program reads each line and prints it back. End the input by pressing Ctrl+Z in Windows (or Ctrl+D if you are using UNIX); the program then quits. As you can see, the program essentially reads from STDIN.

Now run the program in a different manner. Use the same command line as before, but add a few filenames to that command line. Try the following command:

```
perl print.pl print.pl
```

The resulting output is:

```
# File: print.pl
   print while(<>);
```

which is the content of the print.pl file. In this case, the <> operator takes its input from the file whose name you provide as a command line argument.

NOTE **If you provide a few more filenames on the command line, the <> expression magically reads all the lines from all the files you mention on the command line. For example, if you were to type the following command:**

```
perl print.pl file1 file2 file3
```

the `print.pl` program prints the lines from the files file1, file2, **and** file3. It's as if all the files mentioned on the command line are concatenated into a single file and the `<>` operator reads the contents of that single concatenated file.

Printing Output to STDOUT

In Perl programs, you typically use the `print` function to send output to standard output. For example, the following Perl statement:

```
print "Hello, World!\n";
```

prints the `Hello, World!` message on `STDOUT` — the display screen. You can get the same result with the following equivalent statement:

```
print STDOUT "Hello, World!\n";
```

In this case, you are explicitly instructing the `print` function to send its output to `STDOUT`.

TIP **If you want to send output to an open file (identified by a filehandle), all you have to do is use the `print` function with that filehandle as an argument, as follows:**

```
print FILEHANDLE, "Whatever you want to print";
```

One caveat is that the file must be open for writing. As you learn in Chapter 10 and in the Bonus section of this chapter, you can open a file for writing by following a specific syntax when you use the `open` function.

In addition to the `print` function, Perl includes the `printf` function, which works like the `printf` function in the C programming language. You learn a bit more about both `print` and `printf` in the following sections.

Using the `print` function

The `print` function prints a single string or a comma-separated list of strings to a file specified by a filehandle. The general syntax of the `print` function is as follows:

```
print FILEHANDLE $string1, "another string", $string2;
```

As this syntax shows, the `print` function expects a filehandle followed by a list of strings.

If you omit the `FILEHANDLE`, the print function sends its output to `STDOUT` — the standard output. Thus, the following program sends its output to `STDOUT`:

```
$firstname = "Naba";
$lastname = "Barkakati";
print "My name is: ", $firstname, " ", $lastname, "\n";
```

When you run this program, it prints the following line on the display:

```
My name is: Naba Barkakati
```

As you can see, the `print` function simply prints the list of strings one after another. In the list of strings, you can have scalar variables as well as strings within double quotes.

You can embed scalar and array variables in double-quoted strings. Perl replaces such variables with their values.

DEFAULT ARGUMENT FOR PRINT

If you omit both the filehandle and the strings, the `print` function prints the current value of the `$_` variable. The following Perl code illustrates this feature of the `print` function:

```
$_ = "This is a test.\n";
print; # prints $_
```

Typically, you use print without any arguments in situations where `$_` contains the string that your program is processing. A good example is a `while` loop that reads from `STDIN`. If the line read from `STDIN` is not assigned to a specific variable, then Perl assigns that line to `$_`. Here's a `while` loop that prints everything you type on standard input:

```
while(<STDIN>)  # line of text assigned to $_
{
  print;  # prints $_
}
```

Of course, you could have written this `while` loop in a much more concise form, as follows:

```
print while(<STDIN>);
```

PRINT UP TO HERE

There is a special use of the `print` function that's useful for printing a number of lines of text. Actually, you can use the syntax to define string variables, but it's most often used as the argument for the `print` function.

Suppose that you want to print an entire HTML document by using the `print` function. (HTML stands for Hypertext Markup Language, which you learn more about in Chapter 14.) Instead of printing the lines by using them as comma-separated arguments to the print function, you can use the so-called "print up to HERE" syntax, as shown here:

```
# File: prhtml.pl

# Define a few variables
$title = "Thank you";
$website = "http://www.lnbsoft.com/";

# Print the HTML document
print <<END_OF_TEXT;
<html>
<head>
<title>$title</title>
</head>

<body>
Thank you for visiting my
<a href="$website">Web site</a>.
</body>
</html>
END_OF_TEXT
```

When you run this program, it prints the following output:
```
<html>
<head>
<title>Thank you</title>
</head>

<body>
Thank you for visiting my
<a href="http://www.lnbsoft.com/">Web site</a>.
</body>
</html>
```

Incidentally, if you want to see how this HTML text looks in a Web browser, run the program and send its output to a file. If the program file is called prhtml.pl, for example, run it with this command:

```
perl prhtml.pl > sample.html
```

Then use the Open File option of your favorite Web browser to load the sample.html file. Figure 5-4 shows how Netscape Navigator renders the HTML text.

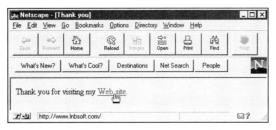

Figure 5-4 The HTML text as rendered by Netscape Navigator

As you can see, when you position the cursor on the hypertext link labeled Web site, the status bar shows the address of the link, which happens to be http://www.lnbsoft.com/.

From this example, you can see what the "print up to HERE" syntax does. The general syntax is as follows:

```
print <<HERE;
... lines of text
to be printed ...
HERE
```

All these lines constitute a single Perl statement that instructs the print function to print the lines of text until it encounters the string that follows the << characters. You can use any text in place of HERE. That text serves as the marker that indicates the end of the text to be printed. Typically, Perl programmers use a string with all capital letters.

The lines of text between the print function and the HERE may include line breaks, blank lines, and other Perl variables. You can place variable names in the text; Perl replaces each variable name with its value before the print function prints the text.

Using the `printf` function

The C programming language includes a function called printf that serves as an all-purpose output function. Perl also includes a printf function that's similar to its namesake in C. The printf function is more complex than print, but it offers you more control over how the output is formatted — for example, you can control details such as the number of digits after a decimal point or the number of characters used to print a string.

TIP If you are a C programmer and already know how to use printf, you'll feel right at home with Perl's printf (even though the syntax is a bit flexible and it can look different from C). If you don't know C, however, it's perfectly adequate to stick to the simpler print function.

AN EXAMPLE OF PRINTF

Before you learn the details of how to use the `printf` function, you should see how `printf` works. Here is a Perl program that prints out a formatted invoice using the `printf` function:

```
#!/usr/local/bin/perl

# Define a few arrays
   @items = ("Coffee", "Tea", "Cookies");
   @prices = (12.10, 25.30, 3.99);
   @how_many = (6, 3.5, 8);
   $separator = "-" x 40;

# Compute some values and print a
# formatted invoice

# First print a header
   print $separator, "\n";
   printf "%-12s %8s %8s %8s\n",
          "Item", "Pounds", "Price/lb", "Total";
   print $separator, "\n";

# Print each item
   foreach $i (0..$#items)
   {
      $total = $how_many[$i] * $prices[$i];
      printf "%-12s %8.2f %8.2f %8.2f\n", $items[$i],
             $how_many[$i], $prices[$i], $total;

      $grand_total += $total;
   }

# Print the grand total
   print $separator, "\n";
   printf "%-30s %8.2f\n", "Grand total", $grand_total;
```

Save the program in a file and run it. When you run the program, it produces the following output:

```
Item           Pounds Price/lb   Total

Coffee           6.00   12.10    72.60
Tea              3.50   25.30    88.55
```

```
Cookies            8.00    3.99   31.92
_____

Grand total                       193.07
```

In this output, all lines, except the ones consisting of the dashes, are generated by the `printf` function. What appears on the line depends on the arguments passed to the `printf` function.

Consider the following `printf` function:

```
printf "%-12s %8s %8s %8s\n",
        "Item", "Pounds", "Price/lb", "Total";
```

This function generates the following line of output:

```
Item            Pounds Price/lb    Total
```

Figure 5-5 illustrates how this `printf` function converts its arguments into the output.

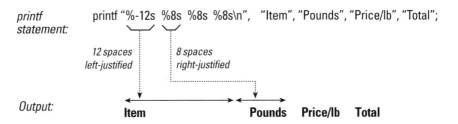

Figure 5-5   A typical use of the printf function with the resulting output

Here's how you can interpret this particular use of `printf`:

* The first argument of the `printf` function is a string that describes the format of the output. In this case, the format string is:

    ```
    "%-12s %8s %8s %8s\n"
    ```

* Each percent sign (%) in the format string marks the beginning of a format specification. The `printf` function expects a format specification for each argument following the format string. In this case, there are four format specifications for the four string arguments.

* The first format specification (%-12s) is applied to the first string ("Item"), the second one (%8s) is applied to the second string ("Pounds"), and so on.

* Each format specification begins with a percent sign followed by some optional numbers and a letter. That letter determines the type of data you are printing. For example, the %-12s format specification has the letter s, which specifies format for strings. The -12 part says that you want the string to occupy 12 spaces and the string should be left-justified (the minus sign specifies left justification).

✳ Besides the format specifications, all the other characters in the format string are printed as is. In other words, the `printf` function prints verbatim any spaces or text you add in the format string (the first argument to `printf`).

FORMAT FOR STRINGS

The simplest way to print a string with `printf` is to use the following format:

```
printf "%s\n", "Hello";
```

This produces the same result as the following `print` function call:

```
print "Hello\n";
```

Note that "`%s`" is the bare minimum format specification for a string. Use `printf` when you want more control over the formatting. More control over formatting is available through a few more additions to the format specification.

For example, if you want to print two strings using 20 spaces each, you can write:

```
$title = "Discovering Perl 5";
printf "%20s %20s\n", "Title:", $title;
```

The result is as follows:

```
              Title:    Discovering Perl 5
```

Each string takes up 20 spaces and is right-justified within its allotted space. If you want to left-justify a string, simply add a minus sign right after the % sign. For example, use the following `printf` function call to print the first string left-justified:

```
printf "%-20s %20s\n", "Title:", $title;
```

With the minus sign in the format specification, the output now looks like this:

```
Title:                 Discovering Perl 5
```

 TIP Note that the "`%20s`" means at least 20 character positions should be used when printing the string. If you want to constrain a string to *at most* 20 characters, add a decimal point in front of the number. For example, here's how you can print the $title string using at most 16 characters:

```
$title = "Discovering Perl 5";
printf "%-20s %.16s\n", "Title:", $title;
```

The result of this `printf` statement is as follows:

```
Title:                 Discovering Perl
```

As you can see, the "%.16s" format specification forces only the first 16 characters of $title to be printed.

FORMAT FOR INTEGERS

To print a value as an integer, use the "%d" format with the printf function. Consider the following example:

```
$reason = "10 Reasons to Buy 'Discovering Perl 5'";
printf "String:  %s\n", $reason;
printf "Integer: %d\n", $reason;
```

Here, $reason is a string that begins with a number. The first printf function prints the string with a string format specification; the second printf function is used with the "%d" format to print the string as an integer. When this code runs, it produces the following output:

```
String:  10 Reasons to Buy 'Discovering Perl 5'
Integer: 10
```

As you can see from the output, the "%d" format prints the string as an integer. In this case, the value is 10 because the characters following 10 are not numbers.

If you want to print an integer value using a specified number of character positions, you can do so by adding the number next to the %, as follows:

```
$count = 1001;
printf "Count = %8d\n", $count;
```

This printf function produces the following output:

```
Count =     1001
```

where the integer value is printed right-justified, using eight character positions.

FORMAT FOR FLOATING-POINT NUMBERS

The common format for printing floating-point numbers with printf is "%f". Suppose that you want to print the total cost of a number of books using the printf function. Here's how you might use the printf function with the "%f" format:

```
$price = 24.99;
$sales_tax_rate = 0.05;
$num_copies = 5;
$total = $num_copies * $price * (1 + $sales_tax_rate);
printf "Total cost = \$%f\n", $total;
```

The resulting output of this program is as follows:

```
Total cost = $131.197500
```

Because this is an amount of money, you might want to print it with at most two decimal places. That's something you can do easily with the `printf` function — all you need is an appropriate format specification for floating-point numbers.

> **TIP** **To print a floating-point number with at most two digits after the decimal place, use the "%.2f" format specification. Here's how the `printf` function looks with this change:**

```
printf "Total cost = \$%.2f\n", $total;
```

With that small change, the output of `printf` changes to the following:

```
Total cost = $131.20
```

which is exactly what you want for a dollar amount — the amount rounded off to the nearest cents.

If, in addition to printing only two digits after the decimal point, you want to take up 10 spaces to print the value, you can add 10 right after the % in the format specification. Here is how the new format looks:

```
printf "Total cost = \$%10.2f\n", $total;
```

The resulting output now becomes:

```
Total cost = $    131.20
```

Figure 5-6 illustrates the effect of a "%10.2f" format specification when printing a floating-point value with the `printf` function.

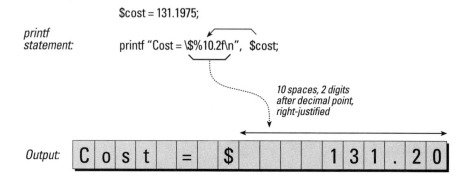

Figure 5-6 Formatting a floating-point value with the printf function

Being able to specify the number of character positions for the floating-point value is useful when you want to prepare a tabular output (you can ensure that all the numbers are aligned properly).

BONUS

Opening a File for Reading and Writing

This chapter showed you how to read from STDIN using the <> operator and how to write to STDOUT using the print and printf functions. You can use these same functions to read from or write to any file. All you have to do is open the file and get a filehandle. Although you learn more about files and directories in Chapter 10, this section gives you a quick introduction to the subject of opening a file.

Filenames in MS-DOS and UNIX

On most systems, files are organized into directories and you can refer to any file in the system by a name. The exact format of the name depends on the operating system. In Windows 95 or Windows NT, the naming convention harks back to the days of MS-DOS, which still remains underneath the graphical exterior of Windows. A typical MS-DOS filename is C:\WINDOWS\SYSTEM\PSCRIPT.INI. You can understand this filename as follows:

* C: is the drive letter designating the physical disk, diskette, or CD-ROM drive.
* \WINDOWS\SYSTEM\ is the directory hierarchy, also called the *path name.*
* PSCRIPT.INI is the name of the file.

In UNIX, a typical filename might be /usr/local/src/perl5.003/Changes. Conf. Unlike MS-DOS, there is no drive letter in UNIX. The /usr/local/src/ perl5.003/ is the path name that tells you where in the directory hierarchy you can find the file. The file's name is Changes.Conf. Unlike MS-DOS filenames, UNIX filenames are case-sensitive.

Open the file or die!

Given a filename, you can open the file with Perl's open function, as follows:

```
open(FILEHANDLE, "file_name_string");
```

Here, FILEHANDLE is the identifier you want to use when referring to this file after it has been opened. The filename itself should be the second argument to the open function.

You should always check whether the open function succeeded. If open succeeds, it returns 1; otherwise, it returns 0. A popular way to check for error is to use a logical OR expression in which the first operand is the open function and the second operand is a die function. Here is a typical open-die logical OR expression:

```
open(FILEHANDLE, "file_name_string") ||
die("Could not open file");
```

This particular use of open and die in a logical expression is often read as "open the file or die!".

Here is how this logical expression works:

* If the open function succeeds, it returns 1. That means the first operand of the logical expression is 1 (true). Because the logical OR of 1 with any other value is 1, the Perl interpreter does not evaluate the second operand of the logical OR (after all, the result is going to be true anyway). The end result is that your Perl program continues with the next statement (skipping over the die function).

* If open fails, it returns 0 (false). Now, the Perl interpreter must evaluate the second operand to determine the value of this logical expression. The second operand being the die function, the net effect of calling die is that the program quits with an error message.

As you can see, the use of logical OR expressions provides a clean and concise way of handling errors in a Perl program.

File open modes

When you open a file in your Perl program, you have to decide what you want to do with the file:

* Read from the file (input)
* Write to the file (output)
* Read from and write to the file (input and output)

You can indicate your intent by the way you specify the file's name when you open the file. Suppose that you are going to work with a file named error-log.txt that presumably contains a log of any errors that may have occurred. When you want to read the error log, you open the file with an open function such as the following:

```
$errfile = "errorlog.txt";
open(ERROR_LOG, "$errfile") ||
die("Cannot open $errfile");
```

After that, you can read from this file as follows:

```
$line = <ERROR_LOG>;
```

If you want to write error messages to the error log, however, you have to open the file for output. In this case, the open function has the following form:

```
open(ERROR_LOG, ">$errfile") ||
    die("Cannot open $errfile");
```

TIP As you can see from this example, simply add a greater-than sign (>) prefix to the filename when you want to open the file for output.

X-REF There are many other ways to open a file. You can even launch another program and set up a pipe to that program (so you can send input to that program). You learn these details in Chapter 10.

The close **function**

When you are finished with a file and you no longer need the filehandle, you should close the file by calling the close function, as follows:

```
close FILEHANDLE;
```

Here FILEHANDLE is the filehandle you used in a previous call to the open function.

Summary

Most Perl programs read input from standard input and print output to standard output. You can think of standard input and standard output as files. In Perl, you refer to a file with an identifier known as a filehandle. Usually, you have to use the open function to open a file and get a filehandle. Perl, however, automatically defines STDIN and STDOUT as the filehandles for standard input and standard output, respectively.

By default, standard input is the keyboard and standard output is the display screen. You can use the operating system's redirection command, however, to connect STDIN and STDOUT to files.

This chapter shows you how to read from STDIN and write to STDOUT. You learn to use the angle operator (<STDIN>) to read input and the print and printf functions to write output.

As a bonus, you get a preview of how to use the open function to open a file for reading and writing.

The next chapter introduces the concept of regular expressions, which forms the basis of Perl's powerful string search capability.

PART TWO

LEARNING TO USE PERL

THIS PART CONTAINS THE FOLLOWING CHAPTERS

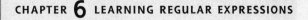

I n the *Old Possum's Book of Practical Cats,* T.S. Eliot writes that "The Naming of Cats is a difficult matter[.]" That enigmatic poem, immortalized by Sir Andrew Lloyd Webber's long-running Broadway production of *Cats,* could very well apply to the naming of things in UNIX.

UNIX is full of names that seem to have a secret inner meaning known only to insiders. And, unlike Eliot's cats, UNIX commands and concepts are lacking names "that the family use daily," so to speak.

For example, you may have heard UNIX users talking about "grep-ing for a string." What they mean is "looking for some text," but why the name grep? For the real scoop, we go to Dennis Ritchie, one of the developers of UNIX from the old Bell Labs.

According to Ritchie, the original UNIX text editor (called "ed") had a command that went like this: g/re/p, where "re" was supposed to stand for a regular expression (a text pattern). This command caused the editor to globally search for all matches with the text pattern and print the lines containing them. This feature was used so often that a separate command was added to UNIX just for searching text. Guess what that command was called. Yep — grep.

In UNIX systems, grep is widely used to rapidly scan one or more files in a search for a particular text pattern. When browsing through a large number of files, UNIX users often speak of "grep-ing around the files."

So, what does grep have to do with Perl? The answer is right in the middle of grep — the "re" part that stands for *regular expression*, which, as you'll learn from this book, is basically a shorthand notation for writing text patterns. Perl uses regular expressions just as the UNIX grep command does.

Of course, UNIX (and Perl) gurus refrain from uttering long words such as "regular expressions." Instead, they refer to regular expressions as regexp, or, even shorter, regex.

When it comes to shortening names, no one can beat the UNIX programmers. I guess if "grep" were called "text finder," they would probably reduce it to "tf" and leave you wondering what that mysterious command called "tf" does!

LEARNING REGULAR EXPRESSIONS

IN THIS CHAPTER YOU LEARN THESE KEY SKILLS

Many programming tasks involve processing text data: locating lines that contain a specific text pattern, replacing one string with another, and so on. Perl has powerful text-processing features that are patterned after UNIX tools such as sed (stream editor — a text editor), grep (a text search utility), and vi (another text editor). All of these text-processing tools support the concept of text patterns that enable you to perform searches such as *find all lines that begin with six blank spaces followed by any alphabetic character.*

Regular expression is a fancy term for text pattern (in fact, this chapter uses the term pattern and regular expression interchangeably). As you will learn, a regular expression is a sequence of characters that uses a concise syntax to describe a large number of fixed patterns. For example, you might write A.E to indicate any 3-character sequence that begins with A and ends with E. Thus, A.E matches ACE, AcE, APE, and ALE.

Regular expressions appear to be cryptic and magical when you first encounter them, but they are not that difficult to understand. Even as a beginner, you'll use a few of these regular expressions in your programs. You use them in pattern matching — selecting lines containing a specific pattern of text from the program's input. You typically use regular expressions to perform tasks such as "if the text contains this pattern somewhere, then do this task" (for example, change the pattern text in some way — such as replacing a string with another string). As you might guess, a word processing search-and-replace operation is analogous to pattern matching.

Because regular expressions are very important in text-processing, this book devotes two chapters to this subject. This chapter familiarizes you with regular expressions, by using tutorials and simple examples. The next chapter shows you how to use regular expressions in Perl programs.

Understanding Regular Expressions

You're most likely to have used regular expressions if you are a UNIX user. All variants of UNIX include the grep command, which enables you to search files for a text pattern. As with any new concept, the best way to understand regular expressions is to see them in action. The grep command is a good way to try out regular expressions.

TIP   If you are not on a UNIX system, you cannot use the grep command to try out regular expressions. You can, however, use Perl to mimic the behavior of grep. Jump to the "Trying out regular expressions in Perl" section if you are learning Perl on a Windows 95 or Windows NT system.

Using regular expressions with grep in UNIX

Suppose that you have the Perl source code in your UNIX system in the /usr/local/src/perl5.003 directory and you want to locate all the C source files that include header files. Because C programmers use the #include directive to include header files, you can use the grep command as follows:

```
cd /usr/local/src/perl5.003
grep include *.c
```

The first command simply takes you to the directory where the Perl source code is located. The second line shows the grep command that searches for the include string in all files that end with a .c (which are the C source files).

The grep command has the following syntax:

```
grep pattern_to_find  files_to_search
```

where *pattern_to_find* is a string that tells grep what you are trying to find and *files_to_search* is one or more files to search.

In the grep include *.c example, the pattern is include, which is just that — the fixed sequence of characters i, n, c, l, u, d, and e. As you'll see soon, the pattern may contain special characters, such as backslash and asterisk. In that case, you have to enclose the pattern in double quotes to satisfy the UNIX shell (command processor).

You usually use wildcard characters such as *.c in the *files_to_search* argument to grep so that you can search through many files.

When you use grep to look for all instances of the pattern include, you get any line that contains the include string. For example, here are some of the lines that the grep include *.c command prints:

```
pp_sys.c:#include "EXTERN.h"
pp_sys.c:#include "perl.h"
pp_sys.c:#  include <unistd.h>
pp_sys.c:/* Put this after #includes because fork and vfork
   prototypes may
```

The grep command prints the filename followed by a colon and then the line containing the specified text. In this case, the first three lines indeed show the occurrence of include you want (the inclusion of a header file). However, you also end up with other lines that contain the include string elsewhere in the line.

What you really want is to look for the following pattern:

* A line that begins with a # character
* Followed by zero or more blank spaces
* And, finally, the include string

A regular expression enables you to describe such a string. Here is how to construct a regular expression that describes this pattern:

```
^# *include
```

Figure 6-1 illustrates how this regular expression relates to the text pattern you want.

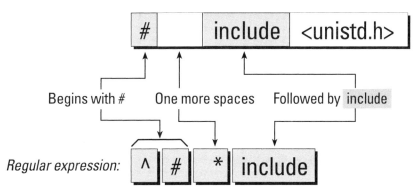

Figure 6-1 A regular expression for a specific text pattern

Here is how you can interpret the various parts of the `^# *include` regular expression:

* The `^` character means beginning of the line. In other words, `^` matches the beginning of a line. Thus, `^#` means the `#` character at the beginning of a line.

* A single space followed by an asterisk means zero or more spaces (in fact, a character followed by an asterisk means zero or more instances of the preceding character).

* The `include` string means the fixed sequence of characters `i`, `n`, `c`, `l`, `u`, `d`, and `e`.

With this regular expression, you can perform the search again with the following `grep` command:

```
grep "^# *include" *.c
```

This time around, the output lists files with the text pattern you are looking for: any line beginning with # followed by zero or more blank spaces and then `include`.

TIP **Note that regular expressions look somewhat similar to filenames with wildcard characters such as `*.c`. As you might already know, most operating systems enable you to specify filenames with wildcards — for example, the file name `*.c` means any file name ending with a `.c`. Just remember that the meaning of the asterisk is totally different when used in regular expressions — in filenames `*` means any character; in regular expressions `*` means zero or more copies of the preceding character.**

Trying out regular expressions in Perl

You cannot try out the `grep` command if you do not have UNIX. No matter. You can get the functionality of `grep` by running Perl with some command-line options.

Suppose that you want to search for a string in a file on your Windows 95 or Windows NT system. To be more specific, suppose that you want to search the `README.TXT` file in the `\PERL5` directory (that's where Perl should be installed on your PC) for any occurrence of the string `Microsoft` or `microsoft`. To do this, type the following commands in an MS-DOS prompt window:

```
cd \perl5
perl -ne "print if /[Mm]icrosoft/" readme.txt
```

This results in the following output:

```
from ftp://ftp.microsoft.com/bussys/winnt/winnt-
    public/reskit/nt351/
"Windows NT" is a registered trademark of Microsoft Corporation.
Portions (C) 1995 Microsoft Corporation. All rights reserved.
Perl for Win32 has been built using Microsoft Visual C++
    version 2.x.
ftp://ftp.microsoft.com/bussys/winnt/winnt-public/reskit/nt351/
```

The first command changes the current directory to \PERL5. The second command runs the Perl interpreter with the -ne options, which have the following meanings:

* The -n option causes the Perl interpreter to read each line of any file named on the command line. In this case, the specified filename is readme.txt.

* The -e option causes the Perl interpreter to execute the Perl code that follows on the command line. In this example, the code is as follows:

```
print if /[Mm]icrosoft/
```

The end result is that the Perl interpreter reads each line of text from the file readme.txt and executes the specified Perl code on that line. Implicitly, the line of text gets stored in the $_ variable and the print statement prints that line if that line contains the pattern [Mm]icrosoft. (In Perl code, patterns are usually enclosed within a pair of forward slashes.)

As the lines following the Perl command show, this example indeed prints those lines of text that contain any occurrence of the string Microsoft or microsoft.

That expression [Mm]icrosoft is a *regular expression* — a pattern that matches a set of strings. You construct a regular expression with a small set of operators and rules that are similar to the ones for writing arithmetic expressions. A list of characters inside brackets ([. . .]), for example, matches any single character in the list. Thus, the regular expression [Mm]icrosoft is a set of two strings, as follows:

```
Microsoft    microsoft
```

NOTE **Perl supports regular expressions just as many UNIX programs, such as grep and the vi editor, do. Most of Perl's regular expression syntax is similar to that used by the UNIX egrep program (egrep is a version of grep).**

As you can see from the examples, a regular expression defines a pattern of strings. Although it may take you a while to master regular expressions, you should be able to begin constructing and using regular expressions easily.

Learning Basic Regular Expressions

Now that you have seen examples of regular expressions, you need to learn the rules for writing regular expressions. As the examples show, regular expressions are like arithmetic expressions — you combine alphanumeric characters with special characters such as ^ and * to construct expressions. Unlike arithmetic expressions, the meaning of the special characters is different in a regular expression.

Just as you need to know the meaning of the symbols +, -, *, and / to write arithmetic expressions, so you have to learn the meaning of a similar set of special characters to construct regular expressions that define specific text patterns.

Understanding the general form of a regular expression

As you might expect, a *pattern* is a sequence of characters, such as `sion`. The exact sequence of characters is all you need when you are interested in a fixed pattern. Often, however, you want to specify a set of patterns, such as *all words ending with the character sequence* `sion`. Regular expressions enable you to describe such pattern sets in a concise manner. The idea is to use special characters (often called *meta-characters* because they modify the meaning of other characters), such as *, ., and \, to extend the meaning of a pattern.

To define a pattern that matches words ending with `sion`, for example, you have to concatenate the following components:

* The \b sequence that matches beginning of a word.
* The \w sequence that denotes any "word" character (in Perl, a "word" character is any alphanumeric character and the underscore).
* A * to specify that the pattern has one or more "word" characters.
* The sequence `sion`, which must be matched exactly.
* Another \b sequence that matches the end of a word (\b matches any word boundary — both the beginning and the end of a word).

Thus, \b\w*sion\b is the regular expression that represents all words that end with the sequence `sion`. In Perl, when you use a regular expression to find any matching patterns in a line of text, you typically enclose the regular expressions inside a pair of slashes. Thus, the regular expression is used as follows:

```
/\b\w*sion\b/
```

Now you can use this pattern match expression to find in a text file all lines that contain a word ending with `sion`. To find such lines in the file named README, for example, use the following command:

```
perl -ne "print if /\b\w*sion\b/" README
```

As you can see from the example, a typical regular expression has three types of elements:

* *Anchors* that specify the location of the pattern in a line of text
* *Character sets* that match one or more characters
* *Modifiers* that specify how many times the preceding character (or character sets) are repeated

The caret (^) is an anchor that means the beginning of a line. A text sequence such as The is a character set that matches the exact sequence of characters T, h, and e, in that order. The asterisk (*) is a commonly used modifier that says "repeat the preceding character zero or more times."

When you enclose a regular expression in a pair of slashes (/. . ./), Perl matches that regular expression with the current content of the special variable $_. Perl includes other pattern-matching operators that you can use to find matches in any string variable. Chapter 7 shows you how to use pattern matching operators.

Anchoring your patterns

Perl's pattern-matching facilities are patterned after UNIX tools and, as in UNIX, Perl's text facilities are meant to work with lines of text. If you want to search for a pattern that is located at the beginning or the end of a line, you have to use *anchors*. Perl's regular expression syntax also recognizes anchors that specify a word boundary (beginning or end of a word).

MATCHING THE START AND END OF A LINE

The caret (^) is the starting anchor and the dollar sign ($) is the end anchor. Figure 6-2 illustrates how these anchors denote the two ends of a line of text.

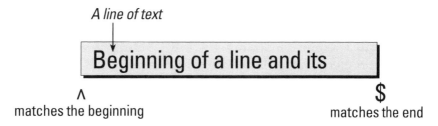

Figure 6-2 Anchors ^ and $ denote the beginning and end of a line.

A regular expression, such as ^The, matches any line that begins with the sequence The. That means ^The matches any of the following lines:

```
The book you want is "Discovering Perl 5."
Then you should buy the book.
Therefore, I recommend "Discovering Perl 5."
```

It matches because all of these lines have The as the first three characters on the line.

On the other hand, if you want to write a regular expression that looks for the Perl 5." that occurs at the end of a line, the regular expression takes the following form:

```
/Perl 5\.\"$/
```

To understand this regular expression, go through the following list:

* The first and the last slashes are the delimiters for the pattern match. In Perl, you enclose regular expressions in a pair of slashes (/. . ./) to match the pattern in a line of text. By default, Perl performs the pattern-matching operation on the special variable $_. (You learn more about pattern matching in Chapter 7).

* The dollar sign ($) at the end anchors this pattern to the end of a line.

* The rest of the pattern is simply the text: Perl 5.". It looks complicated because you have to add backslashes in front of characters that have special meaning — which is why the period and the double quote are preceded by backslashes. Thus, you end up writing Perl 5." as Perl 5\.\".

The regular expression Perl 5\.\"$ matches the following lines:

```
The book you want is "Discovering Perl 5."
Therefore, I recommend "Discovering Perl 5."
```

It matches because each of these lines has Perl 5." at the end of the line.

The ^ and $ act as anchors only when they occur at the proper end of a regular expression. In other words, ^ is only an anchor if it is the first character of a regular expression. Similarly, $ is an anchor marking the end of a line only when it is the last character in a regular expression. If the $ or ^ appear elsewhere in the regular expression, these characters have the same meanings as when they appear in a double-quoted string. Thus, the $ is treated as a prefix for a scalar variable's name and ^ means a control character (in other words, ^x becomes Ctrl+X, ^a is Ctrl+A, and so on).

TIP If you want to match the characters ^ and $ without interpreting them in any special way (even when they occur at the end of a pattern), just add a backslash (\) prefix to the characters. Thus, to match ^, use \^ in the pattern and to match $, use \$. In other words, if you are looking for a literal dollar sign, you use \$.

MATCHING A WORD BOUNDARY

In addition to anchoring patterns at the end of a line, you can specify patterns that begin at a *word boundary* — the beginning or the end of a word. As far as Perl is concerned, word boundaries have the following meaning:

* A word begins when a word character occurs. In Perl, a word character is any alphanumeric character or an underscore.

* A word ends when a nonword character appears following the word. A nonword character is anything but an alphanumeric character or an underscore.

Thus, if you want to look for the word `able` (but not words such as `capable` and `reliable`), you use the following regular expression:

```
/\bable\b/
```

This regular expression matches lines such as the following, which contain `able` as a whole word:

```
Were you able to solve the problem?
Picks up $%able#@ as well.
```

As you can see from the second line, the word boundary matches the nonword character before and after a word. Special characters such as % and # are nonword characters; therefore, `$%able#@` is seen as an occurrence of the word `able`.

Figure 6-3 illustrates Perl's word boundary anchors.

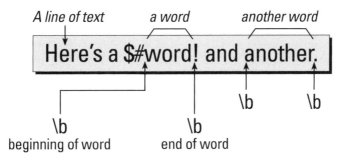

Figure 6-3 The \b sequence matches a word boundary.

As Figure 6-3 illustrates, \b matches both the beginning and the end of a word. Although you may typically think of blank spaces as the separators between words, Perl recognizes any nonalphanumeric character (besides an underscore) as the start or end of a word.

Using Character Sets in Regular Expressions

The simplest character set is a single character. For example, the regular expression /The/ contains three character sets: T, h, and e. The pattern /The/ will match any occurrence of these three characters in a line of text. Thus, it matches lines containing the words The, There, and Therefore. If you want to limit the match to the word The, add the word boundary anchor (\b) at the beginning and end of the word and write the regular expression as /\bThe\b/.

You can do a lot with simple character sets and anchors. For example, mail messages are often stored in text files and the sender is identified by a line that begins with From: followed by a space. You can use the pattern /^From: / to find the addresses in a file of mail messages, as follows:

```
perl -ne "print if /^From: /" mbox
```

where *mbox* is the name of your mail box (the name depends on your e-mail system; on most UNIX systems, incoming mail is often stored in the file /usr/spool/mail/*username* or /var/spool/mail/*username*, where *username* is your login name).

Specifying a range of characters

In addition to single characters, you can use special meta-characters to specify a more complex character set. One such character set is a range of characters, such as the set of all lowercase letters, a through z. The way you indicate this character set is quite intuitive:

* Use a hyphen between the first and last characters to write the range. Thus, the lowercase letters become a-z.
* Place the range of characters inside a pair of square brackets. Thus the character set consisting of lowercase letters is [a-z].

With this character set syntax, you can use [a-z] to match any lowercase letter. What if you want to match any letter regardless of case? Simple. Just concatenate the two character ranges in square brackets, as follows:

```
[a-zA-Z]
```

Another interesting range of characters is `[0-9]`, which denotes a single digit.

In fact, you can match one of a set of characters by enclosing the characters within square brackets. For example, if you want to look for a vowel, just write `[aeiou]`.

Inside the square brackets, you can intermix ranges of characters with explicit characters. For example, Perl's word characters belong to the set `[A-Za-z0-9_]`, which means a letter, a digit, or underscore.

Now that you know the basic syntax of a character set, Table 6-1 shows you some examples of regular expressions that use character sets.

TABLE 6-1 Examples of regular expressions with character sets

Regular expression	Matches
`/a-zA-Z/`	Any letter
`/b[aeiou]g/`	Any of the sequences bag, beg, big, bog, and bug
`/[A-Z][A-Z]/`	Two uppercase letters next to each other (for example, a U.S. postal abbreviation for a state, such as MD, MA, CA, IN, as well as abbreviations, such as MX and NB, that do not correspond to any U.S. state)
`/[A-Z]*/`	Zero or more uppercase letters (for example, A, AB, ABC, and so on)
`/[567]/`	One of the numbers 5, 6, or 7

Excluding some characters

So far, you have seen character sets that specify the characters that you want to match. You can also define a character set that excludes some characters. You can easily match all characters except those inside the square brackets by putting a caret (^) as the first character after the left bracket ([). For example, if you want to match any character other than a digit, use the following regular expression:

`/[^0-9]/`

Thus, to pick out lines of text that do not contain any digits, you might use this pattern:

`/^[^0-9]*$/`

Here, the first caret (^) matches the beginning of the line. Then, `[^0-9]*` matches zero or more non-numeric characters. Finally, the dollar sign ($) matches the end of the line. The net effect is that the pattern matches any line that does not contain a digit.

The caret (^) has a different meaning when it appears as the first character inside a square bracket, as opposed to when it appears as the first character in a regular expression. That means the expression `/^x/` behaves quite differently from `/[^x]/`. The `/^x/` pattern matches an x at the beginning of a line (in this case, ^ matches the beginning of the line). On the other hand, `/[^x]/` matches any character except x. (Here, ^ means exclude the characters inside the square brackets).

Matching any character

You can use the dot, or the period (.), to match any single character. That means a pattern such as `/A./` matches A followed by any character. If you want to find all lines that contain a single character, use the following pattern:

    /^.$/

In this pattern, the caret matches the beginning of the line, the period matches any single character, and the dollar sign matches the end of the line.

Repeating a character set

So far, you have seen the anchors and character sets in regular expressions. The third type of element in a regular expression is a modifier. The asterisk (*) is a common modifier that means *zero or more copies* of the preceding character set. For example, if you were to write:

    /x*/

the pattern would match zero or more occurrences of the letter x.

A pattern such as `/x*/` is useless, because it matches any number of letter x, including zero. That means the pattern will match any line (because a line without any x contains zero number of x).

However, it's still useful to have the asterisk match zero or more instances of a character. For example, often you want to ignore leading spaces in a line. Suppose that after skipping any spaces, you want to match a digit. You can do so with the following regular expression:

    /^ *[0-9]/

This pattern matches each of the following lines with zero or more leading spaces:

```
911
 301-555-1212
   300 pages
```

You can repeat any character set (enclosed in square brackets) by placing an asterisk after the character set. For example, to match zero or more digits, use the following pattern:

```
/[0-9]*/
```

To match one or more digits, simply repeat the character set in the pattern, as in this example:

```
/[0-9][0-9]*/
```

Now this pattern matches any line that contains at least one digit.

TIP   **There is another way to specify that you want to match one or more occurrences of a character set (as opposed to zero or more). Write the character set you want and then add a plus sign (+). Thus, the following pattern matches one or more digits:**

```
/[0-9]+/
```

Matching a specific number of character sets

Sometimes you need to match a specific number of characters. For example, you might want to look for exactly five digits to match a U.S. postal ZIP code. You cannot use the * modifier for such patterns, because you cannot specify a maximum number of characters to match with the * modifier. In this case, you have to use another special pattern that enables you to specify the minimum and maximum number of characters to match. The pattern takes the form of two comma-separated numbers enclosed in curly braces.

To see a concrete example, suppose that you want to match at least five and at most nine digits. Here's a regular expression for such a match:

```
/\b[0-9]{5,9}\b/
```

The \b at the beginning and the end of the pattern matches word boundaries. The rest of the pattern consists of the character set [0-9] (which means a digit) followed by the sequence {5,9}. The {5,9} sequence means that the digit must occur at least 5 times but no more than 9 times. That means the pattern matches any sequence of 5 to 9 digits.

If you want to match exactly 5 digits, you can use the following regular expression:

```
/[0-9]{5}/
```

TIP You can use this feature to validate data entered by the user. Suppose that your Perl program accepts a U.S. social security number from the user and the program prompts the user for the social security number in its well-known form of XXX-XX-XXXX, where each X denotes a digit. You can then use the following regular expression to check whether the input data is valid:

```
/[0-9]{3}-[0-9]{2}-[0-9]{4}/
```

If you study this expression, you'll notice that this pattern represents the 3-2-4 sequence of digits used to write U.S. social security numbers. For example, the first three digits are specified by [0-9]{3}. The hyphens separating the digits appear in their respective positions in the pattern.

Matching one fixed sequence or another

Sometimes, you may want to match one of several fixed text sequences. To construct a regular expression that accomplishes this, just list the text sequences separated by vertical bars (|). Thus, the following regular expression matches any one of the U.S. state abbreviations MA, MD, VA, or CA:

```
/MA|MD|VA|CA/
```

As a Perl operator, the vertical bar (|) means OR. In the regular expression, the vertical bar has the same meaning. Any of the sequences MA, MD, VA, or CA matches this regular expression.

If you want to match one of the selected two-letter state abbreviations followed by a five-digit U.S. postal ZIP code, you can do so by grouping the state codes as follows:

```
/(MA|MD|VA|CA) [0-9]{5}/
```

This regular expression matches a text sequence such as MD 20910.

Matching special characters

In addition to matching specific characters and character sets (such as [0-9] denoting any digit), you may have to match special characters, such as a tab or any whitespace character. (Perl considers space, tab, newline, carriage return, and form feed whitespace characters.)

In regular expressions, you can specify special characters by using special character sequences consisting of a backslash followed by one or more letters or numbers. You have already seen some of these character sequences in previous sections. For example, \w means a word character (any letter or an underscore) and \b means a word boundary.

There are quite a few other backslash sequences with special meanings. Table 6-2 summarizes these backslash sequences.

TABLE 6-2 Backslashed letters with special meaning in regular expressions

Character	Meaning
\d	Any digit
\D	Anything other than a digit (opposite of \d)
\t	Tab
\f	Form feed
\e	Escape (Character ASCII code 27 decimal)
\cX	Ctrl+X, where X is any character
\w	Word character (letters, numbers, and underscore)
\W	Anything but a word character (opposite of \w)
\s	A whitespace character (space, tab, newline, carriage return, or form feed)
\S	Anything but a whitespace character (opposite of \s)

Another use of a backslash (\) prefix is to reverse the meaning of some characters that have special meaning when used in a regular expression. For example, the dollar sign ($) matches the end of a line, but if you add a backslash prefix and write \$, Perl interprets that as a literal dollar sign.

TIP In a regular expression, if you want to match one of the characters $, |, *, ^, [,], \, and /, you have to place a backslash before it. Thus, when you want to refer to these characters literally, you type them as \$, \|, *, \^, \[, \], \\, and \/. Regular expressions often look confusing because of the preponderance of strange character sequences and the generous sprinkling of backslashes. As with anything else, however, you can start slowly and use only a few of the features in the beginning.

BONUS

Regular Expressions at a Glance

The previous sections give you a tutorial introduction to regular expressions. After you know the basic concepts, however, you may want a quick listing of Perl's regular expression syntax as a refresher. As you know, a regular expression is a sequence of characters in which some characters have special meaning. Table 6-3 lists the basic rules of interpreting the characters.

TABLE 6-3 Rules for interpreting regular expression characters

Expression	Meaning
.	Matches any single character except the newline character
x	Matches zero or more occurrences of the character *x*
x+	Matches one or more occurrences of the character *x*
x?	Matches zero or one occurrence of the character *x*
[. . .]	Matches any of the characters inside the brackets
[^...]	Matches anything *but* the characters inside the brackets
x{n}	Matches exactly *n* occurrences of the character *x*
x{n,}	Matches *n* or more occurrences of the character *x*
x{,m}	Matches zero or, at most, *m* occurrences of the character *x*
x{n,m}	Matches at least *n* occurrences, but no more than *m* occurrences of the character *x*
$	Matches the end of a line
\0	Matches a null character
\B	Matches any character that's not at the beginning or the end of a word
\b	Matches the beginning or end of a word (when not inside brackets)
\c*X*	Matches Ctrl-*X*
\d	Matches a single digit

Expression	Meaning
\D	Matches a nonnumeric character
\f	Matches a form feed
\n	Matches a newline (line feed) character
\ooo	Matches the octal value specified by the digits *ooo* (where each *o* is a digit between 0 and 7)
\r	Matches a carriage return
\S	Matches a non-whitespace character
\s	Matches a whitespace character (space, tab, or newline)
\t	Matches a tab
\W	Matches a nonword character (see \w)
\w	Matches a word character (alphanumeric character or underscore)
\xhh	Matches the hexadecimal value specified by the digits *hh* (where each *h* is a hexadecimal digit between 0 and f)
^	Matches the beginning of a line

Summary

Regular expressions enable you to specify a whole set of text patterns in a concise manner. For example, just by writing /b.g/ you can represent all three-character text patterns with a b followed by any character and then a g. Thus, /b.g/ matches patterns such as big, bug, bag, and bfg. This chapter's goal is to get you familiar with regular expressions, and to help you understand the concept and learn how to construct regular expressions

As a bonus, you get a summary of the rules for interpreting regular expressions. After reading this chapter, regular expressions should be a little less mysterious and a lot more useful in writing effective Perl programs.

The next chapter shows you how to use regular expressions for text searches and text substitutions.

WORKING WITH REGULAR EXPRESSIONS

IN THIS CHAPTER YOU LEARN THESE KEY SKILLS

In Chapter 6, you learn that regular expressions are text patterns — a sequence of characters that represent a set of fixed character patterns. For example, /U[A-Z]*X/ is a regular expression that matches zero or more uppercase letters sandwiched between the letters U and X. Thus, /U[A-Z]*X/ matches sequences such as UX, USX, UNIX, and so on.

Perl's text-processing capabilities rely heavily on regular expressions. Typically, you use regular expressions to search for specific patterns, and sometimes replace one text pattern with another. Your Perl program might use regular expressions to locate a specific piece of data stored in a text file (which is usually the case with many system configuration files in UNIX). Or, you might use regular expressions to check the validity of data entered by the user (for example, to check whether a U.S. social security number has the right number of digits).

This chapter shows you how to use regular expressions in your Perl programs. You learn how to find pattern matches and how to search and replace strings. Some of the material is meant to reinforce what you already learned in Chapter 6 — you see specific examples of regular expressions used in example programs.

Looking for Patterns

One of the common uses of regular expressions is to find lines of text containing a specific pattern. In Chapter 6, you have already seen simple examples of pattern matching in action. This section shows you several ways you can use Perl to search for patterns in a file.

Using Perl for simple text searches

For simple text searches, you can use the Perl interpreter with a special command-line argument. Figure 7-1 illustrates the concept.

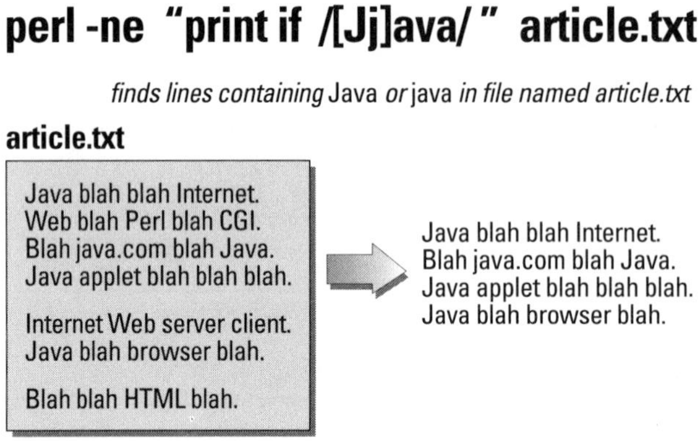

perl -ne "print if /[Jj]ava/ " article.txt

finds lines containing Java or java in file named article.txt

article.txt

Java blah blah Internet.
Web blah Perl blah CGI.
Blah java.com blah Java.
Java applet blah blah blah.

Internet Web server client.
Java blah browser blah.

Blah blah HTML blah.

Java blah blah Internet.
Blah java.com blah Java.
Java applet blah blah blah.
Java blah browser blah.

Figure 7-1   Using Perl for simple text searches

As Figure 7-1 shows, you can specify a search pattern and search one or more files for lines that contain the specified search pattern.

Using the approach illustrated in Figure 7-1, you can find the lines containing the text config or Config in a file named README by using the following command:

```
perl -ne "print if /[cC]onfig/" README
```

This command causes the Perl interpreter to execute the Perl code enclosed in double quotes for each line of text in the README file. By default, each line is read into the $_ special variable and the Perl code print if /[cC]onfig/ is executed. Here /[cC]onfig/ is a regular expression that matches the text patterns config or Config.

The expression /[cC]onfig/ automatically searches the current value of $_ for any match of the regular expression. If the pattern is found, the if statement is true and the print function prints $_. As you can see, the simple statement print if /[cC]onfig/ does quite a lot, thanks to the implicit use of the $_ variable.

To understand the simple pattern-matching operation better, write a Perl program as follows:

1. Assign a string to $_, as follows:

```
$_ = "This string ends with a digit 1";
```

2. Assign the regular expression for the pattern "digit at the end of line" to a scalar variable:

```
$result = /[0-9]$/;
```

The regular expression automatically attempts a match with the current value of $_. In this case, there is a match, so $result will be true (a nonzero value, usually 1).

3. Call the print function if $result is true:

```
print if $result;
```

This should print $_ because $result happens to be true.

That gives you the following program:

```
$_ = "This string ends with a digit 1";
$result = /[0-9]$/;
print if $result;
```

When you run this program, it prints the following:

```
This string ends with a digit 1
```

which is the value of $_.

NOTE To summarize, you can search for a pattern in a text file by running the Perl interpreter with the following command:

```
perl -ne "print if /regex/" filename
```

where regex is a regular expression that specifies the text patterns you want to match and filename is the name of the file being searched.

Writing Perl programs for text searches

The command-line use of Perl interpreter to search a text file is useful for simple searches. For anything complex, such as checking for multiple pattern matches on the same line of text, you'll want to write a Perl program to perform the search.

When writing Perl programs to perform text searches, you'll mostly rely on the pattern-matching expression written by enclosing a regular expression in a pair of forward slashes (/. ./). Figure 7-2 illustrates the pattern-matching expression and how it matches selected lines from a set of input lines.

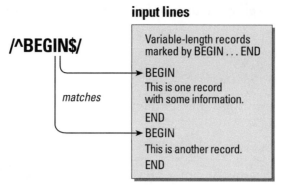

input lines

/^BEGIN$/

matches

Variable-length records
marked by BEGIN...END

BEGIN
This is one record
with some information.
END
BEGIN
This is another record.
END

Figure 7-2 The pattern-matching expression in Perl

The basic pattern-matching expression operates on the current value of the special variable $_. The "Matching Patterns in Any String" section shows you how to match patterns with any string.

An example is the best way to illustrate how to write a Perl program that performs text searches. Suppose that you have a collection of text files containing recent magazine articles and you want to find out how many times the words Java and java occur in these text files. You have also decided to rate the magazines based on a Java index — the percentage of lines that contain the word Java.

Here's how you might proceed to write this program:

1. Use the following form of input loop to process all the lines in all the filenames specified on the command-line:

```
while(<>)
{
# ... perform pattern match ...
}
```

As Chapter 5 explains, this while loop reads lines of text from all the files specified in the command-line. The current line of text is stored in the special variable $_.

2. Use the regular expression \b[Jj]ava\b to match either Java or java as a word (remember that \b matches the beginning and the end of a word).

3. Inside the while loop, the current line of text is available in the special variable $_. Increment a count if the line has a pattern match. By relying on the $_ variable, you can write this line as follows:

```
$count++ if /\b[Jj]ava\b/;
```

That line says: increment $count if the pattern \b[Jj]ava\b is contained in $_ (which contains the current line of text read from the file).

4. Count all the lines with another variable, say, $lines. Just include the following line in the while statement to keep count of all the lines that have been processed thus far:

```
$lines++;
```

5. When the while loop ends (that happens after all the files have been read), compute the Java index:

```
$Jindex = (100 * $count) / $lines;
```

and print the result.

Putting this approach into practice, you might write the following program to count the number of times "Java" occurs in a bunch of text files:

```
#!/usr/local/bin/perl

# Count the number of lines that contain
# the word Java or java in a number of files

  while(<>)
  {
    $count++ if /\b[Jj]ava\b/;

    $lines++;  # count all lines
  }

# Compute Java index (% lines with Java)
  $Jindex = (100 * $count) / $lines;

# Print the result
  print "Out of $lines lines, ",
        "$count contain \"Java\"\n";
  printf "Java index = %.2f\%\n", $Jindex;
```

Save this program in a file named jindex.pl. Then you can run it on your files as follows:

```
perl jindex.pl file1 file2 . . .
```

where file1 file2 . . . is a list of files you want to search for lines containing Java. If all of the articles are stored in files with names that begin with article and end with .txt, you can use the program as follows:

```
perl jindex.pl article*.txt
```

A typical output might look this way:

```
Out of 2721 lines, 16 contain "Java"
Java index = 0.59
```

Although the example is a bit tongue-in-cheek with its definition of Java index, the basic structure of this Perl program serves as a good template for typical pattern-matching programs that you might write.

Finding lines that do not match

So far, you have seen example programs that find lines of text containing a specific pattern. Sometimes you may want just the opposite — the lines that do *not* contain the pattern.

As you have seen, to print the lines containing a pattern such as [Jj]ava, you can use a simple program such as the following:

```
while(<>)
{
  print if /[Jj]ava/;
}
```

Here, the if /[Jj]ava/ statement is true when the line contains the pattern.

TIP **If you want to print lines that *do not* contain the pattern, all you have to do is add a logical NOT operator (denoted by !) to the if statement. Thus, the following loop prints the lines that *do not* contain the pattern [Jj]ava:**

```
while(<>)
{
  print if !/[Jj]ava/;
}
```

Processing a data file with variable-length records

Most of the time, you'll use matching as well as nonmatching lines to process data files. Often, data files (that Perl programs deal with) store information organized into variable-length records, where each record's beginning and end are marked by a special line.

As an example, consider a text file that contains data organized as records, with each record having the following format:

```
BEGIN
... line 1...
... line 2 ...
... number of lines vary ...
END
```

In other words, each record begins with a `BEGIN` line and ends with an `END` line. The lines in between constitute the data for this record. This is a typical way to store data in text files (usually, the data inside each record has more structure — for instance, each record may include name and address fields).

Suppose that your job is to write a Perl program that extracts the records in the file and prints out each record (in a more useful program, you might locate a specific record and do something else, such as update the record). To do this, you could use the following logic:

1. Read a line of text.

2. Repeat Step 1 if the line does not contain the pattern `^BEGIN$` (that the line starts with `BEGIN` and then it ends).

3. After finding the `BEGIN`, keep reading and printing the lines. End the loop when the line matches the pattern `^END$`.

4. After finding the `END` line, go back to Step 1 for the next record.

You can essentially implement this logic in a `while` loop that keeps reading and processing lines of text. A second `while` loop can handle reading the lines of a record once the `BEGIN` line is located.

So that the program can work on any data file, you can write the `while` loop to read from `STDIN`. Then you can process any file by redirecting `STDIN` to that file (an example appears later in this section). That means the basic structure of the program is as follows:

```
while(<STDIN>)
{
# Line is in $_
# ... skip if line does not match ^BEGIN$
   while(<STDIN>)
   {
# ... end loop if line matches ^END$
      print;  # this prints $_
   }
}
```

In the outer `while` loop, you can skip a line that does not match `^BEGIN$` by using the `next` statement with an `if` statement, as follows:

```
next if !/^BEGIN$/;
```

In the inner `while` loop, you can end the loop when you find a line that matches `^END$` by using a combination of `last` and `if` statements, as follows:

```
last if /^END$/;
```

Now you have all the information you need to write the Perl program. Based on these ideas, you might write the following Perl program to print out the records from a data file that uses the BEGIN. . .END block structure:

```perl
#!/usr/local/bin/perl
# extract.pl — extract records from a data file

    $count = 0;
    $separator = "-" x 40;

# Read lines of text and process
    while(<STDIN>)
    {
# Skip if not BEGIN line
        next if !/^BEGIN$/;

# Found a record
        $count++;
        print "$separator\n";
        print "Record #$count:\n\n";

# Print all the lines until an END

        while(<STDIN>)
        {
            last if /^END$/;
            print;
        }
    }

# Print a summary
    print "$separator\n";
    print "Total: $count records.\n";
```

Save this program in a file named extract.pl. To test the extract.pl program, save the following text in a file named data.txt:

```
This is a data file that uses
BEGIN...END blocks to delimit
records. Lines up to the first
BEGIN are ignored.
_____


BEGIN
This is record number 1.
Each record begins with BEGIN
```

```
and ends with an END line.
END

There can be comments of blank
lines between

BEGIN
This is another block
of information.
END

Lines at the end are ignored
as well.
```

Now you can run the extract.pl program and process the data.txt file with the following command:

```
perl extract.pl < data.txt
```

This command generates the following output:

```
_____

Record #1:

This is record number 1.
Each record begins with BEGIN
and ends with an END line.
_____

Record #2:

This is another block
of information.
_____

Total: 2 records.
```

If you compare the output with the content of the data.txt file, you'll notice that the extract.pl program correctly extracts the records between BEGIN and END lines.

NOTE   Perl CGI programs often use variable-length records with well-defined delimiters (such as BEGIN and END) to store information. For example, when you offer a guest book or a feedback form for user input, the Perl CGI program that processes that input might store the data in such a file. Then you can use this section's approach to process the data. Note that you can choose other record delimiters besides BEGIN and END; it takes only a few small changes to make the extract.pl program work with a new set of delimiters.

Matching Patterns in Any String

When you place a regular expression inside a pair of forward slashes (/. . ./), Perl matches the pattern with the current contents of the special variable $_. Sometimes, however, you may have to look for a match in another string variable. For this, Perl provides the pattern-binding operators =~ and !~. These operators force Perl to look for a match (or non-match) in a specified string variable. An example should clarify the concept.

Suppose that you are prompting the user for a U.S. social security number. You read the input line into a variable named $line and you want to check whether the input is a valid social security number of the form XXX-XX-XXXX, where each X is a digit. You can perform the check by defining a pattern for social security and looking for a match in the $line variable. Using the information you learn in Chapter 5, a workable pattern is as follows:

```
/^[0-9]{3}-[0-9]{2}-[0-9]{4}$/
```

This regular expression looks for a sequence of 3 digits followed by a hyphen, then 2 digits followed by a hyphen, and finally 4 more digits. Also, the line must end after this 3-2-4 digit sequence. To look for this pattern's match in the $line variable, you can use the =~ operator as follows:

```
if($line =~ /^[0-9]{3}-[0-9]{2}-[0-9]{4}$/)
{
# ... valid social security number ...
}
```

Here is a complete ssn.pl program to demonstrate how you can use the =~ operator to match a pattern in a string variable other than $_:

```
#!/usr/local/bin/perl
# ssn.pl — reads and validates a U.S. social
#          security number

# Display a prompt and read input
EnterSSN:
  print "Enter social security number (XXX-XX-XXXX):";
  $line = <STDIN>;

# Check if this is a valid social security number
  if($line =~ /^[0-9]{3}-[0-9]{2}-[0-9]{4}$/)
  {
# Successful match, good Social Security Number
    print "Social Security Number = $line\n";
  }
```

```
    else
    {
# Did not match, try again
      print "Invalid social security number: $line\n";
      goto EnterSSN;
    }
```

Here is a trial session showing how a user might interact with the `ssn.pl` program (user input is in boldface):

```
perl ssn.pl
```

The program prompts you for input. In the following listing you see a typical session with the program. Your input is shown in boldface:

```
Enter social security number (XXX-XX-XXXX):123456789
Invalid social security number: 123456789

Enter social security number (XXX-XX-XXXX):123-45-6789
Social Security Number = 123-45-6789
```

You can rearrange the logic in the `ssn.pl` program and look for a nonmatch instead of a match. That requires the use of the `!~` operator, as illustrated in the following lines of code:

```
    if($line !~ /^[0-9]{3}-[0-9]{2}-[0-9]{4}$/)
    {
# Did not match, try again
      print "Invalid social security number: $line\n";
      goto EnterSSN;
    }
    else
    {
# Successful match, good Social Security Number
      print "Social Security Number = $line\n";
    }
```

NOTE Thus, the pattern-binding operators `=~` and `!~` enable you to perform the match and nonmatch operations on a scalar variable other than the default `$_`. To look for a match, write the following:

```
if($string =~ /regex/)
{
# Yes, pattern matches
}
```

where `regex` is the regular expression for the pattern and `$string` is the variable in which Perl should look for a match of the pattern. Similarly, when you want to check whether a variable does not match a pattern, use the !~ operator, as follows:

```
if($string !~ /regex/)
{
# No pattern match
}
```

Modifying the Pattern-Matching Criteria

The previous sections showed you how to match a pattern in any string. There are several useful features of pattern matching that you have not yet seen. In particular, you have not yet seen:

* How to do a case-insensitive search
* How to find all occurrences of a pattern

You can accomplish these tasks easily by using single-letter modifiers.

Making the pattern match case-insensitive

Often, you may want to search for a string without regard to case. Suppose that you want to locate the lines that contain all variations of the word image, such as Image, IMAGE, or even iMaGe. Here is a Perl program that accomplishes this task:

```
#!/usr/local/bin/perl
# imgsrch.pl — case-insensitive search for "image"

   while(<>)
   {
# case-insensitive pattern match
      print if /\bimage\b/i;
   }
```

If you were to save this program in a file named imgsrch.pl, you could perform a case-insensitive search of the word image in a file named access_log with the following command:

```
perl imgsrch.pl access_log
```

NOTE As you can see, for case-insensitive pattern matches, all you need to do is append an i to the pattern enclosed in a pair of forward slashes (/. . ./), as follows:

```
/pattern/i
```

That letter i is called a *modifier*. Figure 7-3 illustrates the use of the i modifier to match a pattern regardless of case.

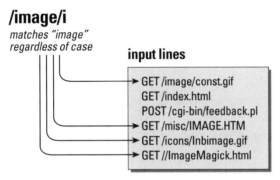

Figure 7-3   Use the i modifier for case-insensitive pattern matching.

In addition to the i modifier, Perl includes other pattern modifiers that enhance the behavior of pattern matching in different ways. One such modifier is the g modifier, described in the next section.

Finding all occurrences of a pattern

Earlier in this chapter is an example program that counts the number of lines containing the words java or Java. That example uses the pattern-matching expression /\b[Jj]ava\b/ to find the lines that contain one or more occurrences of the words Java or java. What if you want to count all occurrences of the words instead of just the lines? In that case, you need a way to search for multiple occurrences of a pattern.

NOTE Just as you append an i to make a pattern match case-insensitive, you can make a pattern match *global,* (that is, the match finds all occurrences) by appending a g to the pattern-matching expression.

Thus, if you want to match all occurrences of the words java or Java, you write the pattern-matching expression as follows:

```
/\b[Jj]ava\b/g
```

Suppose that you want to use this feature — matching a pattern globally — to count all occurrences of the words java or Java in one or more text files. In an earlier example, I used the following statement to count the lines containing the pattern /\b[Jj]ava\b/:

```
$count++ if /\b[Jj]ava\b/;
```

If you simply append g to the pattern, that does not count all occurrences of the pattern. Because this is a scalar context (the expected result is a single value), Perl iterates through the string and returns true each time a match is found, but in the end all you get is a single increment of $count.

NOTE   **To count all the matches in each line, you have to use the global pattern-matching expression /\b[Jj]ava\b/g in a list context. Simply assign the pattern to an array variable as follows:**

```
@matches = /\b[Jj]ava\b/g
```

Then the array @matches will contain all the substrings matched by the pattern. To count the occurrences, all you have to do is add to $count the number of items in @matches as follows:

```
$count += @matches;
```

Remember that the value of an array in a scalar context (when the array is assigned to a scalar variable) is the number of elements in the array. Thus, the following Perl program — jcount.pl — counts all occurrences of the words java or Java in the files you specify in the command line:

```
#!/usr/local/bin/perl
# jcount.pl — count all occurrences
#                 of java or Java

# Count the all occurrences of the words
# Java or java in a number of files

   while(<>)
   {
     @matches = /\b[Jj]ava\b/g;
     $count += @matches;   # count all matches

     $lines++;   # count all lines
   }

# Print the result
   print "In $lines lines, \"Java\" occurs ",
         "$count times.\n"
```

For example, here's this program with the readme file that comes with the Java Developers Kit (JDK):

```
perl jcount.pl readme
```

The following line shows the output from the program:

```
In 243 lines, "Java" occurs 43 times.
```

Replacing a Pattern

When you search for a pattern, sometimes you want to replace the pattern with a different string. Perl provides a pattern substitution operator that performs this task.

Using the substitution operator

Basically, the pattern substitution operator takes the following form:

```
s/pattern/substitution/;
```

where `pattern` is a regular expression describing what you want to replace and `substitution` is the string that replaces `pattern`. The shorthand version of referring to this substitution pattern is `s///` (without explicitly showing the pattern and its substitution). In practice, you actually have to fill out the patterns before using this function. Incidentally, Perl implements `s///` as a built-in function (built-in functions are described in Chapter 9).

Note that the `substitution` is a plain string, not a regular expression. However, you can use the `e` modifier and make Perl evaluate an expression as the `substitution` pattern. In other words, you can substitute a pattern with the result of evaluating an expression (which may include a function call). You'll learn about this in the section "Substituting with result of an expression."

NOTE Just like the pattern-matching operation, pattern substitution works on the `$_` variable. If you want to apply the substitution on a different variable, you have to use the pattern-binding operator =~ as follows:

```
$string =~ s/pattern/substitution/;
```

where `$string` denotes the variable on which Perl performs the substitution specified on the right-hand side of the =~ operator.

You can try out the substitution operator with the following example program:

```
$string = "Then we had Windows 95 in 1995."
$string =~ s/95/97/; # Change 95 to 97
print "$string\n";
```

When you run this code, it generates the following output:

```
Then we had Windows 97 in 1995.
```

As you can see, only the first instance of 95 changed to 97; the second one remains unchanged. That's because the substitution operator matches the pattern only once in a line. You have to use a modifier to change all occurrences of the pattern.

Substituting globally

To make a global substitution of the pattern, append g to the pattern. Thus, if you want to replace all occurrences of 95 with 97, modify the previous example as follows:

```
$string =~ s/95/97/g; # Globally change 95 to 97
print "$string\n";
```

This time around the output is as follows:

```
Then we had Windows 97 in 1997.
```

Just what you want!

Most of the time, you'll want to apply the substitutions globally throughout a string. Remember to add the g modifier to make this happen.

Substituting with the result of an expression

Sometimes you may have to substitute a pattern with a string that's the result of evaluating an expression rather than a fixed string. Suppose that you have some text that includes the <date> tag (a *tag* is simply a short string with a special meaning) and you want to replace all occurrences of <date> with the current date and time.

Although you may not know this yet, Perl provides the localtime function (described in Chapter 9) that returns the current time. If you call localtime in a scalar context, as follows:

```
$date = scalar localtime;
```

then $date will be a string containing the current date and time in the following format:

```
Sat Jan 25 17:22:15 1997
```

Now your problem is to use the s/// operator to perform the substitution: Find all occurrences of <date> and replace each one with the result of evaluating the expression scalar localtime.

The implementation is very simple. All you have to do is append the e modifier to the s/// operator to evaluate an expression. You also have to add a g modifier if you want the substitution to apply globally throughout the string. Here's the substitution operator you need to use:

```
s/<date>/scalar localtime/ge;
```

The following program demonstrates how this substitution works:

```
$sample =
"<date>: This is a date stamp.\
Here's another: <date>\
The idea is to use a tag that\
is globally replaced by the current\
date like this: <date>\n";

$sample =~ s/<date>/scalar localtime/ge;
print "$sample\n";
```

When you run this program, it displays the following output:

```
Sat Jan 25 17:52:44 1997: This is a date stamp.
Here's another: Sat Jan 25 17:52:44 1997
The idea is to use a tag that
is globally replaced by the current
date like this: Sat Jan 25 17:52:44 1997
```

As you can see, each occurrence of the <date> tag has been replaced by the date and time (this reflects the time when the program is run).

NOTE **If you want to replace a pattern with the result of an expression, use the e modifier with the s/// operator (in other words, the operator takes the form s//e).**

Referring to a previous match

Sometimes when you are substituting a pattern, you may have to refer to the exact substring that had just matched a pattern you specified. This need arises specifically when you are writing Perl programs to handle form input on the Web — you'll learn all the details in Chapters 14 and 15, but here is the gist of the problem.

When your Perl program receives information, many special characters are provided in an encoded form. For example, a tilde appears as %7e and a space is encoded as %20. The encoding is quite simple — each special character is replaced with a percent sign (%) followed by a two digit hexadecimal number representing the ASCII code for that symbol.

The Perl program has to locate each occurrence of % followed by two hexadecimal digits and replace those three characters with a single character whose

ASCII code matches the hexadecimal digits. Given the hexadecimal digits, you can find the character using the `pack` function, as illustrated in the following:

```
$hexdigits = "7e";  # This should be a tilde (~)

# The "c" in pack tells the function that you
# are looking for a single character and the
# second argument uses the hex() function to
# convert the hexadecimal number into decimal
#
$char = pack("c",hex($hexdigits));
print "ASCII code $hexdigits corresponds to $char\n";
```

This code prints the following output:

```
ASCII code 7e corresponds to ~
```

Now that you know about the encoding and how to convert the hexadecimal digits to a character, the only remaining problem is that you must find the two hexadecimal digits that follow the % and use them as the argument in the `pack` function. You can do this by writing the substitution operator `s///` as follows:

```
s/%(..)/pack("c",hex($1))/ge;
```

Notice that the pattern to match is written as `%(..)`, which means % followed by two digits. These are enclosed in parentheses for a reason. Because this pattern is in parentheses, after a match you can refer to the two digits with the special variable $1. As you can see, the substitution string uses the `pack` function, within which $1 appears. Because you want Perl to evaluate the `pack` function, you have to specify the e modifier with `s///` (and the g modifier ensures that the replacement happens for all occurrences of the pattern).

The following example program illustrates this idea of performing pattern substitutions that require you to refer to the string that has been matched:

```
$input =
"This%20is%20an%20encoded%20string.\
Here%20is%20a%20space%20followed%20by%20a%20tilde%20%7e\n";

$input =~ s/%(..)/pack("c",hex($1))/ge;

print $input;
```

When you run this program, it prints the following output:

```
This is an encoded string.
Here is a space followed by a tilde ~
```

As you can see, each occurrence of %20 has been replaced by a space, and the %7e has been replaced by a tilde (~).

NOTE Here's what you have to do when you need to refer to a matched string:

* Define the pattern as usual, but enclose in parentheses anything you have to refer to later on. For example, in the pattern /%../ (that's a percent sign followed by two characters), you want to refer to the two characters later. So, you write the pattern as /%(..)/

* Where you need to refer to whatever matched the parts of the pattern inside parentheses, use the special variable $1. Thus, if the pattern is 174, then $1 refers to the two characters following the percent sign in a matched string. If the match is with %7e, then $1 is 7e.

This technique of using parentheses and $1 extends to multiple pairs of parentheses. Suppose that you are matching a time in the following *hour:minute:second* format:

```
10:43:23
```

If you specify the pattern as follows:

```
/(..):(..):(..)/
```

then, after a match, $1, $2, and $3 refer to the hour, minute, and second digits, respectively. Here's an example program that illustrates this:

```
$time = "10:43:23";

$time =~ /(..):(..):(..)/;

print
"  Hours = $1\
Minutes = $2\
Seconds = $3\n";
```

When you run this program, it prints the following output:

```
  Hours = 10
Minutes = 43
Seconds = 23
```

That shows you how you could use the special variables $1, $2, $3, (if you have more parentheses in the pattern, you can use more variable names, such as $4 and $5) to refer to other matches.

Trying out substitution

As a more interesting example, suppose that you have a text file with an advertisement that talks about a C++ code generator that's part of a product your company sells. Recently, your company has converted that code generator to generate Java code. Now you want to change all occurrences of the string C++ in the advertisement copy to Java. This is an ideal job for Perl's pattern substitution operator.

Here's the strategy for the Perl program (change.pl):

* So that you can use the program to process other files, write the program to read from STDIN in a while loop, make the substitution, and send the output to STDOUT. That way, you can process any file by redirecting the input and save the output in any file by redirecting the output. The basic program structure is as follows:

```
while(<STDIN>)
{
  s/pattern/substitution/; # Works implicitly on $_
  print;
}
```

* The substitution expression can use the pattern C\+\+ for the pattern to be replaced. You need the backslashes because + has a special meaning in regular expressions. Use the g modifier for global substitution, as follows:

```
s/C\+\+/Java/g;
```

Figure 7-4 illustrates how this pattern substitution program works.

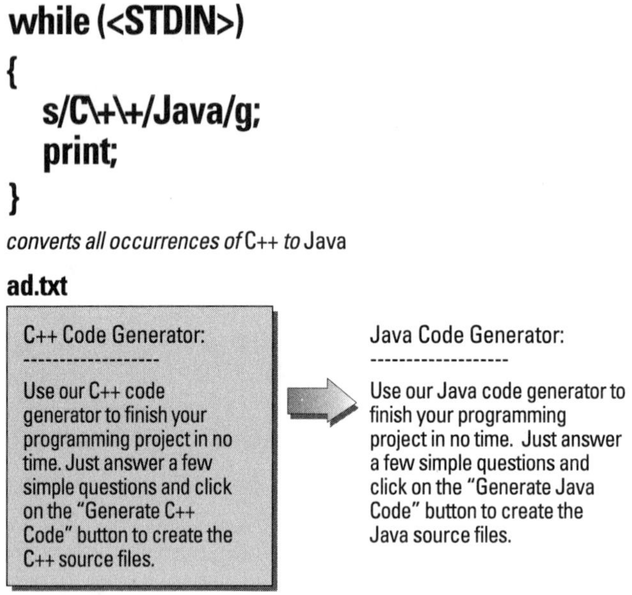

while (<STDIN>)
{
  s/C\+\+/Java/g;
  print;
}

converts all occurrences of C++ *to* Java

ad.txt

C++ Code Generator:

Use our C++ code generator to finish your programming project in no time. Just answer a few simple questions and click on the "Generate C++ Code" button to create the C++ source files.

Java Code Generator:

Use our Java code generator to finish your programming project in no time. Just answer a few simple questions and click on the "Generate Java Code" button to create the Java source files.

Figure 7-4   A program that changes all occurrences of C++ to Java

Based on these ideas, here's how you might write the `change.pl` program:

```perl
#!/usr/local/bin/perl
# change.pl — substitute Java for C++
# Usage: perl change.pl <infile >outfile

while(<STDIN>)
{
  s/C\+\+/Java/g; # global substitution on $_
  print;          # print modified $_
}
```

To test the program, prepare the file `ad.txt` with the following text:

```
C++ Code Generator:
_____

Use our C++ code generator to
finish your programming project
in no time.  Just answer a few
simple questions and click on
the "Generate C++ Code" button
to create the C++ source files.
```

Now run the `change.pl` program with the following command:

```
perl change.pl < ad.txt
```

This command generates the following output:

```
Java Code Generator:
_____

Use our Java code generator to
finish your programming project
in no time.  Just answer a few
simple questions and click on
the "Generate Java Code" button
to create the Java source files.
```

As you can see, all occurrences of C++ have been replaced by Java (sounds ominous, doesn't it?). If you would want to save the modified advertisement copy in a file named `java-ad.txt`, you would use the following command line:

```
perl change.pl < ad.txt > java-ad.txt
```

BONUS

Changing the Pattern Delimiter

So far, I have shown you the simple form of a pattern-matching operator, in which the pattern is always enclosed in forward slashes (/. . ./). On UNIX systems, however, you often need to search for patterns containing filenames that also use / as a delimiter (a filename such as `/usr/local/etc/httpd/htdocs/index.html`, for example). In such situations, if you use / as the pattern delimiter, you have to place a backslash (\) in front of any forward slash in the pattern.

Suppose that you want to look for the specific directory prefix `/usr/local/etc/httpd/htdocs/`. If you must use the forward slash delimiter, the pattern is as follows:

```
/\/usr\/local\/etc\/httpd\/htdocs\//
```

Basically, each / in the directory name becomes \/ (with the backslash prefix), giving rise to what Larry Wall, Tom Christiansen, and Randall Schwartz calls LTS — the *leaning toothpick syndrome* — because all those forward and backward slashes look like toothpicks leaning against each other.

To avoid the leaning toothpick syndrome and to make the pattern easier to read, you need another pattern delimiter besides the forward slash. Knowing how flexible Perl is, you may have already guessed that Perl probably includes a way to change the pattern delimiter. And you're right. Perl does enable you to use some other character besides the forward slash to enclose patterns.

NOTE To enclose a pattern inside a different pair of delimiters than /, you have to use the m operator. The m operator is the match operator, which has the following syntax:

```
m/regex/
```

where / is the pattern delimiter and `regex` is the regular expression that specifies the pattern. If you choose to use / as a pattern delimiter, you do not need to use the m prefix. If you choose a different pattern delimiter, however, you must include the m prefix.

With the m operator, you could write a simpler pattern to look for the UNIX directory name `/usr/local/etc/httpd/htdocs/`:

```
m|/usr/local/etc/httpd/htdocs/|
```

As you can see, just a simple change of the pattern delimiter enables you to write a much more readable pattern.

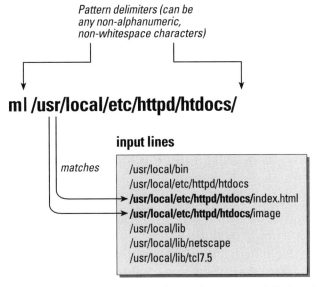

NOTE With the m operator, you can use any non-alphanumeric and non-whitespace characters as delimiters. That means you can use characters such as @, ~, !, #, |, and so on. The vertical bar is often a good choice for a separator. Essentially, you should pick as the delimiter a character that does not occur in your pattern.

Figure 7-5 shows the use of the m operator with a vertical bar (|) as the pattern delimiter.

Pattern delimiters (can be any non-alphanumeric, non-whitespace characters)

m| /usr/local/etc/httpd/htdocs/

input lines

matches

/usr/local/bin
/usr/local/etc/httpd/htdocs
➤ **/usr/local/etc/httpd/htdocs/**index.html
➤ **/usr/local/etc/httpd/htdocs/**image
/usr/local/lib
/usr/local/lib/netscape
/usr/local/lib/tcl7.5

Figure 7-5 The m operator allows other pattern delimiters besides /.

As with the standard pattern-matching expression /pattern/, you can use modifiers with the m operator as well. For example, to match a pattern globally, use the g modifier in the following manner:

```
m/pattern/g
```

For a case-insensitive match, use the i modifier, as follows:

```
m/pattern/i
```

Summary

A significant aspect of text processing is searching for specific patterns of text and then performing some task, such as replacing the pattern with another string. For such tasks, Perl provides pattern-matching and pattern substitution operators. This chapter shows you how to perform pattern matches and substitutions in Perl programs. The default pattern-matching expression is very simple: You merely enclose a regular expression in a pair of forward slashes (/ . . ./).

As one of the example programs shows, you can use pattern matching to verify that the user has entered valid data in a form (for example, you can check whether an account number matches a specific pattern of digits).

As a bonus, you learn how to use the m/PATTERN/ form of the pattern-matching operator, which enables you to use other pattern delimiters besides forward slashes.

The next chapter describes Perl subroutines, which enable you to package code for use in many different programs.

PACKAGING CODE IN SUBROUTINES

IN THIS CHAPTER YOU LEARN THESE KEY SKILLS

I n a programming project of any significant size, some tasks are performed often in many different programs. Instead of writing the code again and again wherever you perform that task, it's wiser to package the code so that you can simply invoke the code when needed. Perl already provides some packaged code in the form of built-in functions, such as `print` and `chop`. Additionally, Perl enables you to package a block of code in a subroutine so that you can subsequently invoke that code with a single name. The term *function* is also used to refer to subroutines.

This chapter explains how to write a subroutine and pass arguments to the subroutine. You also learn how to invoke a subroutine in Perl programs.

X-REF   **Perl's built-in functions are just like subroutines you write. The only difference is that the built-in functions are already defined when your Perl program begins running. Chapter 9 provides an overview of Perl's built-in functions.**

8

Understanding Subroutines

A *subroutine* is a block of Perl statements with a name. The idea is to write a subroutine that groups together the Perl statements to perform a specific task. Then you can perform that task anywhere in your Perl program by invoking that subroutine by name. You can best understand a subroutine by trying out a simple example.

A simple subroutine

Consider a subroutine that prints a message. Following Perl's subroutine syntax (which you learn in detail later in this chapter), you might write this subroutine as follows:

```
sub message
{
   print "Hello, there.\n";
}
```

As you can see, the structure of a subroutine is simple. You use the `sub` keyword to define a subroutine. The name of the subroutine comes after the `sub`. The body of the subroutine is a block of Perl statements enclosed in curly braces (`{...}`).

To invoke the `message` subroutine, you just have to write the subroutine's name with an ampersand (&) prefix, like this:

```
&message;
```

This causes the `message` subroutine's statement block to execute, and the result is the following output:

```
Hello, there.
```

This output is generated by the single `print` statement that constitutes the statement block of the `message` subroutine.

Subroutine arguments

As it stands now, the `message` subroutine is not that exciting, because it always prints the same message. Suppose, however, that you want to print the message addressed to a specific person. That's where the concept of subroutine arguments comes in.

When you invoke a subroutine, you can provide it a list of items by placing the list inside parentheses following the subroutine's name. These are the subroutine's *arguments*. For example, you could call the `message` subroutine as follows:

```
&message("John", "Doe");
```

The result is still the same `Hello, there.` message, because the `message` subroutine is not written to handle arguments.

When you call a subroutine with an argument list, Perl places this list in the array named @_. Thus, you can handle arguments in a subroutine by accessing and using the contents of the @_ array. What you do with those arguments depends on the purpose of the subroutine. In the `message` subroutine, you might want simply to print the contents of array as follows:

```
sub message
{
  print "Hello, there @_.\n";
}
```

As you can see, the `print` statement now includes the @_ array in the output. With this definition of the `message` subroutine, if you call it with the following argument list:

```
&message("John", "Doe");
```

the resulting output will be the following:

```
Hello, there John Doe.
```

This example and Figure 8-1 illustrate the basic concept of a subroutine and how you can pass arguments to the subroutine. You do not have to do anything special to define the @_ array that contains the arguments passed to the subroutine; the Perl interpreter automatically sets up the @_ array when the subroutine is called with any arguments. If your subroutine requires arguments, you simply refer to the @_ array in the subroutine.

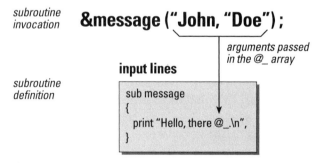

Figure 8-1 Passing arguments to Perl subroutines

Value returned from subroutine

Suppose that you need to write a subroutine that returns the average value of the numbers that you provide as an argument. You plan to use this `average` subroutine as follows:

```
$avg = &average(1, 2, 3); # $avg = (1+2+3)/3 = 2
```

That means the `average` subroutine has to return a value, which you can assign to any scalar variable. Here is how you might write this subroutine:

```
sub average
{
# Declare local variables (names that
# do not affect similarly named variables
# outside the subroutine)
    my($avg);
    my($i);

# Add up the numbers passed in the @_ array
    foreach $i (@_)
    {
        $avg += $i;
    }

# Divide by the total number of elements
# in @_ array
    if(@_ > 0)
    {
      $avg /= @_;
    }

# Return the computed average value
    return($avg);
}
```

This implementation of the `average` subroutine illustrates the following key features of Perl subroutines:

* The `my` function enables you to declare variable names local to the subroutine. You can use such local variables inside the subroutine without worrying whether the name conflicts with other variables already in use outside the subroutine.
* Use the `@_` array to access the arguments that are used when the subroutine is called.
* Use the `return` function to return a value from the subroutine.

 NOTE Note that Perl has another way to return a value from a subroutine. If you do not use a `return` function, the return value is the last expression evaluated in the subroutine. That means all you have to do is place the return value at the very end of the subroutine.

Learning the Basic Form of Subroutines

The preceding section shows you the main features of a subroutine through some simple examples. Now you can turn to the details of writing subroutines.

Perl provides a keyword called sub that you use to define a subroutine. You have to use the sub keyword to write a subroutine with the following structure:

```
sub SubroutineName
{
... Perl statements constituting body of subroutine ...
}
```

Every Perl subroutine has this basic structure:

* Start the subroutine definition with sub followed by the subroutine name. Like any variable name, subroutine names begin with a letter followed by one or more letters, digits, or underscores.

* Inside a pair of curly braces ({. . . }) place the Perl statements that constitute the body of the subroutine. The statements in the subroutine can include calls to other subroutines, if necessary.

As an example, suppose that you want to write a subroutine that prints a line of text. Let's assume you want to print out a line in Hypertext Markup Language (HTML) with a link to your World Wide Web site. You might write such a subroutine as follows:

```
sub LinkHome
{
    print "<a href=\"http://www.mysite.net\">Home</a>\n";
}
```

where www.mysite.net is the hostname of your Web server. You can then call this subroutine as follows:

```
&LinkHome;
```

whenever you need to add a hyperlink to your home page.

NOTE You can define the subroutine anywhere in your Perl program. To make your programs readable, however, it's best to place the subroutine definitions at the very beginning or the end of a program. As you learn in the section "Packaging Subroutines in a File," you can also place several related subroutines in a separate file and use them in any program.

Using Local Variables

Often you need to use variables inside a subroutine. You need to learn some rules for this, because variable names are global in Perl. For example, consider the following program:

```
sub message
{
  $count++;
  print "In subroutine: count = $count\n";
}

$count = 10;
print "Count BEFORE subroutine call = $count\n";
&message;  # call the subroutine
print "Count AFTER subroutine call = $count\n";
```

When you run this program, it prints the following result:

```
Count BEFORE subroutine call = 10
In subroutine: count = 11
Count AFTER subroutine call = 11
```

As you can see, the `$count++` in the subroutine's body increments the `$count` variable that exists outside the subroutine. This shows that whatever you do to a variable inside a subroutine affects the variable with the same name anywhere else in your program. You have to use a local variable inside a subroutine if you do not want to mess up a similarly named variable elsewhere in your program.

There is a way in which you can use a variable name inside the subroutine without conflicting with any outside variable with the same name. All you have to do is add a line that declares the variable to be local to the subroutine. Perl 4 had one way to declare a local variable; Perl 5 introduces a new way (as well as preserves the old way). In Perl 4, you can make `$count` local by adding the following statement at the beginning of the subroutine:

```
local($count);
```

After adding this line to the `message` subroutine and running the program, it prints the following output:

```
Count BEFORE subroutine call = 10
In subroutine: count = 1
Count AFTER subroutine call = 10
```

As this output shows, the value of `$count` outside the subroutine is no longer affected by the `$count++` statement inside the subroutine. The reason is that `$count` inside the subroutine is only defined within the subroutine. The other `$count` is a variable separate from the one inside the subroutine.

NOTE In Perl 5, you can define a local variable in another way. Use the `my` keyword (which is provided as a built-in function) to make a variable local, as follows:

```
my($count);
```

The net effect of `my` is the same as `local` — the `$count` variable becomes local to the subroutine, and anything you do to the variable inside the subroutine does not affect the `$count` that exists outside the subroutine.

TIP Inside a subroutine, you should use either `my` or `local` to define all variables to avoid potential conflicts with variables declared in programs that may use the subroutine.

To declare a number of local variables, simply provide a comma-separated list of variable names as argument to either the `local` or `my` function, as follows:

```
local($i, $key, $val);
my($param, @value, $var);
```

When you declare only one variable, the parentheses are optional; they are required for multiple variables.

You can also initialize a local variable as you declare it:

```
my $name = "Naba";
my @names = ("Joe", "Bill", "Mary", "Susan");
my(%days) = ( 1 => "Mon",
              2 => "Tue",
              3 => "Wed",
              4 => "Thu",
              5 => "Fri",
              6 => "Sat",
              7 => "Sun");
local $control = 1;
```

As you can see, you can declare and initialize any type of variable as local in a subroutine. A common practice is to initialize local variables from arguments so that you can refer to the arguments by a meaningful name.

Passing Arguments to Subroutines

Although you can write subroutines that do not accept any arguments, most useful subroutines accept arguments and produce some result based on the argument. For example, if you write a subroutine to compute the average value of a series of numbers, those numbers are the arguments to the subroutine; the average is the return value (which is a subject of the "Returning Values from Subroutines" section).

Understanding argument passing

In most programming languages, the syntax for subroutine definition requires you to specify the arguments that a subroutine accepts. In Perl, the arguments are not defined in the subroutine. Instead, Perl passes the arguments in a special array variable named @_.

To see how this works, try out the following program:

```
sub printarg
{
# Print the @_ array which contains
# the arguments

    my($arg);
    if(@_)
    {
      print "Here are the arguments:\n";
      foreach $arg (@_)
      {
          print "$arg\n";
      }
    }
    else
    {
      print "No arguments\n";
    }
    print "————————\n";
}


# Call the subroutine with various arguments

&printarg;
&printarg(1, 2, 3);
&printarg("John", "Mary", "Joe", "Jane");

# If the subroutine is defined above, you can
# also call the subroutine without the &
printarg "price", 24.99;
printarg 100, 200, 300;
```

When you run this program, it prints the following output:

```
No arguments
_____

Here are the arguments:
1
2
3
_____

Here are the arguments:
John
Mary
Joe
Jane
_____

Here are the arguments:
price
24.99
_____

Here are the arguments:
100
200
300
_____
```

In this program, the `printarg` subroutine prints the contents of the @_ array that contains the arguments passed to the subroutine. Essentially, when you call a subroutine such as `printarg`, you can provide a list of arguments. This list is what is passed in the @_ array.

NOTE Because Perl passes arguments in a special array, Perl subroutines can, by design, accept a variable number of arguments. It's up to the subroutine to use these arguments appropriately. For example, if a subroutine does not expect arguments, it ignores any argument you provide when you call the subroutine. You have to know what a subroutine does and what arguments it expects before you call it in your program.

Initializing local variables from arguments

Instead of working with the elements of the @_ array, it's more readable if you can define local variables with meaningful names and use them in your subroutine. Suppose that your subroutine expects a single argument — a scalar variable with your Web server's name. You might then initialize a local variable from the @_ array as follows:

```
my($hostname) = @_;
```

which initializes the `$hostname` variable with the first element in the array `@_`. Here's a more complete program that uses this approach to initialize a local variable from `@_`:

```
sub MakeLink
{
# Expects hostname of server
  my($hostname) = @_;
  print "<a href=\"http://$hostname/\">Home</a>\n";
# ...
}
# Sample call
MakeLink "www.lnbsoft.com";
```

When you run this program, it prints the following:

```
<a href="http://www.lnbsoft.com/">Home</a>
```

If your subroutine expects several scalar values, you can initialize them in a similar manner. Suppose that you are writing a subroutine that expects two arguments, a last name and an identifier. You might then initialize the local variables as follows:

```
my($lastname, $id) = @_;
```

 NOTE When you copy argument values from the `@_` array into a local variable, any changes you make to the local copies do not affect the argument that was passed during the call. The only way to get those changes back to the calling program is to return the values (you learn about this in the "Returning Values from Subroutines" section).

Modifying the argument value

If you directly manipulate the `@_` array inside the subroutine, any changes you make to the values in `@_` do affect the arguments passed during the subroutine call. Sometimes this may be a desirable way to implement a subroutine. An example might be a subroutine that converts its arguments into lowercase. The conversion is performed in-place — meaning that the subroutine makes the change directly in the `@_` array. The `makelc` subroutine in the following program demonstrates how you can do this:

```
sub makelc
{
    foreach (@_)
```

```
        {
            tr/A-Z/a-z/;   # converts $_ into lowercase
        }
    }

    $string = "I WANT THIS IN LOWERCASE!";
    &makelc($string);
    print "$string\n";
```

When you run this program, it displays the following output:

```
i want this in lowercase!
```

As you can see, the `makelc` subroutine modifies the argument that was passed to it.

You can get the same effect by using a special type of local variable. Here is a version of the `makelc` subroutine that has been written using the special type of local variable:

```
sub  makelc_new
{
# Use a special form of local
# variable called "typeglob"
    local(*input) = @_;

# Now convert the $input variable into lowercase
    $input =~  tr/A-Z/a-z/;
}

$newstring = "CHANGE THIS TO LOWERCASE!";
&makelc_new(*newstring);
print "$newstring\n";
```

When you run this program, it produces the following output:

```
change this to lowercase!
```

Again, the revised subroutine `makelc_new` converts its argument to lower-case. This version, however, has the following key differences from the preceding subroutine, which directly manipulated the `@_` array:

✳ The local variable is declared with a * prefix, as follows:

```
local(*input) = @_;
```

   This syntax is known as a *typeglob,* and it works only with the `local` function (and not `my`). The net effect of the `typeglob` is that this local variable matches whatever actual variable you pass in an argument, be it a scalar, an array, or an associative array.

* Inside the subroutine, you have to use the local variable in its expected form. Thus, if the subroutine expects a scalar and you have the typeglob *input, you have to refer to it with the symbol $input.

* When you call the subroutine, pass the argument in typeglob form — replace the funny letter at the beginning of the variable name (such as $, @, or %) with an asterisk (*), like this:

  ```
  &makelc_new(*newstring);
  ```

  where $newstring is the actual variable you want to pass to the subroutine.

Even if you do not use the typeglob form of local variables, you may run into Perl subroutines that use this trick. When you see any subroutine call with arguments that have an asterisk prefix, that means the subroutine directly modifies the argument that's being passed.

Passing a filehandle to a subroutine

Another interesting use of the typeglob format is to pass a filehandle to a subroutine. In fact, you cannot pass filehandles to Perl subroutines without using this special approach, because Perl treats filehandles differently from other variables.

Suppose that you want to pass a filehandle to a subroutine and have the subroutine read from the file (or write to it). Here is a very simple program that passes the STDIN filehandle to a subroutine, and the subroutine reads a line from its filehandle argument:

```perl
sub readline
{
# Use typeglob to get the filehandle
# Note that $_[0] is simply the first element
# of the @_ array that contains the arguments

   local(*FHANDLE) = $_[0];
   local $line;

# Read a line from the filehandle
# Note that filehandles don't have any special
# characters such as $ or @ as prefix

   $line = <FHANDLE>;
}

# Demonstrate how the "readline" subroutine is used
print "Enter input: ";
$line = readline(*STDIN);  # Note the * prefix
```

```
print "You entered = $line";
```

When you run this program, here's how you might interact with it (your input is in boldface):

```
Enter input: Hello
You entered = Hello
```

Note the following key features of the readline subroutine and how it's used:

* The local filehandle is declared as a typeglob consisting of an asterisk followed by the name:

  ```
  local(*FHANDLE) = $_[0]; # refer to filehandle
  ```

* To use the filehandle in the subroutine, use the plain name without any special character prefix, as follows:

  ```
  $line = <FHANDLE>;
  ```

* In the subroutine call, pass the filehandle argument with an asterisk prefix. Thus, to pass STDIN to the subroutine, you write:

  ```
  $line = readline(*STDIN);
  ```

This program also returns a value by placing the return value as the last expression in the subroutine's body. The next section covers the subject of returning values from subroutines.

Returning Values from Subroutines

Perl has a simple scheme for returning values from a subroutine. All you need to do is place the return value (or values, in case you are returning a list of items) at the very end of your subroutine. Perl returns the value of the last expression in the subroutine.

You can use the return function to explicitly return a value from a Perl subroutine.

Returning the last expression

Most Perl subroutines return values by making the return value the last expression in the subroutine. A few simple examples can show you how this works.

Here is a subroutine that returns a single scalar value:

```
sub doubleit
{
# Returns 2 times the argument
```

```
    my($x) = $_[0];
    $x *= 2;
}

$y = doubleit(2);
print "Result = $y\n";
```

As you can see, the `doubleit` subroutine simply computes the value and leaves it as the last line in the subroutine. That then becomes the return value of the subroutine. When you run the program, it prints the expected output:

```
Result = 4
```

If you want to return a list of items, you can do so by placing that list as the last line of your subroutine. Here is a contrived example that returns a list of values (and does nothing else):

```
sub retarray
{
# Returns a fixed list of items
   (1, 2, 3);
}

# Call retarray and store value in an array
@result = retarray;

print "Result = @result\n";
```

This program generates the following output:

```
Result = 1 2 3
```

which is what the `retarray` subroutine returns.

Using the `return` function

Perl includes a built-in function called `return` that enables you to explicitly return a value from a subroutine. If you have programmed in C, C++, or Java, then you are already familiar with the `return` statement. To return a value, you write the following:

```
return(EXPRESSION);
```

where *EXPRESSION* is a Perl expression containing the value returned. As in all Perl function calls, the parentheses are optional.

For example, to return a scalar variable, you might write this code:

```
sub doubleit
{
```

```
# Returns 2 times the argument
    my($x) = $_[0];
    $x *= 2;

# Return the result
    return($x);
}
```

where you explicitly return the result with the `return` function.

You can also return a literal value, such as a double-quoted string, like this:

```
return "</BODY></HTML>";
```

Returning an array variable is equally simple; just write the following:

```
return(@result); # to return the @result array
```

You can also return a list of scalar variables:

```
return($name, $account, $amount);
```

BONUS

Packaging Subroutines in a File

A common use of subroutines is to package the code for specific tasks into a set of subroutines and then store the subroutines in a file. Later on, you can use those subroutines in any Perl program by referring to the file where the subroutines are stored. It's worthwhile to store even a single subroutine in its own file, because that makes it easier to use the subroutine in many different Perl programs.

When you want to store one or more subroutines in a file, you have to follow some guidelines for that file. Also, you have to learn how to use subroutines that happen to be in various files. This section shows you how to do this.

Suppose that you need a date string formatted in a specific way. As you learn in Chapter 9, Perl provides the `localtime` function for getting the date and time in the form of a list of numbers (these numbers denote day of the week, day of the month, month number, hour, minute, and so forth). From the elements returned by `localtime`, you can pick out the date part.

You decide to put together a `get_date` subroutine that will return the date in a string, formatted just the way you want it. You also want to keep this subroutine in a file so that you can use it in any Perl program that may need the date and time.

Here is how you might write the subroutine and save it in a file named `date.pl`:

```
# File: date.pl

# Returns current date and time as a string
# Uses the localtime function

# Usage:  require "date.pl";

sub get_date
{
   local($mday, $mon, $year, $wday) =
                     (localtime)[3,4,5,6];
   local $day   = (Sun,Mon,Tue,Wed,Thu,Fri,Sat)[$wday];
   local $month = (Jan,Feb,Mar,Apr,May,Jun,
             Jul,Aug,Sep,Oct,Nov,Dec)[$mon];

   $year += 1900; # localtime subtracts 1900 from the year

   "$day, $month $mday $year";
}

# End the file with a 1 as the last expression
1;
```

As you can see, you define the `get_date` subroutine just as you would in any Perl program. The actual logic of the subroutine depends on the details of the `localtime` function, but you really do not need to understand that to see how to package a subroutine in a file.

NOTE The only key point is that you must include a 1 as the last expression in the subroutine file. The file can have more than one subroutine and may include other variables. Just place all the subroutine definitions one after another and make sure a 1; is at the very end of the file. The Perl interpreter uses the value of the last expression in the file as an indicator of success or failure. By making 1; the last expression, you are indicating that the subroutine file was successfully included.

To use the `get_date` subroutine in a Perl program, incorporate the `date.pl` file into the Perl program and then call the subroutine. Here's an example:

```
require "date.pl";

$date = &get_date;
print $date, "\n";
```

The first line incorporates the file date.pl into the current program (require is a built-in Perl function). After that, you can call any subroutine defined in the date.pl file. In this case, the only subroutine is get_date. This example saves the string returned by get_date in a scalar variable and then prints out the string. When you run the program, it generates output similar to the following:

```
Thu, Jan 30 1997
```

You can actually call the get_date subroutine and directly print the return value, as follows:

```
print &get_date, "\n";
```

From this example, you should note the following key points about placing subroutines in a file and using the subroutines elsewhere:

* Place the subroutines in a file and end the file with a 1; as the last expression.
* To use any of the subroutines in a specific file, use the require function, as follows:

```
require "filename"
```

  where *filename* is the file containing the subroutines.
* After the require function, call the subroutine as usual.

Summary

You can use subroutines to assign a name to a block of Perl statements and then execute those statements in any Perl program by using the subroutine name. You can also pass arguments to subroutines and return results from subroutines. This chapter shows you how to define subroutines using the sub keyword, how to access the arguments passed to a subroutine, and how to return values from a subroutine.

As a bonus, you learn how to place one or more subroutines in a file and then use them in various Perl programs.

The next chapter provides an overview of Perl's built-in functions, which are subroutines that are already defined for you. You can use them in any Perl program.

CHAPTER NINE

USING PERL'S BUILT-IN FUNCTIONS

9

IN THIS CHAPTER YOU LEARN THESE KEY SKILLS

A significant part of Perl's capability comes bundled as built-in functions — subroutines that are predefined and are available for use anywhere in a Perl program. You have already seen many of the built-in functions in the previous chapters. One popular function is the `print` function, which you use to display output in nearly all Perl programs. Other functions include string functions, such as `chop`, `substr`, and `length`, and math functions, such as `abs`, `cos`, `sin`, and `sqrt`. Many more functions are devoted to accessing the operating system and perform tasks such as manipulating files and directories and executing other programs. All in all, Perl 5 has nearly 200 built-in functions (also referred to as the *Perl functions*).

Although you have seen some of Perl's built-in functions in action, you have not yet had an overview of these functions. Even though you may be a Perl beginner, you'll find it beneficial to get a feel for the breadth of capabilities that these functions provide.

This chapter provides an overview of Perl's built-in functions and includes a tutorial introduction to some of the commonly used functions. In particular, you'll see the functions organized into categories, as well as see a list of the functions with a brief description of each function's capability. You do not have to immediately grasp all the information presented in this chapter. All you need to do is to glance through the types of tasks these functions can perform. Later on, when you begin to write Perl programs in earnest, you can look back at the list of functions and find the ones that can help you get the job done.

Appreciating the Built-in Functions

Before you see the details of what Perl's built-in functions provide, you may want to know why the built-in functions are so important. The best way to appreciate the usefulness of the built-in functions is to see how they help you solve various programming problems in Perl. Table 9-1 shows you a list of some "how to" problems that you can solve by using Perl's built-in functions.

As Table 9-1 shows, you can use built-in functions in a variety of situations, from printing output to writing TCP servers.

TABLE 9-1   Typical "how to" problems solved by Perl's built-in functions

How do I . . .	Solution
PRINT OUTPUT	Use the `print` function. To print the value of a variable, embed the variable in a double-quoted string.
PRINT OUTPUT IN SPECIFIC FORMAT	Use the `printf` function.
REMOVE THE TRAILING NEWLINE CHARACTER	Use the `chomp` function to remove any trailing newline character in a string. Use `chop` to indiscriminately remove the last character of a string.
SPLIT A LINE INTO SEVERAL PARTS	Use the `split` function with a regular expression that specifies the separator between the parts.
COMPUTE MATH FORMULAS	Use functions such as `cos`, `sin`, `log`, and `sqrt`.
GENERATE RANDOM NUMBERS	Use the `srand` and `rand` functions.
FIND THE LENGTH OF A STRING	Use the `length` function.
CONVERT CASE	Use `uc` to make a string all uppercase; `lc` to make it lowercase.
FIND A SUBSTRING	Use the `substr` function.
SORT AN ARRAY	Use the `sort` function.

How do I . . .	Solution
GET THE CURRENT DATE AND TIME	Call the `time` function to get the date and time in binary form. Then call `localtime` to convert the binary time into various components of the time, such as hour, minute, day, month, year, and day of the week.
READ DATA FROM A FILE	Use the `open` function to open the file and get a filehandle. Then use the angle operator `<FILEHANDLE>` or functions such as `read` and `sysread` to read from the file. Use the `close` function to close the file when you are finished.
GET A LIST OF ALL FILES IN A DIRECTORY	Use the `glob` function (yes, the name sounds strange, but it works!).
RUN ANOTHER PROGRAM	Use the `system` function or a combination of `fork` and `exec` functions.
WAIT FOR SOME AMOUNT OF TIME	Use the `sleep` or `select` function to wait for a specified amount of time.
CREATE AND ACCESS A DATABASE MANAGEMENT (DBM) FORMAT FILE	Use the `dbmopen` and `dbmclose` functions to work with DBM files — DBM is a simple data storage format commonly used in UNIX.
IMPLEMENT TCP CLIENT OR SERVER	Use the sockets-based network programming functions, such as `socket`, `connect`, `accept`, `bind`, `listen`, `send`, and `recv`.

Taking Stock of the Built-In Functions

Perl's built-in functions are like the C run-time library. The C programming language is built around a small set of core capabilities with a large support library. The core offers a selection of data types and control structures, while all additional tasks, including input and output, graphics, math computations, and access to the operating system, are relegated to a library of functions. In this respect, Perl is similar to C. Many of Perl's capabilities come from its collection of built-in functions. As Figure 9-1 illustrates, you can think of the Perl functions as a toolbox that includes the tools to perform many types of tasks.

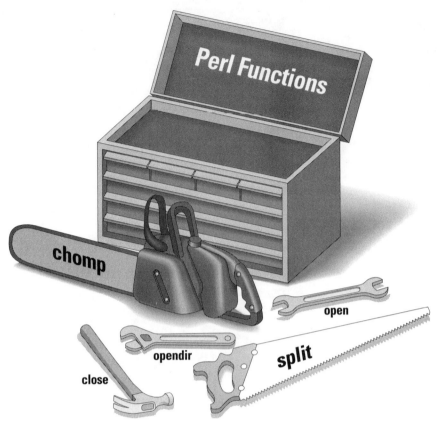

Figure 9-1 You can think of Perl's built-in functions as a toolbox.

X-REF In Perl 5, even more functionality comes in the form of Perl modules. A *module* is essentially a collection of Perl subroutines (that follow some guidelines) in a file. Each Perl module contains Perl scripts stored in files with names ending in .pm. The modules follow a specific set of guidelines and essentially package a related set of subroutines. For example, there are Perl modules for error handling and file access. You learn more Perl modules in Chapter 11, where I discuss the new features of Perl 5.

An overview gives you a view of the functions, arranged by the tasks they perform. For example, many functions are devoted to math, some are meant for manipulating strings, and yet others are for network programming. Table 9-2 shows the Perl functions, organized by task.

TABLE 9-2 An overview of Perl functions by task

Task	Functions
PERFORM INPUT AND OUTPUT	binmode, close, eof, format, formline, getc, open, print, printf, read, seek, sprintf, sysread, syswrite, tell, write
PROCESS DATA IN SCALARS AND ARRAYS	chr, crypt, grep, hex, int, map, oct, ord, pack, reverse, shift, sort, splice, split, unpack, unshift, vec
PROCESS STRINGS	chomp, chop, index, join, lc, lcfirst, length, q/STRING/, qq/STRING/, quotemeta, qw/STRING/, qx/STRING/, rindex, substr, uc, ucfirst
PERFORM PATTERN-MATCHING AND SUBSTITUTIONS	m/PATTERN/, pos, s/ PATTERN /REPLACE/, study, tr/SEARCHLIST/REPLACELIST/, y/SEARCHLIST/REPLACELIST/
PERFORM MATH COMPUTATIONS	abs, atan2, cos, exp, log, rand, sin, sqrt, srand
WORK WITH TIME	gmtime, localtime, time
MANIPULATE FILES AND DIRECTORIES	chdir, chmod, chown, chroot, closedir, fcntl, fileno, flock, glob, ioctl, link, lstat, mkdir, opendir, readdir, readlink, rename, rewinddir, rmdir, seekdir, stat, symlink, telldir, truncate, umask, unlink, utime
USE VARIOUS PERL PROGRAMMING FEATURES	caller, defined, die, do, goto, import, last, local, my, next, pop, push, redo, require, reset, return, scalar, undef, wantarray, warn
WORK WITH ASSOCIATIVE ARRAYS	dbmclose, dbmopen, delete, each, exists, keys, tie, untie, values
START AND CONTROL OTHER PROCESSES	alarm, dump, eval, exec, exit, fork, getpgrp, getppid, getpriority, kill, pipe, select, setpgrp, setpriority, sleep, syscall, system, times, wait, waitpid
DEFINE AND USE PERL MODULES	bless, no, ref, use
FIND USER INFORMATION (UNDER UNIX)	endgrent, endpwent, getgrent, getgrgid, getgrnam, getlogin, getpwent, getpwnam, getpwuid, setgrent, setpwent
INTERPROCESS COMMUNICATION	msgctl, msgget, msgrcv, msgsnd, semctl, semget, semop, shmctl, shmget, shmread, shmwrite

(continued)

TABLE 9-2 An overview of Perl functions by task *(continued)*

Task	Functions
OBTAIN NETWORK INFORMATION	endhostent, endnetent, endprotoent, endservent, gethostbyaddr, gethostbyname, gethostent, getnetbyaddr, getnetbyname, getnetent, getprotobyname, getprotobynumber, getprotoent, getservbyname, getservbyport, getservent, sethostent, setnetent, setprotoent, setservent
WRITE SOCKETS-BASED NETWORK PROGRAMS	accept, bind, connect, getpeername, getsockname, getsockopt, listen, recv, send, setsockopt, shutdown, socket, socketpair

Using the Built-In Functions

In previous chapters, you have seen many of Perl's built-in functions used in example programs. In particular, you'll find the print function in nearly all Perl programs. Functions such as chomp (to get rid of trailing newline characters) and open (to open a file) are also commonplace. The rest of the book also uses Perl functions in various examples. This section provides a tutorial introduction to several important categories of Perl functions. Many of these functions are covered in detail in other relevant chapters.

Input and output functions

The input and output functions read from and write to files. You have to identify the file by a filehandle that you initialize when you open a file. Most of your Perl programs work with standard input and standard output — by default, these refer to the keyboard and the display monitor, respectively. Perl automatically opens the standard input and standard output and assigns the filehandles STDIN and STDOUT to these "files."

You can think of the following set of Perl functions as being used for input or output:

binmode, close, eof, format, formline, getc, open, print, printf, read, seek, sprintf, sysread, syswrite, tell, write

Here is a brief list of tasks that these functions perform:

Task	Functions
OPEN AND CLOSE FILES	`open, close`
INPUT FROM FILE (INCLUDING STDIN)	`getc, read, sysread`
OUTPUT TO FILE (INCLUDING STDOUT)	`print, printf, write, syswrite`
CONTROL OUTPUT FORMAT	`format, formline`
PREPARE FORMATTED OUTPUT IN A STRING	`sprintf`
SET INPUT/OUTPUT TO BINARY MODE	`binmode`
GO TO SPECIFIC POSITION IN FILE	`seek`
GET CURRENT POSITION IN FILE	`tell`
CHECK FOR END OF FILE	`eof`

One of the most commonly used output functions is `print`. You can print output to a file with a call such as the following:

```
print FILEHANDLE "This output goes to the file.\n";
```

where `FILEHANDLE` refers to an open file. If you omit the `FILEHANDLE`, the `print` function sends its output to the standard output.

You can print values of variables with the `print` function. You can also embed variable names in double-quoted strings — Perl replaces the variable names with their values. With the `printf` function, you can more closely control the appearance of the printed output (for example, you can control exactly how many digits to print after the decimal point). Chapter 5 shows you how to use the `printf` function.

 Most of the other functions in this category have to do with reading from and writing to files. To do this, you have to open a file and then perform the read or write operations. You learn more about accessing files in Chapter 10.

String functions

You can manipulate text strings with the string functions. This category includes the following functions:

```
chomp, chop, index, join, lc, lcfirst, length, pos, q/STRING/, qq/STRING/,
quotemeta, qw/STRING/, qx/STRING/, rindex, substr, uc, ucfirst
```

These string functions perform the following types of tasks:

Task	Functions
REMOVE TRAILING NEWLINE CHARACTER	chomp, chop
FIND THE LENGTH OF A STRING	length
FIND POSITION OF A CHARACTER	index, rindex
EXTRACT OR REPLACE A SUBSTRING	substr, rindex
CONVERT CASE	lc, lcfirst, uc, ucfirst
COMBINE SEVERAL STRINGS INTO ONE	join
QUOTE A STRING	q/STRING/, qq/STRING/, quotemeta, qw/STRING/, qx/STRING/

X-REF Chapter 3 describes some of the commonly used string functions.

File and directory functions

Your Perl programs often have to work with files and directories, especially if you are writing Perl programs for a Web site. Typically, you may have to perform tasks such as get the listing of a directory, read data from a binary file (which is different from reading lines of text), and write data to a file.

Perl includes the following built-in functions that enable you to manipulate files and directories:

```
chdir, chmod, chown, chroot, closedir, fcntl, fileno, flock, glob, ioctl,
link, lstat, mkdir, opendir, readdir, readlink, rename, rewinddir, rmdir,
seekdir, stat, symlink, telldir, truncate, umask, unlink, utime
```

Here are the typical tasks that these functions perform:

Task	Functions
CREATE OR DELETE A DIRECTORY	mkdir, rmdir
OPEN, CLOSE, READ, AND USE A DIRECTORY	closedir, opendir, readdir, rewinddir, seekdir, telldir
CHANGE WORKING DIRECTORY	chdir
CHANGE THE ROOT DIRECTORY	chroot
CHANGE FILE OWNER AND PERMISSIONS	chown, chmod, umask

Task	Functions
CHANGE FILE MODIFICATION TIME	utime
DELETE A FILE	unlink
TRUNCATE A FILE	truncate
GET INFORMATION ABOUT A FILE	lstat, stat
GET FILE DESCRIPTOR FOR A FILEHANDLE	fileno
LOCK/UNLOCK AND CONTROL FILES	fcntl, flock, ioctl
EXPAND WILDCARD FILENAMES	glob
CREATE A LINK OR A SYMBOLIC LINK	link, symlink

 X-REF Chapter 10 shows you how to use most of these file and directory functions.

Pattern-matching and substitution functions

As described in Chapters 6 and 7, Perl supports pattern-matching and substitution facilities based on regular expressions. This category of functions includes the following:

```
m/PATTERN/, pos, s/ PATTERN /REPLACE/, study,
tr/SEARCHLIST/REPLACELIST/, y/SEARCHLIST/REPLACELIST/
```

These pattern-based functions perform the following tasks:

Task	Functions
SEARCH FOR A PATTERN MATCH	m/PATTERN/
REPLACE A PATTERN	s/ PATTERN /REPLACE/
RETURN POSITION OF LAST MATCH	pos
STUDY A PATTERN BEFORE ATTEMPTING MATCHES	study
REPLACE ONE SET OF CHARACTERS WITH ANOTHER	tr/SEARCHLIST/REPLACELIST/, y/SEARCHLIST/REPLACELIST/

X-REF Chapter 7 describes the pattern-matching and substitution functions. The only functions that are not covered in Chapter 7 are `tr///` and `y///` (because these functions do not use regular expressions).

The `tr///` and `y///` functions both perform the same task — replace all occurrences of one set of characters with corresponding letters in another set. The syntax is as follows:

```
tr/SEARCHLIST/REPLACELIST/
```

where *SEARCHLIST* and *REPLACELIST* are lists of characters. For example, to convert all letters to lowercase, write:

```
tr/[A-Z]/[a-z]/;
```

This converts the letters in `$_` to lowercase. If you want to perform the conversion on another scalar variable, you can do so with the `=~` operator, as follows:

```
$string =~ tr/[A-Z]/[a-z]/;
```

In this case, the `tr///` function replaces all occurrences of the characters `A` through `Z` with the corresponding characters from `a` through `z`. The net effect is to convert all letters to lowercase.

NOTE Another use of the `tr///` function is to delete unwanted characters. For example, each line in an MS-DOS text file ends with a carriage return followed by a line feed character. In UNIX, you do not want the carriage return character. Here's a Perl program that can get rid of the carriage return from lines of text:

```
while(<>)
{
  tr/\015//d;  # delete octal 15 (carriage return)
  print;
}
```

Suppose that you save this program in a file named `nocr.pl`. Then, to convert the MS-DOS file `dosfile.txt` into a UNIX text file `unix.txt`, use the following command:

```
perl nocr.pl dosfile.txt > unix.txt
```

The program uses the `tr///` function with the `d` modifier to delete all occurrences of characters whose ASCII code is octal 15 (which happens to be the ASCII code for a carriage return).

Time functions

Sometimes you need the current date and time in a Perl program. For example, in a Perl program that accepts and saves some user comments in a file, you may want to add a time stamp with the current date and time. For such tasks, Perl provides the following time functions:

```
gmtime, localtime, time
```

These functions perform the following tasks:

Task	Functions
GET CURRENT DATE AND TIME IN BINARY FORM	time
CONVERT TIME TO GMT OR LOCAL TIME	gmtime, localtime

Local time refers to the time at a specific locality (in the case of a Perl program, it's the time where the computer is located). As you know, the local time is different at different places in the world. For example, when it's 10:00 a.m. in Washington, D.C., it is already 3:00 p.m. in London, England, but it's only 7:00 a.m. in Los Angeles, California. When computers communicate and exchange e-mail messages and other documents, computers need a standard reference time.

Greenwich Mean Time (or GMT, for short) is the standard reference time that all computers use. GMT is also known as Zulu time or Universal Coordinated Time (the acronym is UTC, which is short for the French translation of Universal Coordinated Time). GMT refers to the local time in Greenwich, England (the zero meridian of longitude passes through Greenwich, England).

When you call the time function, it returns the seconds elapsed since 00:00:00 hours GMT on January 1, 1970. The gmtime and localtime functions convert the binary time into a list of items, as illustrated by the following example program:

```
# First print the time as a string by calling
# localtime in a scalar context

print scalar localtime,
"\n—————————\n";

# Now call localtime and get the components of
# current date and time.

# Note that these are numerical values
```

```
($sec, $min, $hour, $mday, $mon, $year, $wday,
 $yday, $isdst) = localtime(time);

print
"seconds           = $sec\
minutes            = $min\
hours              = $hour\
day of the month   = $mday\
month              = $mon\
year               = $year\
day of the week    = $wday\
day of the year    = $yday\
Daylight saving    = $isdst\n";
```

When you run this program, it produces the following output:

```
Tue Jan 28 20:11:06 1997
_____

seconds           = 6
minutes            = 11
hours              = 20
day of the month   = 28
month              = 0
year               = 97
day of the week    = 2
day of the year    = 27
Daylight saving    = 0
```

The first line is the date and time string returned by the scalar localtime call. Following that you see the result returned by the localtime call in an array context. By correlating the numerical values with the date and time shown on the first line, you can figure out what the numerical values mean. Here is how to interpret the return values (described in terms of the scalar variables that appear in the program):

$sec   = seconds after the minute (0 - 59)

$min   = minutes after the hour (0 - 59)

$hour   = hours since midnight (0 - 23)

$mday   = day of the month (1 - 31)

$mon   = months since January (0 - 11)

$year   = years since 1900 (add 1900 to get actual year)

$wday   = days since Sunday (0 - 6)

$yday   = days since January 1 (0 - 365); this is same as one less than the Julian date

$isdst   = daylight savings time flag (0 or 1; 1 means Daylight Savings Time)

The gmtime function works the same way as localtime, except that gmtime returns the time in GMT.

BONUS

A Catalog of Perl's Built-in Functions

The previous sections provided you with an overview of Perl's built-in functions and showed you how to use several important categories of functions. Although this book's philosophy is to provide you with just enough information to get you started with Perl programming, it's really handy to have a list of functions at the ready. Table 9-3 is such a list. You can browse the list to see the breadth of capabilities that these functions provide. Additionally, you can use this list as a quick reference guide for the functions. Each entry provides a one-line description that should give you an idea what the function does.

WEB
PATH   If you need more information on any of these functions, an online manual is available at the following URL:

ftp://ftp.digital.com/pub/plan/perl/CPAN/doc/manual/html/
perlfunc-all.html

The same document, in HTML format, appears on this book's companion CD-ROM. You can view that document by using a Web browser. Follow these instructions to view the documentation:

1. Place the companion CD-ROM in your system's CD-ROM drive.

2. Start a Web browser (such as Netscape Navigator or Microsoft Internet Explorer).

3. Select File → Open File . An Open dialog box appears.

4. From the Open dialog box, open the `\perl5\docs` directory on the CD-ROM drive. From the files in that directory, select the `perlfunc.htm` file (see Figure 9-2).

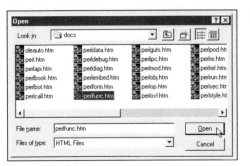

Figure 9-2 Selecting the `perlfunc.htm` file from the `\perl5\docs` directory of the CD-ROM

This causes the HTML document to appear in the browser. Figure 9-3 shows a typical entry in the online reference.

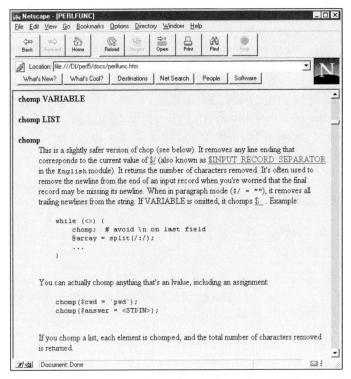

Figure 9-3 A typical function reference from the `perlfunc.htm` file

As you can see, the reference entries in the `perlfunc.htm` file provide enough detail to be helpful.

TABLE 9-3 A quick reference guide to Perl functions

Function call	Description
`abs(VALUE)`	Returns the absolute value of the argument
`accept(NEWSOCKET, GENERICSOCKET)`	Waits for connection on a socket
`alarm(SECONDS)`	Sends an alarm signal after a specified number of seconds
`atan2(Y,X)`	Returns the arctangent of Y/X
`bind(SOCKET,NAME)`	Associates a name to an already opened socket
`binmode(FILEHANDLE)`	Arranges for a file to be treated as binary
`bless(REF,PACKAGE)`	Makes a referenced item an object in a package
`caller(EXPR)`	Returns information about current subroutine calls
`chdir(EXPR)`	Changes directory to directory specified by EXPR
`chmod(LIST)`	Changes the permissions of a list of files
`chomp(VARIABLE)`	Removes trailing characters that match the current value of the special variable $/
`chop(VARIABLE)`	Chops off last character (useful for removing the trailing newline character in a string)
`chown(LIST)`	Changes the owner of a list of files
`chr(NUMBER)`	Returns the character whose ASCII code is NUMBER
`chroot(FILENAME)`	Changes root directory to specified FILENAME
`close(FILEHANDLE)`	Closes the specified file
`closedir(DIRHANDLE)`	Closes directory that had been opened by opendir
`connect(SOCKET,NAME)`	Initiates a connection to another system using a socket
`cos(EXPR)`	Returns the cosine of the angle EXPR (radians)
`crypt(PLAINTEXT,SALT)`	Encrypts string
`dbmclose(ASSOC_ARRAY)`	Disassociates an associative array from a DBM file
`dbmopen(ASSOC, DBNAME,MODE)`	Associates an associative array with a DBM file
`defined(EXPR)`	Returns true if EXPR is defined

(continued)

TABLE 9-3 A quick reference guide to Perl functions (*continued*)

Function call	Description
`delete $ASSOC{KEY}`	Deletes a value from an associative array
`die(LIST)`	Prints LIST to standard error and exits the Perl program
`do SUBROUTINE (LIST)`	Calls subroutine
`dump(LABEL)`	Causes a core dump
`each(ASSOC_ARRAY)`	Returns next key-value pair of an associative array
`endgrent`	Closes the `/etc/group` file in UNIX
`endhostent`	Closes the `/etc/hosts` file in UNIX
`endnetent`	Closes the `/etc/networks` file in UNIX
`endprotoent`	Closes the `/etc/protocols` file in UNIX
`endpwent`	Closes the `/etc/passwd` file in UNIX
`endservent`	Closes the `/etc/services` file in UNIX
`eof(FILEHANDLE)`	Returns true if end-of-file is reached
`eval(EXPR)`	Executes the `EXPR` as if it were a Perl program
`exec(LIST)`	Terminates the current Perl program by running another program (specified by `LIST`) in its place
`exists($ASSOC($KEY))`	Returns true if the specified key exists in the associative array
`exit(EXPR)`	Exits the Perl program and returns `EXPR`
`exp(EXPR)`	Returns e raised to the power `EXPR`
`fcntl(FILEHANDLE, FUNCTION,SCALAR)`	Performs various control operations on a file
`fileno(FILEHANDLE)`	Returns file descriptor for a filehandle
`flock(FILEHANDLE, OPERATION)`	Locks a file so that other processes cannot change the file (useful when multiple processes need to access a single file)
`fork`	Creates a child process and returns the child process ID
`format NAME =picture line value list`	Defines an output format to be used by the write function

Function call	Description
formline(PICTURE, LIST)	Formats a list of values according to contents of PICTURE
getc(FILEHANDLE)	Reads next character from file
getgrent	Returns group information from /etc/group
getgrgid(GID)	Looks up a group file entry by group number
getgrnam(NAME)	Looks up a group file entry by group name
gethostbyaddr(ADDR, ADDRTYPE)	Translates a network address to a name
gethostbyname(NAME)	Translates a network hostname to corresponding addresses
gethostent	Gets entries from /etc/hosts file in UNIX
getlogin	Returns current login information in UNIX
getnetbyaddr(ADDR, ADDRTYPE)	Translates a network address to corresponding network name
getnetbyname(NAME)	Translates a network name to its corresponding network address
getnetent	Gets entries from the /etc/networks file (or equivalent on non-UNIX systems)
getpeername(SOCKET)	Returns the socket address of the other end of a socket connection
getpgrp(PID)	Returns the current process group for the specified process ID
getppid	Returns the process ID of the parent process
getpriority(WHICH, WHO)	Returns the current priority of a process
getprotobyname(NAME)	Translates a protocol name into a number
getprotobynumber (NUMBER)	Translates a protocol number into a name
getprotoent	Gets networking protocol information from /etc/networks file in UNIX
getpwent	Gets entry from password file (/etc/passwd in UNIX)

(continued)

TABLE 9-3   A quick reference guide to Perl functions *(continued)*

Function call	Description
getpwnam(NAME)	Translates a user name into the corresponding entry in the password file
getpwuid(UID)	Translates a numeric user ID into the corresponding entry in the password file
getservbyname(NAME, PROTO)	Translates a service (port) name into the corresponding port number
getservbyport(PORT, PROTO)	Translates the service (port) number into a name
getservent	Gets entries from the /etc/services file in UNIX
getsockname(SOCKET)	Returns the address of this end of a socket connection
getsockopt(SOCKET, LEVEL,OPTNAME)	Returns the requested socket options
glob(EXPR)	Returns filenames corresponding to a wildcard expression
gmtime(EXPR)	Converts binary time into a 9-element list corresponding to Greenwich Mean Time (GMT)
goto(LABEL)	Jumps to the statement identified by the LABEL
grep(EXPR,LIST)	Searches LIST for occurrences of expression
hex(EXPR)	Returns decimal value corresponding to hexadecimal EXPR
index(STR,SUBSTR, POSITION)	Returns position of first occurrence of a string (search begins at character location specified by POSITION)
int(EXPR)	Returns integer portion of EXPR
ioctl(FILEHANDLE, FUNCTION,SCALAR)	Controls various aspects of FILEHANDLE
join(EXPR,LIST)	Returns a single string by joining list elements
keys(ASSOC_ARRAY)	Returns an array of keys for an associative array
kill(LIST)	Sends a signal to a list of processes
last(LABEL)	Exits the loop identified by LABEL
lc(EXPR)	Returns lowercase version of EXPR
lcfirst(EXPR)	Returns EXPR after changing the first character to lowercase

Function call	Description
length(EXPR)	Returns the length of EXPR in number of characters
link(OLDFILE, NEWFILE)	Creates NEWFILE as link to OLDFILE
listen(SOCKET, QUEUESIZE)	Waits for incoming connections on a socket
local(LIST)	Makes a list of variables local to a subroutine
localtime(EXPR)	Converts binary time into a 9-element list corresponding to local time
log(EXPR)	Returns the logarithm (to base e) of EXPR
lstat(FILEHANDLE)	Returns file statistics for a file (if file refers to a symbolic link, returns information about the symbolic link)
m/PATTERN/gimosx	Performs pattern matching
map(EXPR,LIST)	Evaluates the expression EXPR for each item of LIST
mkdir(FILENAME,MODE)	Creates the directory specified by FILENAME
msgctl(ID,CMD,ARG)	Performs message control operations on message queues
msgget(KEY,FLAGS)	Gets a message queue identifier corresponding to KEY
msgrcv(ID,VAR,SIZE, TYPE,FLAGS)	Receives a message from the message queue identifier ID
msgsnd(ID,MSG,FLAGS)	Sends a message to message queue identifier ID
my(EXPR)	Declares one or more private variables that exist in a subroutine or a block enclosed in curly braces ({. . .})
next(LABEL)	Starts the next iteration of the loop identified by LABEL
no(Module LIST)	Stops using a Perl module
oct(EXPR)	Returns the decimal equivalent of an octal number in EXPR
open(FILEHANDLE,EXPR)	Opens a file whose name is in EXPR and associates that file with FILEHANDLE
opendir(DIRHANDLE, EXPR)	Opens a directory whose name is in EXPR and associates that directory with DIRHANDLE
ord(EXPR)	Returns the numeric ASCII code of the first character in EXPR

(continued)

TABLE 9-3 A quick reference guide to Perl functions *(continued)*

Function call	Description
pack(TEMPLATE,LIST)	Takes a list of values and returns a string containing a packed binary structure (TEMPLATE specifies the packing)
pipe(READHANDLE, WRITEHANDLE)	Opens a pipe for reading and writing
pop(ARRAY)	Removes and returns the last element of an array
pos(SCALAR)	Returns the position where the last pattern match occurred (applies when a global search is performed with /PATTERN/g)
print(FILEHANDLE LIST)	Prints a list of items to a file identified by FILEHANDLE
printf(FILEHANDLE LIST)	Prints formatted output to a file
push(ARRAY,LIST)	Appends values in LIST to end of ARRAY
q/STRING/	Quotes a STRING without replacing variable names with values (similar to single-quoted string)
qq/STRING/	Quotes a STRING but replaces variable names with values (similar to double-quoted string)
quotemeta(EXPR)	Returns the value of EXPR after adding a backslash prefix for all characters that take on special meaning in regular expressions
qw/STRING/	Quotes a word list (similar to parentheses used in patterns)
qx/STRING/	Quotes a command (similar to backquotes)
rand(EXPR)	Returns random value between 0 and EXPR
read(FILEHANDLE, SCALAR,LENGTH)	Reads specified number of bytes from file
readdir(DIRHANDLE)	Reads directory entries from a directory handle
readlink(EXPR)	Returns the filename pointed to by a symbolic link
recv(SOCKET,SCALAR, LEN,FLAGS)	Receives a message from a socket
redo(LABEL)	Restarts the loop identified by LABEL

Function call	Description
ref(EXPR)	Returns true if EXPR is a reference (a reference points to an object)
rename(OLDNAME, NEWNAME)	Changes the name of a file from OLDNAME to NEWNAME
require(FNAME)	Includes the file specified by FNAME and executes the Perl code in that file
reset(EXPR)	Clears global variables
return(LIST)	Returns from subroutine with the specified values
reverse(LIST)	Reverses the order of elements in LIST
rewinddir(DIRHANDLE)	Sets current position to the beginning of the directory identified by DIRHANDLE
rindex(STR,SUBSTR)	Returns the last position of a substring in a string
rindex(STR,SUBSTR, POSITION)	Returns the position of last occurrence of a substring in a string
rmdir(FILENAME)	Deletes the directory specified by FILENAME
s/PATTERN/ REPLACEMENT/egimosx	Replaces PATTERN (a regular expression) with REPLACEMENT
scalar(EXPR)	Evaluates the expression EXPR in a scalar context
seek(FILEHANDLE, POSITION,WHENCE)	Moves to new location in file
seekdir(DIRHANDLE,POS)	Moves to a new position in a directory
select(FILEHANDLE)	Returns the currently selected filehandle and sets FILEHANDLE as the default filehandle for output
select(RBITS,WBITS, EBITS,TIMEOUT)	Checks if one or more files are ready for input or output
semctl(ID,SEMNUM, CMD,ARG)	Controls the semaphores used for interprocess communication
semget(KEY,NSEMS, FLAGS)	Returns the semaphore ID corresponding to a key
semop(KEY,OPSTRING)	Performs a semaphore operation (semaphores are used for interprocess communications in UNIX System V)

(continued)

TABLE 9-3   A quick reference guide to Perl functions *(continued)*

Function call	Description
`send(SOCKET,MSG, FLAGS,TO)`	Sends a message to a socket
`setgrent`	Sets group information in `/etc/group`
`sethostent(STAYOPEN)`	Opens the host database (`/etc/hosts` file in UNIX)
`setnetent(STAYOPEN)`	Opens the network database (`/etc/networks` file in UNIX)
`setpgrp(PID,PGRP)`	Sets the current process group of a process
`setpriority(WHICH, WHO,PRIORITY)`	Sets the priority for a process
`setprotoent(STAYOPEN)`	Opens the protocol database (`/etc/protocols` file in UNIX)
`setpwent`	Opens the `/etc/passwd` file in UNIX
`setservent(STAYOPEN)`	Opens the `/etc/services` file in UNIX
`setsockopt(SOCKET, LEVEL,OPTNAME,OPTVAL)`	Sets the specified socket options
`shift(ARRAY)`	Removes the first value from the array and returns it
`shmctl(ID,CMD,ARG)`	Controls shared memory settings such as permission
`shmget(KEY,SIZE,FLAGS)`	Allocates a shared memory segment
`shmread(ID,VAR, POS,SIZE)`	Reads from the shared memory segment identified by ID
`shmwrite(ID,STRING, POS,SIZE)`	Writes to the shared memory segment identified by ID
`shutdown(SOCKET,HOW)`	Shuts down a socket connection
`sin(EXPR)`	Returns the sine of the angle specified by `EXPR` (in radians)
`sleep(EXPR)`	Sleeps for `EXPR` seconds
`socket(SOCKET, DOMAIN,TYPE,PROTOCOL)`	Opens a socket for a specified kind and attaches it to the filehandle `SOCKET`
`socketpair(SOCKET1, SOCKET2,DOMAIN,TYPE, PROTOCOL)`	Creates an unnamed pair of sockets

Function call	Description
sort(LIST)	Sorts a list and returns the sorted list in an array
splice(ARRAY, OFFSET,LENGTH,LIST)	Replaces some ARRAY elements with LIST
split(/PATTERN/, EXPR,LIMIT)	Splits EXPR into an array of strings
sprintf(FORMAT,LIST)	Returns a string containing formatted output consisting of list elements formatted according to the FORMAT string
sqrt(EXPR)	Returns the square root of EXPR
srand(EXPR)	Sets the seed for random number generation
stat(FILEHANDLE)	Returns a 13-element list with statistics for a file
study(STRING)	Examines STRING in anticipation of doing many pattern matches on the string
substr(EXPR,OFFSET, LEN)	Returns a substring from the string EXPR
symlink(OLDFILE, NEWFILE)	Creates NEWFILE as a symbolic link to OLDFILE
syscall(LIST)	Calls the system function specified in the first element of LIST (and passes to that call the remaining list elements as arguments)
sysopen(FILEHANDLE, FILENAME,MODE,PERMS)	Opens a file named FILENAME and associates it with FILEHANDLE
sysread(FILEHANDLE, SCALAR,LENGTH,OFFSET)	Reads a specified number of bytes from a file
system(LIST)	Executes the shell commands in LIST
syswrite(FILEHANDLE, SCALAR,LENGTH,OFFSET)	Writes a specified number of bytes to a file
tell(FILEHANDLE)	Returns the current file position in bytes from beginning of file
telldir(DIRHANDLE)	Returns current position where the readdir function can read from a directory handle
tie(VARIABLE, PACKAGENAME,LIST)	Associates a variable to a package that implements the variable

(continued)

TABLE 9-3 A quick reference guide to Perl functions *(continued)*

Function call	Description
`time`	Returns the number of seconds since 00:00:00 GMT 1/1/1970
`times`	Returns time in seconds for this process
`tr/SEARCHLIST/ REPLACE_LIST/cds`	Translates search list into replacement list
`truncate(FILEHANDLE, LENGTH)`	Truncates the file `FILEHANDLE` to a specified `LENGTH`
`uc(EXPR)`	Returns uppercase version of `EXPR`
`ucfirst(EXPR)`	Returns `EXPR` after changing the first character to uppercase
`umask(EXPR)`	Sets the permission mask to be used when creating a file (this specifies what operations are not allowed on the file)
`undef(EXPR)`	Undefines `EXPR`
`unlink(LIST)`	Deletes a list of files
`unpack(TEMPLATE,EXPR)`	Unpacks a string into an array and returns the array
`unshift(ARRAY,LIST)`	Adds `LIST` to the beginning of `ARRAY`
`untie(VARIABLE)`	Breaks the binding between a variable and a package
`use(MODULE)`	Starts using a Perl module
`utime(LIST)`	Changes the access and modification time of a list of files
`values(ASSOC_ARRAY)`	Returns an array containing all values from an associative array
`vec(EXPR,OFFSET,BITS)`	Treats the string `EXPR` as a vector of integers and returns a specified element of the vector
`wait`	Waits for any of the child processes to terminate
`waitpid(PID,FLAGS)`	Waits for a specific child process (identified by `PID`) to terminate
`wantarray`	Returns TRUE if the current subroutine has been called in an array context
`warn(LIST)`	Produces a warning message (specified by `LIST`) on the standard error file (the screen)

Function call	Description
write(FILEHANDLE)	Writes a formatted record to a file
y/SEARCHLIST/REPLACE_LIST/cds	Translates search list into replacement list

Summary

Perl includes a large assortment of built-in functions. These are subroutines that are already defined when your program begins running. These functions are also referred to as Perl functions. These functions provide a wide variety of capabilities that can be very useful in your Perl programs. Although you may not be able to learn about all the functions right away, it's important to know the categories of functions that Perl provides.

This chapter provides an overview of Perl's built-in functions and shows you how to use some of them. Many of the functions are described in detail elsewhere in the book. Here, you primarily learn about the important groups of functions.

As a bonus, you get a quick reference guide to all the Perl functions. You can consult this quick reference table when you want to find summary information about a specific function.

The next chapter shows you how to access and use files and directories from a Perl program.

WORKING WITH FILES AND DIRECTORIES

10

IN THIS CHAPTER YOU LEARN THESE KEY SKILLS

Computer systems use files and directories to store information. Your Perl programs often must access and use such information, which means the Perl program needs to read data from a file or write data to a file. For example, a Web page that accepts reader feedback might use a CGI (described in Chapter 14) program that saves the comments in a text file. If you write the CGI program in Perl, you have to open the file, store the comments, and close the file from that Perl program.

This chapter shows you how to work with files and directories. A *directory* is a special file that contains information about files in that directory. Perl provides built-in functions to work with files as well as directories.

To use files and directories, you need to understand the concept of a hierarchical file system. You also need to understand the file-naming conventions, which differ from one operating system to another. This chapter provides an overview of a file system and describes the file-naming conventions for UNIX and MS-DOS (Windows NT and Windows 95 filenames are based on MS-DOS conventions).

Understanding Files and Directories

The files and directories in your PC or UNIX workstation are for storing information in an organized manner, just like paper filing systems. When you store information on paper, you typically put several pages in a folder and then save the folder in a file cabinet. If you have many folders, you probably have some sort of filing system. For instance, you might label each folder's tab and then arrange them alphabetically in the file cabinet. In all likelihood, you probably have several file cabinets, each with lots of drawers, which, in turn, contain folders full of pages.

Operating systems such as UNIX, Windows 95, and Windows NT organize information in your computer in a manner similar to your paper filing system. Each of these operating systems uses a *file system* to organize all information in your computer. Of course, unlike your filing cabinet, the storage medium is not paper. Instead, modern operating systems store information on devices such as a hard disk drive, floppy disk drives, and a CD-ROM drive.

To draw an analogy between your computer's file system and a paper filing system, you might think of a disk drive as the file cabinet. The drawers in the file cabinet correspond to the directories in the file system. The folders in each drawer are also directories — because a directory in a computer file system can contain other directories. You can think of the pages inside a folder as files. The file is where the actual information is stored. Figure 10-1 illustrates the analogy between a file cabinet and the computer's file system.

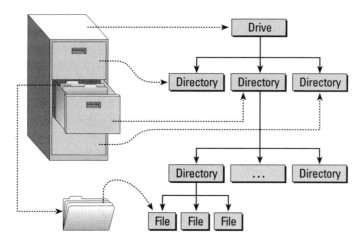

Figure 10-1 Similarities between a file cabinet and a computer's file system

As Figure 10-1 shows, a computer file system has a *hierarchical structure* with individual files stored in directories. A directory, in turn, can contain other directories, which is why the file system is called hierarchical.

To access a file in a computer file system, you need to know how files and directories are named. The naming convention depends on the operating system. Windows 95 and Windows NT filenames are based on conventions that were originally used in MS-DOS (although Windows NT and Windows 95 provide for longer file names than MS-DOS does). UNIX, on the other hand, provides a single unified file system in which various hard drives appear as directories in the file system.

MS-DOS naming conventions

Windows 95 and Windows NT filenames are based on the MS-DOS file-naming conventions, which view a file system in terms of the following three key components:

* *Drives* are the physical devices that hold all information. Some examples of drives are the hard disk, floppy disks, and the CD-ROM drive.
* *Directories* are special files that contain other directories or files.
* *Files* contain the actual information — a Perl program or a text file with data.

MS-DOS identifies each drive by a single letter, such as A, B, C, and so on. The convention is to put a colon after the drive letter. Thus, for example, you see references to the A: drive and C: drive.

As far as the name goes, MS-DOS does not distinguish between directories and files; both have similar naming conventions. This makes sense, because a directory is a special file — one that contains names of other files and directories. For files and directories, MS-DOS uses the so-called 8.3 naming convention. A directory or filename has two parts:

* A *name* with up to eight characters; the name can have any alphanumeric characters, but you cannot have any spaces
* An *extension* with up to three characters

The term *8.3 filename* comes from the use of an eight-character name and a three-character extension in MS-DOS. Some well-known examples of 8.3 MS-DOS filenames are AUTOEXEC.BAT, CONFIG.SYS, COMMAND.COM, and WIN.INI.

Although a directory can have both a name and an extension — like a file — directory names typically do not have any extension. Some examples of directory names are WINDOWS, PERL5, DOS, and TEMP.

To locate a file, you need more than just the file's name; you also need information about the drive and the directory hierarchy. The term *path name* refers to the complete specification necessary to locate a file — the drive letter, then the hierarchy of directories leading to the file, and finally, the filename. Figure 10-2 shows a typical MS-DOS path name for a file.

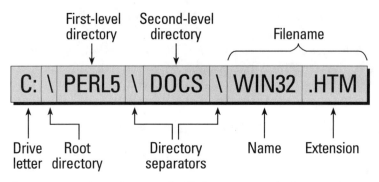

Figure 10-2   The path name of a file in MS-DOS and Windows 95

As you can see, an MS-DOS path name consists of the following sequence of components:

1. A drive letter followed by a colon

2. The root directory, indicated by a backslash (\) character

3. The directory hierarchy, with each directory name separated from the preceding one by a backslash (\) character; a \ appears after the last directory name

4. The filename with a name (up to eight characters) and an optional extension (up to three characters)

This provides enough information to uniquely identify a file in the file system.

NOTE One significant improvement in Windows 95 and Windows NT is the support for longer filenames than in MS-DOS. Windows 95 and Windows NT may have file and directory names up to 255 characters long — and you can have embedded spaces and punctuation in the name. Windows 95 and Windows NT, however, continue to support the MS-DOS 8.3 naming convention, even for files with long filenames. For each file with a long filename, Windows 95 provides an MS-DOS compatible 8.3 name as an alias. For example, for the long filename of the Windows 95 screen saver "Leonardo da Vinci.scr", Windows 95 generates the 8.3 alias LEONAR~1.SCR. Notice that the 8.3 alias uses the first few letters of the long filename, converted to uppercase, and adds a tilde character followed by a number. That is the general pattern of the 8.3 alias for a long filename in Windows 95 and Windows NT.

NOTE When you specify an MS-DOS path name in a Perl program, you have to add an extra backslash prefix for each backslash in the path name. For example, when you want to open the C:\PERL5\DOCS\WIN32.HTM, you have to specify the path name as follows:

```
open(FILEHANDLE, "C:\\PERL5\\DOCS\\WIN32.HTM");
```

where *FILEHANDLE* is the filehandle that will be associated with the open file. Note that each backslash in the path name becomes a pair of backslashes when used in the quoted string. The reason is that Perl associates special meaning to the backslash character — you need a *pair* of backslashes to tell Perl that you really want a backslash character without any special meaning. By the way, in your Perl program, when you refer to files with long Windows 95 filenames, you can use the truncated MS-DOS filename.

UNIX naming conventions

The UNIX file system provides a unified model of all storage in the system. The file system has a single root, indicated by a forward slash (/). Then there is a hierarchy of files and directories. Parts of the file system can be in different physical drives. Figure 10-3 illustrates the concept of the UNIX file system and how it spans multiple physical drives.

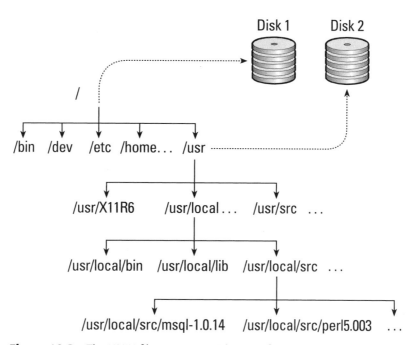

Figure 10-3 The UNIX file system provides a unified view of storage that may span multiple drives.

If you are familiar with MS-DOS or Windows 95 and Windows NT, you'll note that there is no concept of a drive letter in UNIX. Also, filenames do not have a strict 8.3 name-extension format. In UNIX, you can have long filenames, and filenames are case-sensitive. Often, UNIX filenames have multiple extensions, such as `sample.tar.Z`. Here are some examples of UNIX filenames:

```
index.html, Makefile, AnyDBM_File.pm, apache_1.0.3.tar.gz, httpd_src.tar.
gz, libwww_2.17_src.tar.Z.
```

As discussed in the "MS-DOS naming conventions" section, you need a path name — the complete hierarchy of directories leading to the file — to locate a file in the UNIX file system. Figure 10-4 illustrates a typical UNIX path name.

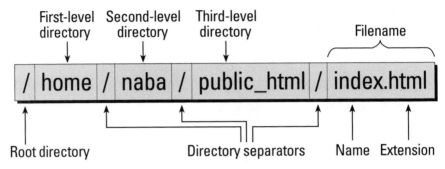

Figure 10-4 A typical UNIX path name

A UNIX path name consists of the following parts:

1. The root directory, indicated by a forward slash (/) character

2. The directory hierarchy, with each directory name separated from the preceding one by a forward slash (/) character. A / appears after the last directory name.

3. The filename, with a name and an optional extension

Opening and Closing Files

Whether you read from a file or write to a file, the first step is to open the file. After completing various input/output operations, the final step is to close the file. You have to use the open and close functions for these tasks. To open a file, you need to specify the filename — that's why the previous sections of this chapter discuss filenames in detail.

The overall sequence of a Perl program that performs some file input/output operations is as follows:

```
# Open the file
open(FILEHANDLE, "filename");
# Perform read/write operations using FILEHANDLE
# ...

# Close the file
close FILEHANDLE;
```

The `open` function opens the file and associates the identifier *FILEHANDLE* with the open file. From then on, you can use *FILEHANDLE* in various input and output operations. For example, you can read text data from the file with the angle bracket (*<FILEHANDLE>*) operator and use the `print` function to write data to the file.

Closing the file is straightforward and always involves calling the `close` function as follows:

```
close FILEHANDLE;
```

NOTE The `open` function, on the other hand, accepts several different forms of the filename argument. You have to use the right form of the filename for the specific operations you want to perform on that file.

Using the `open` function

You use the `open` function to open a file for input/output operations. As Figure 10-5 illustrates, the `open` function opens a file specified by a name and associates a filehandle with that file.

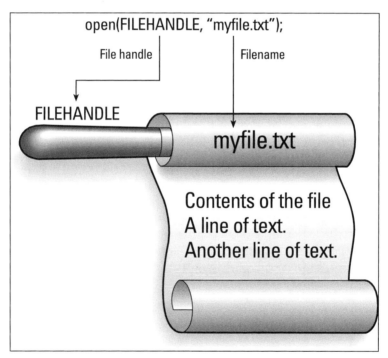

open(FILEHANDLE, "myfile.txt");

File handle   Filename

FILEHANDLE

myfile.txt

Contents of the file
A line of text.
Another line of text.

Figure 10-5 The `open` function opens a file for input/output operations.

You can call the `open` function with the following syntax:

```
open(FILEHANDLE, "filename");
```

The first argument is an identifier, called a *filehandle*, that you want to associate with the file after it has been opened. Perl programmers typically use all capital letters for filehandles. However, you can use any name you want for a filehandle.

The second argument is the filename, which may be a scalar variable or a double-quoted string. As you will see in the next few sections, special characters at the beginning or end of the filename add special meaning to what the `open` function does.

When you use a filename such as `data.txt`, the Perl interpreter expects that file to be in the current directory (typically, the directory from which you ran your Perl program). However, you can always specify a path name that uniquely identifies a file somewhere in your computer's file system. The path name syntax depends on your operating system. For example, to open the `/etc/passwd` file in UNIX, you write:

```
open(PASSWD, "/etc/passwd");
```

On the other hand, to open the `c:\perl5\lib\ole.pm` file in Windows 95, you have to write:

```
open(OLE_PM, "c:\\perl5\\lib\\ole.pm");
```

Note that you must add an extra backslash in front of each backslash in the Windows 95 path name.

TIP **When you use the `open` function, you should always check whether the open function succeeded before you use other Perl functions to perform input or output operations on the file. A common technique is to use a logical OR (denoted by `||`) and combine the `open` function call with a call to the `die` function, as follows:**

```
open(FILEHANDLE, "filename") ||
die "Error opening file!";
```

If the `open` function succeeds, it returns true and the `die` function is never called (because the logical OR of true with anything else is going to be true anyway). When `open` fails, the `die` function is called and it exits the program with an error message. You can accomplish the same objective by using the `unless` keyword, as follows:

```
die "Error opening file!" unless
open(FILEHANDLE, "filename");
```

This works exactly as it sounds: "die unless open succeeds" — that means the program quits with an error message unless the `open` function returns true (meaning that the file opened successfully).

TIP If you add a newline in the message passed to the die function, die only prints the message and exits. If the text does not have a newline, however, die prints the message and adds some more useful information, such as the name of the Perl program and the line number where the error occurred. Because the extra information is helpful, I usually leave the newline out of the error message passed to die.

TIP If you do not want to quit the program when open fails, you can simply check the return value of the open function call and perform some tasks, such as reading from the file, only if the return value is true. In other words, use an if statement like this:

```
if(open(FILEHANDLE, "filename"))
{
# Open succeeded. Perform read/write operations
# ...

# Close file
   close FILEHANDLE;
}
```

Opening a file for input only

When you open a file with the following form of the open function:

```
open(FILEHANDLE, "filename");
```

the open function expects an existing file with the specified filename, and it opens that file for reading only. If the specified file does not already exist, the open function fails and returns false.

After opening a file this way, you can use the filehandle to read from the file with the angle operator (<FILEHANDLE>) or one of the read functions, such as read or sysread.

As you see in the next few sections, you use a special character prefix (sometimes a two-character prefix) to indicate what you want to do with the file after it's open. If you do not use any prefix character, the open function opens the file for reading. However, you can also add a < prefix to explicitly indicate that you want to open the file for reading, as follows:

```
open(PASSWD, "</etc/passwd"); # Open for reading
```

The prefix is more important when you want to open a file for writing (or both reading and writing).

Opening a file for output only

What if you want to create a new file to store data? For that, you must call the `open` function with the filename in a special format. To create a new file and write output to that file, use a > prefix in the filename, as follows:

```
# Open file for output. Create new file if needed.
# Destroy content of existing file.
if(open(DATA, ">current.dat"))
{
# File successfully opened for writing
# Now you can write to file
   print DATA "A line of text\n";
# ...
# Close file when done
   close DATA;
}
```

When you use a > prefix, the `open` function:

* Creates the file, if it does not already exist
* Deletes everything in the file, if it already exists

NOTE **Often you want to keep adding new information to a file. For example, if you are saving user feedback in a file, you'll want to keep appending new comments to that file. To open a file for appending, use >> as the prefix — that's two greater-than signs — as follows:**

```
# Open the feedback.txt file for appending
open(COMMENTS, ">feedback.txt");
```

In this case, the `open` function creates the file if it does not already exist. If the file exists, however, the `open` function opens the file and any output to the file is appended to the file. In other words, anything you write to the file is added at the end of the file.

Reading from and Writing to a File

You may not have thought about this until now, but there are two types of data files:

* *Text files* contain data that's organized into lines of characters. The characters are printable characters — alphanumeric characters and punctuation marks. Some examples of text files are Perl programs,

World Wide Web documents in HTML, and many system configuration files in UNIX and Windows.

* *Binary files* contain data that does not have lines ending with the newline character, nor does the data consist of printable characters only. You can think of the data as a sequence of "characters" (each occupying a byte), but the characters can have any value from 0 through 255 (the maximum value that can be held in a byte). Examples of binary files include GIF (Graphics Interchange Format) images used in HTML documents, executable programs, spreadsheets, word processor documents, and so on.

So far, you have primarily seen how to read and write text files. Later in this section, you learn how to read and write binary files.

Reading and writing text files

Text files store information as lines of text. The characters are printable characters such as alphanumeric characters and punctuation marks. Each line of text ends with one or more characters that mark the end of a line. The exact end-of-line indicator depends on the operating system:

* In UNIX, each line of text ends with a single newline character. A newline character is a line feed, which has an ASCII code of 10 (expressed in decimal). In Perl strings, the newline character is denoted by \n.

* In MS-DOS (as well as in Windows 95 and Windows NT), text files use a "carriage return-line feed" pair (commonly denoted as CR-LF) to mark the end of a line of text. The CR-LF pair is denoted by the sequence \r\n in Perl (\r is the carriage return character — ASCII 13 in decimal notation).

X-REF In Chapter 5, you have seen examples of how to read lines of text from a file as well as how to write text output to a file. Although Chapter 5 discusses how to read from standard input and write to standard output, the techniques apply equally well to any filehandle. For example, to read a line of text from an open file, you write the following:

```
$line = <FILEHANDLE>; # Read a line of text
```

where FILEHANDLE is the filehandle you used when you opened the file by calling open.

To write a line of text to the file, you can simply use the print function with FILEHANDLE as the first argument, followed by a list of other scalar variables or quoted strings, as shown here:

```
print FILEHANDLE "The result is: ", $result, "\n";
```

Reading and writing binary files

You read and write binary data in chunks — bigger chunks than the typical line of text, which contains around 80 characters. The functions for binary read and write are as follows:

* The read and sysread functions read a specified number of bytes from a file. You should not mix calls to read and sysread. (The read function is similar to the fread function in the C run-time library, whereas sysread is an operating-system-level function.)
* The syswrite function writes a specified number of bytes to a file.

 Note that there is a write function, but that function is not the counterpart of read. Instead, the write function is for writing formatted reports. Chapter 13 shows you how to use the write function.

The syntax of the read and sysread functions are as follows:

```
$bytes_read = read(FILEHANDLE, $buffer,
                   $length, $offset);
$bytes_read = sysread(FILEHANDLE, $buffer,
                      $length, $offset);
```

As you can see, the syntax is identical, even the arguments and return values have the same meaning:

* FILEHANDLE is the filehandle of an open file from which you want to read data.
* $buffer is the string into which data is to be read.
* $length is an integer value that specifies how many bytes of data are to be read from FILEHANDLE.
* $offset is an integer value that specifies where in the $buffer variable to put the bytes (thus, you can read into the middle of a string). You can omit the $offset, if you want to put data at the beginning of $buffer.
* $bytes_read will be the number of bytes actually read from FILEHANDLE.

The syswrite function has a syntax similar to that of sysread (and read):

```
$bytes_written = sysread(FILEHANDLE, $buffer,
                         $length, $offset);
```

This function writes $length bytes from the string $buffer to FILEHANDLE (which must refer to a file that has been opened for writing). Use the $offset variable if you want to begin writing from somewhere other than the beginning of the $buffer string.

Binary mode file access in MS-DOS

NOTE In MS-DOS (and in Windows 95 and Windows NT which also use MS-DOS file conventions), you must also specify the binary mode of file access before reading binary data. By default, MS-DOS accesses files in text mode. In text mode access, each CR-LF pair is translated into a single line feed (LF) character. This approach provides compatibility with operating systems, such as UNIX, that use only one character to mark the end of a line of text. You must set the file access mode to binary before reading or writing binary data in MS-DOS; otherwise, any CR-LF pair is translated to an LF, which ruins the binary data. To set the file access mode to binary, call the `binmode` function as follows:

```
binmode(FILEHANDLE);
```

where `FILEHANDLE` is the filehandle of an open file. The `binmode` function has no effect on UNIX. Because it's required in MS-DOS, you can include a call to `binmode` in any program that performs binary read/write operations.

An example of binary read/write

A Web page written to display a different image depending on the season could use the binary read and write functions. For instance, when a new year approaches, the image might depict a "Happy New Year" theme. To get this effect, you might replace the image filename with a CGI script written in Perl that checks the current date and sends back an appropriate GIF image.

The logic might be as follows:

1. Get today's date.

2. If date is in winter season, write a winter GIF image to STDOUT.

3. If date is in spring season, write the spring GIF image to STDOUT.

4. If the date is around New Year's Day, send New Year's GIF image to STDOUT and so on.

Anyway, you get the idea. The part that needs the binary read and write capability is when a GIF image file is selected and written to STDOUT. Here's the block of code that implements this capability:

```
# Assume that the image file's name is in $imagefile
unless(open(IMAGE, "$imagefile"))
{
    exit(0);
}
```

```
# Change access mode to binary (needed in Windows)
binmode IMAGE;

# Send back a response header (required by HTTP)
print "Content-type: image/gif\n\n";

# Read binary data from image file and
# write it to STDOUT
while($len = sysread(IMAGE, $buf, 8192))
{
    syswrite(STDOUT, $buf, $len);
}
close IMAGE;
exit(0);
```

Here are the significant steps in this program:

* An open for the image file whose name is assumed to be in the `$imagefile` variable

* A change of the access mode to binary by calling `binmode`

* A `print` statement to send back a header that indicates that a GIF image is about to follow

* A `while` loop to read the image data in 8,192 byte chunks and write it to STDOUT; the read operation calls `sysread` and reads the image data into the `$buf` variable, the `$len` variable holds the actual number of bytes read, then the `syswrite` function writes `$len` bytes of data from `$buf` to STDOUT.

Working with Directories

D irectories are special files that contain information about other directories and files. Perl provides several functions to access and use information in a directory. As with ordinary files, some of the tasks you might perform on a directory are the following:

* Open a directory (use the `opendir` function).
* Read its contents (use the `readdir` function).
* Go back to the beginning of the directory (use the `rewinddir` function).
* Close a directory when you are finished (use the `closedir` function).

Just as you initialize a filehandle when you open a file, so you set up a directory handle when you open a directory. The only difference is that you call the `opendir` function when you want to open a directory, as shown here:

```
opendir(DIRHANDLE, "dirname") ||
    die("Cannot open directory!");
```

where *dirname* is the name of the directory and *DIRHANDLE* is the directory handle that you can use later on to read the contents of the directory. The use of the logical OR with the die function is the conventional way of quitting the program if the opendir function fails.

When you no longer need the directory, call closedir to close the directory, as follows:

```
closedir(DIRHANDLE);
```

Sometimes, you may need to go back to the beginning of the directory after you have read some of the entries. To do so, you have to call the rewinddir function as follows:

```
rewindir(DIRHANDLE);
```

Listing all files in a directory

After the directory is open, you can read its contents by using the readdir function. The contents of the directory is a list of the files in that directory. You can read the directory entries in two ways:

* Read each entry into a scalar variable one at a time, calling readdir repeatedly to go through all the entries.
* Read all the directory entries into an array with a single call to the readdir function.

To read the directory entries one at a time, use a while loop and assign the readdir function to a scalar variable, as follows:

```
while($file = readdir(DIRHANDLE))
{
    print "$file\n";
}
```

This while loop prints the list of files in the directory identified by *DIRHANDLE*.

To read all the directory entries into an array, call the readdir function in an array context by assigning the return value to an array, like this:

```
@filelist = readdir(DIRHANDLE);
```

After the readdir function returns, the @filelist array will contain a list of all files in the directory identified by *DIRHANDLE*.

If you read all the directory entries into an array, you can, for example, sort it and then print it. Here is a program that does just that:

```
# File: dirlist.pl
```

```
# Print sorted list of all files in
# the current directory

# Open the current directory
opendir(CURDIR, ".") ||
die("Cannot open directory!");

# Read the contents of the directory into an array
@files = readdir(CURDIR);

# Sort the list of files
@sorted_files = sort(@files);

# Print the sorted list

print "Current directory contains:\n\n";

for $file(@sorted_files)
{
  print "$file\n";
}

# Close the directory
closedir(CURDIR);
```

On a Web server, you might use a similar Perl script as a CGI program that generates a list of a directory's contents on the fly. You can use the `opendir` function to open a directory, call `readdir` to read the file list into an array, and then create an HTML document with appropriate icons for the selected files.

Listing directory contents with `glob`

Another, easier way to get a listing of all files in a directory is to use the `glob` function. Although the name sounds a bit strange, the `glob` function is quite useful for expanding wildcards in filenames.

The `glob` function expands a filename with a wildcard (such as `*.pl`) into a list of all files that match the wildcard.

Suppose that you want to list all files with names ending in `.pl`. You can do so with the following Perl script:

```
@names = glob("*.pl");
print "@names";
```

Note that the `glob` function works with wildcards, not regular expressions. When it comes to expanding wildcards, the behavior of the `glob` function is similar to that of the UNIX shell or MS-DOS command processor.

Creating, removing, and changing directories

In addition to accessing a directory to obtain a list of files in that directory, Perl includes functions for performing some other common actions on directories:

* Create a new directory by using the `mkdir` function.
* Remove a directory by using the `rmdir` function.
* Change the current directory using the `chdir` function.

The `mkdir`, `rmdir`, and `chdir` commands originated in UNIX. They are also supported in MS-DOS. Perl provides functions with the same names so that you can accomplish these tasks from within your Perl script.

These directory functions are straightforward to use. For example, on a Windows system, you can change to the `\windows` directory with the following statement:

```
chdir "\\windows";
```

Note, again, that you need to put two backslashes for each backslash in the directory name. On a UNIX system, you have to use a directory name syntax appropriate for UNIX (such as `/etc`).

To create a directory named `temp` that anyone can access for reading, but only you can read and write, call `mkdir` as follows:

```
mkdir("temp", 644);
```

That 644 denotes the read, write, and execute permissions of the directory. This is a feature of how UNIX controls access to files; this is not applicable to Windows 95 or Windows NT.

To remove a directory, call the `rmdir` function with a directory name as argument. If the directory contains any files, the `rmdir` function does not remove the directory.

BONUS

Testing Files and Directories

Sometimes, you need to check whether a file or directory exists before you try to access it. Even when a file exists, you may want to see whether the file can be read, written to, or executed. Perl includes a handy set of file test operators to test files and directories.

These file test operators have a syntax borrowed from UNIX shell programming. Suppose that you want to test whether a file named config.dat exists. Here is how you can use the -e operator to test for that file's existence:

```
if(-e "config.dat")
{
    print "File exists.\n";
}
```

All the other file and directory test operators have similar syntax. Each operator is denoted by a single letter with a dash (-) prefix. To test a file or a directory, you use the operator with an if statement, as follows:

```
if(-O $name)
{
# Test succeeded...
}
```

where O represents the operator and $name is the name of the file or directory. Table 10-1 lists some of the useful file test operators in Perl.

TABLE 10-1   Some useful file test operators

Operator	Returns
-r $filename	True if file is readable.
-w $filename	True if file is writable.
-x $filename	True if file is executable.
-e $filename	True if file exists.
-z $filename	True if file has zero size.
-s $filename	True if file has nonzero size (returns size).

Operator	Returns
-f $filename	True if file is a plain file.
-d $filename	True if file is a directory.
-l $filename	True if file is a symbolic link (applies to UNIX). (A *symbolic link* is a file that refers to another file.)
-p $filename	True if file is a named pipe (first-in first-out buffer).
-S $filename	True if file is a socket.
-T $filename	True if file is a text file.
-B $filename	True if file is a binary file (opposite of -T).

There are a few other file operators that are useful for finding out how old a file is and how long ago a file was accessed. You can use the -M operator to get the number of days (including fractional days) since the file was last modified, as follows:

```
$days_old = -M $filename;
```

After this statement executes, the $days_old contains the number of days (including fractional days) since the file was last modified. You can use this operator to test whether a file is too old (or not old enough to throw away):

```
if(-M $filename > 0.5)
{
# File is older than 12 hours.
# Purge it...
}
```

The -A operator, on the other hand, returns the days since the file was last accessed. Suppose that you want to archive files that have not been accessed in the last 90 days. You can perform this test as follows:

```
if(-A $filename > 90)
{
# File last accessed over 90 days ago
# User does not need file. Archive it!
# ...
}
```

Summary

Because computers store information in files that are organized into directories, you often have to access and use files from your Perl programs. You have to understand the hierarchical organization of the directories and the way files and directories are named. Then you have to learn to use Perl's file and directory manipulation functions.

This chapter introduces you to the basic concepts of files and directories. You learn the naming conventions used by Windows and UNIX. You also learn to use functions such as `open`, `close`, `sysread`, and `syswrite` to read from and write to files.

As a bonus, you learn about a number of special operators that can come in handy when you have to test whether a file exists or find out the last time a file was accessed.

The next chapter provides you with an overview of the new features of Perl 5. The focus is on two useful features — references and Perl modules — that enable you to use objects in your Perl programs.

LEARNING THE NEW FEATURES OF PERL 5

IN THIS CHAPTER YOU LEARN THESE KEY SKILLS

T he previous chapters do not make much mention of Perl 5, the latest version of Perl. That's because what you have learned about Perl programming applies equally well to both Perl 4, the older version of Perl, and Perl 5, the newest version. Although the basic features of Perl did not change in going from Perl 4 to Perl 5, several key features were added to Perl 5 to make it even more powerful.

This chapter provides a gentle introduction to the new Perl 5 features. In particular, the new reference variable enables you to create useful data structures. Reference also supports object-oriented programming. Modules are another useful addition in Perl 5. You'll learn about references and see how Perl supports object-oriented programming through its modules.

NOTE You do not have to learn how to write new Perl modules, but you should know how to use existing Perl modules. For example, a module named CGI.pm is commonly used in Perl CGI programs. To use CGI.pm, you need to know how to create an object in Perl and invoke methods that operate on the object. This chapter teaches you how to create and use existing Perl 5 modules. Because modules implement objects in Perl 5, you also learn how to use objects in your Perl programs.

Understanding References

In Perl 4, you have no way of creating a variable that refers to another variable. Sometimes, however, it's convenient to have a variable that simply points to another variable. This helps you create useful data structures, such as a linked list. Figure 11-1 illustrates how a linked list needs a variable that points to the next item in the link.

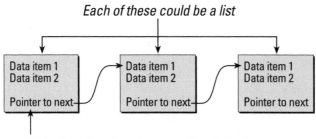

Each of these could be a list

This variable has to refer to another list

Figure 11-1   Linked lists need a reference variable type.

As Figure 11-1 shows, a linked list consists of a number of data structures, where each structure has a link to the next structure. For example, in a Perl program, the structure may be a simple list of scalar variables (think of an employee structure that has fields such as name, social security number, and so forth). However, the variable that acts as the link to the next structure needs to refer to another structure. This is where you need a reference variable.

A *reference* is nothing more than a scalar value that refers to another variable. For those of you who know C or C++ programming, a reference is like a pointer in C or C++. With the introduction of the reference type, Perl 5 also adds some new syntax to initialize a reference and to access the variable that's referred to by the reference.

You probably won't have to use references in your programs, but it's useful to know the syntax of references so you can recognize them when you see them in Perl 5 programs. The following sections introduce you to references. Unfortunately, references (like pointers in C and C++) look somewhat confusing when you first encounter them.

Defining a reference

A *reference* is a scalar variable and, as described in Chapter 2, scalar variable names begin with a dollar sign ($) prefix. Therefore, a reference looks just like any other scalar variable. What's new is the way you assign a value to a reference.

The syntax for defining a reference is quite simple. Suppose that you have a scalar variable named $x; you then can initialize reference to the $x variable, as follows:

```
$x = 24.99;
$rx = \$x; # A backslash prefix indicates reference
```

In this case, $rx is a reference to the variable $x. As you can see, you can refer to a variable by adding a backslash prefix to the variable's name. Figure 11-2 illustrates the relationship between the reference and the variable it references.

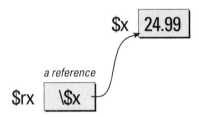

Figure 11-2 A reference to a variable

You can also access the value of $x through the reference $rx. This is known as *dereferencing*. Use the following syntax for this:

```
$y = $$rx;
```

This statement sets $y to the value of the variable being referred to by $rx. Thus, you can dereference a reference variable by adding an extra $ prefix to the reference variable's name.

Understanding various reference types

From Chapter 2, you know that there are three types of variables: scalar, array, and associative array (also called *hash*). You can have a reference to any of these variables. Here is how you define these references and dereference them:

✴ To refer to a variable, add a backslash prefix to the variable's name. Here are some examples of references to different types of variables:

```
$r_scalar = \$scalar;
$r_array = \@array;
$r_hash = \%hash;
```

✴ To dereference a reference variable, add the prefix corresponding to the variable type. Here are some examples of dereferencing:

```
$x = $$r_scalar;
@y = @{$r_array};
%z = %{r_hash};
```

In addition to these three reference types, you can have two more types of references:

* Reference to a subroutine (or a built-in function)
* Reference to another reference

To define a reference to a subroutine, you follow a syntax that's similar to the way you define a reference to any other variable. Here is a reference to a subroutine named process_data:

```
$rproc = \&process_data;
```

To call this function through the reference, use the ampersand notation of the function call as follows:

```
# Call the process_data function with "test" as argument
  &{$rproc}("test");
```

A reference to a reference looks just like a reference to a scalar variable, because a reference is a scalar variable (albeit with a special meaning):

```
$r_ref = \$ref; # Assume $ref is a reference
```

Now, if you were to write $$r_ref, you would end up with the reference $ref. You have to further dereference that variable to access the actual value. Here is a bit of code that illustrates the problem using a scalar variable:

```
$x = 100;      # a scalar
$rx = \$x;     # $rx is a reference to a scalar
$rrx = \$rx;   # Now $rrx is a reference to $rx
# Access the value of $x
$value = $$$rrx;
```

Figure 11-3 illustrates the relationship between the variables $x, $rx, and $rrx.

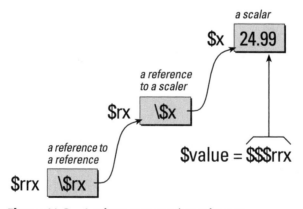

Figure 11-3 A reference to another reference

Here $x is a scalar variable; $rx is a reference to $x, and $rrx, in turn, is a reference to $rx. To dereference $rrx, you have to use two $ prefixes, because $rrx is a reference that refers to another reference.

To summarize, in Perl 5, you can define the following five types of reference variables:

* Reference to a scalar
* Reference to an array
* Reference to an associative array (also called a hash)
* Reference to a subroutine
* Reference to another reference

Using the arrow operator to dereference

When you see objects used in Perl 5 programs, you'll see the use of the arrow operator, written as -> (a minus sign followed by the greater-than sign). For example, a popular Perl module called CGI.pm implements a CGI object that you can use to parse user inputs received through Web forms and to create new Web pages. When the CGI object is used, you'll see Perl statements such as the following:

```
use CGI;          # Required to use the CGI.pm module
$form = new CGI;  # create a CGI object
print $form->header;  # call the "header" method
```

That new CGI statement calls the CGI.pm module's new subroutine, which returns a reference to a new CGI object. From then on, you can call subroutines of the object by using the arrow operator with the object reference.

The arrow operator is actually a way to dereference a reference to an array or a hash. Perl 5 implements objects as a reference to a hash; that's why you use the arrow operator to call a subroutine in an object.

The following example shows how you might use the arrow operator to call subroutines in a hash through a reference:

```
#!/usr/local/bin/perl -w
# Calling subroutines via hash reference

# Define some subroutines
sub start
{
  print "Starting\n";
}
sub run
{
```

```
   print "Running: @_\n";
}
sub stop
{
   print "Stopping\n";
}

# Define a hash with subroutine references
%SUBS = ( 'Start' => \&start,
          'Run'   => \&run,
          'Stop'  => \&stop);

# Define a reference to the %SUBS hash
$Object = \%SUBS;

# Now call subroutines via the hash reference
&{$Object->{Start}};
&{$Object->{Run}}("This", "and", "That");
&{$Object->{Stop}};
```

Run this program. It should generate the following:

```
Starting
Running: This and That
Stopping
```

If you look at the subroutines start, run, and stop in the example program, you'll see that this output is the result of calling those subroutines — it's just that the subroutine calls are not that obvious, because they are called via references. Here is how you should interpret the program:

* The program begins with the definition of three subroutines — start, run, and stop — that simply print specific text messages.

* Then it defines a hash (associative array) named %SUBS that associates text labels with references to the subroutines, as follows:

```
%SUBS = ( 'Start' => \&start,
          'Run'   => \&run,
          'Stop'  => \&stop);
```

   Thus, you can get a reference to the start subroutine by writing $SUBS{Start}, and you can call the subroutine with the syntax &{$SUBS{Start}}.

* To show you how to use the arrow operator to access a hash reference, I defined a reference to %SUBS as follows (I called it $Object, because a Perl object is a reference to a hash):

```
$Object = \%SUBS;
```

✳ After the hash reference, `$Object`, is defined, it is used to access the subroutines by name and call them. For example, the call to the `start` subroutine is as follows:

```
&{$Object->{Start}};
```

To interpret this expression, first focus on `$Object->{Start}`. Here, the arrow (`->`) operator dereferences `$Object` (remember, it's a reference to the hash `%SUBS`) and accesses the item associated with the `Start` key. The item accessed by `$Object->{Start}` happens to be the reference to the `start` subroutine, which is called by adding an ampersand prefix.

If a subroutine needs arguments, you can append the argument list, as follows:

```
&{$Object->{Run}}("This", "and", "That");
```

For object-oriented programming, Perl 5 provides a few additional features that result in a simpler syntax for using subroutines defined in an object. In addition to use of references, Perl objects rely on modules, which are basically collections of subroutines and variables.

Understanding Perl Packages and Modules

A Perl package is a way to group together data and subroutines. Essentially, it's a way to use variable and subroutine names without conflicting with any names used in other parts of a program. The concept of a package existed in Perl 4.

The package provides a way to control the *namespace* — the collection of variable and subroutine names. Even though you may not be aware of this, when you write a Perl program, it automatically belongs to a package named `main`. Besides `main`, there are other Perl packages in the Perl library (that's in the `lib` subdirectory of the Perl 5 installation directory), and you can define your own package as well.

Perl modules, as you'll learn soon, are packages that follow some specific guidelines.

Perl packages

You can think of a Perl package as a convenient way to organize a set of related Perl subroutines. Another benefit is that variable and subroutine names defined in a package do not conflict with names used elsewhere in the program. Thus, a variable named `$count` in one package remains unique to that package and does not conflict with a `$count` variable name used elsewhere in a Perl program.

A Perl package is in a single file. The `package` statement is used at the beginning of the file to declare the file as a package and to give a package name. For example, the file `timelocal.pl` defines a number of subroutines and variables in a package named `timelocal`. The `timelocal.pl` file has the following package statement in various places:

```
package timelocal;
```

The effect of this package declaration is that all subsequent variable and subroutine names are considered to be in the `timelocal` package. You can put such a `package` statement at the very beginning of the file that implements the package.

What if you are implementing a package and you need to refer to a subroutine or variable in another package? As you might guess, all you need to do is specify both the package name and the variable (or subroutine) name. Perl 5 provides the following syntax for referring to a variable in another package:

```
$Package::Variable
```

where *Package* is the name of the package and *Variable* is the name of the variable in that package. If you omit the package name, Perl assumes that you are referring to a variable in the `main` package.

NOTE In Perl 4, you refer to a variable in another package with the `$Package'Variable` syntax — that's a single quote between the package name and the variable name. The double colon syntax (`$Package::Variable`) is new in Perl 5. The pair of colons are more readable than a single quote. Also, C++ happens to use a similar syntax when referring to variables in another C++ class (a class is basically a collection of data and functions — a template for an object).

To use a package in your program, you can simply call the `require` function with the package filename as an argument. For instance, there is a package named `ctime` defined in the file `ctime.pl`. That package includes the `ctime` subroutine, which converts a binary time into a string. Here is a simple program that uses the `ctime` package from the `ctime.pl` file:

```
#!/usr/local/bin/perl -w

# Use the ctime package defined in ctime.pl file
require 'ctime.pl';

# Call the ctime subroutine
$time = ctime(time());

# Print the time string
print $time;
```

As you can see, this program uses the `require` function to bring in the `ctime.pl` file into the program. When you run this program, it should print the current date and time formatted as shown in the sample output:

```
Sun Feb 16 19:06:32 1997
```

Perl modules

Perl 5 takes the concept of package one step further and introduces a *module*, which is a package that follows certain guidelines and that's designed to be reusable. Each module is a package that is defined in a file with the same name as the package, but with a `.pm` extension. Each Perl object is implemented as a module. For example, the CGI object is implemented as the CGI module, stored in the file named `CGI.pm`.

Perl 5 comes with a number of modules. You'll find these modules in the `lib` subdirectory of the Perl 5 installation directory. Thus, if on your Windows 95 system you installed Perl 5 in the `C:\PERL5` directory, the Perl modules are in the `C:\PERL5\LIB` directory. Look for files with names that end in `.PM`.

If you use a UNIX system and you have installed the Perl 5 distribution in the `/usr/local/src/perl5.003` directory, you'll find the Perl modules in the `/usr/local/src/perl5.003/lib` directory.

Using a module

You can call the `require` or the `use` function to include a Perl module in your program. For example, there is a Perl module named `Cwd` (defined, as expected, in the `Cwd.pm` file) that provides a `getcwd` subroutine that returns the current directory. You can call the `require` function to include the `Cwd` module and call `getcwd` as follows:

```
require Cwd;  # You do not need the full filename
$curdir = Cwd::getcwd();
print "Current directory = $curdir\n";
```

The first line brings the `Cwd.pm` file into this program — you do not have to specify the full filename; the `require` function automatically appends `.pm` to the module's name to figure out which file to include. The second line shows how you call a subroutine from the `Cwd` module. When you use `require` to include a module, you must invoke each subroutine with the `Module::subroutine` format.

If you run this program on a Windows 95 or Windows NT system, it prints the current directory in the following format:

```
Current directory = C:\idg\dp\perl
```

On the other hand, if you run the program on a UNIX system, the output is of the following form:

```
Current directory = /usr/local/naba/perl
```

If you rewrite this example program with the `use` function in place of `require`, it takes the following form:

```
use Cwd;
$curdir = getcwd(); # no need for Cwd:: prefix
print "Current directory = $curdir\n";
```

The most significant difference is that you no longer need to qualify a subroutine name with the module name prefix (such as `Cwd::`).

> **NOTE** You can call either `require` or `use` to include a module in your program. You need to know the following nuances when you use these functions:
>
> * When you include a module by calling `require`, the module is included only when the `require` function is invoked as the program runs. You must use the `Module::subroutine` syntax to invoke any subroutines from a module you include with the `require` function.
>
> * When you include a module by calling `use`, the module is included in the program as soon as the `use` statement is processed. Thus, you can invoke subroutines and variables from the module as if they were part of your program. You do not need to qualify subroutine and variable names with a `Module::` prefix.

> **TIP** You may want to stick to the `use Module;` syntax to include modules in your program because this lets you use a simpler syntax when you call subroutines from the module.

Using Objects in Perl 5

An *object* is a data structure together with the functions that operate on that data. Each object is an instance of a *class* that defines the type of the object. For example, a rectangle class may have as data the four corners of the rectangle and functions, such as one that computes the rectangle's area and another that draws the rectangle. Then each rectangle object can be an instance of the rectangle class with different coordinates for the four corners. It's in this sense that an object is an instance of a class.

The functions (or subroutines) that implement the operations on an object's data are known as *methods*. That's a terminology borrowed from Smalltalk, one of the earliest object-oriented programming languages.

Classes also have the notion of *inheritance.* You can define a new class of objects by extending the data or methods (or both) of an existing class. A common use of inheritance is to express the IS A relationship among various classes of objects. Consider, for example, the geometric shapes. Because a circle IS A shape and a rectangle IS A shape, you could says that the circle and rectangle classes inherit from the shape class. In this case, the shape class is called a *parent class,* or *base class.*

NOTE The basic idea behind object-oriented programming is that you can package the data and the associated methods (subroutines) of an object as a black box. Programmers access the object only through advertised methods, without having to know the inner workings of the methods. Typically, a programmer can create an object, invoke its methods to get or set *attributes* (that's another name for the object's data), and destroy the object. This section shows you how to use objects in Perl 5. With this knowledge in hand, you'll be able to exploit objects as building blocks for your Perl programs.

Understanding Perl objects

Perl 5 implements objects using modules, which package data and subroutines in a file. Perl 5 presents the following simple model of objects:

* An *object* is denoted by a reference (objects are implemented as references to a hash).
* A *class* is a Perl module that provides the methods to work with the object.
* A *method* is a Perl subroutine that expects the object reference as the first argument.

Programmers who implement objects have to follow certain rules and provide certain methods in a module that represents a class. However, you really don't need to know much about an object's implementation to use it in your Perl program. All you need to know are the steps you have to follow when you use an object.

Creating and accessing Perl objects

WEB PATH A useful Perl object is Lincoln Stein's CGI object, which is implemented by the Perl module `CGI.pm`. That module together with complete documentation is available from the following Web page:

```
http://www-genome.wi.mit.edu/ftp/pub/software/WWW/cgi_docs.html
```

X-REF You can use the `CGI.pm` module after you copy the file into the Perl library directory on your system (you learn how to find and install the `CGI.pm` module in Chapter 15).

As the name implies, the CGI object is meant for writing Common Gateway Interface applications for World Wide Web servers. A CGI program accepts queries submitted by a user and writes back an HTML document with a response (this is the document that the user sees in the Web browser).

When you create a CGI object, it automatically parses a query string submitted by the user via an HTML form (these are forms that you see on many Web pages; you can essentially fill in and submit information through these forms). The CGI object provides methods to access the parameters entered by the user on a form, creates headers needed for Web pages, and generates HTML code for the Web page that will be sent back by the CGI program.

To use the CGI object, you follow these general steps:

1. Place the following line to include the CGI module in your program:

   ```
   use CGI;
   ```

   You must include this line before you create a CGI object.

2. To create a CGI object, use the following syntax:

   ```
   $query = new CGI;
   ```

   where `$query` is the reference to the CGI object. In the case of the CGI object, creating the object automatically parses the query and sets up the internal variables of the object.

3. Invoke methods from the CGI object, as illustrated by the following examples:

   ```
   print $query->header;  // Send the HTTP header
   print $query->start_html("Title of document");
   print $query->end_html; // End HTML document
   ```

   Here `$query->header` calls the `header` method of the `$query` CGI object. Similarly, `start_html` and `end_html` are methods in the CGI object. All of these methods return strings, which is why they are used as arguments to the `print` function.

You access the object's methods by using the arrow operator and the object reference that you obtain after creating the object.

How do you know which methods to call and in what order to call them? The answer is that you have to read the object's documentation before you can use the object. The method names and the sequences of method invocation depend on what the object does.

BONUS

Using the English Module

By now you have seen that Perl includes a lot of special variables with strange names, such as $_ for the default argument and $! for the error message corresponding to the last error. When you read a program, it can be difficult to guess what a special variable means. The result is that you may end up avoiding a special variable that could be really useful in your program.

As a helpful gesture, Perl 5 provides the English module (English.pm), which enables you to use understandable names for various special variables in Perl. Simply by using the English module you can refer to the strange variables by meaningful names instead of the cryptic ones.

To make use of the English module, include the following line in your Perl program:

```
use English;
```

After that, you can refer to $_ as $ARG and $! as $ERRNO (these "English" names can still be a bit cryptic, but they're definitely better than the punctuation marks). Table 11-1 lists some important special variables and their English names.

TABLE 11-1 Some Perl special variables and their English names

Variable	English name	Description
$^A	$ACCUMULATOR	Current value of the accumulator used by the write function
$_	$ARG	Default input argument
$^T	$BASETIME	Time at which the script began running, in seconds, since 00:00:00 GMT, January 1, 1970
$?	$CHILD_ERROR	Status returned by last child process (see Chapter 12)
$^D	$DEBUGGING	Current value of Perl's debugging flags
$)	$EFFECTIVE_GROUP_ID	Effective group ID of this process (in UNIX)

(continued)

Variable	English name	Description
$>	$EFFECTIVE_USER_ID	Effective user ID of this process (in UNIX)
$!	$ERRNO	Last error number or error message
$@	$EVAL_ERROR	Perl syntax error message from the last `eval` function
$^X	$EXECUTABLE_NAME	Name of the Perl interpreter (`perl` in UNIX, something like `C:\PERL5\BIN\PERL.EXE` in Windows)
$^L	$FORMAT_FORMFEED	What formats print to perform a form feed
$:	$FORMAT_LINE_BREAK_CHARACTERS	Current set of characters, after which a string may be broken to fill continuation fields (starting with ^) in a format (default is space, newline, or hyphen)
$-	$FORMAT_LINES_LEFT	Number of lines left on the page of the current report
$=	$FORMAT_LINES_PER_PAGE	Current page length (printable lines) for reports (default is 60)
$~	$FORMAT_NAME	Name of the current report format for the currently selected output filehandle (default is name of the filehandle)
$%	$FORMAT_PAGE_NUMBER	Current page number for formatted reports
$^	$FORMAT_TOP_NAME	Name of the current top-of-page format for the currently selected output filehandle (default is name of the filehandle with _TOP appended)
$.	$INPUT_LINE_NUMBER	Current input line number of the last filehandle that was read
$/	$INPUT_RECORD_SEPARATOR	Input record separator (newline by default)
$+	$LAST_PAREN_MATCH	Last bracket matched by the last search pattern

Variable	English name	Description
$&	$MATCH	String matched by the last successful pattern match
$*	$MULTILINE_MATCHING	Performs multiline searching within a string (that contains embedded newline characters) when this variable is set to 1
$#	$OFMT	Output format for printed numbers
$|	$OUTPUT_AUTOFLUSH	When this variable is nonzero, output is flushed after each write
$,	$OUTPUT_FIELD_SEPARATOR	Output field separator for the print function
$]	$PERL_VERSION	The version number that's printed out when you type perl -v (for example, "5.003" for Perl version 5.003)
$'	$POSTMATCH	String following whatever was matched by the last successful pattern match
$`	$PREMATCH	String preceding whatever was matched by the last successful pattern match
$$	$PROCESS_ID	Process ID of the process running this script
$0	$PROGRAM_NAME	Name of the file containing the Perl script being executed
$(	$REAL_GROUP_ID	Real group ID of this process (in UNIX)
$<	$REAL_USER_ID	Real user ID of this process (in UNIX)
$;	$SUBSEP	Subscript separator for multidimensional arrays
$^F	$SYSTEM_FD_MAX	Maximum system file descriptor (typically, 2)
$^W	$WARNING	True if warnings have been turned on by the -w switch (by running Perl with perl -w)

Here is a program that uses the English module and prints out a few interesting variables:

```
# File: english.pl

use English;
```

```
print "Perl version = $PERL_VERSION\n";
print "Perl executable = $EXECUTABLE_NAME\n";
print "Script name = $PROGRAM_NAME\n";
```

Running this script on my Windows 95 system with the command `perl eng-lish.pl`, generates the following output:

```
Perl version = 5.001
Perl executable = C:\PERL5\BIN\PERL.EXE
Script name = english.pl
```

On the other hand, on my Linux system (which runs a later version of Perl), the output appears as follows:

```
Perl version = 5.003
Perl executable = perl
Script name = english.pl
```

All in all, the English module is handy, because it enables you to refer to the special variables by meaningful names.

Summary

Perl 5, the latest version of Perl (and the one included on this book's companion CD-ROM), includes a number of helpful features. A key feature is the *reference* — a new data type that can refer to another variable. Another feature is the Perl *module*, which is a package of subroutines that follow certain guidelines. References and modules make it possible to implement objects in Perl.

This chapter introduces you to the concept of references and shows you how to use existing modules in your programs. Objects are also implemented in Perl modules, and you learn how to create an object and call its methods.

As a bonus, you learn about the English module, which enables you to use meaningful names for the special variables that usually have cryptic names, such as $_ and $!.

The next chapter shows you how to run other programs from a Perl script.

## PART THREE

USING PERL IN WEB PROGRAMMING

THIS PART CONTAINS THE FOLLOWING CHAPTERS

Joey Hess, Perl programmer for the IDG Books Web sites (http://www.idg-books.com and http://www.dummies.com), is staring intently at the screen in front of him. Look closely, and you see that Hess is editing a Perl script. It happens to be a Common Gateway Interface — CGI — program for IDG's Web sites. This particular CGI script will enable users to search IDG's database and report the results in a nicely formatted Web page.

Thousands of Webmasters across the world rely on Perl to create CGI programs. These are the helper programs that enable the Web server to access various data sources, such as commercial databases or plain-text files.

"If it were not for the explosive growth of the Web, Perl might have remained an esoteric tool for UNIX system administrators," says Hess when asked about Perl's role in the World Wide Web.

"You see, Web sites want to provide customized information to users, and CGI — Common Gateway Interface — is the way to do that. For UNIX experts such as myself, Perl scripts are the way to go. After all, I already know Perl, so I can whip out a Perl CGI script in no time. It's kind of like Basic for PC programmers. Then again, Perl is available for Windows as well." says Hess, IDG's Perl programmer.

Hess is right on the mark. CGI programming has definitely made Perl extremely popular. That, in turn, has fueled the demand for more Perl books — like this one.

By the way, if you were to search for Perl books at IDG's Web sites, you should find *Discover Perl 5*, thanks to Hess, the Webmaster, and a Perl CGI script he wrote.

RUNNING OTHER PROGRAMS FROM A PERL SCRIPT

IN THIS CHAPTER YOU LEARN THESE KEY SKILLS

12

O ne way to reduce software development time is to reuse existing code. I don't mean just reusing Perl subroutines, but using any program that helps you do the job. In your Perl program, you may want to make use of many programs and utilities that are available for your operating system. For example, in a Perl CGI program, you might want to run a `mail` command (which exists as a separate program) and send mail to a user. To do this, you need to learn how to run other programs from a Perl script — in particular, how to provide input to another program and how to use the output generated by the program being run from the Perl script.

Perl provides quite a few ways to launch another program, send it input, and use the output from that program. Some of the ways may come as a surprise to you — for example, you can use the `open` function (that you may typically associate with opening a file) to launch a program and read the output of that program. You can also execute an operating system command and get that command's output simply by enclosing that command inside a pair of backquotes (` . . . `). This chapter shows you these and other ways to run external programs from your Perl scripts.

Running External Programs

Perl provides a number of ways to run external programs from a Perl script. Here, the term *external program* refers to any program other than the current Perl program — this includes operating system commands, any program installed on your system, and even other Perl scripts. This section shows you several ways of launching external programs.

Before jumping into a discussion of how to run other programs from a Perl script, you need to know the following terminology and concepts:

* A *program* is an executable file on disk. The exact steps for running a program depend on the operating system. Typically, you can run a program by typing the program's name on the command-line. Perl programs have to be executed by the Perl interpreter.

* A *process* is a program that has been loaded into the computer's memory and is being executed by the computer's central processing unit (CPU) — the microprocessor.

* A process can start other *child* processes. The original process is referred to as the *parent* process.

* In UNIX, the term *fork* refers to the act of cloning a process. The `fork` function creates a copy of an existing process. The `fork` function does not work in Windows 95 or Windows NT.

* In UNIX, a process can call the `exec` function to overwrite the current process with a new one. The `exec` function works in Windows NT and Windows 95 as well (you see examples later in this chapter).

* UNIX uses the `fork` and `exec` method to start new processes. First, the parent process calls `fork` to create a child process that's a copy of itself. Then the child process calls `exec` to begin a new process by loading a new program.

Starting a program with the `exec` function

The `exec` function provides a good way to start another program at the very end of your Perl script. In other words, you can use `exec` to chain one program into another. A simple example can show you how `exec` works.

Here are two Perl programs which illustrate the use of the `exec` function: The first one invokes the second program, and the second one enables you to run the first program. Each program uses the `exec` function to do its job.

The first program, called first.pl, is implemented as follows:

```
# File: first.pl

print "First: press <Enter> to start Second\n",
```

```
            "        type something else to quit\n";

$input = <STDIN>;

# If user has pressed Enter, call exec and
# launch the Perl interpreter with "second.pl"
# as the argument

if($input eq "\n")
{
    exec("perl", "second.pl");
}
```

As you can see, the program prompts the user to press Enter to start the second program. The program reads the user's input into the $input variable. If the user presses Enter, $input is "\n" and the program calls the exec function, as follows:

```
exec("perl", "second.pl");
```

This runs the Perl interpreter with the second.pl script as argument — the net effect is to run the second Perl program, which is stored in the file second.pl.

The second program, called second.pl, is a reciprocal version of first.pl — as shown here, it launches the Perl interpreter and runs the first.pl program if the user presses Enter:

```
# File: second.pl

print "Second: press <Enter> to start First\n",
        "        type something else to quit\n";

$input = <STDIN>;

# If user has pressed Enter, call exec and
# launch the Perl interpreter with "first.pl"
# as the argument

if($input eq "\n")
{
    exec("perl", "first.pl");
}
```

To try these programs and see the exec function in action, start any one of them. A typical session is as follows (user input is shown in boldface):

```
First: press <Enter> to start Second
        type something else to quit
```

```
Second: press <Enter> to start First
        type something else to quit

First: press <Enter> to start Second
       type something else to quit
q
```

The first two lines show the output from the first.pl program. When the user presses Enter, that program calls the exec function to run the second.pl program. When the user presses Enter again, the second.pl program, in turn, runs the first.pl program, and so on.

Launching a Windows program with exec

An interesting use of exec is to launch a Windows program from a Perl script. Suppose that you want the user to edit a set of configuration parameters. You can write a Perl script that stores a default set of parameters in a file and then lets the user edit the file using the Notepad program. Here is how you might implement such a Perl script:

```
# File: config.pl
# Writes configuration parameters to a file and lets
# user edit the file using NOTEPAD

# Open a file to save configuration parameters

open(CONFIG, ">config.dat") || die ("Cannot open file!");

# Save configuration parameters in the file

print CONFIG <<END;
Data Purge Configuration Parameters
_____

Data directory       : C:\\DATA
Purge every (days)   : 3
Retain (versions)    : 5
Backup old versions  : No
Backup device        : U:
END

close CONFIG;

# Let user edit file with NOTEPAD

exec("notepad", "config.dat");
```

When you run this program, it creates the `config.dat` file and then launches the Notepad program to edit that file. Figure 12-1 shows the result of launching the Notepad program from the Perl script.

Figure 12-1 The Notepad program launched from a Perl script

TIP If you use this approach to create a script that launches a Windows program, you can define a shortcut icon on the Windows 95 desktop.

You can set up a shortcut for a Perl script as follows:

1. Click the right mouse button in an empty area of the Windows 95 desktop. Windows 95, in turn, displays a pop-up menu.

2. Select `New` → `Shortcut`. A Create Shortcut dialog box appears.

3. Fill in the command to launch the Perl script. Remember to fill in the full path name of the script (for example, if the script `config.pl` is in the directory `c:\proj\perl`, enter the command **perl c:\proj\perl\config.pl**).

4. Click the Next button. The next page of the dialog box appears.

5. You can assign a name for the shortcut (or accept the default name suggested in the dialog box) and click on the Finish button. A shortcut icon appears on the Windows 95 desktop (see Figure 12-2).

Figure 12-2 shows a shortcut icon on the Windows 95 desktop. You can then run that script by double-clicking on the icon. The script, in turn, can launch a Windows program by calling the `exec` function.

Figure 12-2 A shortcut icon to launch a Perl script in Windows 95

Continuing after the External Program

So far, you have seen how to use the `exec` function to run another program from your Perl program. The `exec` function essentially replaces your Perl script with the new program. Sometimes, however, you may want to start another program and continue with your Perl program. To do this, you should use the `system` function.

In the preceding section's example, you have seen the `config.pl` Perl script that prepares a configuration file and then uses the `exec` function to launch the Notepad program so that the user may edit the configuration data. That example program ends when the user quits the Notepad program.

A more realistic example, however, might be to return to the Perl script after the user has saved the edited configuration data and then use the data to configure something. You can get that behavior with the `system` function.

 TIP **The only catch is that if you launch a graphical program such as Notepad (which has its own window), your Perl program does not wait for the graphical program to finish; instead, it continues with the statements that follow the `system` function call. In this case, you can get the desired behavior (wait until the user finishes editing the configuration file) by launching a text editor.**

Here is a UNIX implementation of the a script that enables the user to edit the configuration parameters using the `vi` editor. The script then prints the edited parameters:

```
#!/usr/local/bin/perl -w
# File: newcfg.pl
# Writes configuration parameters to a file and lets
# user edit the file using vi and then prints new
# configuration parameters

# Open a file to save configuration parameters

open(CONFIG, ">config.dat") || die ("Cannot open file!");

# Save configuration parameters in the file

print CONFIG <<END;
Data Purge Configuration Parameters
_____


Data directory      : /usr/local/data
Purge every (days)  : 3
```

```
Retain (versions)    : 5
Backup old versions  : No
Backup device        : /dev/rmt0m
END

close CONFIG;

# Let user edit file with the vi editor

system("vi", "config.dat");

# Reopen the config.dat file and print its contents

open(CONFIG, "<config.dat") || die ("Cannot open file!");

print "config.dat file contains:\n\n";
while($line = <CONFIG>)
{
  print $line;
}
```

When you run this program, it brings up the configuration parameters in the vi editor, as shown in Figure 12-3 (after the file has already been edited).

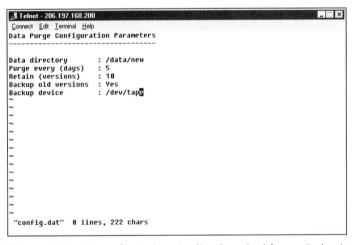

Figure 12-3 A text file in the vi editor launched from a Perl script

After you edit the file's contents and save it, the Perl script opens the file again and prints the contents, as shown in Figure 12-4.

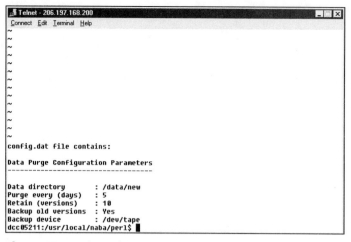

Figure 12-4 The Perl script prints the edited configuration parameters.

As the example program shows, the basic steps in the `newcfg.pl` script are as follows:

1. Open the configuration data file (`config.dat`) and store the initial configuration parameters in that file.

2. Call the `system` function to run the `vi` editor and edit the `config.dat` file.

3. Open the `config.dat` file again and print its contents (which should reflect any changes made by the user in Step 2).

Of course, in a more realistic program, your Perl script may actually make use of the edited configuration parameters for some specific task, such as setting up the appropriate processes to periodically purge old files from a specific directory.

Capturing Output of the External Program

When you run an external program by using the `exec` or `system` function, output from the external program shows up in the standard output. For example, when I run the following Perl program:

```
print "Current directory contains:\n";
system "dir /w";
```

in an MS-DOS prompt window in Windows 95, the program prints the following output (in this case, the current directory is `C:\MSOFFICE`):

```
Current directory contains:

 Volume in drive C is LNBSOFT
 Volume Serial Number is 384C-15D4
 Directory of C:\MSOffice

[.]              [..]             [ACCESS]         [BOOKS95]
  [SCHEDULE]
[SOUNDS]         MICROS~3.LNK     MICROS~7.LNK     SETUP.LNK
  [OFFICE]
[POWERPNT]       [TEMPLA~1]       [WINWORD]        [EXCEL]
  [CLIPART]
MICROS~1.LNK     MICROS~2.LNK     MSACCE~1.LNK     MICROS~5.LNK
  GETTIN~1.LNK
MICROS~6.LNK
            9 file(s)          2,872 bytes
           12 dir(s)      768,507,904 bytes free
```

As you can see, the output consists of the line `Current directory contains:` followed by the output of the `dir /w` command, which prints a directory listing in a "wide" format with several filenames on a single line.

Using backquotes to capture external program output

What if you want to capture the output of the `dir` command in an array variable? Suppose that you want to capture the directory listing and then print it in a different format. You can run a program and capture its output by using *backquotes*. To capture the output of the `dir` command in an array, for example, you write the following Perl statement:

```
@listing = `dir`;
```

After this statement executes, the `@listing` array contains the lines of text that constitute the output of the `dir` command.

To see the use of backquotes, consider an example program that captures the output from the `dir` command and generates a new listing of the files. In Windows 95, when you type `dir` in an MS-DOS prompt window, the output has the following form:

```
 Volume in drive C is LNBSOFT
 Volume Serial Number is 384C-15D4
 Directory of C:\MSOffice

 .               <DIR>        04-03-96  2:17p .
 ..              <DIR>        04-03-96  2:17p ..
ACCESS           <DIR>        04-03-96  2:19p Access
```

```
BOOKS95          <DIR>              04-03-96  2:19p Books95
SCHEDULE         <DIR>              04-03-96  2:19p Schedule
SOUNDS           <DIR>              04-03-96  2:19p Sounds
MICROS~3 LNK               314      12-19-95  8:50a Microsoft Access.lnk
... lines deleted ...
```

After a few lines of header, the output shows each filename, file size (or the word <DIR> if the file is a directory), date and time stamp of the file, and a long name for the file. Suppose that you want the program to capture the output of the dir command and print a new report that shows the long filename and the file size.

Here is how you might implement such a program:

```perl
# File: dirnew.pl
# Captures output of the dir command and
# presents a differently formatted list

# Define format of output report
format =
@<<<<<<<<<<<<<<<<<<<<<<<<<<<<<<<<<<<<<<<< @>>>>>>
         $longname,                          $size
.


format STDOUT_TOP =
Long file name                                   Size
========================================= =============

.


# Get the current directory name by capturing
# the output of the cd command
$curdir = `cd`;
print "Current directory: $curdir\n";

# Run the dir command and capture the output
# by enclosing it within backquotes

@dirlist = `dir`;

# Process the each line of text in @dirlist

$skip = 1;

for $line(@dirlist)
{
  chomp $line;
```

```
# Keep skipping lines until we reach a line
# that begins with ..
  if(substr($line, 0, 2) eq "..")
  {
    $skip = 0;
    next;
  }
  next if $skip;

# Also skip any line that begins with a blank
  next if (substr($line, 0, 2) eq "  ");

# Separate out filename, extension, size etc.
  $name = substr($line, 0, 8);
  $ext = substr($line, 9, 3);
  $rest = substr($line, 12);
  $longname = substr($line, 44);

  ($blank, $size, $date, $time) =
                              split(/  */, $rest, 4);
  $size = "Directory" if($size eq "<DIR>");

# Print a line of the report
  write;
}
```

The program uses backquotes to capture the output of two commands:

* The cd command that returns the current directory name in MS-DOS
* The dir command that prints a directory listing in a specific format

The rest of the program is focused on manipulating the lines of output (from the dir command) that have been captured in the @dirlist array. The output is processed in a for loop as follows:

* Lines are skipped until the for loop reaches the line that begins with two periods (..).
* The filename and file extension are extracted using the substr function.
* The long filename begins at the 44th character in the line. So, the long filename is extracted with the following call to the substr function:

  ```
  $longname = substr($line, 44);
  ```

* The rest of the line is broken up by calling the split function.
* Each line is printed in a report format defined by the format functions

you see in the program. Chapter 13 covers the general topic of formatting reports and how to use the `format` function.

✳ The last few lines of the `dir` command's output are ignored; these lines begin with blank spaces, so any line that begins with two blank spaces is skipped with the following statement:

```
next if (substr($line, 0, 2) eq "  ");
```

Here is a typical output generated by this program:

```
Current directory: C:\MSOffice

Long file name                              Size
========================================= ===============
Access                                    Directory
Books95                                   Directory
Schedule                                  Directory
Sounds                                    Directory
Microsoft Access.lnk                            314
Microsoft PowerPoint.lnk                        322
Setup.lnk                                       357
Office                                    Directory
Powerpnt                                  Directory
Templates                                 Directory
Winword                                   Directory
Excel                                     Directory
Clipart                                   Directory
Microsoft Binder.lnk                            318
Microsoft Word.lnk                              315
MS Access Workgroup Administrator.lnk           311
Microsoft Schedule+.lnk                         322
Getting Results Book.lnk                        299
Microsoft Office Shortcut Bar.lnk               314
```

TIP Whenever you have to write a Perl program, you should take stock of the available operating system commands and see whether any of the commands can do part of the job. Then you can simply place each command within backquotes and capture their output for use elsewhere in your program.

Capturing external program output with open

The preceding section shows you how to capture the output of any operating system command by placing that command within backquotes. True to its philosophy of providing more than one way to do any job, Perl provides another way to capture the output of an external program: You can essentially open a filehandle to read the output generated by an external program.

To open a filehandle that's set up to read the output of a command, you have to call the open function with a filename constructed by appending a vertical bar (|) to the external program's name. Thus, if you want to read the output of the dir command, for example, you call open as follows:

```
open(DIR, "dir|") || die("Cannot run command!");
```

The logical OR with the die function is used to quit the program in case the open function fails to run the external program.

After you use the open function to set up a filehandle, you can read from that handle by using the input operator (< . . .>), as follows:

```
@filelist = <DIR>;
```

Sending Input to an External Program

Some external programs require user input to work. For example, the MS-DOS command date prints the current date and then prompts you for a new date. Here is a typical interaction (user input shown in boldface):

```
date
Current date is Sat 03-01-1997
Enter new date (mm-dd-yy): 12-31-99
```

That sets the current date to December 31, 1999. You might do this, for instance, if you were testing to see whether a program works when the year is 2000.

Because changing the date to the year 2000 may potentially damage your system or data, you should experiment with the date only in a controlled environment and with the consent of the system's owner. To be safe, you may want to try this section's setdate.pl script only after changing the date string ("12-31-99\n") to a date that your system can handle correctly.

Suppose that you want to run the date command from a Perl script and set a new date directly from the script. To do this, you have to send input to the date command from your Perl script.

You can run the `date` command and send it an input string by using the `open` function. Essentially, you call the `open` function as follows:

```
open(DATE, "|date");
```

where the filename is constructed by adding a vertical bar prefix to the command you want to run. After that, you can send input to that command by printing to the `DATE` filehandle.

Here is a Perl script that sets the date to December 31, 1999:

```perl
# File: setdate.pl
# Sets the date to Dec 31, 1999 in MS-DOS

# Open a filehandle to the date command
open(DATE, "|date") || die("Cannot run command!");

# Send the input that "date" expects
print DATE "12-31-99\n";

close DATE;
print "Done.\n";
```

When you run this program in an MS-DOS prompt window in Windows 95 or Windows NT, its output should be something like this (the exact output depends on the date when you run the program):

```
Current date is Sun 03-02-1997
Enter new date (mm-dd-yy): 12-31-99
Done.
```

TIP After running this Perl script, your PC's date will be set to 12-31-99. To set the date back to the correct date, type `date` in the MS-DOS prompt window and enter the current date.

TIP Another example of sending input to an external program is to send mail by running the `sendmail` program (on UNIX systems) and sending it the necessary input. A typical use of a Perl CGI program is to accept user feedback from a Web page and then send the feedback to an appropriate person (the Webmaster) by mail. You'll see such a script in Chapter 15.

BONUS

Using the OLE Module in Windows

Object Linking and Embedding (OLE) is a collection of features and supporting technologies that forms the basis of Microsoft's strategy for supporting Windows objects. OLE is built upon the foundation of Microsoft's Component Object Model (COM), which specifies the interfaces between component objects within a single application or between applications. COM provides a mechanism for dynamically discovering the interfaces that a component object supports and how to invoke the interfaces. Thus, COM provides the "plumbing and wiring" of OLE. Because of the interfaces defined by COM, for example, a spreadsheet object from one vendor can be seamlessly embedded into a word-processing document created by an application from another vendor. The spreadsheet and word processor do not need to know anything about each other's implementation; they only need to know how to connect through the interface provided by the component object model.

A key concept of OLE is *automation,* or *scripting.* OLE automation enables an application to provide a programmable interface. Other applications can then use a scripting language such as Visual Basic to manipulate OLE objects within the automation server. For example, a user can invoke a command from a word-processing program that sorts a range of cells in a spreadsheet created by a different application.

You might say that OLE automation allows one application to control (or "drive") another application. The *automation client* is the controlling application, whereas the *automation server* is the application being controlled. Most automation servers support verbs such as OPEN and EDIT.

Perl 5 for Windows NT includes an OLE automation module (OLE.pm) that enables you to write Perl scripts capable of running and controlling any Windows application that supports OLE automation. Microsoft Office applications such as Excel and Word support OLE automation.

Controlling Excel from a Perl script

The OLE module, OLE.pm, enables you to create an OLE object by running a Windows application such as Excel. Then you can send commands to that OLE object from your Perl script. For example, here's how you can create an OLE object corresponding to Microsoft Excel and send commands to create a simple spreadsheet:

```perl
# Use the OLE module

use OLE;

# Create Microsoft Excel application object

$app = CreateObject OLE 'Excel.Application' || die $!;

# Make the window visible
$app->{'Visible'} = 1;

# Add a new workbook
$workbook = $app->Workbooks->Add();

# Use the first worksheet (Sheet1)
$worksheet = $workbook->Worksheets(1);

# Fill in a few cells of the spreadsheet
$worksheet->Range("A1:B1")->{'Value'} =
                                ["Task","Due date"];
$worksheet->Range("A2")->{'Value'} =
                                "Code and Unit Test";
$worksheet->Range("B2")->{'Value'} = "8/16/97";
$worksheet->Range("A3")->{'Value'} = "Integration Test";
$worksheet->Range("B3")->{'Value'} = "9/16/97";

# Set the first column's width to 30 characters
$worksheet->Range("A1:A3")->{'ColumnWidth'} = 30;

# Leave Excel running. If you want to quit
# from the script, uncomment the following line
# (this will prompt if you want to save the sheet):
#$app->Quit();
```

When you run this program, it runs Microsoft Excel (assuming you have Excel installed on your PC) and sets up a spreadsheet, as shown in Figure 12-5.

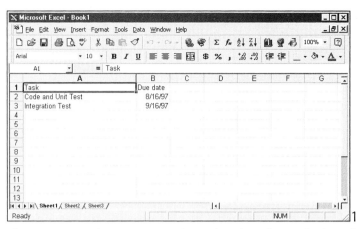

Figure 12-5 Using OLE automation to launch and control Microsoft Excel

Here are the key steps you can learn from this program:

1. Add the following line to include the OLE module:

   ```
   use OLE;
   ```

2. Call the `CreateObject` function to create the Excel application object:

   ```
   $app = CreateObject OLE 'Excel.Application' || die $!;
   ```

   The logical OR with the `die` function is the conventional way to check for errors in Perl scripts. In this case, the program quits with an error message if the `CreateObject` function cannot create the Excel object.

3. Use the `$app` variable (which is a reference to the Excel object) to call methods or to access other objects that are in the Excel object. To make the application window visible, for example, you have to set the Excel object's `Visible` property, as follows:

   ```
   $app->{'Visible'} = 1;
   ```

   To add a new workbook, you have to access the `Workbooks` object and call the `Add` method, as follows:

   ```
   $workbook = $app->Workbooks->Add();
   ```

NOTE As you probably realize by now, to make use of an object (such as the Excel application), you need to know what other objects it contains and what the properties and methods of those objects are. A good source of such information is the Microsoft Office Developer's Kit, available from Microsoft.

Loading an Excel spreadsheet from a data file

You can use the OLE module to load an Excel spreadsheet with information from a data file. As an example, consider the following `prod.db` data file:

```
9702101|166MHz Pentium, 16MB/2.1GB|1795.50
9702103|166MHz Pentium MMX, 32MB/3.2GB|2375.95
9702201|17" Color monitor|789.95
9702303|12ppm Laser printer, PostScript|775.99
9702901|32-bit PCI 10BASE-T card|109.95
9702905|4-port Mini Hub 10BASE-T|79.50
```

The file is ostensibly the inventory of a computer store (a real store would have a much larger inventory, of course; this one simply shows you the format).

Suppose that you want to display the inventory as a spreadsheet that users can view and edit. If you are doing this in Windows, you can make use of Microsoft Excel to do the job. The following Perl script uses OLE automation to launch Microsoft Excel (assuming, of course, that you have Excel installed on the system) and to load the spreadsheet cells with data from a file:

```perl
# File: loadprod.pl
# Runs Excel and loads product list into
# a spreadsheet. Must run on a Windows system
# with Microsoft Excel installed.
#
# Usage: perl loadprod.pl <prodfile>

# Use the OLE module
use OLE;

# Create an Excel object
$app = CreateObject OLE 'Excel.Application' || die $!;

# Make the Excel window visible
$app->{'Visible'} = 1;

# Add a new worksheet
$workbook = $app->Workbooks->Add();
$worksheet = $workbook->Worksheets(1);

# Define the column headers
$worksheet->Range("A1:C1")->{'Value'} =
                    ["Order#","Description", "Price"];

# Set column B width to 40 characters
$worksheet->Range("B1")->{'ColumnWidth'} = 40;
```

```
# Process each line in data file and add a row to
# the spreadsheet. The line is in $_. First get rid
# of trailing newline. Then, extract the fields
# into variables. Finally, use OLE automation to
# add a new row to the spreadsheet.

$row = 1;

while(<>)
{
  chomp;
  ($prodnum, $desc, $price) = split(/\|/, $_);
  $row++;
  $worksheet->Range("A".$row.":C".$row)->{'Value'} =
                            [$prodnum, $desc, $price];
}

# Leave Excel running for user to see
# You can quit by calling the following function:
#$app->Quit();
```

If you save this program in a file named `loadprod.pl`, you can display the contents of the `prod.db` file with the following command:

```
perl loadprod.pl prod.db
```

Figure 12-6 shows the Excel window with the new spreadsheet created by the Perl script.

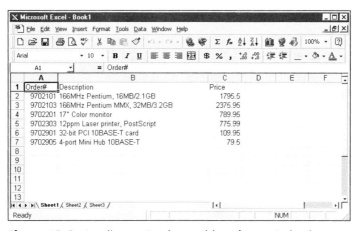

Figure 12-6   Loading an Excel spreadsheet from a Perl script

As you can see from this example, the OLE automation module enables you to run and control Windows applications from a Perl script.

Summary

O ften, your Perl program needs some functionality that already exists in the form of an external program. For example, to send mail from a Perl program, you may want to use the mail program on your UNIX system. Or, if you need an editor, you may need to run the Notepad program in Windows. Perl provides a number of ways to run an external program from a Perl script.

This chapter shows you how to run external programs with the `exec` and `system` functions. You learn how to capture the output from an external program using backquotes and to send a program input by opening a filehandle that's connected to the program's standard input.

As a bonus, you learn about the OLE automation module that enables you to start and control many popular Windows applications, such as Microsoft Excel and Microsoft Word.

The next chapter introduces you to Perl's report-writing capabilities.

WRITING
REPORTS IN PERL

IN THIS CHAPTER YOU LEARN THESE KEY SKILLS

13

From Chapter 1, you may recall that Perl stands for *Practical Extraction and Report Language*. As such, Perl has many built-in features that enable you to generate formatted reports. By formatted reports, I mean old-fashioned formatted reports — the kind we used to have in the days of the typewriter (before word processing and laser printers). These are reports that use fixed-pitch characters to lay down tables and use a line of dashes as a separator. Although old-fashioned, you can still use these report generation facilities to create output that can be very useful (whether printed or as text files disseminated via the World Wide Web).

This chapter describes Perl's report-writing features. You learn how to use the format function to define the layout of a report and the write function to actually send the formatted output to a file.

Generating a Simple Report

The idea of a report starts with the premise that you have lots of data, but the data is not in a readily usable form. You want to print out the data in a nice format so that you can actually use the information. Suppose that you have a database of inventory for a computer store). Each month, you may want to print out a list of items on sale. A typical list might be formatted as follows:

```
Order #   Description                       Sale Price
=====================================================
9702101   166MHz Pentium, 16MB/2.1GB           1795.50
9702103   166MHz Pentium MMX, 32MB/3.2GB       2375.95
9702201   17" Color monitor                     789.95
9702303   12ppm Laser printer, PostScript       775.99
9702901   32-bit PCI 10BASE-T card              109.95
9702905   4-port Mini Hub 10BASE-T               79.50
```

This is a typical report you can generate by using Perl's report-formatting capabilities. To create a report like this, you follow these general steps:

* Use the `format` function to specify a format for the report. With this step, you essentially paint a picture of how each line of the report should look.

* Call the `write` function to print each line of the report according to the format specified by the `format` function.

Of course, you need the data from which you generate the reports. That data may be in a text file or a commercial database. Often, Perl programs manipulate data stored in a text file.

Organizing data in text files

To print reports you need a source of data. Before showing you how to generate formatted reports, this section focuses on data storage in text files. You can store a lot of useful information in an organized format in a plain text file.

One common way to organize information is to present it in a tabular form. You can store such tabular information in a text file as follows:

* Think of each row of data as consisting of fields that appear in different columns.

* Convert each row into a line of text by writing the fields one after another with a unique character (such as |) as the separator between fields.

* Store each line of text in the file.

UNIX uses this approach to store system administration information in text files. A good example is the /etc/passwd file, which contains information about users. A typical line in the /etc/passwd file has the following form:

```
naba:UbAWIPSb3LO6g:501:100:Naba B:/home/naba:/bin/csh
```

In the /etc/passwd file, each line contains a number of fields separated by colons (:). The first field is the user name (that's what the user must type to log in to the computer) and the second field is the password in encoded format. The other fields contain various pieces of information about the user.

You can store the sample inventory information by using this approach of separating the fields with a special character. If you were to use the vertical bar (|) as a separator, the text file containing the inventory information might have the following appearance:

```
9702101|166MHz Pentium, 16MB/2.1GB|1795.50
9702103|166MHz Pentium MMX, 32MB/3.2GB|2375.95
9702201|17" Color monitor|789.95
9702303|12ppm Laser printer, PostScript|775.99
9702901|32-bit PCI 10BASE-T card|109.95
9702905|4-port Mini Hub 10BASE-T|79.50
```

This file can serve as the inventory database, with each line containing the information about a specific item.

TIP   **When you write Perl programs to work with such data files, you can use the split function to separate out the fields contained in each line of text. For example, if $line contains a line of data and the field separator is the vertical bar, you can obtain the array of fields with the following line of code:**

```
@fields = split(/\|/, $line);
```

The first argument to the split function is a pattern that specifies where to break the fields. In this case, the pattern consists of a vertical bar (you need that backslash prefix to ensure that the vertical bar is used literally). Recall that the split function (described in Chapter 3) breaks up a line of text into separate fields. The first argument to split is a pattern that specifies the character or characters that delineate the fields. The second argument is the string to be split into fields.

Writing a report-generation program

To generate a formatted report from a raw data file, you typically go through the following steps:

1. Use the `format` function and define a format for the report.
2. Open the data file.
3. Read a line, separate the fields.
4. Print a line of the report using selected fields.
5. Repeat Steps 3 and 4 until the file ends.

For the preceding section's inventory data, you might write a Perl program such as the following to generate a formatted report:

```perl
#!/usr/local/bin/perl -w

# File: irpt.pl
# Usage: perl irpt.pl <datafile>

# Define format for the report
format =
@<<<<<<<  @<<<<<<<<<<<<<<<<<<<<<<<<<<<<<<  @#####.##
$prodnum, $desc,                          $price
.


# Define a header (use the format name
# STDOUT_TOP because this report is printed
# on the standard output)

format STDOUT_TOP =
Order #   Description                     Sale Price
===================================================
.


# Process each line in data file and print report
# The line is in $_. First get rid of trailing newline.
# Then, extract the fields into variables.
# Finally, call write to print a line of the report.

while(<>)
{
  chomp;
  ($prodnum, $desc, $price) = split(/\|/, $_);
```

```
    write;
}
```

Suppose that you have stored this program in a file named `irpt.pl` and the inventory data is in another file named `prod.db`. You then can process that data file and generate a report with the following command:

```
perl irpt.pl prod.db
```

For the preceding section's inventory data, this program generates the following output:

```
Order #   Description                        Sale Price
======================================================
9702101   166MHz Pentium, 16MB/2.1GB           1795.50
9702103   166MHz Pentium MMX, 32MB/3.2GB       2375.95
9702201   17" Color monitor                     789.95
9702303   12ppm Laser printer, PostScript       775.99
9702901   32-bit PCI 10BASE-T card              109.95
9702905   4-port Mini Hub 10BASE-T               79.50
```

Understanding the report-generation program

The preceding section's example program shows you report generation in Perl. The program uses Perl's report-formatting functions: `format` and `write`. Before you learn the detailed syntax of these functions, here is an overview of the sample program. That should help you better understand the overall structure of typical report-generation programs.

Here is an example program that prints the inventory list:

1. Use the `format` function to define a template for each line of the report:

```
format =
@<<<<<<<   @<<<<<<<<<<<<<<<<<<<<<<<<<<<<<<<<   @####.##
$prodnum,  $desc,                             $price
.
```

   You'll learn the complete syntax of `format` function later in this chapter. This `format` function call specifies the layout of the three fields (represented by the variables $prodnum, $desc, and $price). A single period (.) on a line marks the end of the `format` function call.

2. To add a header to the report, use the `format` function again. By convention, you can add a header to a report by defining an additional template with a special name. If you are printing the report on STDOUT, the name is STDOUT_TOP. Here's how to define the report header:

```
format STDOUT_TOP =
Order #    Description                        Sale Price
========================================================
.
```

As usual, the `format` function begins with the name of a format and ends with a period on a single line. In between, place the lines that should appear in the header. In this case, the lines contain only literal characters, but you can also include arguments in the header. For example, you could use the `$%` argument in the header to print a page number.

3. After the report template is defined, it's simple to generate the report. Use a `while` loop to process each line in the data file:

```
while(<>)
{
  chomp;
  ($prodnum, $desc, $price) = split(/\|/, $_);
  write;
}
```

In the `while` loop, remove the trailing newline character from the line, extract the fields, and call the `write` function to print a line of the report.

Defining a Report Template

As you have seen from the examples in the previous sections, Perl includes the facilities for generating simple, formatted reports. Perl's reporting function can do a lot of things, such as keep track of the number of lines on each page and add a header at the beginning of each page. The function names are borrowed from FORTRAN. The `format` function defines the format of the report. The `write` function prints the report — you can print to the standard output or any other file.

 NOTE Although Perl borrows the `format` and `write` keywords from FORTRAN, Perl's reporting functionality is more comprehensive than what FORTRAN offers. Perl's `write` function is more like the PRINT USING statement in BASIC.

Using the `format` function

You use the `format` function to specify the layout of a report. The syntax of the `format` function is as follows:

```
format NAME =
# Comment lines that begin with a #
# Pairs of picture and argument lines. If a picture
# line does not have arguments, there is no need for
# any argument line. Do not place a comment between
# the picture line and the argument line.
PICTURE LINE
ARGUMENT LINE
# A single period on a line ends the format
.
```

The first line starts with the format function, which is followed by a name for this report template. The name of the format should be the same as the name of the filehandle where the report is printed. If you omit the filehandle, NAME is assumed to be STDOUT (in other words, the report is being printed on standard output). The format definition ends with a line containing a single period.

Between the first and last lines, you can have some comment lines — the convention is the same as other Perl comments; a comment line begins with a #. Besides the comments (which may explain the layout of the report), the format specification contains pairs of PICTURE LINE and ARGUMENT LINE.

 Do not place any comments between a PICTURE LINE **and the corresponding** ARGUMENT LINE. **The report output will not be correct if you insert a comment between these two lines. Each** PICTURE LINE **defines the layout of a line in the report. Special symbols designate fields, the amount of space assigned to a field, and the alignment of the value (for example, right-justified) in the field. The** ARGUMENT LINE **immediately following a** PICTURE LINE **provides the arguments that are used for that line of output. If a** PICTURE LINE **does not have an argument, you do not need an** ARGUMENT LINE **following that** PICTURE LINE.

You can have as many pairs of picture and argument lines as you need for a report. For many tabular reports, you typically have a single pair of picture and argument lines. On the other hand, for more complex reports, you may need several pairs of picture and argument lines.

 TIP The format **function declares the layout of lines, which the Perl interpreter accepts as information. However, nothing happens as a result of the** format **function; the result occurs only when the** write **function is called to generate the report. That means you can place the formats anywhere in the program. It's a good idea, however, to keep them all together in one place — either at the beginning or at the end of a program.**

Specifying the picture line

To define the layout of a line in the report, you need to provide a picture line and an argument line containing any argument (variable names) that you want to print on that line of the report. The picture line can contain literal characters (they are printed as is) plus layout for specific fields that are to appear on that line of the report.

For example, here is a format specification with a picture line that contains two fields plus some literal characters:

```
format =
From: @<<<<<<<<<<<<<<<<<<<<        Message#: @####
          $name,                             $msgnum
      .
```

In this case the picture line is:

```
From: @<<<<<<<<<<<<<<<<<<<<        Message#: @####
```

The two fields are identified by the @ symbol followed by a number of special characters. The @ symbol plus the number of special characters determine the amount of space to be used for that field and the character itself specifies the alignment type. In this example, the first field is a left-justified 20-character field, the second one is a right-justified four-digit number.

The argument line contains the names of the variables that are to be printed in each field. In this case, the $name variable is to be printed in the first field; $msgnum is destined for the second field.

To see the effect of this picture line, try the following program:

```
format =
From: @<<<<<<<<<<<<<<<<<<<<        Message#: @####
          $name,                             $msgnum
      .

$name = "John Doe";
$msgnum = 141;

write;
```

When you run this program, it prints the following output:

```
From: John Doe                    Message#:  141
```

As you can see, the fields (represented by the @ character) in the picture line are replaced by values of the variables specified in the argument line (in this case, $name and $msgnum). The other characters in the picture line appear as is.

In the picture line, you specify the fields by using the following syntax:

✳ Each field begins with the @ character.

✳ The @ character is followed by a number of special characters. First, choose the character you want from the following set:

- For left-justified field
- For right-justified field
- For centered field
- For numeric field

✳ Repeat the character one less than the number of characters you want to use when printing that field. Thus, to specify a six-character, left-justified field, you use @<<<<< (that's the @ symbol followed by five occurrences of <).

In a numeric field, you can embed a period where you want the decimal point to appear. Thus, if you expect a dollar amount to be of the form 9999.99, you use the field specification @####.##. Note that numeric fields (denoted by #) are right-justified.

NOTE It's important to note that you have to count the @ symbol plus the special characters to arrive at the total number of characters that will be used by a field. Thus, @#### means a five-character numeric field (not a four-character-wide field). This point is emphasized because it is easy to forget to include the @ sign when figuring out the space being reserved for a field.

Table 13-1 summarizes the field specifications. The sample field specifications show six-character-wide fields. When you specify a field, just make sure that the @ symbol and the special characters add up to the number of spaces you want reserved for that field. For example, if you want an eight-character, left-justified field, use @<<<<<<< as the field specifier.

TABLE 13-1   Field specifications for formatting reports

Field specification	Meaning
@<<<<<	Six-character-wide, left-justified field
@>>>>>>	Six-character-wide, right-justified field
@|||||	Six-character-wide, centered field
@#####	Six-digit numeric field (right-justified)
@###.##	Six-character-wide numeric field with numbers of the form 999.99 (right-justified)

Specifying the argument line

If a picture line includes one or more fields (each field begins with the @ symbol), the next line is an argument line with a comma-separated list of arguments. Typically, the arguments are variable names. For example, the following format prints four variables in four fields:

```
format =
@####### @##### @<<<<<<<<<<<<<<<<<<<<<<<<<<<<<<<< @####.##
$refid,  $num,   $desc,                           $price
.
```

In this format specification, the picture line and the argument lines are as follows:

```
@####### @##### @<<<<<<<<<<<<<<<<<<<<<<<<<<<<<<<< @####.##
$refid,  $num,   $desc,                           $price
```

As you can see from the @ symbols, the picture line has four fields. The next line is the argument line, with four comma-separated variable names. Typically, Perl programmers place the variable names underneath the field where that variable will be printed.

Adding a Header

Typically, printed reports contain a header on each page. The header contains information that helps the user understand the report. In a tabular report, the header usually identifies the columns.

You can define a top-of-page header very easily. Suppose that you have a format defined for a specific filehandle:

```
format FILEHANDLE =
PICTURE LINE
ARGUMENT LINE
.
```

Then you can define the header for this report with the following format:

```
format FILEHANDLE_TOP =
PICTURE LINE
ARGUMENT LINE

.
```

You have to append _TOP to the format name of the report. Other than that, you can define the format just as you define the report format.

If you are specifying a report format without a name (which means the report is intended for STDOUT), you have to use STDOUT_TOP for the header format. For example, a typical column header format for STDOUT might be defined as follows:

```
format STDOUT_TOP =
Ref no.   Item            Description            Price
===============================================================
.
```

In this case, the header does not include any variable. Perl prints this header at the top of each page (by default, each page consists of 60 lines).

You can, of course, include fields in the header. For example, the special variable named $% contains the current page number. Thus, you can print the page number in the header with the following addition to the header format:

```
format STDOUT_TOP =
Page @<<
      $%

Ref no.   Item            Description            Price
===============================================================
.
```

With this header format, each page will include a page number at the top of the page, as shown here:

```
Page 1

Ref no.   Item            Description            Price
===============================================================
```

You can similarly embed other variables in the header.

Writing the Report

You have already seen examples of how to write the formatted report. Essentially, you specify the format and then call the write function to generate the report. So far, the examples have shown how to print the report to the STDOUT filehandle. As you see later in this section, it's equally easy to print a report to another file. Before discussing how to print the report to a file other than STDOUT, here is a review of another sample report.

Printing a summary of credit card purchases

Suppose that the following text file holds information about purchases made by a credit card:

```
501211|Music Boulevard, 1 CD|13.96
501215|Java Beans Intl, 4lbs|42.00
501321|Bombay Cafe, food/beverage|39.24
501445|National Theater, Ticket CATS|300.00
501233|John F. Kennedy Center, Tickets|65.40
```

Each line has three fields: a reference number, a description of the purchase, and an amount. You want to write a Perl program that prints a summary of charges. You want to print the report in the following form:

```
Ref no.    Item            Description                    Price
==============================================================
 501211      1  Music Boulevard, 1 CD                     13.96
```

The first two lines show the header, and the last line is a typical line of the report. The Item column is simply a running count of the purchases.

Here is how you might implement such a program:

```perl
#!/usr/local/bin/perl -w
# File: charges.pl
# Usage: perl charges.pl <datafile>

# Define report header
format STDOUT_TOP =
Ref no.    Item            Description                    Price
==============================================================
.
# Define format of each line
format =
@######   @####   @<<<<<<<<<<<<<<<<<<<<<<<<<<<<<<<   @####.##
$refid,   $num,   $desc,                              $price
.

# Process the data file and print formatted lines

while(<>)
{
  chomp;
  $num++;
  ($refid, $desc, $price) = split(/\|/, $_);
  write;
}
```

In this program, the format STDOUT_TOP defines the header for the report. The second format (without a name) specifies the format of each line of the report. As usual, a while loop reads each line of data, separates the fields, and calls the write function to print the report to standard output. The item number is simply a count, implemented by the $num variable, that's incremented as each line is processed.

If the credit card charges are stored in the file charges.db and this program is named charges.pl, you can generate the report with the following command:

```
perl charges.pl charges.db
```

The program prints the following output:

```
Ref no.    Item          Description               Price
============================================================
  501211      1   Music Boulevard, 1 CD             13.96
  501215      2   Java Beans Intl, 4lbs             42.00
  501321      3   Bombay Cafe, food/beverage        39.24
  501445      4   National Theater, Ticket CATS    300.00
  501233      5   John F. Kennedy Center, Tickets   65.40
```

Writing a report to a file

You can write a report to a specific file by calling the write function with the file-handle as argument. You also need a corresponding format definition for that filehandle. Suppose that you want to alter the preceding section's example so that the program writes the report to a file named report.397 instead of STD-OUT. Here is a revised program that writes the report to a file (changes from the preceding section's example program appear in boldface):

```
#!/usr/local/bin/perl -w
# File: charges.pl
# Usage: perl charges.pl <datafile>

# Define report header
format REPORT_TOP =
Ref no.    Item          Description               Price
============================================================
.

# Define format of each line
format REPORT =
@#######   @####   @<<<<<<<<<<<<<<<<<<<<<<<<<<<   @#####.##
$refid,  $num, $desc,                             $price
.
```

```
# Open the file to write the report
open(REPORT, ">report.397") ||
die("Error opening file!");

# Process the data file and print formatted lines

while(<>)
{
  chomp;
  $num++;
  ($refid, $desc, $price) = split(/\|/, $_);
  write REPORT;
}
```

To summarize, here are the steps to follow when you want to write a report to a file:

1. Call the `format` function and define a format with the same name as the filehandle that you plan to use when you open the file for writing. For example, if the filehandle is named REPORT, the `format` function call has the following form:

   ```
   format REPORT =
   picture line
   argument line
   .
   ```

   You can also specify a header by defining a format named REPORT_TOP.

2. Open the report file by calling the `open` function. Here is how you open a file named `report.397` for a report:

   ```
   open(REPORT, ">report.397") ||
   die("Error opening file!");
   ```

3. Call the `write` function with the filehandle as an argument. For example, to print to the filehandle REPORT, you call the `write` function as follows:

   ```
   write REPORT;
   ```

BONUS

Printing Long Text Fields

Sometimes, you may have to print a report with a field that's too long to fit in the space available for that column. For example, a formatted product list might have an entry that spans multiple lines, as follows:

```
Item no.      Description                           Price
========================================================
537-276 Ergonomic adjustable chair with             99.99
        pneumatic lift, manual adjustment of
        back height and depth. Available in
        gray, blue, and burgundy.
```

You can easily specify such a report format with Perl's `format` function. An example can show you how to do this.

Suppose that the inventory of an office supply store is kept in a text file. Here is the format of a few entries from the inventory file:

```
840-167
399.99
HP Office Jet 300. Combination ink
jet printer, fax, and copier. 24 page
fax memory. Up to 99 copies with
reduction capabilities.

575-954
3.99
Laser printer paper, white, 20 lb.,
84 brightness, 500-sheet ream.
```

As this example illustrates, each entry is stored in multiple lines with the following conventions:

* The first line is an item number.
* The second line has the item's price.
* The next few lines contain the product's description.
* A blank line marks the end of an entry.

Of these fields, the product description is troublesome for the report, because it can span multiple lines. After you see the following program (`prods.pl`) in action, you'll realize that it's simple to handle such long text fields in a report:

```perl
#!/usr/local/bin/perl -w
# File: prods.pl
# Usage: perl prods.pl < datafile

# Define report header
format STDOUT_TOP =
Item no.     Description                              Price
===========================================================
.

# Define format of each line
format =
@<<<<<< ^<<<<<<<<<<<<<<<<<<<<<<<<<<<<<<<<<<<<<<  @####.##
$refid, $desc,                                  $price
        ^<<<<<<<<<<<<<<<<<<<<<<<<<<<<<<<<<<<<<< ~~
          $desc

.

# Process the data file and print the report

while($refid = <STDIN>)
{
  chomp $refid;

  $price = <STDIN>;
  last unless $price;
  chomp $price;

  $desc = <STDIN>;
  last unless $desc;
  chomp $desc;
  while(1)
  {
    $line = <STDIN>;
    last unless $line;
    last if($line eq "\n");
    chomp $line;

    $desc = $desc." ".$line;
  }
  write;
}
```

Suppose that the inventory is in a file named prodlist. You can try this program with the following command:

```
perl prods.pl < prodlist
```

The program prints the following report:

```
Item no.      Description                                         Price
===========================================================
537-276 Ergonomic adjustable chair with                          99.99
        pneumatic lift, manual adjustment of
        back height and depth. Available in
        gray, blue, and burgundy.

840-167 HP Office Jet 300. Combination ink jet                   399.99
        printer, fax, and copier. 24 page fax
        memory. Up to 99 copies with reduction
        capabilities.

575-954 Laser printer paper, white, 20 lb., 84                     3.99
        brightness, 500-sheet ream.

500-122 Rollerball pens, black, 1 doz.                            12.99
```

As you can see, the product description spans as many lines as necessary. The key to generating a report is the format definition, which looks like this:

```
format =
@<<<<<<  ^<<<<<<<<<<<<<<<<<<<<<<<<<<<<<<<<<<<<<<<   @#####.##
$refid,  $desc,                                      $price
         ^<<<<<<<<<<<<<<<<<<<<<<<<<<<<<<<<<<<<<<< ~~
            $desc

.
```

Note that the second field in the picture line begins with a caret (^) instead of the usual *at* sign (@). That means the field is split across multiple lines. Then you provide a second picture line, which also begins with a caret (^), and add two tilde (~) characters at the end. This ensures that Perl repeats the field over as many lines as it needs.

When you use a picture field that begins with a caret (^), Perl alters the variable during the report-generation process. In the example, for instance, the $desc variable is altered as each line of the report is generated. If you need the variable for other reasons, you should make a copy of the variable before calling the write function.

Summary

Perl was originally created as a report-writing language, and, as such, it includes convenient facilities for creating formatted reports — the kind that relies on fixed-pitch characters to lay down tables and uses a line of dashes as a separator. Although old-fashioned, you can still use Perl's report-generation facilities to create output that can be very useful.

This chapter shows you how to use the `format` function to define report templates. You learn how to specify report headers and print the report with the `write` function.

As a bonus, you learn how to print reports with long text fields that span multiple lines.

The next two chapters focus on another exciting topic — writing CGI programs for World Wide Web servers. You can use CGI scripts on your Web site to serve dynamic Web pages whose content depends on user input.

LEARNING CGI PROGRAMMING

IN THIS CHAPTER YOU LEARN THESE KEY SKILLS

LEARNING HTML   PAGE 303

UNDERSTANDING HTML FORMS   PAGE 307

UNDERSTANDING COMMON GATEWAY INTERFACE (CGI)
PAGE 319

Y ou may have started learning Perl because you want to write CGI programs for your Web page. This chapter explains the basic concepts of a CGI program. An introduction to HTML is also included because CGI programs work closely with Web pages that are written in HTML.

The recent popularity of the Internet is primarily due to the World Wide Web, or Web, which makes it easy to access information residing on computers throughout the Internet. Although the Internet — a set of interconnected computer networks that spans the globe — has been around for quite a while, its benefits did not reach the masses until the Web came along in 1993.

Before the Web, you had to use arcane UNIX commands to access and use information available on the Internet. Now that you have the Web, you can enjoy the benefits of the Internet by using a Web Browser — a graphical application that retrieves and displays Web documents. A click of the mouse is all it takes to go from reading a document to downloading a file through the File Transfer Protocol (FTP) — one of many Internet services. You can read news and even send mail from the Web browser.

The magic of the Web is possible because of the Web sites around the world — these are the computers running Web servers that make Web documents (or *Web pages*, as they are commonly called) available on demand.

NOTE **The standard Web document format is Hypertext Markup Language (HTML), and the standard protocol for exchanging Web documents is Hypertext Transfer Protocol (HTTP). The location of a Web document is specified by an address called a Uniform Resource Locator (URL). For example, the URL of the IDG Books Web page is** `http://www.idgbooks.com/`**. A URL uniquely identifies the location of a file on a computer on the Internet.**

NOTE **A *Web server* is the software that provides HTML documents to any client that makes the appropriate HTTP requests. A *Web browser* is the client software that actually downloads an HTML document from a Web server and displays the contents graphically.**

One interesting aspect of a Web server is that you can add special computer programs that can accept user input and create a Web page on the fly. Unlike static Web pages that display some preset information, these *interactive* Web pages enable the user to send information to the Web server and get back a response that depends on the input. A Web search engine such as Alta Vista (`http://www.altavista.digital.com/`) is a good example of an interactive Web page; the user enters one or more keywords, and the Web index returns a list of Web pages that contain the search words. The Web page returned by the Web index is also *dynamic,* because the content of that page depends on what the user types as search words — it's not a predefined static document.

Another example of an interactive and dynamic Web page might be a form in which the user can enter a stock symbol and receive the latest stock quote for that stock. Yet another example might provide the user with a way to subscribe to a magazine or register for a conference. The interaction might be as simple as having users fill out a feedback form and submit comments that are then recorded in a file at the Web site.

To create an interactive Web page, you have to use certain HTML elements (to display the form that solicits user input) and implement special computer programs on the Web server. These computer programs process the user input and return requested information to the user, usually in the form of a dynamic Web page — a page that is constructed on the fly by a computer program. These programs are known as *gateways* because they typically act as a conduit between the Web server and an external source of information, such as a database (even if the database may be a collection of UNIX files).

NOTE The gateway programs exchange information with the Web server using a standard known as *Common Gateway Interface* (*CGI*). That's why the term *CGI programming* is used to describe the task of writing computer programs that handle user requests for information.

If you have a Web site and you want to provide dynamic content, you have to learn the details of how CGI programs work with the Web server and become familiar with CGI programming.

This chapter provides the details of CGI — how the Web server provides necessary information to CGI programs and how CGI programs return information to the Web server. You also receive an overview of HTML and learn how to use HTML to create forms.

Learning HTML

Before you can begin to prepare interactive Web pages and write Perl CGI scripts, you need to become familiar with HTML — the lingua franca of the Web. This section provides an overview of HTML. You'll learn more about HTML forms in a later section.

Markup languages

Although the name Hypertext Markup Language sounds like a programming language, HTML is really much simpler than a programming language. As its name suggests, HTML is a *markup* language, which means that you embed special *tags* — formatting commands — in the text to describe how the text should be rendered (that is, displayed or printed).

The idea of markup languages has been around for a while. Before the days of graphical interfaces, typesetting with the computer meant preparing a text file with embedded typesetting commands and then processing that marked-up text file with a computer program that generated commands for the output device: a printer or some other typesetter.

For example, in the late '70s and early '80s, I prepared all my correspondence and reports on a DEC VAX/VMS system, using a program named RUNOFF. That program formatted output for a line printer or a daisy wheel printer. That VAX/VMS RUNOFF program accepted embedded commands such as these:

```
.page size 58,80
.spacing 2
.no autojustify
```

As you might guess, the first command sets the number of lines per page and the number of characters on each line. The second command generates double-spaced output. The last command turns off justification. Essentially, I would pepper a text file with these commands, run it through RUNOFF, and send RUNOFF's output to the line printer. The resulting output looked as good as a typewritten document, which was good enough for most work in those days.

UNIX came with a more advanced typesetting program called `troff` (which stands for *typesetting runoff*) that could send output to a special device called a *typesetter.* A typesetter could produce much better output than a line printer. `troff` enables you to choose different fonts and to print text in bold and italic. To handle output on simpler printers, UNIX also included `nroff` (which stands for *nontypesetting runoff*) to process `troff` files and generate output, ignore fancy output commands, and generate output on a line printer.

Although markup languages were originally used to generate printed output, they have also been used to format output on your computer's monitor. For example, on UNIX systems, the `troff` markup language is used to prepare the man pages that provide online help to users.

Man pages are the files that contain the information that users can view by typing the command `man progname`. This command shows online help information on `progname`. The subject of a man page can be anything from an overview of a software package to the programming information for a specific C function, such as `fopen` (for example, try `man fopen` on your UNIX system).

Markup languages such as `troff` are device-specific because the markup commands specify exact fonts to be used for specific parts of the document. A more general approach is to specify the layout of a document and leave the final processing to the software that renders the document. That's where the concept of generalized markup languages comes in.

> **NOTE** In a generalized markup language, you specify *what* you want to display, not *how* you want to display it. For example, instead of saying you want some text typeset in italics, you say that you want the text emphasized, with tags such as `<em>this text is emphasized</em>`. In this case, the software that renders the document displays the text within the `<em>. . .</em>` tags emphasized in some way (typically by using italics).

There is, in fact, a Standard Generalized Markup Language (SGML) that standardizes the concept of generalized markup language by defining parts of the document and the way tags are used to define a document's layout. SGML was standardized by the International Standards Organization (ISO) in 1986 (ISO standard 8879).

HTML is an SGML-derived language with a set of tags that includes support for hypertext links (also known as *hyperlinks*).

HTML by example

NOTE HTML includes tags to denote parts of a document such as headers, bulleted lists, and parts that should be emphasized. The Web browser interprets these tags and displays a formatted document. In addition to tags that control the document's layout, HTML includes tags that enable you to embed images and even applications (such as a Java applet) in a document. You can also ask the user for input and have the Web browser send the user's response back to the Web server.

To give you a feel for HTML, here's a complete HTML document (this example shows only a few HTML tags):

```
<TITLE>A Sample HTML Document</TITLE>
<HTML>
<BODY>
<H1>Sample Document</H1>
This is a sample HTML document. It shows a
few HTML tags to give you a feel for what
the tags do.
<P>
This is a new paragraph and here's a bulleted
list.
<H2>Web servers for UNIX</H2>
<UL>
<LI> NCSA Web server is a popular <EM>public-domain</EM>
Web server.
<LI> CERN Web server is another public-domain server.
</UL>
</BODY>
</HTML>
```

NOTE For a small file such as this one, you would type this into a file using your favorite text editor. On UNIX systems, HTML files usually have the .html file extension. On Windows 95 and Windows NT, you would use an .HTM extension for HTML files.

X-REF In HTML, angle brackets (<. . .>) enclose the tags. For example, you can see how the document title appears within a pair of tags (<TITLE> and </TITLE>). The <H1> and <H2> tags denote first and second level headers. <P> means a paragraph break. Bulleted lists use the <UL> and <LI> tags. The <EM> and </EM> tags enclose text to be emphasized. The interpretation of what *emphasize* means is left up to the Web browser. Most Web browsers render emphasized text in italics.

By the way, you do not have to enter the HTML tags in uppercase. I have shown the tags in uppercase so that they stand out in the document.

 NOTE These HTML tags identify the parts of the document (such as a header or bulleted list), but the tags do not specify the font size or style. The Web browser decides how to display these document parts. For example, Figure 14-1 shows how the Netscape Navigator Web browser displays the sample HTML file.

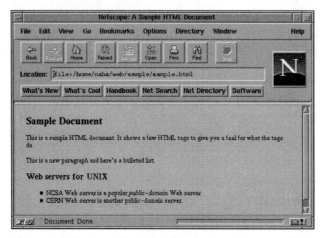

Figure 14-1 A sample HTML file displayed by a popular Web browser

Overview of HTML tags

TIP The best way to learn HTML is to prepare a simple HTML document and view it in a Web browser. Then keep adding new HTML elements to that document and see the effect in the rendered version in a Web browser's window. You can use this technique to learn HTML even if you do not have access to the Internet, because Web browsers enable you to open files that are on your computer's file system.

To help you get a feel for the HTML tags, Table 14-1 summarizes the HTML tags by category.

TABLE 14-1   HTML tags by category

Category	Tags
COMMENTS	`<!— comment—>`
OVERALL STRUCTURE	`<html> <head> <body> <title> <link> <base>` `<isindex> <meta> <nextid>`
HEADER LEVELS	`<h1> <h2> <h3> <h3> <h4> <h5> <h6>`
HYPERLINKS (ANCHORS)	`<a>`
IMAGES AND RULES	`<img> <hr>`
APPLET	`<applet> <param>`
CLIENT-SIDE IMAGE MAP	`<map> <area>`
CONTENT FLOW	`  <p> <pre> <blockquote> <div>`
PHYSICAL STYLES	`<b> <big> <font> <i> <small> <strike> <sub> <sup>` `<tt> <u>`
LOGICAL STYLES	`<address> <cite> <code> <dfn> <em> <kbd> <samp>` `<strong> <var>`
LISTS	`<ul> <ol> <li> <dir> <menu> <dl> <dt> <dd>`
FORMS	`<form> <input> <select> <option> <textarea>`
TABLES	`<table> <tr> <th> <td> <caption>`
RESERVED FOR FUTURE USE	`<script> <style>`

Understanding HTML Forms

Before describing the inner workings of CGI, here is some detailed information that you need to prepare interactive Web pages — those Web pages that look like data-entry forms, where you can type in the requested information and click on a Submit button to send the information back to the Web server. CGI specifies how the Web server uses external programs to handle the input you submit through HTML forms. But, if you maintain your own Web page, you also need to know how to create the data entry forms through which you can solicit information from users.

There is also a relationship between CGI programs and HTML forms, because CGI programs process the data that the user enters in the form. One of the attributes of the form specifies the name of the CGI program that receives the input from the form. Additionally, each element of the form has an identifying name that helps the CGI program separate out the user's input for each form element. You'll learn these details in the next few sections.

A form in action

In HTML, you have to use the `<form>` . . . `</form>` tags to provide the user interface through which the user sends data back to a designated Web server. In many Web pages, one of the links is for user feedback — an example of requesting user input.

Suppose that you want to provide a multiple-line text-entry area where the user can enter comments in free-form text. Then you might prompt specifically for an e-mail address. A button labeled *Submit* enables the user to send the completed form to the server. Another button, marked *Reset*, causes the form to revert to its initial state. For this form, the sample HTML page looks like this:

```
<html>

<head>
<TITLE>
LNB Software: Feedback
</TITLE>
</head>
<body>

<center>
<h2>
Feedback
</h2>
</center>

<hr>
<form method="post" action="/cgi-bin/test-post">

<h3>
Comments:
<br>
<textarea name="feedback" rows="10" cols="40">
```

```
</textarea>
<br>

E-mail address:
<br>
<input type="text" name="e-mail" size=40 maxlength=60>
<br>

<input type=submit> <input type=reset>
</h3>
</form>

<hr>

Copyright &copy; 1996 LNB Software, Inc.
<a href="mailto:webmaster@lnbsoft.com">
<address>
webmaster@lnbsoft.com
</address>
</a>
<p>

<h2>
Back to
<a href="http://www.lnbsoft.com/">Home Page</a>

</body>
</html>
```

The form part of the listing appears in boldface. Figure 14-2 shows the appearance of the form in Netscape.

All the user has to do is click in a text-entry area and type. After typing the input, the user clicks on the Submit[pc1] button to send the input to the server specified in the `action` attribute of the form.

This is a good example of the typical HTML elements that you can use for interactive forms. Also, you can see how the `<form>` element associates a CGI program with a form. Here are the key points to note in this HTML sample:

* The form begins with a `<form>` tag and ends with a closing `</form>` tag.
* The `<input>` tag defines a number of common form elements, such as text fields, option menus, and Submit buttons.
* The `<textarea>` element defines a multiple-line text input area.

You learn more about these form elements (and others) in the next few sections.

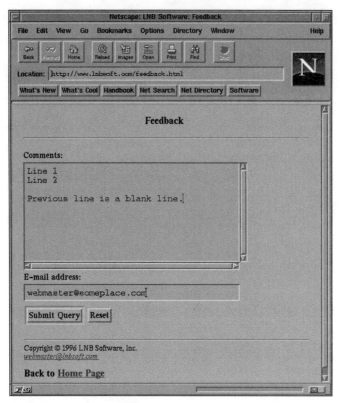

Figure 14-2 An HTML form enables the user to send input to a Web server.

THE `<FORM>` ELEMENT

At the heart of an HTML form is a `<form>` element — the entire form must begin with a `<form>` tag and end with a closing `</form>` tag. The attributes of the starting `<form>` tag specify the CGI program that processes this form's input and how the Web browser sends the user's input to the Web server (which, in turn, forwards this information to the CGI program).

A typical `<form>` element definition has the following structure:

```
<form method="post" action="/cgi-bin/cgi-prog">
...(other form elements appear here)
</form>
```

The attributes of the `<form . . .>` element control how and where the Web browser delivers the user's input. Notice that the `<form . . .>` element has the following attributes:

* `action` specifies the CGI program to be executed when the form is submitted to the server.

* `method` specifies the manner in which the user input is sent to the Web server. There are two methods: `GET` and `POST`.

THE action ATTRIBUTE

The <form> tag's action attribute specifies a URL for the CGI program that you have designed to handle this form's input. You can use an absolute URL that specifies the full server name as well as the path name for the CGI program. Often, however, you use a relative URL that identifies the directory on your Web server where the CGI programs reside.

The exact URL for CGI programs depends on the Web server and how your Internet Service Provider (ISP) has set up the server for users. In many popular UNIX Web servers, /cgi-bin is the default directory where the CGI programs reside. That's why you typically see /cgi-bin in the action URL of most HTML forms.

THE method ATTRIBUTE

The method attribute indicates how the Web browser sends form input back to the server. You can specify one of the following submission methods:

* The POST method causes the browser to send the data in a two-step process. First, the browser contacts the server specified in the action URL. Then, after a successful connection is established, the browser sends the form's data to the server, which, in turn, sends the data to the CGI program.

* The GET method causes the browser to append the form's data to the URL specified in the action attribute and to send everything to the Web server in a single step. A question mark (?) separates the data from the URL.

If you don't specify a method, the browser uses the GET method by default.

Fields in the form

You have to use a handful of other HTML tags to specify the different fields in an HTML form:

* The <input> tag specifies a number of different input fields — the type attribute indicates which type of input field you want.

* The <textarea> element is for multiple-line text fields.

* The <select> and <option> tags are for creating menus.

USING <input> TAGS

You can use the <input> tag for several different input fields, from text entry to the Submit button that actually sends the form's data to the Web server. Table 14-2 summarizes the syntax of the <input> tag in its various forms:

TABLE 14-2 Various forms of the `<input>` tag

Type of input	Sample `<input>` tag
SINGLE LINE TEXT	`<input type=text name=fname value="default" size=num>`
PASSWORD	`<input type=password name=fname value="default" size=num>`
HIDDEN FIELD	`<input type=hidden name=fname value="default">`
CHECK BOX	`<input type=checkbox name=fname value="default">`
RADIO BUTTON	`<input type=radio name=fname value="default">`
SUBMIT BUTTON	`<input type=submit value="button label">`
RESET BUTTON	`<input type=reset value="button label">`
CUSTOM BUTTON	`<input type=image src="path/to/image.gif" name=fname>`

The first three `<input>` tags specify text fields; the last five are for check boxes and buttons. Of these, the Submit and Reset buttons are used on most forms. As you might guess, the Submit button causes the browser to send the form's data to the server. The Reset button changes all fields to their default values (the default value of a field is the value that you assign when you define the field; these values appear when the browser initially displays the form).

TEXT AND PASSWORD FIELDS

The single line text and password `<input>` tags enable the user to enter text; when you use the password type, the browser does not echo the user's input (just what you expect to see in a password field). For example, Figure 14-3 shows a form where the user has to sign in by entering a name and a password.

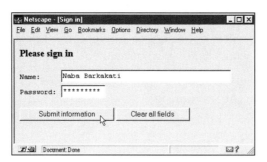

Figure 14-3 A form with text and password fields

Here's the HTML source that creates the form shown in Figure 14-3:

```
<head>
<title>Sign in</title>
</head>
```

```
<body>
<form action="/cgi-bin/login.pl" method=post>
<h3> Please sign in

<pre>
Name:     <input type=text size=40 name=username>
Password: <input type=password size=10 name=passwd>
</pre>

<input type=submit value="Submit information">
<input type=reset value="Clear all fields">

</form>
</body>
```

As this example shows, you can use plain text as well as `<input>` tags inside the `<form>` element. You have to use normal HTML formatting tags (such as `<pre>` and `<br>`) to provide line breaks and align various fields.

The `size` attribute specifies the maximum number of characters that the user can enter in that text field. The Web browser uses the field name when sending the form's data to the Web server.

TIP   The hidden field `<input>` tag (specified by `type=hidden`) — is useful for storing information on the form. When the user clicks on the Submit button of a form, the browser sends the content of any hidden fields (along with the other fields) to the server. As the name implies, the Web browser does not display the contents of any hidden `<input>` tags on the HTML form.

CAUTION   Although the password text (`type=password`) does not appear on the form (as the user types the text), the Web browser does not use any encryption when sending that text to the server. The upshot is that password text is not really protected as it's sent over the network. Therefore, you should not assume that you can use password text to securely accept and transmit sensitive information such as credit card numbers.

RADIO BUTTONS AND CHECK BOXES

Forms sometimes need radio buttons and check boxes to enable the user to select one or more items from a group of choices. Use radio buttons to display a number of options from which the user can select one; use check boxes to let the user choose multiple options from a set.

You can understand the use of radio buttons and check boxes better through a simple example. Suppose that you want to display an HTML form that lets the user order a serving of ice cream. Figure 14-4 shows the appearance of the form after the user has selected some items.

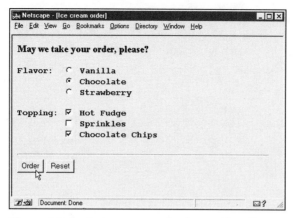

Figure 14-4 An ice cream order form with radio buttons and check boxes

This form shows the ice cream flavors as a collection of radio buttons — that means the user can select only one flavor. On the other hand, the user may choose more than one topping, so the toppings are listed in a group of check boxes.

Here is the HTML source that generates the form shown in Figure 14-4:

```
<head>
<title>Ice cream order</title>
</head>
<body>
<form action="/cgi-bin/icecream.pl" method=post>
<h3> May we take your order, please.

<pre>
Flavor:  <input type=radio checked name=flavor value="Vanilla">
   Vanilla
         <input type=radio name=flavor value="Chocolate"> Chocolate
         <input type=radio name=flavor value="Strawberry">
   Strawberry

Topping: <input type=checkbox checked name=topping value="Hot
   Fudge"> Hot Fudge
         <input type=checkbox name=topping value="Sprinkles">
   Sprinkles
         <input type=checkbox name=topping value="Chocolate
   Chips"> Chocolate Chips
</pre>
```

```
<hr>
<input type=submit value="Order">
<input type=reset>

</form>
</body>
```

Here are the key points to note when you use radio buttons and check boxes in a form:

* Use `type=radio` for radio buttons and `type=checkbox` for check boxes.
* Present a collection of radio buttons (or check boxes) as a group. Indicate a group by using the same `name` attribute for all items in a group.
* Add a `checked` attribute (without any value) to indicate which items are selected by default.
* Provide text next to each `<input>` tag to label the radio buttons and check boxes.
* Use HTML formatting tags such as `<pre>` or `<br>` to break lines and arrange the items on the form.

As long as you give the same name to all radio buttons (or check boxes) in a group, the Web browser treats the group as a collection. For a group of radio buttons, the browser sends the user's selection in a `name=value` format. For check boxes, multiple selections are sent as a comma-separated list in the `name=value1,value2,. . .` format.

For the ice cream flavor and topping selections shown in Figure 14-4, the browser sends `flavor=Chocolate` and `topping=Hot Fudge,Chocolate Chips` to the server. The CGI program at the server has to parse these strings and recognize the user's selections (and send back the right serving of ice cream).

CREATING MENUS WITH `<select>` AND `<option>`

You can create option menus and scrolled lists by placing a number of `<option>` tags inside a `<select>` element. Suppose that you need a book order form that lets the user select one or more books, select the payment option, fill out the credit card information, and submit the order. Figure 14-5 shows a simple book order.

In this example, the list of books and the payment options use the `<select>` and `<option>` tags. As the highlighted entries in Figure 14-5 show, users can select multiple items from the scrolled list. You get the multiple selection behavior by using the `multiple` attribute in the `<select>` tag.

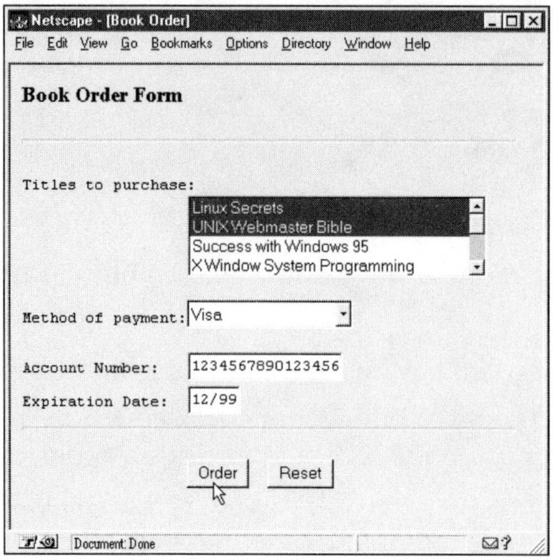

Figure 14-5 A book order form that uses an option menu and scrolled list

The following listing shows the HTML source that implements the book order form shown in Figure 14-5:

```
<head>
<title>Book Order</title>
</head>
<body>
<form action="/cgi-bin/bkorder.pl" method=post>
<h3> Book Order Form
<hr>
<pre>
Titles to purchase:
                  <select name=books size=4 multiple>
                    <option>Linux Secrets
                    <option>UNIX Webmaster Bible
                    <option>Success with Windows 95
                    <option>X Window System Programming
                    <option>Object-oriented programming in C++
                    <option>Visual C++ Developer's Guide
                    <option>Borland C++ Developer's Guide
                    <option>Turbo C++ Bible
                    <option>Microsoft Macro Assembler Bible
                  </select>

Method of payment:<select name=card size=1>
                    <option>Visa
                    <option>MasterCard
```

```
                        <option>American Express
                    </select>
                    </select>

Account Number:     <input type=text name=acct size=16>
Expiration Date:    <input type=text name=expire size=5>
<hr>
                    <input type=submit value="Order">  <input
   type=reset>
</pre>
</form>
</body>
```

You should note the following as you compare the HTML listing with the form in Figure 14-5:

* The entire list or menu appears between the `<select>` and `</select>` tags.
* The `<option>` tag defines items in the list.
* The appearance of the `<select>` element depends on the value of the `size` attribute.
* If you specify `size=1`, the browser displays the `<select>` element as an option menu (the list of items appears in a drop-down list box when you click on the arrow next to a single visible item).
* If the value of `size` is more than 1, the browser displays the `<select>` element as a scrolled list. The browser makes the list box large enough to display the number of items you specify in the `size` attribute. Thus, `size=4` means the list box should make four items visible.
* If you want the user to be able to select more than one item from the list, include the `multiple` attribute in the `<select>` tag (the `multiple` attribute does not need any value).

USING THE `<textarea>` ELEMENT

You must have seen many feedback forms that let you type your comments in a large text-entry area. Unlike the one-line text fields that let you type only your name or password, the comment fields accept multiple lines of text. The `<textarea>` element enables you to provide such multiple-line text-entry fields.

The following example illustrates the syntax of the `<textarea>` element:

```
<textarea name="feedback" rows="10" cols="40">
This is the default text.  This is what
the user sees when the browser
initially displays the form.
</textarea>
```

The element begins with a `<textarea>` tag and ends with a `</textarea>` tag. You may provide some text between the `<textarea>` and `</textarea>` tags — the browser uses this text when initially displaying the text area. If you do not provide any text between the `<textarea>` tags, the text-entry field is empty when first displayed.

The `<textarea>` tag accepts the following attributes:

* `name` identifies this text-entry field. The browser uses the name when it sends the contents of this field to the server.

* `rows` specifies the height of the text-entry area. This defines the visible rows of text; the user can enter more lines of text than that specified by the value of the `rows` attribute.

* `cols` specifies the width of the text-entry area. This defines the visible number of characters per line; the user can enter longer lines than that specified by the value of the `cols` attribute.

Netscape Navigator supports a fourth attribute — `wrap` — that automatically wraps the text as the user types in the text-entry field.

Typically, you use `<textarea>` elements when soliciting comments through a text-entry area. For example, Figure 14-6 shows a feedback form that uses a `<textarea>` element.

Figure 14-6   The `<textarea>` element is useful for soliciting user feedback.

The following HTML text creates the form shown in Figure 14-6:

```
<head>
<title>Feedback</title>
```

```
</head>

<body>
<h2>Your feedback is welcome.</h2>
<hr>

<form method="post" action="/cgi-bin/test-post">
<h3>
Comments:<br>

<textarea name="feedback" rows="10" cols="40">
</textarea><br>

E-mail address:<br>
<input type="text" name="e-mail" size=40 maxlength=60><br><br>
<input type=submit>  <input type=reset>
</h3>
</form>
</body>
```

Understanding CGI

I f you have set up a Web server, you know how the Web server provides documents from a specific directory. The Web server can provide a variety of documents, but a key characteristic of these documents is that their content is
static — the document does not change unless you, as the Webmaster, explicitly
edit the document.

On the other hand, sometimes a document's content may not be known in
advance. For example, if a Web site provides a search capability, the result of a
search depends on which keywords the user enters in the search form. To handle
these needs, the Web server relies on external programs called *gateways*.

A gateway program accepts the user input and responds with the requested
data formatted as an HTML document. Often, the gateway program acts as a
bridge between the Web server and some other repository of information, such
as a database.

Gateway programs have to interact with the Web server. To enable anyone
to write a gateway program, the method of interaction between the Web server
and the gateway program had to be specified completely. This is where
Common Gateway Interface (CGI) comes in. CGI defines how the Web server
and external gateway programs communicate. Figure 14-7 shows the interrela-
tionship of the Web browser, Web server, and CGI programs.

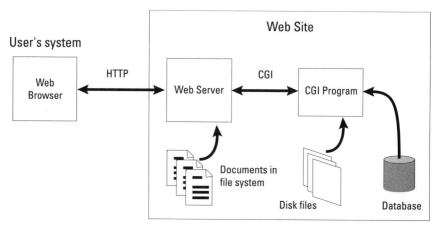

Figure 14-7 The Web server can access external resources through CGI programs.

As Figure 14-7 shows, the Web browser running on the user's system exchanges information with a Web server using HTTP. The Web server and the CGI programs typically run on the same system where the Web server resides. Depending on the type of request from the browser, the Web server either provides a document from its own document directory or executes a CGI program.

CGI in action

When the user retrieves a dynamic HTML document through CGI, the basic sequence of events is as follows:

1. The user clicks on some link that causes the Web browser to request an HTML document that contains a form.

2. The Web server sends the HTML form, which the browser displays.

3. The user fills in the fields of the form and clicks on the Submit button. The browser, in turn, sends the form's data using the GET or POST method (as specified by the method attribute of the <form> tag in the HTML form). In either method, the browser sends the URL specified in the <form> tag's action attribute.

4. From the URL, the Web server determines that it should activate the gateway program listed in the URL and send the information to that program. (The "How a Web browser sends form data to the Web server" section explains this.)

5. The gateway program processes the information and returns HTML text to the Web server (which reads the output of the gateway program). The server, in turn, adds a MIME header and returns the HTML text to the Web browser.

6. The Web browser displays the document received from the Web server. That document contains information that depends on what the user entered in the HTML form (often the information may be nothing more than a confirmation from the server that the user's input has been received).

After reading this sequence of events, you probably have the following questions:

* How does the Web browser send data using the GET and POST methods?
* How does the Web server determine that a URL specifies a gateway program and not a normal document?
* How does the Web server send information to the gateway program and receive information from the program?
* How does the gateway program process the information sent by the Web server?
* How does the gateway program return information to the server?

You'll find answers to these questions and more in the followings sections.

How a Web browser sends form data to the Web server

The Web browser uses the method attribute of the <form> tag to determine how to send the form's data to the Web server. There are two submission methods:

* GET: The Web browser submits the form's data as a part of the URL.
* POST: The Web browser sends the form's data separately from the URL; the server then sends the data to the CGI program's standard input (that means in a Perl CGI program, you'll read the input with the <STDIN> syntax).

Because you design the form as well as the CGI program that processes the form's data, you can select a method that best suits your needs. The "GET versus POST" section provides some guidelines to help you choose the appropriate data submission method for your forms.

NOTE If you do not specify a `method` attribute in the `<form>` tag, the browser uses the `GET` method by default.

THE GET METHOD OF DATA SUBMISSION

The `GET` method is so called because the browser uses the HTTP `GET` command to submit the data. The `GET` command sends a URL to the Web server. That means that if you want to send a form's contents to the server using the `GET` method, the browser must include all data in the URL.

The key features of the `GET` method of data submission are as follows:

✳ The values of all the fields are concatenated to the URL specified in the `action` attribute of the `<form>` tag. Each field's value appears in the `name=value` format (you specify each field's name with the `name` attribute of various elements, such as `<input>`, `<select>`, and `<textarea>`, that constitute an HTML form).

✳ To ensure that the Web server is not confused by special characters that may appear in the form's data, any character with special meaning is encoded using a special encoding scheme.

For example, the Alta Vista Web index (`http://www.altavista.digital.com/`) uses a form with the `GET` method of data submission. When you submit a query with the following search keywords:

```
"fairy tale" +frog -dragon
```

the Web browser sends the following URL back to the Alta Vista server:

```
http://www.altavista.digital.com/cgi-
    bin/query?pg=q&what=web&fmt=.&q=%22fairy+tale%22+%2Bfrog+-
    dragon
```

In this URL, everything following the question mark (?) constitutes form data. Each field is separated by an ampersand (&). Each blank space is converted to a plus sign (+); an actual plus sign becomes `%2B` (that means ASCII code 2B in hexadecimal); and each double quote is changed to `%22`.

THE POST METHOD OF DATA SUBMISSION

In the `POST` method of data submission, the Web browser sends the `POST` command (another HTTP command) to the server and includes the form's data in the body of that command.

NOTE The Web browser encodes the form's data identically whether you use the GET or the POST method of data submission. However, as you will see in the "How the Web server sends data to the CGI program" section, the CGI program receives the information in a different manner when you specify the POST method.

GET **VERSUS** POST

When you design an HTML form, you have the option of specifying either GET or POST as the data submission method. In the early days of the Web, the GET method was the only way a browser could send form data to the server. The server, in turn, passes the data to the CGI program in an environment variable. Both the URL and environment variables have upper limits on length — that means the GET method could not be used to transfer large amounts of form data from the browser to the server. (The upper limit on the length of environment variables depends on your system — some systems can handle only 1KB of data in an environment variable.)

The POST method was defined as a new way to transfer data without the limitations of GET. POST can handle any amount of data, because the browser sends the data as a separate stream (which the Web server then sends to the standard input of the CGI program).

GET and POST are both useful ways of sending data from the browser to the server. The basic guidelines for choosing a data submission method are as follows:

✳ Use GET to transfer a small amount of data and POST to send potentially large amounts of data. For example, GET is appropriate for a search form that solicits a few keywords from the user. On the other hand, you would want to use POST for a feedback form with a free-form text-entry area, because the user might enter a considerable amount of text.

✳ Use the GET method if you want to access the CGI program without using a form. For example, if you want to access a CGI program at the URL http://www.someplace.com/cgi-bin/dbquery with a field named keyword as input, you could invoke the CGI program with a URL such as the following:

http://www.someplace.com/cgi-bin/dbquery?keyword=Linux

If a CGI program is designed to receive data with the POST method, you cannot activate that program with a URL like this one.

When you define a form in an HTML document, use the preceding guidelines to decide whether to use the GET or the POST method of data submission.

How the Web server interprets a CGI URL

The URL specifying a CGI program looks like any other URL, but the Web server can examine the directory name and determine whether the URL is a normal document or a CGI program.

NOTE The conversion of a CGI URL into the complete path name of the CGI program depends on the Web server. In popular UNIX Web servers, a specific directive in a configuration file defines where the CGI programs are located. Typically, on UNIX systems, the `/cgi-bin` directory translates to `/usr/local/etc/httpd/cgi-bin` directory. If your Internet Service Provider (ISP) allows CGI scripts, the ISP should provide you with instructions on where to place the scripts and how to refer to the CGI scripts in a URL.

The Web server expects the CGI program's name to appear immediately following the CGI directory alias (such as `/cgi-bin/`). If the URL includes other path information following the program name, the Web server passes that information to the CGI program in an environment variable named `PATH_INFO`. For example, if you were to invoke the `/cgi-bin/dbquery` program with the following URL:

```
http://www.someplace.com/cgi-bin/dbquery/misc/items
```

the Web server places the string `/misc/items` in the `PATH_INFO` environment variable before running the `/cgi-bin/dbquery` program. This example illustrates another way to pass extra information to a CGI program.

How the Web server sends data to the CGI program

Some details of how the Web server sends data to the CGI program depend on whether the browser uses the `GET` or `POST` method to submit a form's data. The browser selects the method from the `method` attribute of the `<form>` tag which you wrote in the first place. That means you are in charge of deciding how you want your CGI program to accept input — through the `GET` or the `POST` method.

INFORMATION THROUGH ENVIRONMENT VARIABLES

Whether you use the `GET` or the `POST` method, the Web server uses a number of environment variables (see sidebar) to transfer helpful information to the CGI program. On a UNIX system that runs an NCSA (National Center for Supercomputing Applications) or Apache Web server, you can see these environment variables using a sample CGI program (called `/cgi-bin/test-cgi`) that comes with the NCSA Web server. The `/cgi-bin/test-cgi` program echoes back the relevant environment variables in an HTML document.

You can also see the effect of various query strings on the environment variables through the examples at the following URL:

```
http://hoohoo.ncsa.uiuc.edu/cgi/examples.html
```

Figure 14-8 shows the result of invoking the /cgi-bin/test-cgi program on a system running an Apache Web server.

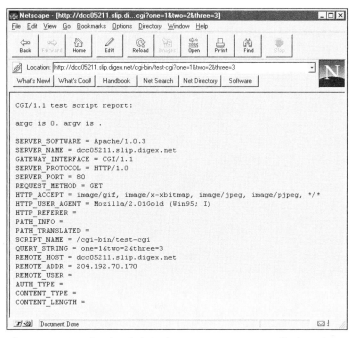

```
Netscape - [http://dcc05211.slip.di...cgi?one=1&two=2&three=3]
File  Edit  View  Go  Bookmarks  Options  Directory  Window  Help

  Back  Forward  Home  Edit  Reload  Images  Open  Print  Find  Stop

  Location: http://dcc05211.slip.digex.net/cgi-bin/test-cgi?one=1&two=2&three=3

  What's New!  What's Cool!  Handbook  Net Search  Net Directory  Software


  CGI/1.1 test script report:

  argc is 0. argv is .

  SERVER_SOFTWARE = Apache/1.0.3
  SERVER_NAME = dcc05211.slip.digex.net
  GATEWAY_INTERFACE = CGI/1.1
  SERVER_PROTOCOL = HTTP/1.0
  SERVER_PORT = 80
  REQUEST_METHOD = GET
  HTTP_ACCEPT = image/gif, image/x-xbitmap, image/jpeg, image/pjpeg, */*
  HTTP_USER_AGENT = Mozilla/2.01Gold (Win95; I)
  HTTP_REFERER =
  PATH_INFO =
  PATH_TRANSLATED =
  SCRIPT_NAME = /cgi-bin/test-cgi
  QUERY_STRING = one=1&two=2&three=3
  REMOTE_HOST = dcc05211.slip.digex.net
  REMOTE_ADDR = 204.192.70.170
  REMOTE_USER =
  AUTH_TYPE =
  CONTENT_TYPE =
  CONTENT_LENGTH =


  Document: Done
```

Figure 14-8   The /cgi-bin/test-cgi program displays the environment variables through which the Web server sends information to a CGI program.

As Figure 14-8 shows, the server defines 20 or so environment variables with a variety of information for the CGI program.

The very fact that the test-cgi program is invoked through a URL implies that the GET method is used to send any data to the server. You can see that the REQUEST_METHOD environment variable is indeed set to GET.

NOTE   Note that everything in the URL after the question mark (?) appears as the value of the environment variable QUERY_STRING. This is how the Web server sends a form's contents to the CGI program when the GET method is used.

ENVIRONMENT VARIABLES

An environment variable is nothing more than a name associated with a string. On a UNIX system, for example, the environment variable named PATH might be defined as follows:

```
PATH=/usr/local/bin:/bin:/usr/bin:/usr/X11/bin:.
```

The string to the right of the equal sign is the value of the PATH environment variable. The meaning of an environment variable depends on the program that uses the environment variable. By convention, the PATH environment variable is a sequence of directory names, each name separated from the preceding one by a colon (:). The period at the end of the list of directories also denotes a directory; it represents the current directory. The forward slash separates a directory name from its subdirectory name.

To see the value of an environment variable in a UNIX shell (the command interpreter for UNIX), use the echo command followed by the environment variable's name with a dollar sign prefix ($). Thus, to see the value of PATH, type the following command:

```
echo $PATH
```

Programs written in Perl can query the values of environment variables through the %ENV associative array. Therefore, the environment variables provide a convenient mechanism to transfer information from one program to another. The Web server uses environment variables to send information to a CGI program.

You'll find it instructive to look at the test-cgi program — that program happens to be a simple shell script. On a UNIX system with a default installation of the NCSA Web server, you can view the file with the following command:

```
cat /usr/local/etc/httpd/cgi-bin/test-cgi
```

Here is the result of this command:

```
#!/bin/sh

echo Content-type: text/plain
echo

echo CGI/1.1 test script report:
echo

echo argc is $#. argv is "$*".
echo
```

```
echo SERVER_SOFTWARE = $SERVER_SOFTWARE
echo SERVER_NAME = $SERVER_NAME
echo GATEWAY_INTERFACE = $GATEWAY_INTERFACE
echo SERVER_PROTOCOL = $SERVER_PROTOCOL
echo SERVER_PORT = $SERVER_PORT
echo REQUEST_METHOD = $REQUEST_METHOD
echo HTTP_ACCEPT = "$HTTP_ACCEPT"
echo HTTP_USER_AGENT = "$HTTP_USER_AGENT"
echo HTTP_REFERER = "$HTTP_REFERER"
echo PATH_INFO = "$PATH_INFO"
echo PATH_TRANSLATED = "$PATH_TRANSLATED"
echo SCRIPT_NAME = "$SCRIPT_NAME"
echo QUERY_STRING = "$QUERY_STRING"
echo REMOTE_HOST = $REMOTE_HOST
echo REMOTE_ADDR = $REMOTE_ADDR
echo REMOTE_USER = $REMOTE_USER
echo AUTH_TYPE = $AUTH_TYPE
echo CONTENT_TYPE = $CONTENT_TYPE
echo CONTENT_LENGTH = $CONTENT_LENGTH
```

This shell script uses the echo command to display the values of the environment variables.

This simple UNIX shell script happens to be a complete CGI program and, as such, demonstrates the basic format of a CGI program's output. Notice the first two echo commands:

```
echo Content-type: text/plain
echo
```

These lines send a header telling the Web server that the CGI program is returning a text document. After that, the script prints out the value of each environment variable on a separate line.

You can guess the meaning of some of the environment variables shown in Figure 14-8. Consult Table 14-3 for a description of some environment variables commonly used in CGI.

TABLE 14-3 Useful CGI environment variables

Environment variable	Description
AUTH_TYPE	Name of authentication method used to validate the user.
CONTENT_LENGTH	Number of bytes of data being sent (used with the POST method).
CONTENT_TYPE	Multimedia Internet Mail Extension (MIME) type of data being sent to the CGI program (used with the POST method).
GATEWAY_INTERFACE	Name and version number of gateway interface (currently CGI/1.1).
HTTP_ACCEPT	MIME types that the Web browser accepts (such as image/gif, image/x-xbitmap, image/jpeg, */*).
HTTP_REFERER	URL of the document from where this request originated.
HTTP_USER_AGENT	Name and version of the Web browser making the request.
PATH_INFO	Any extra path names following the CGI program's name in the URL.
PATH_TRANSLATED	PATH_INFO appended to the server's document root directory.
QUERY_STRING	Everything following the question mark (?) in the URL (this is how a CGI program receives the data from an HTML form that uses the GET method).
REMOTE_ADDR	Internet protocol (IP) address of the system from where this request originated.
REMOTE_HOST	Host name of the system from where this request was made (this is the system where the user is running the Web browser).
REMOTE_USER	Name of authenticated user (if the CGI program is password-protected, this is the user name under which the program is being accessed).
REQUEST_METHOD	Data submission method used (for example, GET or POST).
SCRIPT_NAME	Name of the CGI program (for example, /cgi-bin/test-cgi).
SERVER_NAME	Host name or IP address of system where Web server is running (for example, www.idgbooks.com).
SERVER_PORT	Port number where request was received (for example, 80 for HTTP requests).
SERVER_PROTOCOL	Name and version number of protocol used for this request (for example, HTTP/1.0).

Environment variable	Description
SERVER_SOFTWARE	Name and version of Web server software (such as NCSA/1.5.2 or Apache/1.0.3).

> **NOTE** Note that when you specify the GET method, the Web server places all required data in the QUERY_STRING environment variable.

INFORMATION THROUGH COMMAND-LINE ARGUMENTS

In UNIX, you run most programs with a command that has the following general format:

```
progname option1 option2 ... optionN
```

where *progname* is the name of the program's executable file. A single line of command commonly is referred to as a *command line*. On a command line, you enter the name of a computer program followed by one or more arguments (or *options*) known as *command-line arguments* (or *command-line options*). You pass information to the program through its command-line arguments. Of course, the program must be designed to accept and deal with the command-line arguments.

When the Web server runs a CGI program, the server can use command-line arguments to pass information to the program. Indeed, the CGI specification calls for the Web server to send simple queries to a CGI program through command-line arguments (a *query* is everything following the question mark in a CGI URL). For example, consider the following CGI URL:

```
http://www.someplace.com/cgi-bin/test-cgi?one+two+three
```

In this case, the Web server starts the /cgi-bin/test-cgi program with the following command line:

```
/cgi-bin/test-cgi one two three
```

That means /cgi-bin/test-cgi receives three command-line arguments. By convention, the Web server replaces any plus signs in the query with spaces, and that's how one+two+three becomes a sequence of three arguments: one two three.

> **NOTE** If the query contains an equal sign (=), then the Web server does not provide anything in the command-line arguments. In any case, the entire query is always provided in the QUERY_STRING environment variable.

TIP Note that only the GET method uses command-line arguments to pass information to a CGI program. Even then, the technique is used when the query is simple. Because the query is always available in the QUERY_STRING environment variable, you are better off using that environment variable to access the query.

INFORMATION THROUGH STANDARD INPUT

When you use the POST method in an HTML form, the Web server sends the form's data to the standard input of the CGI program. In other words, a CGI program must read the standard input in order to accept data sent using the POST method.

The CONTENT_LENGTH environment variable indicates the total number of bytes to be read. The MIME type of the input data is specified in the CONTENT_TYPE environment variable.

Unless you specify a different encoding through the enctype attribute of the <form> tag, the CGI program receives the form's data in the application/x-www-form-urlencoded MIME type and the CONTENT_TYPE environment variable is set to application/x-www-form-urlencoded. That means the information is URL encoded: a space is replaced with a plus sign (+), fields are separated by an ampersand (&), and any nonalphanumeric character is replaced with a %*xx* code (where *xx* is the character's ASCII code in hexadecimal format).

How a CGI program processes a form's data

Depending on the data submission method — GET or POST — a CGI program receives information through the QUERY_STRING environment variable or through the standard input. Typically, you associate a CGI program with a form through the <form> tag's action attribute and, at the same time, specify whether the GET or the POST method is to be used to send the form's data. Thus, you could design a CGI program to handle either GET or POST input.

NOTE One school of thought is that you should design your CGI program to handle both GET and POST methods of input. You can do so because you can determine the input method at run time by checking the value of the REQUEST_METHOD environment variable. The reason for handling both GET and POST requests is that you can then use that CGI program in two ways:

✴ To handle input from a form using the POST method

✴ To support predefined requests as part of a URL and submitted using the GET method

Here are the basic steps for a CGI program designed to handle URL-encoded data sent through both GET *and* POST *methods:*

1. Check the REQUEST_METHOD environment variable to determine whether the request is a GET or a POST.

2. If the method is GET, use the value of the QUERY_STRING environment variable as the input. Also check for any extra path information in the PATH_INFO environment variable. Then go to Step 4.

3. If the method is POST, get the length of the input (in number of bytes) from the CONTENT_LENGTH environment variable. Then read that many bytes from the standard input.

4. Extract the *name=value* pairs for various fields by splitting the input data at the ampersand character (&), which separates the values of fields.

5. In each *name=value* pair, convert all %*xx* sequences into ASCII characters (here, *xx* denotes a pair of hexadecimal digits)

6. In each *name=value* pair, convert all plus signs (+) to spaces.

7. Save the *name=value* pairs denoting values of specific fields for later use.

After you decode the input and find the values of all the fields, you know what to do with the fields because you designed the form in the first place. For example, if it's a registration form that solicits the name and e-mail address, you may simply store the decoded information in a database and return an acknowledgment in the form of an HTML document.

How a CGI program returns information to the server

Regardless of how the Web server passes information to the CGI program, the CGI program always returns information to the server by writing to the standard output. In other words, if the CGI program wants to return an HTML document (typically constructed on the fly), the program must write that document to the standard output. The Web server then processes that output and sends the data back to the Web browser that had originally submitted the request.

The CGI program cannot simply begin sending an HTML document back to the server; the program also must send some header information. The Web server accepts the CGI program's output, adds some HTTP codes and a MIME header, and then sends everything to the Web browser.

A CGI program must write at least a minimal MIME header before writing the data to standard output. A minimal header includes the MIME type of the data with a line such as the following:

```
Content-type: text/html
```

The MIME type can be anything consistent with the data the CGI program is returning to the Web server. For example, for a plain text file, the MIME header should be:

```
Content-type: text/plain
```

From a CGI program, you can also send back an image. For a GIF image, you use the following MIME header:

```
Content-type: image/gif
```

TIP If you return binary data (such as a GIF image) from a CGI program, you should include the Content-length header with the size of the data. For example, if you return a GIF image with 10,940 bytes of data, you need the following header line:

```
Content-length: 10940
```

You may also include other header lines. Table 14-4 shows a list of typical header lines:

TABLE 14-4 List of header lines returned by CGI programs

Header	Description
Content-type	MIME type of data being sent to the Web server.
Content-length	Number of bytes being sent (you must provide this for binary data).
Expires	Date and time when document is no longer valid (for example, Expires: Friday, 31-Dec-99 05:15:10 GMT).
Location	New URL that the server should send back to the Web browser (you cannot use the Location header with other headers).
Pragma	Cache control (for example, you can turn off browser-side caching with Pragma: no-cache).
Status	Status code such as Status: 200 OK (you cannot use the Status header with other headers).

TIP The only key point you must remember is that the last line of a MIME header block must end with a blank line. After the blank line marking the end of the header, you can begin the CGI program's output, which is usually an HTML document.

BONUS

Creating Tables in HTML

Tables are clearly a logical way to format and present many different types of information to the user. For example, you can use tables to list products and their prices at a Web site offering products for sale. You can write Perl CGI programs that print results in tabular form. This section shows you how to create tables in HTML.

Initially, HTML did not include support for tabular output. Web browsers such as Netscape Navigator, Mosaic, and Internet Explorer stepped in to correct this deficiency and added extensions that support table layout. By now, the HTML standard includes the capability to display tables. The following HTML elements are meant for displaying tables:

* `<caption>` to specify a table caption
* `<table>` to enclose a table definition (the closing tag is `</table>`)
* `<td>` to define a cell that represents the table's data
* `<th>` to define a cell that constitutes part of the table header
* `<tr>` to define a row in a table

HTML table model

The basic HTML table model encloses an entire table definition inside a pair of `<table>` and `</table>` tags. The table is made up of rows; you have to define each row using the `<tr>` and `</tr>` pair.

Each row consists of a number of cells. There are two types of cells:

* A *table header cell* (enclosed in a pair of `<th>` and `</th>` tags) is a part of the table's header. Table headers can span entire rows or go down a column.
* A *table data cell* (enclosed in a pair of `<td>` and `</td>` tags) is part of the table's data.

The total number of cells in the row's definition is the number of columns in the table. Header and data cells can span multiple columns. If a cell spans more than one column, use the `colspan` attribute to specify the number of columns over which that cell extends. (You'll understand these better when you see an example in the "A sample table" section.)

You can optionally provide a caption for the table by enclosing the caption string in `<caption>` and `</caption>` tags.

Here is the skeleton of a simple table with three columns (the number of columns is determined by the cells in each row):

```
<table border>
<caption>Table's caption</caption>
<tr>
    <th>Col 1 Header</th>
    <th>Col 2 Header</th>
    <th>Col 3 Header</th>
</tr>

<tr>
    <td>Row 1, Col 1</td>
    <td>Row 1, Col 2</td>
    <td>Row 1, Col 3</td>
</tr>

<tr>
    <td>Row 2, Col 1</td>
    <td>Row 2, Col 2</td>
    <td>Row 2, Col 3</td>
</tr>

<tr>
    <td colspan=3 align=center>This spans 3 columns.</td>
</tr>

<!-... more rows...->
</table>
```

You should be able to discern the pattern of tags that constitute the full table. The `<table>` tag includes the `border` attribute — this causes Netscape Navigator to display borders around the cells. Also, the last row shows a data cell that spans across all three columns (the `colspan=3` attribute specifies this) and the contents of that cell are centered (that's indicated by the `align=center` attribute).

In fact, this is a valid table definition that Netscape Navigator renders as shown in Figure 14-9.

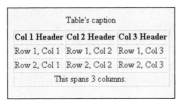

Table's caption		
Col 1 Header	Col 2 Header	Col 3 Header
Row 1, Col 1	Row 1, Col 2	Row 1, Col 3
Row 2, Col 1	Row 2, Col 2	Row 2, Col 3
This spans 3 columns.		

Figure 14-9 A skeletal table rendered by Netscape Navigator

By comparing the HTML source with the rendered form of the table, you should be able to see how the table layout tags (`<table>`, `<tr>`, `<th>`, and `<td>`) work. The next section shows a more complex table layout.

A sample table

For a more realistic table, consider a tax table that shows the amount you owe based on your income range and filing status (whether you are single, married, and so on). Figure 14-10 shows a partial tax table as it appears in Netscape Navigator.

Figure 14-10 A relatively complicated sample table viewed in Netscape Navigator

To format this table, you first have to realize that there are six columns (even though some of the headers span multiple columns). Next, you have to go down the table row-by-row and specify each row. For example, the first row has only two header cells: the first one spans the first two columns and the next one spans the other four columns. You have to use the `colspan` attribute to specify this. Also, to center the text in the cell, use the `align=center` attribute.

Netscape Navigator also accepts the `cellpadding` attribute, whose value determines the spacing between the edge of a cell and its contents. If you do not specify the `cellpadding`, the browser leaves a one-pixel border between a cell's edge and its contents.

Another useful attribute is `cellspacing` — this attribute controls the amount of space between adjacent cells in a table. The value of `cellspacing` is also used as the spacing between the table border and cells that lie along the edges of the table.

If you go through the table row-by-row, here is the HTML source you'll end up creating (Figure 14-10 results from this HTML source):

```
<html>
<head><title>A sample table</title></head>
<body>

<table border cellpadding=4>
<caption>Partial Tax Table</caption>

<tr>
    <th colspan=2 align=center>If line 37 is</th>
    <th colspan=4 align=center>And you are</th>
</tr>

<tr>
    <th>At least</th>
    <th>But less than</th>
    <th>Single</th>
    <th>Married(joint)</th>
    <th>Married(sep)</th>
    <th>Head of House</th>
</tr>

<tr>
    <th colspan=2><br></th>
    <th colspan=4 align=center>Your tax is:</th>
</tr>

<tr>
    <th>48,000</th>
    <th>48,050</th>
    <td>10,412</td>
    <td>8,377</td>
    <td>10,939</td>
    <td>9,385</td>
</tr>

<tr>
    <th>48,050</th>
    <th>48,100</th>
```

```
            <td>10,426</td>
            <td>8,391</td>
            <td>10,955</td>
            <td>9,399</td>
        </tr>

        <tr>
            <th>48,100</th>
            <th>48,150</th>
            <td>10,440</td>
            <td>8,405</td>
            <td>10,970</td>
            <td>9,413</td>
        </tr>

        <tr>
            <th>48,150</th>
            <th>48,200</th>
            <td>10,454</td>
            <td>8,419</td>
            <td>10,86</td>
            <td>9,427</td>
        </tr>

        <tr>
            <td colspan=6 align=center><em>More taxes to come...</em></td>
        </tr>

    </table>

    </body>
    </html>
```

Summary

The most useful Web sites are the ones that provide customized information. That means instead of static Web pages with predetermined content, users get dynamic Web pages created on the fly based on user input. Such dynamic Web pages rely on CGI programs.

This chapter describes how CGI programs work and how you can create HTML forms that invoke CGI programs on the Web server.

As a bonus, you learn how to create HTML tables. Tables can be really useful when displaying results of a search to the user.

The next chapter goes into CGI programming in Perl — the most popular language for CGI programming.

WRITING CGI PROGRAMS IN PERL

IN THIS CHAPTER YOU LEARN THESE KEY SKILLS

Although you can write a CGI program in any language, Perl has become synonymous with CGI programming. Perl's text-processing features make it an excellent tool for writing CGI programs (which involve parsing URLs and preparing HTML text that is sent back to the user).

This chapter introduces you to CGI programming with Perl through examples of typical CGI programs.

Writing a Perl CGI Program

As explained in Chapter 14, the basic steps for a CGI program are as follows:

1. Read the CGI query into a string. Depending on the method of data submission (GET or POST), the input is either in the QUERY_STRING environment variable or read from standard input (STDIN in Perl).

2. Separate out the fields and their values from the query. In Perl, you can use the `split` function to separate the fields.

3. Decode the URL-encoded input values.

4. Store the fields in associative arrays.

5. Process the fields as appropriate.

Of these steps, only the last step is specific to a form. The other steps are performed for all types of form data. That means it's best to implement the first four steps using a library of Perl subroutines. In fact, as you learn in the "Using the `cgi-lib.pl` Library" section, you can perform these steps using Steven Brenner's `cgi-lib.pl` Perl library.

A simple CGI program needs to display the CGI environment variables in an HTML page. (*CGI environment variables* means the environment variables that are used by the Web server to communicate with a CGI program.) You can perform this chore easily in Perl.

Just to make the output interesting, here is a Perl script that presents the environment variables in a tabular format:

```perl
#!/usr/local/bin/perl
# File: showenv.pl
# Print out the environment variables in a tabular form
# Author: Naba Barkakati

# Array of environment variables
@envvars = (SERVER_SOFTWARE, SERVER_NAME,
            GATEWAY_INTERFACE,SERVER_PROTOCOL,
            SERVER_PORT, REQUEST_METHOD,
            PATH_INFO, PATH_TRANSLATED, SCRIPT_NAME,
            QUERY_STRING, REMOTE_HOST, REMOTE_ADDR,
            REMOTE_USER, AUTH_TYPE, CONTENT_TYPE,
            CONTENT_LENGTH, HTTP_ACCEPT,
            HTTP_USER_AGENT, HTTP_REFERER);

# Note the extra newline needed to indicate
# end of MIME header
print "Content-type: text/html\n\n";

# Print HTML tags
print "<html>\n";
print "<head>\n";
print "<title>Environment variables</title>\n";
print "</head>\n";
```

```perl
    print "<body>";

# Display the environment variables as a table

    print "<table border>\n";
    print "<caption>List of environment variables</caption>\n";
    print "<tr><th>Variable</th><th>Value</th></tr>\n";

    foreach $var(@envvars)
    {
        if($ENV{$var})
        {
            print "<tr>\n";
            print "<td><strong>$var</strong></td>\n";
            print "<td>$ENV{$var}</td>\n";
            print "</tr>\n";
        }
    }
    print "</table>\n";
    print "</body>\n";
    print "</html>\n";
```

> **TIP** Remember to edit the first line of the Perl script to reflect the exact location of the `perl` program on the system running your Web server. On most systems, `perl` is in the `/usr/local/bin` directory, but it could be in some other arbitrary location, such as `/usr/contrib/bin`.

To test the sample Perl CGI script, place the script in the location where your server expects CGI programs. Then use a Web browser to invoke the script by providing its URL. For example, on my server, the URL would look this way:

    http://www.lnbsoft.com/exec-bin/showenv.pl

Figure 15-1 shows the result of running the script on my server.

Notice the complete URL shown in the `Location` line of the Netscape browser in Figure 15-1. As the URL shows, you can submit a query to the script by appending the query to the URL — a question mark separates the URL proper from the query string. That query string is reported as the value of the QUERY_STRING environment variable.

This simple script gives you an idea of how to write CGI programs in Perl. The `showenv.pl` script, however, does not show how to process a query from the user. As you'll see in the next section, the best way to process a query is to use a well-known Perl library named `cgi-lib.pl`.

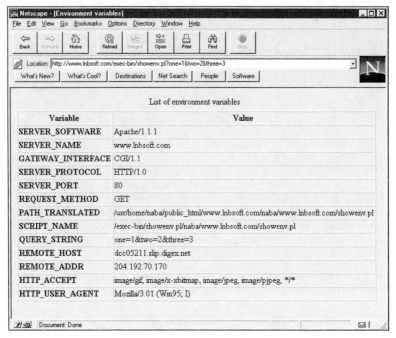

Figure 15-1 The list of environment variables displayed by the showenv.pl program

CGI Programming with the cgi-lib.pl Library

Each CGI program is designed to handle a specific query submitted by the user by filling in a form. However, all form data requires similar processing to extract the fields and their values. For this, you could use a common set of subroutines. As you might expect for a popular tool such as Perl, there is already such a Perl library, and that common library happens to be cgi-lib.pl by Steven Brenner.

TIP Just as Perl is the accepted programming language for CGI programs, cgi-lib.pl is the accepted library for parsing the CGI query string that the Web server sends to the CGI program. By using the cgi-lib.pl library, you can quickly create Perl programs to handle form input.

NOTE The cgi-lib.pl library works with both Perl 4 and Perl 5. If your ISP has Perl 5 installed, you may want to use the CGI module, an object-oriented CGI processing module that works in Perl 5 only. I describe the CGI module in the Bonus section, at the end of this chapter.

Many ISPs and many Web sites still use Perl 4. That's why I present `cgi-lib.pl`, because it works with both Perl 4 and Perl 5.

Obtaining `cgi-lib.pl`

WEB PATH You can download the latest version of `cgi-lib.pl` from the official `cgi-lib.pl` home page at the following URL:

`http://www.bio.cam.ac.uk/cgi-lib/`

As of this writing, version 2.14 is the latest released version of `cgi-lib.pl`. However, it's easier to understand (because there are fewer subroutines) an earlier version (1.14), which is what is described in this chapter. This book's companion CD-ROM includes both version 1.14 and version 2.14 of `cgi-lib.pl`.

TIP On Windows systems, you will find the `cgi-lib.pl` file in `D:\BOOK\WIN\CH15` directory, where `D:` is the CD-ROM drive letter. On UNIX systems, assuming that the CD-ROM is mounted on the `/cdrom` directory, look for the file `/cdrom/book/unix/ch15/cgi-lib.pl`.

Because `cgi-lib.pl` is a library of Perl subroutines in a text file, there is nothing much to install. All you need to do is get the latest version of the file and place it in the `/cgi-bin/` directory of your server (for NCSA and Apache Web servers, the default path name of the CGI binary directory is `/usr/local/etc/httpd/cgi-bin`). If your server is set up to load CGI programs from a different directory, place the `cgi-lib.pl` file in that directory.

Understanding `cgi-lib.pl`

The `cgi-lib.pl` library is popular because it's simple to understand and use. Although version 2.14 is somewhat more complex, you can understand the basic functionality by studying version 1.14, which is shown in the following listing:

```
#!/usr/local/bin/perl

# Perl Routines to Manipulate CGI input
#
# Copyright (c) 1995 Steven E. Brenner
# Permission granted to use and modify this library so long as the
# copyright above is maintained, modifications are documented, and
# credit is given for any use of the library.
#
# Thanks are due to many people for reporting bugs and suggestions
# especially Meng Weng Wong, Maki Watanabe, Bo Frese Rasmussen,
```

```
# Andrew Dalke, Mark-Jason Dominus, Dave Dittrich, Jason Mathews

# For more information, see:
#      http://www.bio.cam.ac.uk/web/form.html
#      http://www.seas.upenn.edu/~mengwong/forms/

# Minimalist http form and script
  (http://www.bio.cam.ac.uk/web/minimal.cgi):
#
# require "cgi-lib.pl";
# if (&ReadParse(*input)) {
#    print &PrintHeader, &PrintVariables(%input);
# } else {
#    print &PrintHeader,'<form><input type="submit"> Data: <input
  name="myfield">';
#}

# ReadParse
# Reads in GET or POST data, converts it to unescaped text,
# creates key/value pairs in %in, using '\0' to separate multiple
# selections

# Returns TRUE if there was input, FALSE if there was no input
# UNDEF may be used in the future to indicate some failure.

# Now that cgi scripts can be put in the normal file space, it is
# useful to combine both the form and the script in one place.
# If no parameters are given (i.e., ReadParse returns FALSE), then
# a form could be output.

# If a variable-glob parameter (e.g., *cgi_input) is passed to
# ReadParse, information is stored there, rather than in $in, @in,
# and %in.

sub ReadParse {
  local (*in) = @_ if @_;
  local ($i, $key, $val);

  # Read in text
  if (&MethGet) {
    $in = $ENV{'QUERY_STRING'};
  } elsif (&MethPost) {
    read(STDIN,$in,$ENV{'CONTENT_LENGTH'});
  }
```

```perl
@in = split(/[&;]/,$in);

foreach $i (0 .. $#in) {
  # Convert plus's to spaces
  $in[$i] =~ s/\+/ /g;

  # Split into key and value.
  ($key, $val) = split(/=/,$in[$i],2); # splits on the first =.

  # Convert %XX from hex numbers to alphanumeric
  $key =~ s/%(..)/pack("c",hex($1))/ge;
  $val =~ s/%(..)/pack("c",hex($1))/ge;

  # Associate key and value
  $in{$key} .= "\0" if (defined($in{$key})); # \0 is the multiple
separator
  $in{$key} .= $val;

}

return scalar(@in);
}


# PrintHeader
# Returns the magic line which tells WWW that we're an HTML document

sub PrintHeader {
  return "Content-type: text/html\n\n";
}


# HtmlTop
# Returns the <head> of a document and the beginning of the body
# with the title and a body <h1> header as specified by the parameter

sub HtmlTop
{
  local ($title) = @_;

  return <<END_OF_TEXT;
<html>
<head>
<title>$title</title>
</head>
```

```
<body>
<h1>$title</h1>
END_OF_TEXT
}

# Html Bot
# Returns the </body>, </html> codes for the bottom of every HTML
# page

sub HtmlBot
{
    return "</body>\n</html>\n";
 }

# MethGet
# Return true if this cgi call was using the GET request, false
# otherwise

sub MethGet {
    return ($ENV{'REQUEST_METHOD'} eq "GET");
}


# MethPost
# Return true if this cgi call was using the POST request, false
# otherwise

sub MethPost {
    return ($ENV{'REQUEST_METHOD'} eq "POST");
}


# MyURL
# Returns a URL to the script

sub MyURL  {
    local ($port);
    $port = ":" . $ENV{'SERVER_PORT'} if  $ENV{'SERVER_PORT'} != 80;
    return  'http://' . $ENV{'SERVER_NAME'} .  $port .
    $ENV{'SCRIPT_NAME'};
}


  # CgiError
```

```perl
# Prints out an error message which contains appropriate headers,
# markup, etcetera.
# Parameters:
#  If no parameters, gives a generic error message
#  Otherwise, the first parameter will be the title and the rest
#  will be given as different paragraphs of the body

sub CgiError {
  local (@msg) = @_;
  local ($i,$name);

  if (!@msg) {
    $name = &MyURL;
    @msg = ("Error: script $name encountered fatal error");
  };

  print &PrintHeader;
  print "<html><head><title>$msg[0]</title></head>\n";
  print "<body><h1>$msg[0]</h1>\n";
  foreach $i (1 .. $#msg) {
    print "<p>$msg[$i]</p>\n";
  }
  print "</body></html>\n";
}


# CgiDie
# Identical to CgiError, but also quits with the passed error
# message.

sub CgiDie {
  local (@msg) = @_;
  &CgiError (@msg);
  die @msg;
}

# PrintVariables
# Nicely formats variables in an associative array passed as a
# parameter
# And returns the HTML string.
sub PrintVariables {
  local (%in) = @_;
  local ($old, $out, $output);
  $old = $*;   $* =1;
```

```
        $output .=  "\n<dl compact>\n";
        foreach $key (sort keys(%in)) {
          foreach (split("\0", $in{$key})) {
            ($out = $_) =~ s/\n/<br>\n/g;
            $output .=  "<dt><b>$key</b>\n <dd><i>$out</i><br>\n";
          }
        }
        $output .=  "</dl>\n";
        $* = $old;

        return $output;
    }

    # PrintVariablesShort
    # Now obsolete; just calls PrintVariables

    sub PrintVariablesShort {
      return &PrintVariables(@_);
    }

    1; #return true
```

The `cgi-lib.pl` library includes the following Perl subroutines:

Name	Description
ReadParse	Reads and parses the CGI query for both GET and PUT methods. Places parsed result in associative array that you provide as an argument. Returns TRUE if there is a query; otherwise, returns FALSE.
PrintHeader	Prints the MIME header (Content-type: text/html) with an extra blank line indicating end-of-header.
HtmlTop	Prints the top of the HTML document, including a title that you provide as argument.
HtmlBot	Prints the bottom of the HTML document with the ending </body> and </html> tags.
MethGet	Returns TRUE if the CGI query came as a GET request.
MethPost	Returns TRUE if the CGI query came as a POST request.
MyURL	Returns a complete HTTP URL for your script (such as http://www.someplace.com:8000/cgi-bin/dbquery.pl).

Name	Description
CgiError	Prints an HTML document with an error message. If you provide an array of strings as an argument, the first string is used as a title and the rest are displayed in the body of the HTML document. If you do not provide any arguments, a generic error message is used as the body of the HTML document.
CgiDie	Calls CgiError and then the script quits with a call to the die function.
PrintVariables	Prints the variables in the associative array that you pass as an argument (use this subroutine to print the fields and their values).

Using cgi-lib.pl

It's straightforward to use the subroutines from the cgi-lib.pl library. The general sequence of subroutine calls is as follows:

1. Call the ReadParse subroutine to process the CGI query.

2. If ReadParse returns TRUE, process the query (which is now available in an associative array). Output the desired HTML document by calling PrintHeader, HtmlTop, and HtmlBot.

3. Call CgiDie or CgiError to report any error conditions through an HTML page.

You can understand this sequence best by studying a skeleton script, such as the one shown here:

```
#!/usr/local/bin/perl

# Include the cgi-lib.pl library with a require function
# require "cgi-lib.pl";

# Read and parse input (in this case result is in the associative
# array named input)

if(&ReadParse(*input))
{

# Successfully read and parsed the query string.
# Access specific fields from the input array. For example,
# if you have a field named keyword, access that field's value with
# the construct $input{'keyword'}
```

```
# Output HTML using the PrintHeader and HtmlTop subroutines
    print &PrintHeader;
    print &HtmlTop("Title of page");

# Print any other text you want

# End with the string returned by HtmlBot
    print &HtmlBot;
}
else
{
# You might want to generate an error message if ReadParse fails
# Call CgiDieor CgiError to do this
    &CgiDie("Error reading form input",
                    "A descriptive error message.");
}
```

In the next section, you see a more complete example of a Perl CGI script that uses the `cgi-lib.pl` library.

Implementing a Feedback Form

One of the common uses of CGI programming is to solicit and accept feedback from users. The next few sections present a simple CGI program to handle the input from a feedback form. The sample Perl program illustrates the use of the `cgi-lib.pl` library and also shows how to send mail from a CGI program. This program assumes that your Web site runs UNIX.

Designing the feedback form

 WEB PATH The first step is to create an HTML form through which the user can submit comments. Figure 15-2 shows a typical feedback form (at the URL `http://www.lnbsoft.com/feedback.html`) with the fields filled in.

Figure 15-2 A feedback form with the fields filled in

This form is used at the site `www.lnbsoft.com` to accept user feedback and mail those comments to myself (the Webmaster). The HTML source for the form shown in Figure 15-2 looks like this:

```
<html>

<head>
<TITLE>
LNB Software: Feedback
</TITLE>
</head>

<body>

<h2>
<center>
Feedback
</center>
</h2>

<hr>
```

```
<form method="post" action="http://www.lnbsoft.com/exec-
  bin/feedback.pl">

<h3>
Comments:
<br>

<textarea name="comment" rows="10" cols="40">
</textarea>
<br>

E-mail address:
<br>
<input type="text" name="e-mail" size=40 maxlength=60>
<br>

<input value="Send feedback" type=submit>  <input value="Clear
  all" type=reset>
</h3>
</form>

<hr>
<p>
Back to
<a href="http://www.lnbsoft.com/">Home Page</a>

</body>

</html>
```

As indicated by the `action` attribute of the `<form>` tag, this form's input is handled by a script named `feedback.pl` at my site. My ISP specifies `/exec-bin/` as the script directory; that's why the script's URL is `http://www.lnbsoft.com/ exec-bin/feedback.pl`. On most sites with NCSA and Apache Web servers, the scripts reside in the `/cgi-bin/` directory (of course, the `/cgi-bin/` directory name is an alias for another real directory on the system, usually `/usr/local/etc/httpd/ cgi-bin/`).

Note that the feedback form (shown in Figure 15-2) has two fields:

* The `comment` field is where the user enters comments.
* The `e-mail` field is where the user enters an e-mail address.

The `method` attribute of the `<form>` tag specifies that the Web browser should send the form's data through a `POST` request.

Processing user feedback

The `feedback.pl` CGI program that processes the feedback form has to perform the following tasks:

* If the method is not `POST`, report an error and exit.
* Read and parse the form's data.
* Save the comment and e-mail fields in a log file with a date and time stamp and any other relevant information (such as the site from which the user sent the feedback).
* Send an e-mail message to the Webmaster with the comment and e-mail fields so that the Webmaster can respond with a reply (provided the user enters an e-mail address in the e-mail field).
* Return a "thank you" note to the user in the form of an HTML document.

Here are some points to help you design the CGI program in Perl:

* Include the `cgi-lib.pl` library to parse the CGI input and the `ctime.pl` library to get the current date and time.
* Use the `MethPost` subroutine from `cgi-lib.pl` to check whether the method is `POST`.
* Call `ReadParse` to parse the input. Then open the log file and append the fields in that file. To add a time stamp, get the date and time by calling the `ctime` subroutine from the `ctime.pl` library.
* To send e-mail, run the `sendmail` program with a `-t` option and send a mail header with the addressee, subject, and body of the message to `sendmail` (see the `send_mail` subroutine in the following listing).

The following listing shows the complete `feedback.pl` program that handles input from the form shown in Figure 15-2:

```
#!/usr/local/bin/perl

# File: feedback.pl
# A simple Perl script to save user comments in a log file.
# Expects a POST request. Mails comment to Webmaster.

# Author: Naba Barkakati

require "cgi-lib.pl";
require "ctime.pl";

# A subroutine to send mail message to the Webmaster
#
```

```perl
# Usage: $to   = "Webmaster@site.com";
#        $sub  = "Feedback from web site";
#        $body = "Body of mail message";
#        &send_mail($to, $sub, $body);

sub send_mail
{
    local($addressee, $subject, $message) = @_;
    local($sendmail) = "/usr/lib/sendmail";

    open(SENDMAIL, "| $sendmail -t");

    print SENDMAIL "To: ", $addressee, "\n";
    print SENDMAIL "Subject: ", $subject, "\n\n",
    print SENDMAIL $message;

    close(SENDMAIL);
}

$my_home_page =
  "<a href=\"http://$ENV{SERVER_NAME}/\">$ENV{SERVER_NAME}</a>.";


# If the method is not POST, display error message and quit.

if(!&MethPost)
{
&send_mail("naba", "mtest", "Mail test from $ENV{SERVER_NAME}");
    &CgiDie("Form input only",
            "You need to submit data from a form to use this
  script.",
            "<hr>",
    "Return to <a
  href=\"http://$ENV{SERVER_NAME}/\">$ENV{SERVER_NAME}</a>.");
}

# If method is POST, process the input

$logfilename = "feedback.log";

$remote_host = $ENV{"REMOTE_HOST"};
$remote_addr = $ENV{"REMOTE_ADDR"};
$date = &ctime(time);
$separator = "-";
```

```perl
$separator x= 65;  # Separator is a line with 65 dashes
$separator .= "\n";

if(&ReadParse(*input))
{
# open the log file
    open(LOGFILE,">$logfilename");

# Lock the file to guard against another process updating the
# file as this script uses it
    $lock_exclusive = 2;
    $unclock = 8;
    flock(LOGFILE, $lock_exclusive);

# Append the comments to the log file
    print LOGFILE $date;
    print LOGFILE "From: $remote_host ($remote_addr)\n\n";
    print LOGFILE "E-mail address: ", $input{'e-mail'}, "\n\n";
    print LOGFILE "Comment: ", $input{'comment'}, "\n";
    print LOGFILE $separator;

# Close the log file
    close(LOGFILE);

# Remember to unlock the file
    flock(LOGFILE, $unlock);

# Send mail message to Webmaster at this host (assumes that server
# name is www.<mailhost> — you may want to change the following)
    $host = substr($ENV{SERVER_NAME}, 4);
    $to = "webmaster\@$host";
    $when = substr($date, 0, 10);
    $sub = "Feedback from: $remote_host on $when";
    $body = "$date\nFrom:$remote_host ($remote_addr)\nE-mail:\
            $input{'e-mail'}\n\nComment: $input{'comment'}\n";

    &send_mail($to, $sub, $body);

# Send back a response
    print &PrintHeader;
    print &HtmlTop("Thank you for the feedback");
    print "Thank you for the feedback. Your input will be
  forwarded \n",
```

```
                    "to the Webmaster ($to). You should receive a response
    soon.\n";
}
else
{
    print &PrintHeader;
    print &HtmlTop("Empty form");
    print "You did not fill out anything!\n";
}

# Output a link to return to home page of this site
    print "<hr>\n";
    print "Return to ", $my_home_page;

    print &HtmlBot;
```

When the user submits the comments from the form shown in Figure 15-2, the `feedback.pl` program appends the comments to the file `feedback.log` and also mails the comments to the Webmaster. Finally, the `feedback.pl` program sends a thank-you message to the user, as shown in Figure 15-3.

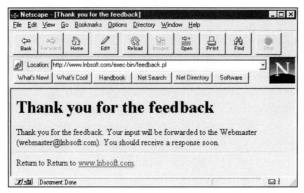

Figure 15-3 The "Thank you" message returned by the
`feedback.pl` CGI program

BONUS

CGI Programming with the CGI Module

The CGI.pm module, developed by Lincoln D. Stein, uses Perl 5's object-oriented style of programming. You need Perl version 5.001 or higher to use the CGI module; Perl 5.003 is the recommended version. If your Web site has Perl 5.001 or higher installed, you would want to use the CGI module in your CGI scripts.

Obtaining `CGI.pm`

CGI.pm is copyrighted by Lincoln D. Stein, but anyone can freely copy and distribute the program. You can download the latest version of CGI.pm from the official CGI.pm home page at the following URL:

```
http://www-genome.wi.mit.edu/ftp/pub/software/WWW/cgi_docs.html
```

On this page, you'll find complete current documentation on CGI.pm and instructions on how to download the module. You should download the CGI.pm file and copy it to the Perl library directory on your system. If you do not have permission to copy files to the Perl library directory, simply leave the CGI.pm file in the same directory as your CGI scripts (that make use of the CGI module).

As of this writing, version 2.31 is the latest released version of CGI.pm. Because CGI.pm can be freely distributed, this book's companion CD-ROM includes version 2.31 of CGI.pm.

TIP On Windows systems, you will find the CGI.pm file in D:\BOOK\WIN\CH15 directory, where D: is the CD-ROM drive letter. On UNIX systems, assuming that the CD-ROM is mounted on the /cdrom directory, look for the file /cdrom/book/unix/ch15/CGI.pm.

Using `CGI.pm`

Like the cgi-lib.pl library, CGI.pm enables you to accept a query (submitted through an HTML form) and easily extract the parameters submitted by the user. Unlike cgi-lib.pl with its procedural interface, CGI.pm provides its functionality through a CGI object. To use the CGI module, you begin by inserting the following statement in your Perl script:

```
use CGI;
```

After that, create a CGI object as follows:

```
$query = new CGI;
```

The creation of the CGI object involves parsing the CGI query string and extracting all environment variables relevant to CGI programming (you can find the details in Chapter 14). The return value, $query, will be a reference to the new CGI object. From then on, you can access the methods of the CGI object through the $query reference.

Parsing a CGI query is only one part of the CGI module, and the parsing occurs when you create the CGI object. Additionally, the CGI object has many more features, such as the following:

* Methods for creating HTTP headers that you need to include in HTML documents being sent back from the script

* Methods for creating HTML forms

* Methods for handling advanced features such as frames, Netscape cookies, and Javascript

You don't have to learn everything about CGI.pm before using it. In fact, you need to learn only a handful of methods to write scripts that handle form input.

After you create a new CGI object and get a reference to that object, you can begin accessing the parameters in the HTML form's data. Suppose that you have the following HTML form for searching documents at a Web site:

```
<form method=GET action="/cgi-bin/search.pl">
<b>Search</b>
<select name=what>
  <option value=all selected>All
  <option value=reports>Reports
  <option value=memos>Memorandums
</select>
<b>for:</b>
  <input name=keyword size=40 maxlength=120 value="">
  <input type=submit value=Submit>
</form>
```

Figure 15-4 shows how this form appears in a Web browser.

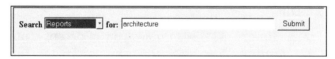

Figure 15-4   A typical HTML form for searching a Web site

This HTML form has two parameters that the user can set:

* An option menu named `what`, from which the user can select one of the following values: `all`, `reports`, and `memos`. This parameter presumably denotes the documents that the user wants to search.
* A text-entry field named `keyword`, where the user enters the search text.

When the user makes the selections and presses the `Submit` button, the Web server invokes the Perl program `search.pl` (this appears in the action attribute of the `<form>` tag). If you were to use `CGI.pm` in `search.pl`, here's how you would extract the values of the user's selections:

```perl
#!/usr/local/bin/perl
# search.pl

use CGI;
$query = new CGI;

# Where to search... (get the "what" parameter)
$source = $query->param('what');

# What to find...(the "keyword" parameter)
$search_string = $query->param('keyword');

# Just print a message with the parameter values

# Send necessary header
print $query->header;
print $query->start_html("Searching...");

print <<END;
<b>Searching: </b> $source
<b>for:</b> $search_string
END
print $query->end_html;
```

A real search script would have reported back the results of the search as an HTML document. This script simply sends back an HTML document repeating the search parameters. Figure 15-5 shows the output corresponding to the selections shown in Figure 15-4.

Searching: reports **for:** architecture

Figure 15-5 HTML document sent back by `search.pl` script

Even though this sample `search.pl` script does not perform an actual search, it illustrates how you use the `CGI.pm` module in a Perl CGI program.

Here is a basic sequence of steps in a Perl CGI script that uses the CGI module:

1. Incorporate the `CGI.pm` module with the following statement:

   ```
   use CGI;
   ```

2. Create a CGI object as follows:

   ```
   $query = new CGI;
   ```

3. To access a parameter by name, call the `param` method with the name as an argument, as follows:

   ```
   $value = $query->param('param_name');
   ```

   where `param_name` is the name you use for that parameter in the HTML form.

4. To send back an HTML document, begin by calling the `print` function and invoke the CGI object's `header` method as argument:

   ```
   print $query->header;
   ```

5. Send the rest of the HTML document as follows:

   ```
   print $query->start_html("Document Title");

   # print other information (that you want
   # to include in the HTML document)

   print $query->end_html;
   ```

Summary

Although you can write CGI programs in any programming language, Perl has become the language of choice. Perl's text-processing capabilities make it ideal for CGI programming where you need to parse and extract information from a query.

This chapter shows how to write CGI programs in Perl. You learn to use the popular `cgi-lib.pl` library to write Perl CGI programs that work with both Perl 4 and Perl 5.

As a bonus, you also learn how to install and use the `CGI.pm` module in CGI programs written in Perl 5.

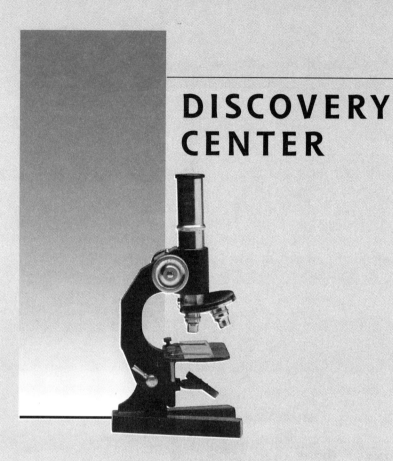

DISCOVERY CENTER

The Discovery Center gives you quick, step-by-step instructions that cover the main skills and concepts in each chapter of *Discover Perl 5*. This special section is broken down by chapter, and each task or explanation gives you a page reference indicating where you can go in the book to find a more detailed discussion of the topic at hand.

CHAPTER 1

To Install Perl on Windows 95 or Windows NT   (page 15)

1. Insert the CD-ROM into your system's CD-ROM drive.

2. Open an MS-DOS window. Create a directory for Perl 5 with the following commands:

```
cd \
md perl5
```

3. Change the directory to the newly created directory and copy the Perl 5 software from the CD-ROM with the following commands (this step assumes that D: is your system's CD-ROM drive):

```
cd \perl5
xcopy /s d:\perl5
```

Note that you have to replace `d:` with the drive letter for your CD-ROM drive.

4. Complete the final installation steps by typing the following command:

```
bin\perlw32-install
```

Press `y` when prompted with questions.

To Check if Perl Is Installed   (page 14)

Type `perl -v`.
   If a message appears with the Perl version number, then you have Perl installed on your system.

To Run a Perl Program   (page 18)

1. To run the program named `hello.pl`, type `perl hello.pl`.

2. Observe the program's output.

CHAPTER 2

To Define Scalar Variables   (page 37)

1. Write the variable name with a `$` prefix and assign the value like this:

```
$pages = 350;
```

2. To define a text string, enclose the text in double quotes, as follows:

```
$title = "Discover Perl 5";
```

To Define Array Variables   (page 43)

1. Write the array variable name with a @ prefix and assign a list of scalar values like this:

```
@names = ("John", "Bill", "Mary", "Susan");
```

2. To access an element of the array, increment the index starting with zero for the first element and then refer to the element, as follows:

```
$names[3]     # this is the fourth element of the array
```

To Define Associative Array Variables   (page 53)

1. Write the associative array variable name with a % prefix and assign a list of pairs of scalar values like this:

```
%expenses = ("John"  => 239.45,
             "Bill"  => 496.75,
             "Mary"  => 365.47,
             "Susan" => 178.94);
```

In each pair, the first item is the *key* and the second one is the *value*.

2. To access an element of the array, replace the % with a $ and append the key within curly braces. For example, to access the value for the key "Bill" in the %expenses associative array, write the following:

```
$expenses{"Bill"}
```

CHAPTER 3

To Perform Arithmetic in Perl   (page 66)

1. Translate names of items in the formula into scalar variable names that begin with $.

2. Replace addition, subtraction, multiplication, and division operations with the corresponding Perl operators: +, -, *, and /.

To Compute Trigonometric Formulas   (page 75)

1. If the variable $a is an angle in radians, compute sine and cosine of $a as follows:

```
$cosine_a = cos($a);
$sine_a = sin ($a);
```

2. To compute the tangent of $a, use the formula tan($a$) = sin($a$)/cos($a$) as follows:

```
$tangent_a = sin($a) / cos($a);
```

To Generate Random Numbers   (page 77)

1. Initialize the seed of the random number generator by calling srand with a numeric argument. A good choice is to use the current time as the seed:

```
srand(time());
```

2. To generate a random integer between 1 and 100, call the rand function as follows:

```
$random_int = int(rand(100) + 1);
```

To Concatenate Strings   (page 80)

Write the strings with periods (.) between them, as shown in the following:

```
$firstname = "Naba";
$lastname = "Barkakati";
$fullname = $firstname." ".$lastname;
# Now $fullname = "Naba Barkakati"
```

To Repeat a String   (page 81)

Use the x operator to repeat a string a number of times. To repeat a string consisting of 5 asterisks 13 times, write:

```
$marker = "*****" x 13;
```

After this, the $marker string contains 65 asterisks.

To Remove the Last Character of a String   (page 83)

Use the `chop` function to remove the last character of a string. Typically, you use `chop` to remove the trailing newline character from a line of text (after reading that line into a string variable):

```
$line = <STDIN>;  # Read a line from standard input
chop($line);      # Remove the trailing newline
```

To Extract a Substring from a String   (page 84)

Use the `substr` function to extract parts of a string. For example, to extract all the text following the first six characters of the string `$line`, write:

```
$last_part = substr($line, 6);
```

To Obtain the Length of a String   (page 85)

Use the `length` function to get the number of characters in a string, as follows:

```
$length = length("Perl");  # $length is 4
```

CHAPTER 4

To Compare Numbers in Perl   (page 94)

* To check if $x is equal to 10, write (`$x == 10`)
* To check if $x is not equal to 10, write (`$x != 10`)
* To check if $x is less than 10, write (`$x < 10`)
* To check if $x is less than or equal to 10, write (`$x <= 10`)
* To check if $x is greater than 10, write (`$x > 10`)
* To check if $x is greater than or equal to 10, write (`$x >= 10`)

To Compare Strings in Perl   (page 95)

* To check if $name is equal to "Perl", write (`$name eq "Perl"`)
* To check if $name is not equal to "Perl", write (`$name ne "Perl"`)
* To check if $name is less than "Perl", write (`$name lt "Perl"`)
* To check if $name is less than or equal to "Perl", write (`$name le "Perl"`)
* To check if $name is greater than "Perl", write (`$name gt "Perl"`)
* To check if $name is greater than or equal to "Perl", write (`$name ge "Perl"`)

1. Use the `if` statement. For example, to exit the program when the input is "quit", write:

```
if($input eq "quit")
{
  print "Quitting program\n";
  exit;
}
```

2. Add an `else` block to execute an alternate block of statements when the condition is false:

```
if($input eq "quit")
{
  print "Quitting program\n";
  exit;
}
else
{
  print "Current input = $input\n";
# other Perl statements...
}
```

Use the `while` statement. To add the numbers from 1 through 10, write:

```
while($i <= 10)
{
  $sum += $i;
  $i++;
}
```

To add the numbers from 1 through 10 with a `for` loop, write the loop as follows:

```
for($i=1; $i <= 10; $i++)
{
    $sum += $i;
}
```

To Execute a Block of Statements for Each Element in an Array (page 106)

Use the `foreach` loop as follows:

```
foreach $Variable (@Array)
{
  statement block
}
```

You can read this `foreach` loop as follows: "for each variable in the array, execute the statement block."

CHAPTER 5

To Redirect STDIN and STDOUT   (page 117)

1. Use the < operator on the command line to redirect STDIN from the keyboard to a file:

```
perl prog.pl < infile
```

This causes STDIN to be associated with the file `infile` (that means input comes from this file).

2. Use the > operator on the command line to redirect STDOUT from the display to a file:

```
perl prog.pl > outfile
```

This causes STDOUT to be associated with the file `outfile` (that means output goes to this file).

3. Use both < and > to simultaneously redirect STDIN and STDOUT:

```
perl prog.pl < infile > outfile
```

To Read from STDIN   (page 120)

1. Read a line of text into a scalar variable named `$line` by writing:

```
$line = <STDIN>;
```

After this, `$line` will contain all the text up to and including a newline character. To remove the trailing newline character, use the `chomp` function, as follows:

```
chomp $line;
```

2. In a `while` loop, the input text is assigned to the special variable `$_`. Thus, you may write a loop of the following form:

```
while(<STDIN>)  # input will be in $_
{
  print;        # prints $_
}
```

3. To read multiple lines from `STDIN` (up to end of file), assign `<STDIN>` to an array variable as follows:

```
@lines = <STDIN>;  # reads lines until end of file
```

To Print to STDOUT (page 124)

✳ Use the print function, as follows:

```
print $string1, "another string", $string2;
```

✳ To print the values of variables, embed the variables in a double-quoted string, as follows:

```
$name = "Joe";
$age = 45;
# The following prints: Name = Joe, Age = 45
print "Name = $name, Age = $age\n";
```

✳ To print a number of lines, use the "print up to HERE" format, as follows:

```
$name = "Joe";
$title = "Discover Perl 5";
$from = "Naba";
print <<HERE;
Dear $name,
  Hope you like "$title."
  Everyone says it's a great book.
— $from
HERE
```

This program prints the following output:

```
Dear Joe,
  Hope you like "Discover Perl 5."
  Everyone says it's a great book.
— Naba
```

CHAPTER 6

To Try Out Regular Expressions in UNIX   (page 140)

1. Go to the directory where Perl 5 is installed and make `lib` the current directory. For example, if Perl 5 is in the `/usr/local/src/perl5.003`, then type:

   ```
   cd /usr/local/src/perl5.003/lib
   ```

2. Use the following `grep` command to locate lines containing `make` or `Make` in all files with names ending in .pl:

   ```
   grep "[Mm]ake" *.pl
   ```

   This causes `grep` to print out lines that contain the search pattern. Here `[Mm]ake` is a regular expression.

To Try Out Regular Expressions in Perl   (page 142)

1. Find all occurrences of words ending with `sion` in a file named `release.txt`, by running Perl with the following command:

   ```
   perl -ne "print if /\b.*sion\b/" release.txt
   ```

   This command runs the Perl interpreter and executes the double-quoted statement for each line in the `release.txt` file. Here, `/\b.*sion\b/` is a regular expression.

2. To find a specific string, such as `Version`, in the file `release.txt`, use the following command:

   ```
   perl -ne "print if /Version/" release.txt
   ```

   In this case, the regular expression is `/Version/`, which represents a fixed string (`Version`).

Basic Regular Expressions   (page 144)

A regular expression is a concise notation for text patterns. For example, `/\b.*sion\b/` means any word that ends with the character sequence `sion`. Interpret this pattern as follows:

* The first and last forward slashes (/) enclose the regular expression.
* The first `\b` matches the beginning of a word; the last `\b` matches the end of the word.
* The period (.) matches any single character.
* The asterisk (*) means zero or more instances of the previous character.

* The `sion` is a literal sequence of characters that matches exactly those characters in that order.

A caret (^) at the beginning of a regular expression matches the beginning of a line. That means /^The/ matches any `The` occurring at the beginning of a line. A dollar sign ($) at the end of a regular expression matches the end of a line. That means /OK$/ matches `OK` at the end of a line. Regular expressions consist of:

* *anchors* that denote specific locations, such as the beginning of a line (denoted by ^)
* *character sets* that match literal character sequences
* *modifiers,* such as *, that modify the meaning of the preceding character

Character Sets in Regular Expressions   (page 148)

A single character is the simplest form of character set. A literal sequence of characters such as `The` consists of three simple character sets: `T`, `h`, and `e`. A more complex character set is of the form `[A-Z]` that denotes any letter from `A` to `Z`. In other words, when you use `[A-Z]` in a regular expression, `[A-Z]` matches exactly one uppercase letter (any letter). Here are some other examples:

* `[0-9]` for any single digit
* `[a-z]` for any lowercase letter
* `[aeiou]` for any vowel
* `[678]` for any one of the digits 6, 7, or 8
* `[a-zA-Z]` for any lowercase or uppercase letter

Thus, the syntax requires enclosing the character sequences of ranges inside square brackets.

Some special characters that modify the meaning of a character set are the following:

* A single period (.) matches any single character.
* An asterisk (*) means zero or more occurrences of the preceding character.
* A plus sign (+) means one or more occurrences of the preceding character.

Some character sequences with a backslash prefix have special meaning:

* `\w`   matches word character (letters, numbers, and underscore)
* `\W`   matches anything but a word character (opposite of `\w`)
* `\s`   matches a whitespace character (space, tab, newline, carriage return, or form feed)
* `\S`   matches anything but a whitespace character (opposite of `\s`)

To match a special character *literally* in a regular expression, add a backslash prefix to the character. For example, to match an asterisk, write *.

CHAPTER 7

To Search for Text Patterns   (page 158)

The simplest way to search for a specific text pattern in a file is to read the lines into the $_ special variable and then use the /PATTERN/ expression to look for a match. Here, PATTERN is a regular expression. Perl evaluates /PATTERN/ by searching $_ for PATTERN. The result is true if PATTERN occurs in the $_ variable. Here is a generic Perl program that looks for PATTERN in a file (it prints out the lines that contain PATTERN):

```
while(<>)
{
    print if /PATTERN/;
}
```

If you save this program in the file named search.pl, you can use it to search a file with the following command:

```
perl search.pl filename
```

To Search for Patterns in an Arbitrary String   (page 166)

* Use the pattern-binding operator =~ to find pattern matches in any arbitrary string:

```
# Assume you want to search for PATTERN in $string
if($string =~ /PATTERN/)
{
# Place here code that should be executed
# when a match occurs
}
```

* Use the pattern-binding operator !~ to look for "nonmatches" in an arbitrary string:

```
while($line = <STDIN>)
{
# Skip to next line if it does not contain PATTERN
    next if($line !~ /PATTERN/);

# Place here code to execute when line
# does contain PATTERN ...
}
```

To Ignore Case in Pattern Matches   (page 168)

Add the i suffix to the pattern-matching expression, as follows:

```
/PATTERN/i
```

This expression ignores case when looking for a match with *PATTERN*.

To Perform a Global Pattern Match   (page 169)

Add the g suffix to the pattern-matching expression, as follows:

```
/PATTERN/g
```

This expression matches all occurrences of *PATTERN* in the $_ variable.

To Substitute a Pattern with a String   (page 171)

1. Use the substitution operator, as follows:

   ```
   s/PATTERN/SUBSTITUTION/;
   ```

   This expression replaces an occurrence of *PATTERN* in the $_ variable with the *SUBSTITUTION* string.

2. To perform the substitution on a specific scalar variable such as $string, write:

   ```
   $string =~ s/PATTERN/SUBSTITUTION/;
   ```

To Perform Global Substitution   (page 172)

Add the g suffix to the substitution operator, as follows:

```
s/PATTERN/SUBSTITUTION/g
```

This expression substitutes all occurrences of *PATTERN* in the $_ variable with the string *SUBSTITUTION*.

To Substitute with the Result of an Expression   (page 172)

Use the e suffix to the substitution operator, as follows:

```
s/PATTERN/EXPRESSION/e
```

This expression substitutes an occurrence of *PATTERN* in the $_ variable with the result of evaluating the expression *EXPRESSION*. For example, to replace the string DATE with the result of evaluating the localtime function in a scalar context (the result is a date string), write:

```
s/DATE/scalar localtime/e
```

For global substitution, remember to add the `g` suffix as well:

```
s/DATE/scalar localtime/ge
```

CHAPTER 8

Basic Form of a Subroutine   (page 185)

A Perl subroutine has the following form:

```
sub SubroutineName
{
... Perl statements constituting body of subroutine ...
}
```

where `SubroutineName` is the name of the subroutine. Like any variable name, subroutine names begin with a letter, followed by one or more letters, digits, or underscores. To call a subroutine in a Perl program, use the following syntax:

```
&SubroutineName;
```

If a subroutine accepts arguments, place the list of arguments after the subroutine name, as follows:

```
&SubroutineName Arg1, Arg2, Arg3;
```

You may also enclose the argument list within parentheses:

```
&SubroutineName(Arg1, Arg2, Arg3);
```

If a subroutine definition precedes the subroutine call, you can drop the ampersand prefix and call the subroutine as follows:

```
# Subroutine definition must occur before the call
SubroutineName(Arg1, Arg2, Arg3);
```

To Use Local Variables in a Subroutine   (page 186)

Use the `local` or `my` functions to declare any local variables, as follows:

```
local($i, $key, $val);
my($param, @value, $var);
```

To Pass Arguments to a Subroutine   (page 187)

In Perl, when you call a subroutine as follows:

```
&SubroutineName(Arg1, Arg2, Arg3);
```

Perl places the list of arguments in the array variable named `@_`. To access the arguments in the subroutine, you may work directly with the `@_` array and refer to the arguments as $_[0], $_[1], $_[3], and so on. You can also initialize local variables from the @_ array with a statement such as the following:

```
my($var1, $var2, $var3) = @_;
```

This initializes the local variables $var1, $var2, and $var3 from the first three elements of the @_ array.

To Return Values from a Subroutine (page 193)

1. Place the value at the very end of the subroutine:

```
sub SubroutineName
{
# Body of subroutine
    $ReturnValue;
}
```

where $ReturnValue is what you want to return from the subroutine.

2. To return an array, place the list of items at the end of the subroutine body:

```
($x, $y, $z);   # To return a list of three variables
```

3. You may also use the return function to end a subroutine execution and return a value. The return function has the following syntax:

```
return(EXPRESSION);
```

CHAPTER 9

Built-in Functions (page 200)

The built-in functions are Perl subroutines that are known to the Perl interpreter before it begins to run your Perl program. The term *Perl functions* is also used to refer to the built-in functions. Perl 5 includes nearly 200 built-in functions that provide a wide range of capabilities, from printing output to handling inter-process communications. To use a built-in function, you need to know the function's name, what it does, the arguments it accepts, and the value it returns. For example, the print function accepts a list of values, which it prints to a specified file. Thus, you can call print as follows:

```
print FILEHANDLE "A string", $var, "\n";
```

If you omit the FILEHANDLE argument, print sends the output to the standard output (which is usually the display screen).

One way to get a feel for the built-in functions is to organize them by task. Perl includes built-in functions in the following broad categories:

- ✳ Input/output
- ✳ Scalar and array processing
- ✳ String functions
- ✳ Pattern matching and pattern substitution
- ✳ Math functions
- ✳ Time functions
- ✳ File and directory functions
- ✳ Programming support
- ✳ Associative array functions
- ✳ Process control functions
- ✳ Perl module functions
- ✳ User information (UNIX)
- ✳ Interprocess communication (IPC)
- ✳ Network information
- ✳ Socket-based network programming

Some of the functions are too advanced to discuss in this book. Many of the important categories of functions are covered in other chapters (cross-reference icons point you to the relevant chapter). An online manual for the Perl functions is available at the following location on the Internet:

```
ftp://ftp.digital.com/pub/plan/perl/CPAN/doc/manual/html/
    perlfunc-all.html
```

The same document, in HTML format, appears on this book's companion CD-ROM (in Windows NT or Windows 95, the filename is `\perl5\docs\perlfunc.htm`).

CHAPTER 10

MS-DOS Filenames   (page 227)

A *path name* is the complete specification necessary to locate a file. MS-DOS path names have the following form:

```
C:\DIR1\SUBDIR1\SUBDIR2\FILENAME.EXT
```

where `C:` denotes a physical disk drive, `\DIR1\SUBDIR1\SUBDIR2\` represents the directory hierarchy, and `FILENAME.EXT` is a filename with up to 8 characters followed by a 3-character extension.

Drives are the physical devices that hold all information. Some examples of drives are the hard disk, floppy disks, and the CD-ROM drive.

Directories are special files that contain other directories or files. Files contain the actual information, such as a Perl program or a text file with data. MS-DOS path names are used in Windows 95 and Windows NT. When you use path names in a Perl program, remember to add an extra backslash prefix for each backslash in the path name. You also have to enclose the path name in double quotes. Thus, you write `C:\PERL5\DOCS\WIN32.HTM` as `"C:\\PERL5\\DOCS\\WIN32.HTM"`.

UNIX Filenames   (page 229)

UNIX path names have the following form:

```
/usr/local/etc/httpd/htdocs/index.html
```

where `/usr/local/etc/httpd/htdocs/` represents the directory hierarchy and `index.html` is a filename with the `html` extension. A UNIX path name begins with the root directory, indicated by a forward slash (/) character. The directory hierarchy shows each directory name separated from the preceding one by a forward slash (/) character. A / appears after the last directory name. The filename has a name and an optional extension.

To Open and Close Files   (page 230)

✳ Use the `open` function, as follows:

```
open(FILEHANDLE, "filename");
```

where *FILEHANDLE* is the filehandle (an identifier) assigned to the open file. This opens the file for reading only.

✳ To open a file for output, use a > prefix in the filename, as follows:

```
open(FILEHANDLE, ">filename"); # open for output
```

✳ To open a file and append to it, add the >> prefix to the filename, as follows:

```
open(FILEHANDLE, ">filename"); # open for appending
```

✳ To close a currently open file, call the `close` function, as follows:

```
close FILEHANDLE;
```

Reading from and Writing to a Text File   (page 234)

✳ To read lines of text from a file, use the angle operator, as follows:

```
$line = <FILEHANDLE>; # Read a line of text
```

where *FILEHANDLE* is the filehandle of an open file. See Chapter 5 for information on how to read from standard input and write to standard output.

* To write a line of text to a file that has been opened for output, use the print function with FILEHANDLE as the first argument, followed by a list of other scalar variables or quoted strings:

```
print FILEHANDLE "The result is: ", $result, "\n";
```

Reading from and Writing to a Binary File   (page 236)

* To read a number of bytes from a binary file, use the sysread function, as follows:

```
$bytes_read = sysread(FILEHANDLE, $buffer, $length, $offset);
```

where FILEHANDLE is the filehandle of the open file, $buffer is the string into which data is to be read, $length specifies how many bytes of data are to be read, and $offset specifies where in the $buffer string to put the bytes.

* To write a number of bytes from a string to a file, use the syswrite function, as follows:

```
$bytes_written = syswrite(FILEHANDLE, $buffer, $length, $offset);
```

Each of the arguments for syswrite has the same meaning as the corresponding argument for sysread.

Opening and Reading Directories   (page 238)

* To open a directory, use the opendir function, as follows:

```
opendir(DIRHANDLE, "dirname") ||
die("Cannot open directory!");
```

where dirname is the name of the directory and DIRHANDLE is the directory handle that you can use later on to read the contents of the directory.

* To read the directory entries one at a time, use a while loop similar to the following:

```
while($file = readdir(DIRHANDLE))
{
    print "$file\n";
}
```

* To read all the entries in a directory into an array, call readdir as follows:

```
@filelist = readdir(DIRHANDLE);
```

* To close an open directory, use the `closedir` function, as follows:

```
closedir(DIRHANDLE);
```

CHAPTER 11

Perl References   (page 246)

A *reference* is a scalar variable that refers to another variable. To define a reference, add a backslash prefix to a variable's name and assign the value to the scalar variable that represents the reference. Here are some examples of references to different types of variables:

```
$r_scalar = \$scalar;
$r_array = \@array;
$r_hash = \%hash;
```

To dereference a reference variable, add the prefix corresponding to the variable type. Here are some examples of dereferencing:

```
$x = $$r_scalar;
@y = @{$r_array};
%z = %{r_hash};
```

To define a reference to a subroutine, add a backslash prefix to the subroutine name (use the ampersand prefix to indicate that it is a subroutine). Here is a reference to a subroutine named `process_data`:

```
$rproc = \&process_data;
```

To call this function through the reference, use the ampersand notation of the function call syntax as follows:

```
# Call the process_data function with "test" as argument
  &{$rproc}("test");
```

A reference to a reference looks just like a reference to a scalar variable, because a reference is a scalar variable (albeit with a special meaning):

```
$r_ref = \$ref; # Assume $ref is a reference
```

Here is an example that shows a reference to a reference:

```
$x = 100;     # a scalar
$rx = \$x;    # $rx is a reference to a scalar
$rrx = \$rx;  # Now $rrx is a reference to $rx
# Access the value of $x
$value = $$$rrx;
```

Perl Packages   (page 251)

A Perl *package* provides a way to control the *namespace* — a term that refers to the collection of variable and subroutine names. When you write a Perl program, it automatically belongs to a package named `main`. A Perl package is in a single file. You use the `package` statement at the beginning of the file to declare the file as a package and to give it a package name. For example, the `timelocal.pl` file has the following `package` statement in various places:

```
package timelocal;
```

To use a package in your program, you call the `require` function with the package filename as an argument. To use the package named `ctime` defined in the file `ctime.pl`, for example, write the following:

```
require 'ctime.pl';
```

To refer to a variable in a package, use the following syntax:

```
$Package::Variable
```

where `Package` is the name of the package and `Variable` is the name of the variable in that package. If you omit the package name, Perl assumes that you are referring to a variable in the `main` package.

Perl Modules   (page 253)

A Perl *module* is a package that follows certain guidelines and is designed to be reusable. Each module is a package that is defined in a file with the same name as the package, but with a `.pm` extension. To use a module, call the `use` function with the module name. For example, to use the Perl module named `Cwd` (defined in the `Cwd.pm` file), call the `use` function as follows:

```
use Cwd;
```

After that, you can call any subroutine from that module.

Perl Objects   (page 255)

An *object* is a data structure together with the functions that operate on that data. Each object is an instance of a *class* that defines the type of the object. The functions (or subroutines) that implement the operations on an object's data are known as *methods*. In Perl 5, an *object* is denoted by a reference (objects are implemented as references to a hash); a *class* is a Perl module that provides the methods to work with the object; and a *method* is a Perl subroutine that expects the object reference as the first argument.

To use an object, include the module in your program by calling the `use` function. For example, to use the CGI object (defined in `CGI.pm`), call the `use` function as follows:

```
use CGI;
```

To create an instance of the object, you typically have to call the `new` function. For instance, here is how you create an instance of the CGI object:

```
$query = new CGI;
```

where `$query` is the reference to the CGI object.

Invoke methods of the object by using the arrow operator. For example, to call the `start_html` method of the CGI object referenced by `$query`, write the following:

```
$query->start_html("Title of document");
```

As this example shows, to make use of an object, you have to know about that object's methods and the arguments that each method expects.

CHAPTER 12

To Run an External Program   (page 264)

1. Call the `exec` function to run a program specified by name. For example, to run a Perl script named `prog.pl`, write the following:

```
exec("perl", "prog.pl");
```

This causes the `exec` function to replace the current script with the Perl interpreter and provide `prog.pl` as an argument to the Perl interpreter.

2. To run the Notepad program in Windows and load the text file `sample.txt`, write the following:

```
exec("notepad", "sample.txt");
```

To Continue after the External Program Finishes   (page 268)

Use the `system` function. For example, to run the `vi` editor (in UNIX) and edit a file named `config.dat`, call `system` as follows:

```
system("vi", "config.dat");
```

To Capture the Output of an External Program   (page 270)

Run the program by enclosing the program name within backquotes. For example, to capture the output of the `dir` command (in Windows) in an array, write the following Perl statement:

```
@listing = 'dir';
```

After this statement executes, the @listing array contains the lines of text that constitute the output of the dir command.

Another way to capture an external program's output is to call the open function with a filename constructed by appending a vertical bar (|) to the external program's name. Thus, if you want to read the output of the dir command, call open as follows:

```
open(DIR, "dir|") || die("Cannot run command!");
```

After you use the open function to set up a filehandle, you can read from that handle by using the input operator (<. . .>), as follows:

```
@filelist = <DIR>;
```

To Send Input to an External Program   (page 275)

1. Call the open function with a filename consisting of a vertical bar (|) prefix followed by the external program's name. This opens a filehandle that enables you to print commands to the external program (assuming the program accepts commands). For example, in Windows, you can run the date command with the open function as follows:

```
open(DATE, "|date");
```

2. After running a command this way, you can send input to the external program by printing to the filehandle. Thus, to set the current date to December 31, 1999, you can use the following statement:

```
print DATE "12-31-99\n";
```

CHAPTER 13

To Define a Report Template   (page 288)

Use the format function to specify the template of a report. For example, the following format defines a layout of a single line:

```
format =
From: @<<<<<<<<<<<<<<<<<<<         Message#: @###
          $name,                             $msgnum
.
```

The first line defines the format. In this case, the format has no name (the name goes between format and =). That means the format is meant for the STD-OUT filehandle. The second line is the *picture line,* which shows the layout with the space allocated for each field indicated by patterns that begin with @. The third line is the *argument line,* which lists the variables that will be printed in each field. The format definition ends with a single period in the last line.

With that format definition, if you were to run the following Perl program

```
$name = "John Doe";
$msgnum = 141;

write;
```

the output line will be as follows:

```
From: John Doe                    Message#:  141
```

1. To format a field, pick the character you want from the following set:

   <   for a left-justified field

   >   for a right-justified field

   | for a centered field

   #   for a numeric field

2. Repeat the character one less than the number of characters you want to use when printing that field. Thus, to specify a six-character, left-justified field, use @<<<<< (that's the @ symbol followed by five occurrences of <).

3. In a numeric field, embed a period where you want the decimal point to appear. Thus, if you want to print a dollar amount of the form 9999.99, use the field specification @####.##. As you can see, the total number of characters including the @, the decimal point, and the #s add up to the number of characters you want to use to display the field.

To add a header to a report being printed to the standard output, define a format with the name STDOUT_TOP. A typical column header for a tabular output might be as follows:

```
format STDOUT_TOP =
Ref no.    Item            Description                Price
============================================================

.
```

Perl prints this header at the top of each page (by default, each page consists of 60 lines).

To include a page number in the header, use the variable name $%, as follows:

```
format STDOUT_TOP =
Page @<<
     $%

.
```

This prints the page number in the left-hand corner of each page.

1. Define a format with no name, like this:

```
format =
@<<<<<<<   @<<<<<<<<<<<<<<<<<<<<<<<<<<<<<<<<<<<   @####.##
$prodnum,  $desc,                                $price
.
```

2. If you want a report header, define a format named STDOUT_TOP, as follows:

```
format STDOUT_TOP =
Order #   Description                         Sale Price
=======================================================
.
```

3. Initialize any variables that appear in the format, as follows:

```
$prodnum = 9702101;
$desc = "166MHz Pentium, 16MB/2.1GB";
$price = 1795.50;
```

4. Call the write function:

```
    write;
```

Here is some sample output (shown with the header):

```
Order #   Description                         Sale Price
=======================================================
9702101   166MHz Pentium, 16MB/2.1GB             1795.50
```

1. Call the format function and define a format with the same name as the filehandle of the file where the report is to be written. For example, if the filehandle is REPORT, the format function call has the following form:

```
format REPORT =
picture line
argument line
.
```

You can also specify a header by defining a format named REPORT_TOP.

2. Open the report file by calling the `open` function. Here is how you open a file named `report.new` for output:

```
open(REPORT, ">report.new") ||
die("Error opening file!");
```

3. Call the `write` function with the filehandle as an argument. For example, to print to the filehandle `REPORT`, call the `write` function as follows:

```
write REPORT;
```

CHAPTER 14

Hypertext Markup Language   (page 301)

HTML provides a set of *tags* — formatting commands — that you embed in the text to specify how the text should be rendered (that is, displayed or printed) as in the following HTML document:

```
<html>
<!- This line is a comment. ->
<head>
<title>Sample Document</title>
</head>
<body>
<h1>Sample Document</h1>
<hr>
This is a sample HTML document.
<strong>This sentence is bold.</strong>
<em>This sentence is emphasized.</em>
</body>
</html>
```

Here, the tags are the text enclosed in angle brackets (<. . .>). Most tags come in pairs — if the start tag is <TAG>, the corresponding end tag has the form </TAG>.

HTML Forms   (page 307)

HTML forms are for soliciting user input. The form definition includes information on how the user input is sent to the Web server and what program the server should execute to process the input. The following is a typical HTML form:

```
<form method=GET action="/cgi-bin/search.pl">
<b>Search</b>
<select name=what>
```

```
    <option value=all selected>All
    <option value=reports>Reports
    <option value=memos>Memorandums
  </select>
  <b>for:</b>
    <input name=keyword size=40 maxlength=120 value="">
    <input type=submit value=Submit>
  </form>
```

The following figure shows how this form appears in a Web browser.

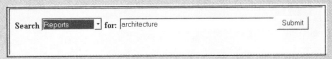

The `method` attribute in the `<form>` tag specifies how data is transferred to the Web server. The `method` can be `GET` or `POST`. The `action` attribute of the `<form>` tag specifies the name of the CGI program that will process the form's data. The form can have various fields, each identified by a `name` attribute. Each field also has a `value` attribute, which happens to be the user's input. When the form's data is sent to the Web server, the user input for each field is sent in the *name=value* format.

Common Gateway Interface   (page 319)

CGI is essentially a set of conventions that specifies how user input from an HTML form finds its way to a computer program on the Web server. A CGI program is a computer program that the Web server starts when the server receives HTML form input from a Web browser. The HTML `<form>` tag's `action` attribute specifies the name of the CGI program (including the server where that program resides). For example, the following `<form>` tag specifies a program named `query` in the `/cgi-bin` directory on the Web server `digital.com`:

```
<FORM method=GET action="http://digital.com/cgi-bin/query">
```

The CGI program receives most of its information through environment variables. The Web browser sends the data entered on the form using a type of encoding commonly referred to as *URL encoding,* in which a space is replaced by a plus sign (+), fields are separated by an ampersand (&), and any nonalphanumeric character is replaced with a *%xx* code (where *xx* is the character's ASCII code in hexadecimal format). The CGI program has to decode this information before using the data. The CGI program sends information back to the Web server by writing to standard output. Typically, the CGI program sends a header (known as a *MIME* header, where MIME is the acronym for Multimedia Internet Mail Extension) followed by HTML text.

You can write a CGI program in any language, but Perl is especially suited for this, because Perl programs are easy to write and Perl has good text-processing capabilities. (CGI programs have to process the URL-encoded text data and print HTML text to standard output.)

CHAPTER 15

To Write a Perl CGI Program   (page 339)

1. Check the REQUEST_METHOD environment variable for the method of data submission (the value is GET or POST).

2. Read the CGI query into a string. Depending on the method of data submission (GET or POST), the input is either in the QUERY_STRING environment variable or read from standard input (STDIN in Perl).

3. Separate out the fields and their values from the query. In Perl, you can use the split function to separate the fields.

4. Decode the URL-encoded input values.

5. Store the fields in associative arrays.

6. Process the fields as appropriate.

7. Because Steps 1 through 5 apply to any HTML form, it's best to use a library of Perl subroutines (such as Steven Brenner's cgi-lib.pl Perl library) to implement Steps 1 through 5.

To Obtain the cgi-lib.pl Library   (page 343)

Steven Brenner's cgi-lib.pl library includes a set of Perl subroutines to read and parse HTML form input and print HTML text. This book's companion CD-ROM includes the cgi-lib.pl library. You can also download the latest version of cgi-lib.pl from the official cgi-lib.pl home page at the following Web address:

```
http://www.bio.cam.ac.uk/cgi-lib/
```

You can either place the cgi-lib.pl library in the Perl library directory or place it in the same directory where the CGI programs are located.

To Use the cgi-lib.pl Library   (page 349)

1. Use the require function to include the cgi-lib.pl library:

```
require "cgi-lib.pl";
```

2. Call the ReadParse subroutine to process the CGI query. Use ReadParse as follows:

```
if(&ReadParse(*input))
{
```

```
# Fields are in the input associative array
# Extract each field using the field's name:
#    $value = $input{'name'};

# Call other subroutines to print HTML text
}
```

3. Print HTML text by calling `PrintHeader`, `HtmlTop`, and `HtmlBot` as follows:

```
print &PrintHeader;
print &HtmlTop("Title of page");

# Print any other HTML test you want. Use the
# the print function.

# End with the string returned by HtmlBot
print &HtmlBot;
```

4. Call `CgiDie` or `CgiError` to report any error conditions.

5. Use the `MethGet` and `MethPost` functions to check if the data submission method is `GET` or `POST`. The `MethGet` function returns True if the CGI query came as a `GET` request. The `MethPost` function returns True if the CGI query came as a `POST` request.

VISUAL INDEX

WRITING A PERL PROGRAM

How to prepare
a Perl program
(page 17)

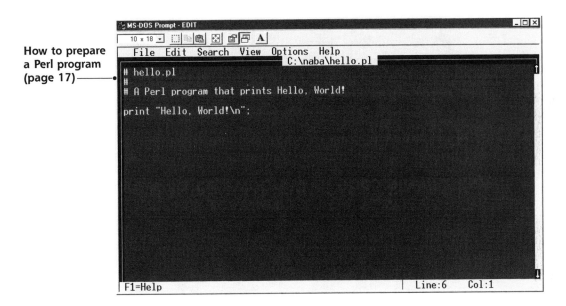

RUNNING A PERL PROGRAM

How to run a
Perl program
(page 18)

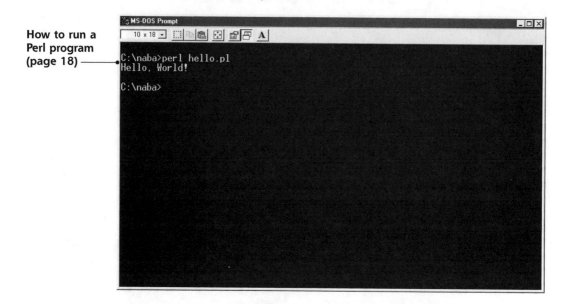

```
C:\naba>perl hello.pl
Hello, World!

C:\naba>
```

USING PERL VARIABLES

How to define
scalar variables
(page 37)

How to define
array variables
(page 43)

How to define
associative
array (hash)
variables
(page 53)

```perl
# Examples of variables in Perl

# Scalar variables
$title = "Discovering Perl 5";
$pages = 350;
$price = 24.99;

# Array variables
@names = ("John", "Bill", "Mary", "Susan");
@amounts = (239.45, 496.75, 365.47, 178.94);

# Associative array
%expenses = ("John"  => 239.45,
             "Bill"  => 496.75,
             "Mary"  => 365.47,
             "Susan" => 178.94);
```

PERFORMING ARITHMETIC IN PERL

How to
perform
arithmetic
in Perl
(page 67)

How to
compute a
trigonometric
formula
(page 76)

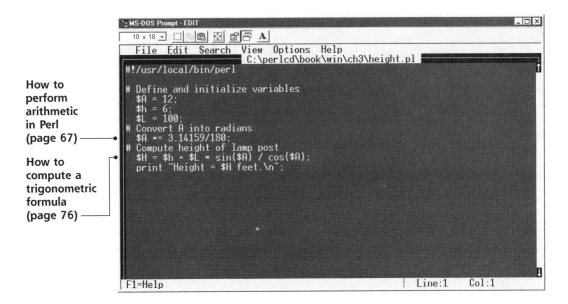

```
MS-DOS Prompt - EDIT                                      _ □ ×
10 x 18 ▼  □ ▣ ▣ ▣ ▣ ☞▭ A
   File  Edit  Search  View  Options  Help
              C:\perlcd\book\win\ch3\height.pl
#!/usr/local/bin/perl

# Define and initialize variables
  $A = 12;
  $h = 6;
  $L = 100;
# Convert A into radians
  $A *= 3.14159/180;
# Compute height of lamp post
  $H = $h + $L * sin($A) / cos($A);
  print "Height = $H feet.\n";




F1=Help                                    Line:1    Col:1
```

CONTROLLING PROGRAM FLOW

How to
compare
numbers in Perl
(page 95)

How to
execute a
statement
block when
a condition
is true
(page 98)

How to
repeatedly
execute a
statement
block
(page 102)

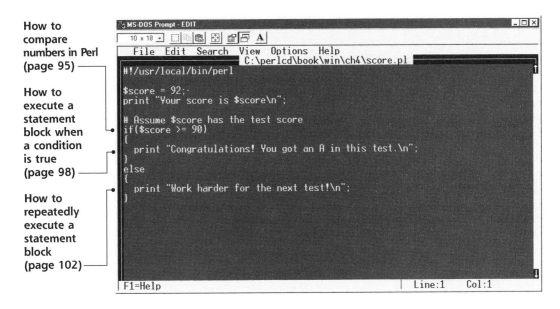

```
MS-DOS Prompt - EDIT                                      _ □ ×
10 x 18 ▼  □ ▣ ▣ ▣ ▣ ☞▭ A
   File  Edit  Search  View  Options  Help
              C:\perlcd\book\win\ch4\score.pl
#!/usr/local/bin/perl

$score = 92;
print "Your score is $score\n";

# Assume $score has the test score
if($score >= 90)
{
   print "Congratulations! You got an A in this test.\n";
}
else
{
   print "Work harder for the next test!\n";
}



F1=Help                                    Line:1    Col:1
```

READING INPUT FROM STDIN AND WRITING TO STDOUT

How to read from STDIN (page 120)

How to print to STDOUT (page 124)

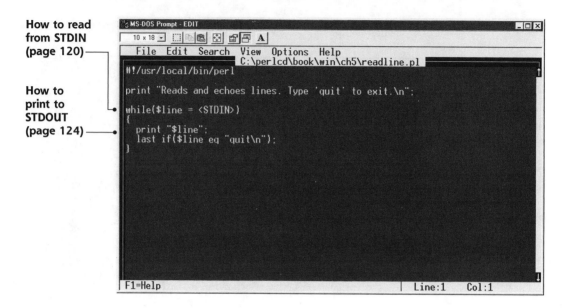

```
#!/usr/local/bin/perl

print "Reads and echoes lines. Type 'quit' to exit.\n";

while($line = <STDIN>)
{
  print "$line";
  last if($line eq "quit\n");
}
```

USING REGULAR EXPRESSIONS

How to search for text patterns (page 158)

How to perform global pattern matching (page 169)

```
#!/usr/local/bin/perl
# ssn.pl -- reads and validates a U.S. social
#           security number

# Display a prompt and read input
EnterSSN:
  print "Enter social security number (XXX-XX-XXXX):";
  $line = <STDIN>;

# Check if this is a valid social security number
if($line =~ /^[0-9]{3}-[0-9]{2}-[0-9]{4}$/)
{
# Successful match, good Social Security Number
    print "Social Security Number = $line\n";
  }
  else
  {
# Did not match, try again
    print "Invalid social security number; $line\n";
    goto EnterSSN;
  }
```

WRITING AND USING SUBROUTINES

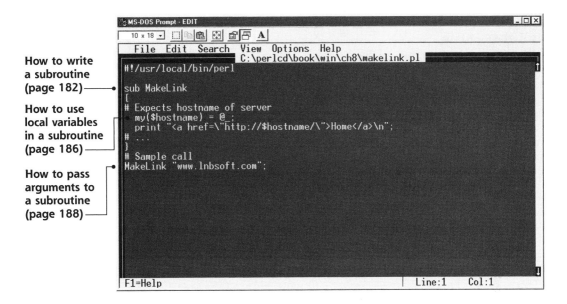

How to write
a subroutine
(page 182)

How to use
local variables
in a subroutine
(page 186)

How to pass
arguments to
a subroutine
(page 188)

```perl
#!/usr/local/bin/perl

sub MakeLink
{
# Expects hostname of server
  my($hostname) = @_;
  print "<a href=\"http://$hostname/\">Home</a>\n";
# ...
}
# Sample call
MakeLink "www.lnbsoft.com";
```

WORKING WITH FILES

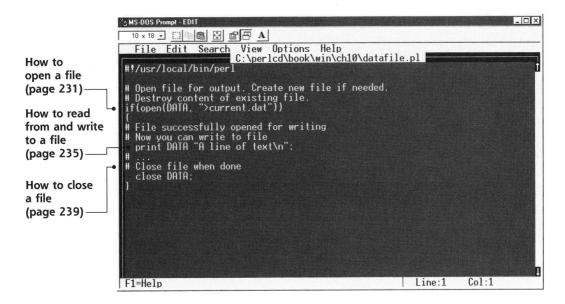

How to
open a file
(page 231)

How to read
from and write
to a file
(page 235)

How to close
a file
(page 239)

```perl
#!/usr/local/bin/perl

# Open file for output. Create new file if needed.
# Destroy content of existing file.
if(open(DATA, ">current.dat"))
{
# File successfully opened for writing
# Now you can write to file
  print DATA "A line of text\n";
# ...
# Close file when done
  close DATA;
}
```

RUNNING OTHER PROGRAMS FROM A PERL SCRIPT

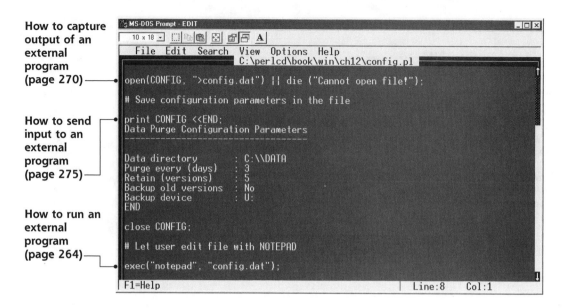

How to capture output of an external program (page 270)

How to send input to an external program (page 275)

How to run an external program (page 264)

```
%MS-DOS Prompt - EDIT                                              _ □ ×
10 x 18 ▾   □ ▤ ▥   ⬚ ⬚ A
   File  Edit  Search  View  Options  Help
               C:\perlcd\book\win\ch12\config.pl

open(CONFIG, ">config.dat") || die ("Cannot open file!");

# Save configuration parameters in the file

print CONFIG <<END;
Data Purge Configuration Parameters
-----------------------------------

Data directory       : C:\\DATA
Purge every (days)   : 3
Retain (versions)    : 5
Backup old versions  : No
Backup device        : U:
END

close CONFIG;

# Let user edit file with NOTEPAD

exec("notepad", "config.dat");

F1=Help                                         Line:8    Col:1
```

GENERATING FORMATTED REPORTS

How to define a report template (page 288)

How to write a report to STDOUT (page 286)

```
%MS-DOS Prompt - EDIT                                              _ □ ×
10 x 18 ▾   □ ▤ ▥   ⬚ ⬚ A
   File  Edit  Search  View  Options  Help
               C:\perlcd\book\win\ch13\charges.pl

# Define report header
format STDOUT_TOP =
Ref no.  Item            Description            Price
=====================================================
.

# Define format of each line
format =
@######  @####  @<<<<<<<<<<<<<<<<<<<<<<<<<<<<<  @####.##
$refid,  $num, $desc,                    .      $price
.

# Process the data file and print formatted lines

while(<>)
{
   chomp;
   $num++;
   ($refid, $desc, $price) = split(/\|/, $_);
   write;
}
F1=Help                                         Line:4    Col:1
```

CREATING HTML FORMS

How to create HTML forms (page 308) —•

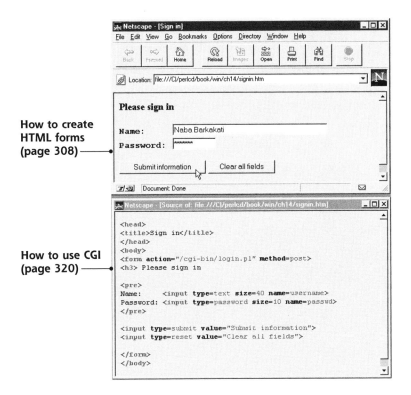

How to use CGI (page 320) —•

WRITING PERL CGI PROGRAMS

How to write CGI programs (page 339) —•

How to create a CGI object (page 360) —•

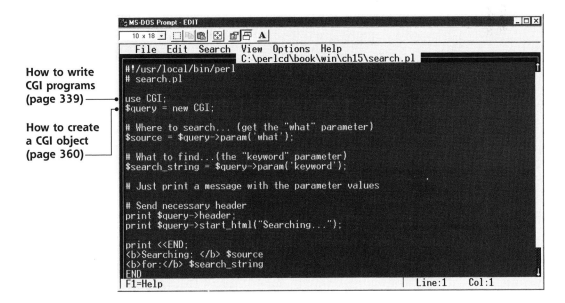

PERL RESOURCES ON THE INTERNET

Throughout this book, there are references to some sources of information, programs, and utilities that can help you learn and use Perl effectively. Most of these resources are located on the Internet, and you can access them from your Web browser. The best part is that most Internet-based resources are updated frequently, so you can always get the latest information or the latest version of a program from the Internet.

To use Internet-based resources, all you need is a starting point, a URL (a Web address) where you can begin your search. Once you have a good starting document, hypertext links within that document should lead you to other relevant resources. This appendix provides that starting point by listing many useful URLs, organized by subject.

TIP For ease of use, these URLs are provided as links in an HTML document on the companion CD-ROM. Use a Web browser to open the `perllink.htm` file in the root directory of the CD-ROM. Then you can visit a site by simply clicking on the appropriate link.

Perl Basics

The Perl home page (for the latest scoop on Perl and lots of useful links)
`http://www.perl.com/perl/`

The Perl Institute home page (a non-profit organization devoted to Perl)
`http://www.perl.org/`

Perl Frequently Asked Questions (FAQ)
`http://www.perl.com/perl/faq/`

Comprehensive Perl Archive Network — CPAN (the following URL connects you to the CPAN site nearest to you)
`http://www.perl.com/CPAN/`

A list of all CPAN sites (same as last URL but without the trailing slash)
`http://www.perl.com/CPAN`

Perl for Win32 (Windows NT and Windows 95) home page
`http://www.hip.activeware.com/`

Internet Basics

Internet Network Information Center (InterNIC) home page
`http://rs.internic.net/`

Templates for IP address application form
`ftp://rs.internic.net/templates`

Request for Comments (RFC) — the working papers of the Internet
`http://www.internic.net/ds/rfc-index.html`

Internet Engineering Task Force (IETF) home page
`http://www.ietf.org/`

History of Internet: Final report of the NSFNET backbone project (1987–1995)
`http://nic.merit.edu/nsfnet/final.report/`

Internet network architecture
`http://nic.merit.edu/.internet.html`

Mecklermedia's list of Internet Service Providers
`http://thelist.iworld.com/`

Yahoo!'s ISP category
`http://www.yahoo.com/Business_and_Economy/Companies/Internet_`
`    Services/Internet_Access_Providers/`

Introduction to the World Wide Web

World Wide Web Consortium (W3C)
`http://www.w3.org/`

Hypertext Transfer Protocol standards news
`http://www.w3.org/pub/WWW/Protocols/`

Hypertext Markup Language news
`http://www.w3.org/pub/WWW/MarkUp/`

Links to information on Web browsers
`http://www.yahoo.com/Computers_and_Internet/Software/Internet/`
`    World_Wide_Web/Browsers/`

Microsoft Internet Explorer (freely available Windows Web browser from Microsoft)

http://www.microsoft.com/ie/

Netscape Navigator (popular commercial Web browser; evaluation copy available)

ftp://ftp.netscape.com/pub/navigator/

Mosaic for X (for UNIX workstations running the X Window System)

ftp://ftp.ncsa.uiuc.edu/Mosaic/Unix/binaries/

Links to information on Web servers

http://www.yahoo.com/Computers_and_Internet/Software/Internet/
  World_Wide_Web/Servers/

NCSA HTTP server and related documentation

http://hoohoo.ncsa.uiuc.edu/

Apache Web server

http://www.apache.org/

Microsoft Personal Web Server (a free Web server for Windows 95 and Windows NT; select Personal Web Server from the option menu on this page)

http://www.microsoft.com/msdownload/ieplatform/iewin95.htm

Some Popular Web Sites

Netscape home page

http://home.netscape.com/

Microsoft home page

http://www.microsoft.com/

Yahoo! (a popular Web directory) home page

http://www.yahoo.com/

Alta Vista (a popular Web index) home page

http://www.altavista.digital.com/

Excite (another popular Web index) home page

http://www.excite.com/

Open Text (full-text search of the Web)

http://search.opentext.com/

Lycos (Web index)

http://www.lycos.com/

WebCrawler (Web index)
`http://www.webcrawler.com/`

DejaNews (keyword search of Internet newsgroups)
`http://www.dejanews.com/`

Web Page Design and HTML

Collection of links to HTML style guides
`http://union.ncsa.uiuc.edu/HyperNews/get/www/html/guides.html`

Yahoo!'s collection of HTML and Web support pages
`http://www.yahoo.com/Computers_and_Internet/Internet/World_Wide_Web`

How Do They Do That With HTML?
`http://www.nashville.net/~carl/htmlguide/index.html`

Common Gateway Interface (CGI)

CGI specification and other related information
`http://hoohoo.ncsa.uiuc.edu/cgi/`

`cgi-lib.pl` (Perl library for CGI programming) home page
`http://www.bio.cam.ac.uk/cgi-lib/`

`CGI.pm` (Perl 5 module for CGI programming) home page
`http://www-genome.wi.mit.edu/ftp/pub/software/WWW/cgi_docs.html`

Web Site Security

CERT (short for Computer Emergency Response Team [Carnegie Mellon University, Pittsburgh, PA, USA]) summaries of known security problems
`http://www.cert.org/`

Internet security and firewall information
`http://www.v-one.com/newpages/faq.htm`

`http://www.netcraft.co.uk/security/http/`

`http://www.netcraft.co.uk/security/diary.html`

`ftp://info.cert.org/pub/cert_summaries/`

Web server security

http://hoohoo.ncsa.uiuc.edu/security/

The World Wide Web Security FAQ (Frequently Asked Questions)

http://www-genome.wi.mit.edu/WWW/faqs/www-security-faq.html

CGI security

http://www.thinkage.on.ca/~mlvanbie/cgisec/

TIS Firewall Toolkit (a freely available firewall from Trusted Information Systems)

http://www.tis.com/docs/products/fwtk/index.html

HOW TO USE THE CD-ROM

In keeping with the spirit of the *Discover* series books, the CD-ROM contains only what you need to get started with Perl 5. The CD-ROM includes the Perl 5 executables for Windows NT and Windows 95, as well as Perl 5 source code for UNIX. In addition to Perl itself, the CD-ROM includes the sample Perl and HTML files from this book.

The way you use the CD-ROM depends on whether you are using Windows or UNIX. You can learn more about the exact contents of the CD-ROM by reading one of the following files:

* `README.win` (on Windows NT and Windows 95)
* `README.unix` (on UNIX)

Windows NT or Windows 95 Installation

You have two installation tasks:

* Install Perl 5.
* Install the sample files from this book.

You can perform these installations separately. If you don't mind typing the examples (which is what I recommend, because you can learn quickly by actually typing the code), you don't even have to install the sample files.

Install Perl 5 on Windows NT or Windows 95

You have two options:

* Install from the self-extracting files in the `Pw32i` directory of the CD-ROM.
* Install by copying preinstalled files from the `Perl5` directory of the CD-ROM.

INSTALL FROM Pw32i DIRECTORY

1. Insert the CD-ROM into your system's CD-ROM drive.

2. Type the following command:

   ```
   d:\Pw32i\Pw32i304
   ```

   where d: is the drive letter for your CD-ROM drive. If the drive letter is something else, replace d: with the appropriate drive letter.

3. Follow the on-screen instructions to complete the installation.

INSTALL FROM Perl5 DIRECTORY

The Perl5 directory has a complete Perl for Win32 installation that will work on Windows 95 and Windows NT (only Intel CPUs). To install from the Perl5 directory, you basically have to copy the files (including all subdirectories) and then run an installation script. Here are the steps:

1. Insert the CD-ROM into your CD-ROM drive.

2. Create a directory for Perl 5 on your hard drive, as follows:

   ```
   c:
   cd \
   md Perl5
   ```

   This assumes that you want to place Perl 5 in the Perl5 directory on the C: drive.

3. Copy the Perl 5 files from the CD-ROM drive's Perl5 directory, as follows:

   ```
   cd \Perl5
   xcopy /s d:\Perl5
   ```

   Note that you have to replace d: with the drive letter for your CD-ROM drive.

4. Complete the installation by typing the following command:

   ```
   c:\Perl5\bin\perlw32-install
   ```

   This runs the batch file perlw32-install.bat in the c:\Perl5\bin directory.

Install sample code in Windows 95 or Windows NT

1. Create a directory where you want to place the code. Suppose that you want to install the code in a directory named DPCODE on the C: drive. Type these commands:

```
c:
cd \
md dpcode
```

2. Copy the sample files from the CD-ROM drive's `book\win` directory, as
   follows:

```
cd \dpcode
xcopy /s d:\book\win
```

Note that you have to replace `d:` with the drive letter for your CD-ROM
drive. This step copies the sample files into a set of subdirectories named
`ch1` through `ch15`.

UNIX Installation

Y ou have two installation tasks:

* Install Perl 5.
* Install the sample files.

You can perform these steps separately.

Install Perl 5 on UNIX

If you work on a UNIX system, you probably have a system administrator who
takes care of installing software on the system. The CD-ROM includes an archive
(`latest.tar`) with the source code for Perl 5. Your system administrator has to
copy the source code archive to the system, unpack the archive, and compile the
files to create the executable. (Unfortunately, there are too many varieties of
UNIX systems to provide ready-to-run Perl software for each UNIX variant.)

If you cannot perform the following steps yourself, ask your system administrator for help:

1. Mount the CD-ROM. A typical UNIX command to mount the CD-ROM
   on the directory named `/cdrom` might be as follows:

```
mount -r /dev/devname /cdrom
```

where you must replace *devname* with the actual device name of the
CD-ROM drive.

2. Unpack the source code in a directory of your choice. For example, you
   might decide to place the source code in the `/usr/local/src` directory.
   To do this, type the following commands:

```
cd /usr/local/src
tar xvf /cdrom/latest.tar
```

This step assumes that the CD-ROM is mounted on `/cdrom`. After this step finishes, you'll find the Perl source code in a directory whose name begins with `perl` (the rest of the directory name depends on the exact version number of Perl).

3. Change the directory to the Perl source directory with the following command:

```
cd perl*
```

4. Configure the Perl software for your system with the following command:

```
sh configure
```

5. To compile and link the Perl software, your system must have a C compiler. Type the following command to build Perl:

```
make
```

6. Complete the installation steps with the following command, which copies the binary files to an appropriate directory:

```
make install
```

After the system administrator completes these steps, you should be able to try out Perl with the `perl -v` command.

Install sample code on UNIX

Once the CD-ROM is mounted on a directory on your UNIX system, you can view or run the Perl programs directly from the CD-ROM. If the CD-ROM is mounted on `/cdrom`, look for the files in the directory `/cdrom/book/unix/ch`X (where X is a chapter number).

If you want to edit the files, you have to copy them to a directory on your UNIX system's hard drive. All the sample files are in the `tar` file named `dpcode.tar`. You can copy the files to a directory by first changing to the target directory and then typing the following command:

```
tar xvf /cdrom/book/unix/dpcode.tar
```

This assumes that the CD-ROM is mounted on `/cdrom`.

MacPerl for Macintosh

Although this book focuses on learning to use Perl on Windows and UNIX systems, Perl is also available for the Macintosh (and many other systems). To get a copy of MacPerl, the version of Perl 5 for the Mac by Matthias Neeracher, visit the following URL:

```
ftp://err.ethz.ch/pub/neeri/MacPerl/
```

Installation is as simple as unstuffing the .SIT file and double-clicking on the Installer icon.

MacPerl is also available from any CPAN site (try `http://www.perl.com/CPAN/` for the nearest CPAN site).

INDEX

SYMBOLS

|. *See* vertical bar (|)

||, logical OR operator, 114, 133–135, 232, 275, 279

!, logical NOT operator, 114, 162

!=. *See* relational operators

". *See* double quotes ("")

#. *See* hash mark (#)

#!, UNIX recognition of, 19–20

$. *See* dollar sign ($)

$], version number variable, 62

$_ default variable, 62
    pattern substitution, 171
    print function, 125, 143
    regular expressions, 143, 145–146, 158

$0 variable, 62

$^X, full path name variable, 62

$< user ID variable, 62

%. *See* percent sign (%)

&. *See* ampersand (&)

&&, logical AND operator, 113–114

'. *See* single quotes ('...')

*. *See* asterisk (*)

**. *See* double asterisk (**)

+. *See* plus sign (+)

++. *See* double plus sign (++)

--. *See* double minus sign (--)

. *See* period (.)

/. *See* forward slash (/)

//. *See* slashes (//)

::. *See* double colon (::)

;. *See* semicolon

==. *See* relational operators

@. *See* at symbol (@)

@_ variable, 28, 183–184, 188–192, 373–374

[]. *See* square brackets ([])

^. *See* caret (^)

<. *See* less than sign (<)

<=. *See* relational operators

<<, left shift operator, 71

<>. *See* angle brackets (<>)

<=>. *See* relational operators

>. *See* greater than sign (>)

->. *See* arrow operator (->)

>=. *See* relational operators

=>, in associative arrays, 54, 59

>>, for appending files, 234

\. *See* backslash (|)

\b. *See* word boundary

\n, newline character, 18

{}. *See* curly braces ({})

~. *See* tilde (~)

!~, pattern-binding operator, 166–168, 371

=~, pattern-binding operator, 166–168, 171, 371

A

-A operator, 243

access mode, 237

action attribute, 309–311, 320, 330

adding array elements, 49

Alta Vista, 302, 322, 399

ampersand (&), 28, 378, 385
    referencing, 248

anchors, regular expression, 145, 370

angle brackets (<>), 30, 120–124, 233, 305, 384

Apache Web server, 324–325, 352

appending
    arrays, 51–52
    to files, 234

argument line, report template, 289–290, 292, 382

arguments
    command-line, 46

subroutine, 182–183, 187–193, 373–374
    initializing local variables, 189–190
    modifying values, 190–192
    passing filehandle, 192–193

@ARGV array, 46–47, 61

arithmetic operations, 66–75, 363, 391

arithmetic operators, 23, 66–75, 363

array-index operator, 23

arrays, 22, 43–52, 363
    accessing elements, 44
    adding elements, 49
    appending, 51–52
    @ARGV, 46–47, 61
    counting elements, 44–45
    multiple lines read to, 122–123
    referencing, 247
    removing elements, 47–49
    reversing element order, 50–51
    sorting elements, 50

arrow operator (->), 249–251, 256

ASCII code, 96–97, 173–174
    carriage return, 208
    end-of-line characters, 235

assignment operators, 66, 73–74

associative array, 22–23, 32, 53–60, 340, 363, 386
    accessing keys and values, 57–59
    deleting elements, 60
    %ENV, 54–56
    functions, 203, 375
    key-value pair retrieval, 59–60

(continued)

memory, 11
menus, 311, 315–317
meta-characters, 144, 148
MethGet subroutine, 346, 348, 387
method attribute, 310–311, 320–324
methods, object, 254–256, 379
MethPost subroutine, 346, 348, 387
Microsoft. *See also* Windows
    Excel, 277–281
    Internet Explorer, 333, 399
    Office Developer's Kit, 279
    Web sites, 399
    Word, 277
MIME (Multipurpose Internet Mail Extension), 32–33, 321, 330–332, 385
mkdir function, 241
modifier, regular expression, 145, 150–151, 169–173, 176, 179, 370
modules, 253–254, 379
    CGI.pm, 255–256, 357–360
    English, 257–260
    functions, 203, 375
    objects, 255–256
    OLE, 277–281
modulo operator, 70, 72–73
Mosaic, 333, 399
MS-DOS
    binary file access mode, 237
    directory commands, 241
    EDIT text editor, 3, 17
    end of file, 121
    end-of-line indicator, 235, 237
    filenames, 133, 227–229, 375–376
    redirection operators, 117–118
    regular expressions, 142–143
multiple conditions, testing, 113–114
my function, 184, 187, 373
MyURL subroutine, 346, 348

N

NCSA (National Center for Supercomputing Applications), 324, 326, 352

Neeracher, Matthias, 407
Netscape Navigator, 306, 309–310, 399
    HTML tables, 333–335
    text wrapping, 318
network information functions, 203, 375
newline, 121
next command, 109–112
Notepad program, 3, 17, 266–267
numbers, comparing, 95, 365, 391. *See also* mathematical operations

O

object code, 13
Object Linking and Embedding (OLE), 277–281
object-oriented programming, 8, 254–255
objects, 254–256, 277–281, 379–380
open function, 30, 133–135, 230–234, 376, 384
    capturing external program output, 275
    sending input, 276
Open Text Web site, 399
opendir function, 238, 377
opening files, 133–135, 230–234, 376, 393
operating system, 12–13
    accessing, 30–31
    command output, 42, 271–274
operator, 23–24. *See also* specific operators
    angle, 120–124, 233
    arithmetic, 23, 66–75, 363
    array-index, 23
    arrow, 249–251, 256
    assignment, 66, 73–74
    bitwise, 70–71, 89–90
    comparison, 23
    concatenation, 80–81
    decrement, 69–70
    dot, 23–24
    exponentiation, 70–72
    file test, 242–243
    increment, 68–69
    logical, 113–114

match (m), 178–179
modulo, 70, 72–73
order of operations, 74–75
pattern-binding, 166–168, 171, 371
precedence, 74–75
range, 107
redirection, 117–118
relational, 94–97
repetition, 81–82
shortcuts, 73–74
strings and, 80–82, 88–90
substitution, 171–177, 372
unary, 88–89
vertical bar (|), 118–120
option tag, 315–317
order of operations, 74–75
output
    capturing external program, 270–275, 380–381, 394
    functions, 203, 204–205, 375
    opening file for, 234
    printing to STDOUT, 124–132, 392
        print function, 124–127
        printf function, 127–132
    redirecting STDOUT, 117–120
    redirecting through command line, 117–118
output redirection operator (>), 117–118

P

pack function, 174
package statement, 252
packages, Perl, 251–253, 379. *See also* modules
password, 312–313
path name, 62, 133, 375–376
    conversion of CGI URL, 324
    MS-DOS, 227–228, 232
    UNIX, 230, 232
pattern-binding operators, 166–168, 171, 371
pattern-matching functions, 159–160, 207–208, 375
patterns, text. *See also* regular expressions
    command-line search, 158–159

IDG BOOKS WORLDWIDE END-USER LICENSE AGREEMENT

retain no copies. If the Software is an update or has been updated, any transfer must include the most recent update and all prior versions.

4. **<u>Restrictions On Use of Individual Programs.</u>** You must follow the individual requirements and restrictions detailed for each individual program in Appendix B, "How to Use the CD-ROM," of this Book. These limitations are also contained in the individual license agreements recorded on the CD-ROM or printed in this book. These limitations may include a requirement that after using the program for a specified period of time, the user must pay a registration fee or discontinue use. By opening the Software packet(s), you will be agreeing to abide by the licenses and restrictions for these individual programs that are detailed in Appendix B and on the Software Media. None of the material on this Software Media or listed in this Book may ever be redistributed, in original or modified form, for commercial purposes.

5. **<u>Limited Warranty.</u>**

   (a) IDGB warrants that the Software and Software Media are free from defects in materials and workmanship under normal use for a period of sixty (60) days from the date of purchase of this Book. If IDGB receives notification within the warranty period of defects in materials or workmanship, IDGB will replace the defective Software Media.

   (b) **IDGB AND THE AUTHOR OF THE BOOK DISCLAIM ALL OTHER WARRANTIES, EXPRESS OR IMPLIED, INCLUDING WITHOUT LIMITATION IMPLIED WARRANTIES OF MERCHANTABILITY AND FITNESS FOR A PARTICULAR PURPOSE, WITH RESPECT TO THE SOFTWARE, THE PROGRAMS, THE SOURCE CODE CONTAINED THEREIN, AND/OR THE TECHNIQUES DESCRIBED IN THIS BOOK. IDGB DOES NOT WARRANT THAT THE FUNCTIONS CONTAINED IN THE SOFTWARE WILL MEET YOUR REQUIREMENTS OR THAT THE OPERATION OF THE SOFTWARE WILL BE ERROR FREE.**

   (c) This limited warranty gives you specific legal rights, and you may have other rights that vary from jurisdiction to jurisdiction.

6. **<u>Remedies.</u>**

   (a) IDGB's entire liability and your exclusive remedy for defects in materials and workmanship shall be limited to replacement of the Software Media, which may be returned to IDGB with a copy of your receipt at the following address: Software Media Fulfillment Department, Attn.: Discover Perl 5, IDG Books

Worldwide, Inc., 7260 Shadeland Station, Ste. 100, Indianapolis, IN 46256, or call 1-800-762-2974. Please allow three to four weeks for delivery. This Limited Warranty is void if failure of the Software Media has resulted from accident, abuse, or misapplication. Any replacement Software Media will be warranted for the remainder of the original warranty period or thirty (30) days, whichever is longer.

(b) In no event shall IDGB or the author be liable for any damages whatsoever (including without limitation damages for loss of business profits, business interruption, loss of business information, or any other pecuniary loss) arising from the use of or inability to use the Book or the Software, even if IDGB has been advised of the possibility of such damages.

(c) Because some jurisdictions do not allow the exclusion or limitation of liability for consequential or incidental damages, the above limitation or exclusion may not apply to you.

7. **U.S. Government Restricted Rights.** Use, duplication, or disclosure of the Software by the U.S. Government is subject to restrictions stated in paragraph (c)(1)(ii) of the Rights in Technical Data and Computer Software clause of DFARS 252.227-7013, and in subparagraphs (a) through (d) of the Commercial Computer—Restricted Rights clause at FAR 52.227-19, and in similar clauses in the NASA FAR supplement, when applicable.

8. **General.** This Agreement constitutes the entire understanding of the parties and revokes and supersedes all prior agreements, oral or written, between them and may not be modified or amended except in a writing signed by both parties hereto that specifically refers to this Agreement. This Agreement shall take precedence over any other documents that may be in conflict herewith. If any one or more provisions contained in this Agreement are held by any court or tribunal to be invalid, illegal, or otherwise unenforceable, each and every other provision shall remain in full force and effect.

GNU General Public License

Version 2, June 1991

Copyright (C) 1989, 1991 Free Software Foundation, Inc., Massachusetts Avenue, Cambridge, MA 02139, USA.

Everyone is permitted to copy and distribute verbatim copies of this license document, but changing it is not allowed.

Preamble

The licenses for most software are designed to take away your freedom to share and change it. By contrast, the GNU General Public License is intended to guarantee your freedom to share and change free software—to make sure the software is free for all its users. This General Public License applies to most of the Free Software Foundation's software and to any other program whose authors commit to using it. (Some other Free Software Foundation software is covered by the GNU Library General Public License instead.) You can apply it to your programs, too.

When we speak of free software, we are referring to freedom, not price. Our General Public Licenses are designed to make sure that you have the freedom to distribute copies of free software (and charge for this service if you wish), that you receive source code or can get it if you want it, that you can change the software or use pieces of it in new free programs; and that you know you can do these things.

To protect your rights, we need to make restrictions that forbid anyone to deny you these rights or to ask you to surrender the rights. These restrictions translate to certain responsibilities for you if you distribute copies of the software, or if you modify it.

For example, if you distribute copies of such a program, whether gratis or for a fee, you must give the recipients all the rights that you have. You must make sure that they, too, receive or can get the source code. And you must show them these terms so they know their rights.

We protect your rights with two steps: (1) copyright the software, and (2) offer you this license which gives you legal permission to copy, distribute and/or modify the software.

Also, for each author's protection and ours, we want to make certain that everyone understands that there is no warranty for this free software. If the software is modified by someone else and passed on, we want its recipients to know that what they have is not the original, so that any problems introduced by others will not reflect on the original authors' reputations.

Finally, any free program is threatened constantly by software patents. We wish to avoid the danger that redistributors of a free program will individually obtain patent licenses, in effect making the program proprietary. To prevent this, we have made it clear that any patent must be licensed for everyone's free use or not licensed at all.

The precise terms and conditions for copying, distribution and modification follow.

GNU General Public License Terms and Conditions for Copying, Distribution, and Modification

0. This License applies to any program or other work which contains a notice placed by the copyright holder saying it may be distributed under the terms of this General Public License. The "Program", below, refers to any such program or work, and a "work based on the Program" means either the Program or any derivative work under copyright law: that is to say, a work containing the Program or a portion of it, either verbatim or with modifications and/or translated into another language. (Hereinafter, translation is included without limitation in the term "modification".) Each licensee is addressed as "you".

Activities other than copying, distribution and modification are not covered by this License; they are outside its scope. The act of running the Program is not restricted, and the output from the Program is covered only if its contents constitute a work based on the Program (independent of having been made by running the Program). Whether that is true depends on what the Program does.

1. You may copy and distribute verbatim copies of the Program's source code as you receive it, in any medium, provided that you conspicuously and appropriately publish on each copy an appropriate copyright notice and disclaimer of warranty; keep intact all the notices that refer to this License and to the absence of any warranty; and give any other recipients of the Program a copy of this License along with the Program.

   You may charge a fee for the physical act of transferring a copy, and you may at your option offer warranty protection in exchange for a fee.

2. You may modify your copy or copies of the Program or any portion of it, thus forming a work based on the Program, and copy and distribute such modifications or work under the terms of Section 1 above, provided that you also meet all of these conditions:

   (a) You must cause the modified files to carry prominent notices stating that you changed the files and the date of any change.

   (b) You must cause any work that you distribute or publish, that in whole or in part contains or is derived from the Program or any part thereof, to be licensed as a whole at no charge to all third parties under the terms of this License.

   (c) If the modified program normally reads commands interactively when run, you must cause it, when started running for such interactive use in the most ordinary way, to print or display an announcement including an appropriate copyright notice and a notice that there is no warranty (or else, saying that you provide a warranty) and that users may redistribute the program under these conditions, and telling the user how to view a copy of this License. (Exception: if the Program itself is interactive but does not normally print such an announcement, your work based on the Program is not required to print an announcement.)

These requirements apply to the modified work as a whole. If identifiable sections of that work are not derived from the Program, and can be reasonably considered independent and separate works in themselves, then this License, and its terms, do not apply to those sections when you distribute them as separate works. But when you distribute the same sections as part of a whole which is a work based on the Program, the distribution of the whole must be on the terms of this License, whose permissions for other licensees extend to the entire whole, and thus to each and every part regardless of who wrote it.

Thus, it is not the intent of this section to claim rights or contest your rights to work written entirely by you; rather, the intent is to exercise the right to control the distribution of derivative or collective works based on the Program.

In addition, mere aggregation of another work not based on the Program with the Program (or with a work based on the Program) on a volume of a storage or distribution medium does not bring the other work under the scope of this License.

3. You may copy and distribute the Program (or a work based on it, under Section 2) in object code or executable form under the terms of Sections 1 and 2 above provided that you also do one of the following:

    (a) Accompany it with the complete corresponding machine-readable source code, which must be distributed under the terms of Sections 1 and 2 above on a medium customarily used for software interchange; or,

    (b) Accompany it with a written offer, valid for at least three years, to give any third party, for a charge no more than your cost of physically performing source distribution, a complete machine-readable copy of the corresponding source code, to be distributed under the terms of Sections 1 and 2 above on a medium customarily used for software interchange; or,

    (c) Accompany it with the information you received as to the offer to distribute corresponding source code. (This alternative is allowed only for noncommercial distribution and only if you received the program in object code or executable form with such an offer, in accord with Subsection b above.)

The source code for a work means the preferred form of the work for making modifications to it. For an executable work, complete source code means all the source code for all modules it contains, plus any associated interface definition files, plus the scripts used to control compilation and installation of the executable. However, as a special exception, the source code distributed need not include anything that is normally distributed (in either source or binary form) with the major components (compiler, kernel, and so on) of the operating system on which the executable runs, unless that component itself accompanies the executable.

If distribution of executable or object code is made by offering access to copy from a designated place, then offering equivalent access to copy the source code from the same place counts as distribution of the source code, even though third parties are not compelled to copy the source along with the object code.

4. You may not copy, modify, sublicense, or distribute the Program except as expressly provided under this License. Any attempt otherwise to copy, modify, sublicense or distribute the Program is void, and will automatically terminate your rights under this License. However, parties who have received copies, or rights, from you under this License will not have their licenses terminated so long as such parties remain in full compliance.

5. You are not required to accept this License, since you have not signed it. However, nothing else grants you permission to modify or distribute the Program or its derivative works. These actions are prohibited by law if you do not accept this License. Therefore, by modifying or distributing the Program (or any work based on the Program), you indicate your acceptance of this License to do so, and all its terms and conditions for copying, distributing or modifying the Program or works based on it.

6. Each time you redistribute the Program (or any work based on the Program), the recipient automatically receives a license from the original licensor to copy, distribute or modify the Program subject to these terms and conditions. You may not impose any further restrictions on the recipients' exercise of the rights granted herein. You are not responsible for enforcing compliance by third parties to this License.

7. If, as a consequence of a court judgment or allegation of patent infringement or for any other reason (not limited to patent issues), conditions are imposed on you (whether by court order, agreement or otherwise) that contradict the conditions of this License, they do not excuse you from the conditions of this License. If you cannot distribute so as to satisfy simultaneously your obligations under this License and any other pertinent obligations, then as a consequence you may not distribute the Program at all. For example, if a patent license would not permit royalty-free redistribution of the Program by all those who receive copies directly or indirectly through you, then the only way you could satisfy both it and this License would be to refrain entirely from distribution of the Program.

If any portion of this section is held invalid or unenforceable under any particular circumstance, the balance of the section is intended to apply and the section as a whole is intended to apply in other circumstances.

It is not the purpose of this section to induce you to infringe any patents or other property right claims or to contest validity of any such claims; this section has the sole purpose of protecting the integrity of the free software distribution system, which is implemented by public license practices. Many people have made generous contributions to the wide range of software distributed through that system in reliance on consistent application of that system; it is up to the author/donor to decide if he or she is willing to distribute software through any other system and a licensee cannot impose that choice.

This section is intended to make thoroughly clear what is believed to be a consequence of the rest of this License.

8. If the distribution and/or use of the Program is restricted in certain countries either by patents or by copyrighted interfaces, the original copyright holder who places the Program under this License may add an explicit geographical distribution limitation excluding those countries, so that distribution is permitted only in or among countries not thus excluded. In such case, this License incorporates the limitation as if written in the body of this License.

9. The Free Software Foundation may publish revised and/or new versions of the General Public License from time to time. Such new versions will be similar in spirit to the present version, but may differ in detail to address new problems or concerns.

   Each version is given a distinguishing version number. If the Program specifies a version number of this License which applies to it and "any later version", you have the option of following the terms and conditions either of that version or of any later version published by the Free Software Foundation. If the Program does not specify a version number of this License, you may choose any version ever published by the Free Software Foundation.

10. If you wish to incorporate parts of the Program into other free programs whose distribution conditions are different, write to the author to ask for permission. For software which is copyrighted by the Free Software Foundation, write to the Free Software Foundation; we sometimes make exceptions for this. Our decision will be guided by the two goals of preserving the free status of all derivatives of our free software and of promoting the sharing and reuse of software generally.

11. BECAUSE THE PROGRAM IS LICENSED FREE OF CHARGE, THERE IS NO WARRANTY FOR THE PROGRAM, TO THE EXTENT PERMITTED BY APPLICABLE LAW. EXCEPT WHEN OTHERWISE STATED IN WRITING THE COPYRIGHT HOLDERS AND/OR OTHER PARTIES PROVIDE THE PROGRAM "AS IS" WITHOUT WARRANTY OF ANY KIND, EITHER EXPRESSED OR IMPLIED, INCLUDING, BUT NOT LIMITED TO, THE IMPLIED WARRANTIES OF MERCHANTABILITY AND FITNESS FOR A PARTICULAR PURPOSE. THE ENTIRE RISK AS TO THE QUALITY AND PERFORMANCE OF THE PROGRAM IS WITH YOU. SHOULD THE PROGRAM PROVE DEFECTIVE, YOU ASSUME THE COST OF ALL NECESSARY SERVICING, REPAIR OR CORRECTION.

12. IN NO EVENT UNLESS REQUIRED BY APPLICABLE LAW OR AGREED TO IN WRITING WILL ANY COPYRIGHT HOLDER, OR ANY OTHER PARTY WHO MAY MODIFY AND/OR REDISTRIBUTE THE PROGRAM AS PERMITTED ABOVE, BE LIABLE TO YOU FOR DAMAGES, INCLUDING ANY GENERAL, SPECIAL, INCIDENTAL OR CONSEQUENTIAL DAMAGES ARISING OUT OF THE USE OR INABILITY TO USE THE PROGRAM (INCLUDING BUT NOT LIMITED TO LOSS OF DATA OR DATA BEING RENDERED INACCURATE OR LOSSES SUSTAINED BY YOU OR THIRD PARTIES OR A FAILURE OF THE PROGRAM TO OPERATE WITH ANY OTHER PROGRAMS), EVEN IF SUCH HOLDER OR OTHER PARTY HAS BEEN ADVISED OF THE POSSIBILITY OF SUCH DAMAGES.

END OF TERMS AND CONDITIONS

Appendix: How to Apply These Terms to Your New Programs

I f you develop a new program, and you want it to be of the greatest possible use to the public, the best way to achieve this is to make it free software which everyone can redistribute and change under these terms.

To do so, attach the following notices to the program. It is safest to attach them to the start of each source file to most effectively convey the exclusion of warranty; and each file should have at least the "copyright" line and a pointer to where the full notice is found.

<one line to give the program's name and a brief idea of what it does> Copyright (C) 19yy <name of author>.

This program is free software; you can redistribute it and/or modify it under the terms of the GNU General Public License as published by the Free Software Foundation; either version 2 of the License, or (at your option) any later version.

This program is distributed in the hope that it will be useful, but WITHOUT ANY WARRANTY; without even the implied warranty of MERCHANTABILITY or FITNESS FOR A PARTICULAR PURPOSE. See the GNU General Public License for more details.

You should have received a copy of the GNU General Public License along with this program; if not, write to the Free Software Foundation, Inc., 675 Mass Ave, Cambridge, MA 02139, USA.

Also add information on how to contact you by electronic and paper mail.

If the program is interactive, make it output a short notice like this when it starts in an interactive mode:

Gnomovision version 69, Copyright (C) 19yy name of author Gnomovision comes with ABSOLUTELY NO WARRANTY; for details type 'show w'. This is free software, and you are welcome to redistribute it under certain conditions; type 'show c' for details.

The hypothetical commands 'show w' and 'show c' should show the appropriate parts of the General Public License. Of course, the commands you use may be called something other than 'show w' and 'show c'; they could even be mouse-clicks or menu items—whatever suits your program.

You should also get your employer (if you work as a programmer) or your school, if any, to sign a "copyright disclaimer" for the program, if necessary. Here is a sample; alter the names:

Yoyodyne, Inc., hereby disclaims all copyright interest in the program 'Gnomovision' (which makes passes at compilers) written by James Hacker.

<signature of Ty Coon>, 1 April 1989

Ty Coon, President of Vice

This General Public License does not permit incorporating your program into proprietary programs. If your program is a subroutine library, you may consider it more useful to permit linking proprietary applications with the library. If this is what you want to do, use the GNU Library General Public License instead of this License.

The "Artistic License"

Preamble

The intent of this document is to state the conditions under which a Package may be copied, such that the Copyright Holder maintains some semblance of artistic control over the development of the package, while giving the users of the package the right to use and distribute the Package in a more-or-less customary fashion, plus the right to make reasonable modifications.

Definitions

"Package" refers to the collection of files distributed by the Copyright Holder, and derivatives of that collection of files created through textual modification.

"Standard Version" refers to such a Package if it has not been modified, or has been modified in accordance with the wishes of the Copyright Holder as specified below.

"Copyright Holder" is whoever is named in the copyright or copyrights for the package.

"You" is you, if you're thinking about copying or distributing this Package.

"Reasonable copying fee" is whatever you can justify on the basis of media cost, duplication charges, time of people involved, and so on. (You will not be required to justify it to the Copyright Holder, but only to the computing community at large as a market that must bear the fee.)

"Freely Available" means that no fee is charged for the item itself, though there may be fees involved in handling the item. It also means that recipients of the item may redistribute it under the same conditions they received it.

1. You may make and give away verbatim copies of the source form of the Standard Version of this Package without restriction, provided that you duplicate all of the original copyright notices and associated disclaimers.

2. You may apply bug fixes, portability fixes and other modifications derived from the Public Domain or from the Copyright Holder. A Package modified in such a way shall still be considered the Standard Version.

3. You may otherwise modify your copy of this Package in any way, provided that you insert a prominent notice in each changed file stating how and when you changed that file, and provided that you do at least ONE of the following:

(a) place your modifications in the Public Domain or otherwise make them Freely Available, such as by posting said modifications to Usenet or an equivalent medium, or placing the modifications on a major archive site such as uunet.uu.net, or by allowing the Copyright Holder to include your modifications in the Standard Version of the Package.

(b) use the modified Package only within your corporation or organization.

(c) rename any non-standard executables so the names do not conflict with standard executables, which must also be provided, and provide a separate manual page for each non-standard executable that clearly documents how it differs from the Standard Version.

(d) make other distribution arrangements with the Copyright Holder.

4. You may distribute the programs of this Package in object code or executable form, provided that you do at least ONE of the following:

(a) distribute a Standard Version of the executables and library files, together with instructions (in the manual page or equivalent) on where to get the Standard Version.

(b) accompany the distribution with the machine-readable source of the Package with your modifications.

(c) give non-standard executables non-standard names, and clearly document the differences in manual pages (or equivalent), together with instructions on where to get the Standard Version.

(d) make other distribution arrangements with the Copyright Holder.

5. You may charge a reasonable copying fee for any distribution of this Package. You may charge any fee you choose for support of this Package. You may not charge a fee for this Package itself. However, you may distribute this Package in aggregate with other (possibly commercial) programs as part of a larger (possibly commercial) software distribution provided that you do not advertise this Package as a product of your own. You may embed this Package's interpreter within an executable of yours (by linking); this shall be construed as a mere form of aggregation, provided that the complete Standard Version of the interpreter is so embedded.

6. The scripts and library files supplied as input to or produced as output from the programs of this Package do not automatically fall under the copyright of this Package, but belong to whomever generated them, and may be sold commercially, and may be aggregated with this Package. If such scripts or library files are aggregated with this Package via the so-called "undump" or "unexec" methods of producing a binary executable image, then distribution of such an image shall neither be construed as a distribution of this Package nor shall it fall under the restrictions of Paragraphs 3 and 4, provided that you do not represent such an executable image as a Standard Version of this Package.

7. C subroutines (or comparably compiled subroutines in other languages) supplied by you and linked into this Package in order to emulate subroutines and variables of the language defined by this Package shall not be considered part of this Package, but are the equivalent of input as in Paragraph 6, provided these subroutines do not change the language in any way that would cause it to fail the regression tests for the language.

8. Aggregation of this Package with a commercial distribution is always permitted provided that the use of this Package is embedded; that is, when no overt attempt is made to make this Package's interfaces visible to the end user of the commercial distribution. Such use shall not be construed as a distribution of this Package.

9. The name of the Copyright Holder may not be used to endorse or promote products derived from this software without specific prior written permission.

10. THIS PACKAGE IS PROVIDED "AS IS" AND WITHOUT ANY EXPRESS OR IMPLIED WARRANTIES, INCLUDING, WITHOUT LIMITATION, THE IMPLIED WARRANTIES OF MERCHANTIBILITY AND FITNESS FOR A PARTICULAR PURPOSE.

The End

CD-ROM Instructions

This CD-ROM contains all you need to get started with Perl 5. The CD-ROM includes the Perl 5 executables for Windows NT and Windows 95, as well as Perl 5 source code for UNIX. In addition to Perl itself, the CD-ROM includes the sample Perl and HTML files from this book. The way you use the CD-ROM depends on whether you are using Windows or UNIX. You can learn more about the exact contents of the CD-ROM by reading one of the following files:

* `README.win` (on Windows NT and Windows 95)
* `README.unix` (on UNIX)

For either Windows or UNIX, you have two installation tasks:

* Install Perl 5.
* Install the sample files from this book.

You can perform these installations separately. If you don't mind typing in the examples (which is what I recommend because you can learn quickly by actually typing the code), you don't even have to install the sample files.

Read Appendix B for complete instructions on installing Perl 5 for Windows 95, Windows NT, and UNIX.